Best–Loved Pot Pies, Casseroles, *and* One–Dish Meals

Betty Crocker

Best-Loved

Pot Pies, Casseroles, and One-Dish Meals

325 comfort food recipes— from Breakfasts to Desserts

RODALE

© 2013 by General Mills, Minneapolis, Minnesota

Front cover photos—*(left, top)* Triple Berry Granola Crisp (page 360); *(left, bottom)* Alfredo Chicken Pot Puff Pies (page 128); and *(right)* Cheesy Rigatoni with Eggplant Sauce (page 245)
Back cover photos—*(top to bottom)* Italian Meatball Pie (page 242); Burger 'n Fries Pot Pie (page 52); and Spicy Pork Chimichurri-Style Casserole (page 62)

Interior and Cover Photography © General Mills Photography Studios and Image Library

Library of Congress Cataloging-in-Publication Data is on file with the publisher.

ISBN 978–1–60961–572–7   direct hardcover

4   6   8   10   9   7   5   direct hardcover

We inspire and enable people to improve their lives and the world around them.

For more of our products visit rodalestore.com or call 800-848-4735

Dear Friends,

There's nothing better than the aroma of a home-cooked meal in the oven to warm hearts and whet the appetite. And with *Betty Crocker Best-Loved Pot Pies, Casseroles, and One-Dish Meals*, you'll be able to choose from hundreds of delicious, family-friendly recipes any day of the week. This high-quality collection provides easy step-by-step directions for every dish as well as plenty of inspiring photographs, to help you put great-tasting meals together quickly, without a lot of prep work.

Best of all, this edition is designed to help you on those nights when you're too busy to cook. You'll find recipes clearly labeled "Make Ahead," if they're suitable for assembling the night before. Look for "Fast" labels when you're searching for something that can be on the table in 30 minutes or less. And if you enjoy having some leftovers available for a quick meal, look for recipes tagged with the "Great Leftovers" label so you can be sure to save the extras. After all, many dishes taste even better the day after they're made. There's also plenty of advice in the front of the book to help you freeze and store your food safely.

So what kind of meals are we talking about? Imagine starting your day with a Blueberry Fold-Over Coffee Cake or a Sausage 'n Apple Cheddar Biscuit Bake. For dinner, you might enjoy Chicken Paprika Shepherd's Pie or, if you're pressed for time, an Italian Crescent Casserole—which only takes 10 minutes to prepare and is on the table in 30 minutes! While most of the recipes are perfect for a one-dish meal, there's also a chapter dedicated to simple side dishes for those occasions when you want to serve a little something extra.

Most important, don't forget dessert! If you already have the oven on, why not whip up a Triple-Berry Granola Crisp or a loaf of Pumpkin Chocolate Chip Bread to end your meal in style? The last chapter is packed with dozens of family favorites. And with so many recipes to choose from in this collection, you're sure to find the perfect combination of meals that works for you.

Here's to happy home cooking!

Betty Crocker®

Contents

Making Meals That Work for You

One of the biggest reasons everyone loves pot pies, casseroles and one-dish meals is because they make weeknight meals extra easy. They're versatile, delicious and quick to prepare. Plus, many of these dishes rely on a similar range of ingredients, so odds are you already have most of what you need on hand. If you're the type of person who really likes getting a head start on the weekly cooking, you'll find plenty of great-tasting recipes that are flexible enough to make ahead of time, freeze or enjoy as a leftover. So what are you waiting for? Let's get started!

CREATIVE POT PIES AND CASSEROLES

Bubbling, steaming, cheesy, pleasing. Nothing says "comfort food" quite like a casserole or pot pie. Try our tips for making these one-dish wonders as easy to share as they are delicious to enjoy.

Wrap it for transport. To keep a casserole or pot pie hot on the way to a potluck, place two kitchen towels in the bottom of a basket and set the hot dish inside. Tuck additional hand towels around and over the top of the dish. Dishes can stay safely at room temperature for 2 hours (an hour if the outside temperature is hot).

Be flexible. As you cook your way through this collection, you'll find that many of the recipes are easy to adapt to whatever you have on hand. Have some leftover turkey? Feel free to use the same amount of chopped cooked turkey for any recipe that calls for chopped cooked chicken. The same logic applies to frozen vegetables. Corn, peas and carrots are all sweet vegetables that can usually be used in place of one another if you don't have the exact amount called for in a recipe.

Let it chill. Many casseroles can be assembled ahead and chilled until it's time to cook them, making them ideal make-ahead dishes. Remove from the refrigerator 20 to 30 minutes before putting it in the oven. You may need to add a few minutes to the baking time.

Try a tasty topping before baking. Bread crumbs on top of a casserole do a couple of things: they provide taste and texture, and they can help prevent excess moisture loss during baking. Enhance your favorite casserole by sprinkling it with something that will lend a distinct flavor to the finished dish. Buttered bread crumbs, French-fried onions, crushed potato chips, shredded cheese or cooked and crumbled bacon are all tasty choices.

Use a disposable foil pan if the dish is going to travel. This is an especially good idea if you're preparing a casserole to take to a potluck or share with a neighbor. Then there's no need to worry about getting your pan back.

Freeze it in a foil sling. When making a casserole to freeze, line the dish with foil, allowing 3 inches of foil to hang over each side. Assemble the casserole as directed, then cover and freeze. When frozen, use the foil to lift the casserole out of the dish. Peel off the foil, wrap the casserole in freezer paper and return it to the freezer. When ready to bake, unwrap and place the casserole back in the pan.

Reheat wisely. If you wish to warm a cold casserole in the microwave, tightly cover your casserole with microwavable plastic food wrap to speed reheating. Fold back a corner or cut a few slits in the plastic wrap to vent the steam. Stir or rotate the casserole once or twice during reheating. For casseroles that can't be stirred, such as lasagna, allow some standing time to let the heat equalize.

When preparing a casserole or pot pie that was frozen before baking, adjust your baking time to keep it in the oven slightly longer than one that's baked immediately after being prepared. Most casseroles and pot pies need an additional 10 to 15 minutes, but it's a good idea to check the dish during baking and adjust the time accordingly.

SUPERB SOUPS AND STEWS

Chicken-Vegetable-Barley Soup? Asian Beef and Noodle Soup or Fire Roasted Tomato-Basil Crab Bisque? Greek Beef Stew or Italian Sausage and Pepper Stew? The possibilities are endless! Serve soups year-round, hot or cold, as a meal starter or main course. While some soups are quick to assemble and serve, others demand to be simmered slowly over low heat for several hours to develop a full, rich flavor. In those cases, you're not limited to the stovetop; slow cookers are ideal for such situations. Whatever recipe and method you choose, try these tips for making your next soup or stew memorable:

Remember that size matters. Be sure to use the pot size called for in the recipe so that the soup or stew heats properly without boiling over.

Slowly heat soups made with dairy products. If soups containing milk, cream, eggs or cheese come to a boil, the ingredients may separate and curdle.

Use a flavor foundation. If you need a quick soup base, try Progresso® Vegetable Classics soups. And for south-of-the border flavor, Old El Paso® taco sauce and Old El Paso® chopped green chiles make perfect additions to soup recipes.

Aim for thick and smooth soups and stews. Keep lumps from forming when thickening soup with flour and water. Here's how: In a separate bowl, thoroughly beat flour into a small amount of cold water using a wire whisk. Whisk into the hot soup mixture.

Consider using vegetables in place of fat. Want to thicken your soup or stew without using a traditional roux (fat and flour mixture)? Stir dry mashed potatoes into the dish. Or use a blender or food processor to puree some cooked vegetables with a little broth; then stir back into the soup.

Lighten up. To remove fat from the soup or stew, refrigerate for 6 to 8 hours or

"SOUPER" SOUP TOPPERS

Make your soup recipes even better with creative toppings. Slip these topper recipes into your soup cookbook.

Crostini Recipe

1. Heat oven to 375°F.
2. Place 12 slices Italian bread, 1/2 inch thick, on ungreased cookie sheet.
3. Drizzle 1 teaspoon olive oil over each slice of bread.
4. Mix 1/2 cup chopped tomatoes, 1 tablespoon chopped fresh basil leaves, 1/4 teaspoon salt and 1/4 teaspoon pepper. Spread over bread slices.
5. Sprinkle 1 tablespoon shredded Parmesan cheese over each slice.
6. Bake about 8 minutes or until bread is hot.

Easy Cheese Biscuits Recipe

1. Heat oven to 450°F.
2. Mix 1 cup Original Bisquick® mix, 1/2 cup milk and 1/4 cup shredded Cheddar cheese until soft dough forms; beat vigorously 30 seconds.
3. Drop dough by 6 to 8 spoonfuls about 2 inches apart onto ungreased cookie sheet.
4. Bake 6 to 8 minutes or until golden brown.

Seasoned Croutons Recipe

1. Cut dry (not hard) bread into 1/2-inch cubes. Toss with olive oil to lightly coat. Or spread one side of dry bread with softened butter or margarine, and cut into 1/2-inch cubes.
2. Sprinkle with grated Parmesan cheese and Italian seasoning, or with your favorite herbs and seasonings.
3. Cook in ungreased skillet over medium heat 4 to 7 minutes, stirring frequently, until golden brown.

Toasted Cheese Slices Recipe

1. Set oven to broil.
2. Place 8 slices French bread, 3/4 to 1 inch thick, on ungreased cookie sheet.
3. Broil with tops about 5 inches from heat 1 to 2 minutes or until golden brown.
4. Turn bread slices over. Top each slice with 2 tablespoons shredded cheese or 1 slice of cheese.
5. Broil 1 to 2 minutes longer or until cheese is melted and golden brown.

Tortilla Strips Toppings Recipe

1. Heat oven to 375°F.
2. Brush 4 small corn or flour tortillas with melted butter or margarine. Sprinkle with chili powder if desired.
3. Cut each tortilla into 2 x 1/2-inch strips or 12 wedges, or cut into shapes with cookie cutters.
4. Place in single layer on 2 ungreased cookie sheets.
5. Bake 6 to 8 minutes or until light brown and crisp. Cool slightly.

overnight. Fat will rise to the surface and solidify. Skim fat with a spoon and discard.

Refrigerate in the right containers. Soup is ideal for making ahead of time, but it's important to store soup in shallow containers for rapid cooling.

Keep track of time. Cover and refrigerate soups for up to 3 days. Soups made with fish or shellfish should be refrigerated no longer than 1 day.

Reheat wisely. Heat broth-based soups over medium heat, stirring occasionally, until hot; or reheat in the microwave. Reheat thick purees or soups containing milk, cream, eggs or cheese over low heat, stirring frequently. Boiling may cause ingredients to separate.

Adjust the consistency as necessary. Thick soups tend to become thicker during storage. Add a little broth, milk or half-and-half while reheating until the soup reaches the desired consistency.

SLOW COOKING MADE SIMPLE

Using your slow cooker is one of the best-kept time-saving secrets of mealtime preparation! Slow cookers offer a great deal of flexibility—and even after your dish is ready, your cooked food can be held up to an hour on the low setting without overcooking. To get the most out of your slow cooker recipes, follow these tips to make recipes their slow-simmered best!

Keep it full. Just as ovens cook differently, so do slow cookers. Some slow cookers may have hotter heating units, and those with auto-shift cook faster. Some come with removable crocks; others do not. For best results, be sure the slow cooker is between one-half and three-quarters full of food.

Coat it before cooking. Before adding food to the slow cooker, spray the inside of it with cooking spray so the cooked food will release easily. You can also purchase a slow cooker with a nonstick interior.

Put your veggies in the right places. Root vegetables, such as potatoes, take longer to cook, so cut them into smaller pieces and place in the bottom of the slow cooker for best results. And remember that small is not always faster. Baby carrots, for example, take longer than some other veggies. Be sure to test for doneness.

Cook meats beforehand. For food safety reasons, always cook and drain ground meats before adding them to the slow cooker. Browning large cuts of meat (roasts, chops) and poultry, although not necessary, can enhance the flavor and appearance of the finished dish. To shorten the cook time, turn the slow cooker to high for 1 hour, which counts as 2 hours on low.

Cook for at least 3 hours. For food safety reasons, slow cooker recipes containing raw poultry or beef should cook a minimum of 3 hours. Do not cook whole chickens in the slow cooker because the temperature of the chicken cannot reach the desired level quickly enough for food safety.

Add tender veggies last. Tender vegetables, such as fresh tomatoes, mushrooms and zucchini, should be added the last 30 minutes to prevent overcooking.

Don't lift the lid! Removing the lid of the slow cooker can delay the cooking time by 15 to 20 minutes. Instead, try spinning the lid until vapors fall off so you can see inside. When you do have an impulse to stir, lift the lid slightly just so you can get the spoon in.

Cover the potatoes with liquid. Prevent the darkening of peeled potatoes by covering them with a liquid when cooking in a slow cooker.

Use the right amount of liquids. Slow cookers do not allow for evaporation, so don't add extra liquids to your recipes. Ingredients may appear dry before cooking, but they should turn out okay if you follow the slow cooker recipe.

SMART SUBSTITUTIONS

Having a variety of baking dishes, baking pans and casserole dishes will help with meal planning by allowing you to make several items and then refrigerate or freeze them. Don't use a smaller dish, but rather use one of a similar size. Take a quick look at this chart to see how easy it is to interchange dishes and pans.

Casserole Size	Substitution	Cup Equivalent
1-quart casserole	9-inch pie plate or 9-inch round pan	4 cups
1½-quart casserole	9-inch square pan or baking dish or 9 x 5-inch loaf pan	6 cups
2-quart casserole	11 x 7- or 8-inch square baking dish	8 cups
2½- to 3-quart casserole	13 x 9-inch baking dish	10 cups

FREEZING AND STORING YOUR MEALS

To ensure your weeknight meals are consistently a pleasure and ready to eat when you are, keep the following tips in mind when cooking ahead:

Start fresh. Always begin with fresh, high-quality foods for do-ahead meals. It's the best way to ensure delicious results.

Know what freezes well. Most casseroles may be frozen either before or after they are baked, but it's important to know what can freeze well. Recipes with a low-fat sauce or condensed soup base usually freeze well. Fresh potatoes do not freeze well. Some dairy products, such as sour cream, half-and-half, ricotta and cottage cheese, are also not recommended for freezing.

Cook just until done. To make sure meats, vegetables, pastas and grains don't overcook when reheated, cook them just until tender the first time around.

Know what to add last. If a recipe calls for a sour cream topping, add it after thawing and reheating the dish. Likewise, crisp toppings, such as nuts, crushed chips or bacon bits, should be added after the dish is thawed.

Cool cooked food before freezing. When you want to make something ahead (or save the leftovers), keep in mind that cooked foods need to be at room temperature (about 100°F) before freezing to retain the best quality and flavor. This is especially true of soups, stews and sauces, because you want to minimize ice crystal formation (which makes food mushy when thawed).

Keep it moving. To ensure even cooling, stir your dish every 15 minutes during the cool-down period.

Use ice. Transfer warm food from the cooking pan to a large, shallow pan set in a sink full of ice.

Refrigerate. Hot food should be placed in the fridge uncovered in a shallow container.

Keep containers cold. For long-term storage, hold foods in the coldest part of your freezer at 0°F or colder.

Select the right containers. Freeze food in sizes that are suitable for your family's needs. Individual sizes, enough for one family meal, are usually a good idea. Ideally, use airtight containers that can go in the microwave or can go directly from the freezer to the oven. Heavy-duty plastic bags specifically designed for freezer temperatures of 0°F and below are another good resource to consider.

Pack food containers tightly to almost full. Allow about ¼-inch to ½-inch headspace for expansion during freezing (especially important for chunky soups, stews and sauces). When headspace is more than $\frac{1}{4}$ inch, place foil (the quick-release variety) or plastic wrap directly on top of the food before covering to protect from freezer burn discoloration. Remove wrapping before baking or heating (loosen with a wet towel).

Maintain ideal freezer temperature and efficiency. Don't freeze more food than about one-tenth of the capacity of the freezer at one time. Set freezer thermostat to –10°F to speed freezing; once food is frozen (usually 24 hours), reset temperature to 0°F.

Pot Pie, Casserole and One-Dish Meals Q&A

Is it better to bake casseroles covered or uncovered?

It's best to follow the recipe since there is no one rule for when to cover. Generally, casseroles with grains, rice or pasta that will cook during the baking process are usually covered for at least part of the time. Casseroles made of cooked ingredients are usually baked uncovered. If you like a crisper, browner top, be sure the casserole is uncovered for at least part of the bake time. Pot pies made with a pie crust are typically baked uncovered.

I want to make and freeze an egg-based casserole about 1 month ahead, then defrost and reheat it. Can I freeze a casserole with eggs in it?

Yes, you can. Raw eggs are fairly stable in the freezer, especially when beaten or mixed with other ingredients. Check to see what else is in the casserole, though. Hard-cooked eggs, potatoes, rice and pasta don't freeze particularly well because they break down and lose their texture.

Can I use instant rice in place of regular rice or wild rice in a casserole?

Maybe, maybe not! If the recipe calls for cooked rice, go ahead and substitute an equal amount of cooked instant rice for the cooked regular or wild rice. However, you should not make an equal substitution if the recipe calls for uncooked rice. The amounts of liquid and rice and the cooking time will all be different.

Should I grease the casserole dish? What should I use?

For easier release and cleanup, grease the casserole dish. For the quickest cleanup, line the dish with heavy-duty foil and then grease the foil with shortening, oil or cooking spray before filling and baking—or use nonstick foil.

Should I freeze casseroles before they are baked or after baking?

Both! You can actually do either, but the most important thing is to cool the casserole before freezing. If the casserole has a topping, freeze it without the topping. Then, add the topping the last 10 to 20 minutes of the bake time. You should also thaw the casserole overnight in the refrigerator before baking. When you're ready to bake, start by adding 15 minutes to the suggested bake time, then check to see if more time is needed. The center of the casserole should reach 160°F.

How long can I keep a casserole frozen?

For best quality, use frozen casseroles within 3 months. Although the casserole will still be safe to eat after that, as more moisture is lost, the texture and flavor will deteriorate.

How long can I keep soups frozen?

Soups and broths can be kept frozen for 2 to 3 months.

When I took my main ingredients out of the slow cooker, a tasty-looking juice was in the bottom of the pot. I hate to throw all that flavor out of my finished dish. How can I thicken the juices instead?

Liquids tend to be thin after you remove the meat and vegetables from the slow cooker. You might want to thicken these juices before serving your meal. This usually takes about 10 to 15 minutes and is worth the time. Use flour to thicken and cook for the recommended time according to the slow cooker recipe.

Why should I cool down foods before freezing?

It's always a good idea to avoid adding hot food to a freezer. The freezer has to work harder, you create extra moisture and the heat can partially thaw already-frozen foods.

I'd like to freeze several dishes at the same time. How can I maximize my freezer space?

When freezing several food packages at once, place in a single layer in the coldest part of the freezer, leaving space for air circulation. Once solidly frozen, packages can be stacked.

To quick-freeze foods, arrange separately in a single layer on a cookie sheet or jelly roll pan. Freeze uncovered (or covered with an inverted pan as a lid) until solid (12 to 24 hours) and then repackage.

How can I use plastic freezer bags most effectively?

When food is exposed to air in the freezer, freezer burn can occur. To effectively shrink-wrap foods packaged in freezer bags, you need to press out as much air as possible before sealing.

Close the bag, leaving a $\frac{1}{2}$-inch opening. Then use either of these air-sealing methods:

1) Insert a drinking straw in the opening and suck out any remaining air until the bag shrinks around the food. Quickly slip the straw out and seal the bag completely.

2) Or submerge the filled bag in a container of water, pushing air out of the bag, and then seal the bag.

REHEATING FOODS IN THE MICROWAVE—ZAP IT!

A microwave is a quick and easy way to reheat one-dish meals. Here's what you need to know to get the most reliable results:

For food safety reasons, bring the internal temperature to 160°F. Use an instant-read thermometer to determine whether the food is hot enough at its center. Don't leave the thermometer in the food while the microwave is heating; use it to check the temperature only after reheating.

Consider the consistency of the food. Moist foods reheat best, and covering foods will allow for faster and more even heating. Pizzas and other crisp or crunchy foods reheat best when heated on a browning dish or a microwave rack, so the bottom doesn't get soggy.

Keep it small. Individual servings heat more quickly than the entire recipe yield, because the microwave can penetrate the food more deeply and heat the center more quickly.

Avoid overcooking. Make sure to heat casseroles with eggs, cheese or large chunks of meat at a lower power setting.

Breakfasts

Bacon and Hash Brown Egg Bake

PREP TIME: *30 minutes*
TOTAL TIME: *9 hours 40 minutes*
MAKES 12 SERVINGS

1 pound bacon, cut into 1-inch pieces

1 medium onion, chopped (½ cup)

1 medium red bell pepper, chopped (¾ cup)

1 package (8 ounces) sliced fresh mushrooms

2 tablespoons Dijon mustard

½ teaspoon salt

½ teaspoon black pepper

¾ cup milk

12 eggs

1 package (2 pounds) frozen hash browns, thawed

2 cups shredded Cheddar cheese (16 ounces)

In 12-inch skillet, cook bacon until crisp. Using slotted spoon, remove from pan to small bowl. Cover and refrigerate. Drain drippings, reserving 1 tablespoon in pan. Add onion, bell pepper and mushrooms; cook 4 minutes over medium heat, stirring occasionally. Stir in mustard, salt and pepper. In large bowl, beat milk and eggs with wire whisk.

Spray 13 × 9-inch (3-quart) baking dish with cooking spray. Spread half of the hash browns in baking dish. Spread onion mixture evenly on top. Sprinkle with 1 cup of the cheese. Spread remaining hash browns over top. Pour egg mixture on top. Cover; refrigerate 8 hours or overnight.

Heat oven to 325°F. Uncover; bake 50 to 60 minutes or until thermometer inserted in center reads 160°F. Sprinkle with remaining 1 cup cheese and the bacon. Bake 3 to 5 minutes longer or until knife inserted in center comes out clean, top is puffed and cheese is melted. Let stand 5 minutes.

1 SERVING: Calories 410; Total Fat 24g (Saturated Fat 12g, Trans Fat 0g); Cholesterol 265mg; Sodium 740mg; Total Carbohydrate 25g (Dietary Fiber 3g, Sugars 4g); Protein 22g; EXCHANGES: 1½ Starch; 2½ High-Fat Meat; 1 Fat; CARBOHYDRATE CHOICES: 1½

Sausage 'n Apple Cheddar Biscuit Bake

- 1 package (1 pound) bulk pork sausage
- 4 medium cooking apples, coarsely chopped (4 cups)
- 1 large onion, chopped (1 cup)
- 6 eggs
- 1/2 teaspoon salt
- 2 1/4 cups Gold Medal® all-purpose flour
- 2 1/2 teaspoons baking powder
- 2 teaspoons sugar
- 3/4 teaspoon baking soda
- 1 teaspoon salt
- 6 tablespoons firm butter or margarine, cut into 1/2-inch cubes
- 1 1/2 cups shredded Cheddar cheese (6 ounces)
- 2 medium green onions, finely chopped (2 tablespoons)
- 1 cup buttermilk

Heat oven to 425°F. Spray bottom and sides of 13 × 9-inch (3-quart) glass baking dish with cooking spray or grease with shortening. In 12-inch skillet, cook sausage, apples and onion over medium-high heat 8 to 10 minutes, stirring frequently, until sausage is no longer pink; drain if necessary. Spoon into baking dish.

In medium bowl, beat eggs and 1/2 teaspoon salt with wire whisk or fork until well mixed. Pour eggs over sausage mixture.

In large bowl, mix flour, baking powder, sugar, baking soda and 1 teaspoon salt. Cut in butter, using pastry blender (or pulling 2 table knives through ingredients in opposite directions), until mixture looks like coarse crumbs. Stir in cheese and green onions. Add buttermilk; stir just until combined. Drop dough by rounded tablespoonfuls evenly onto sausage mixture.

Bake uncovered 20 to 30 minutes or until biscuits are deep golden brown and done in the middle. Let stand 10 minutes before serving.

1 SERVING: Calories 340; Total Fat 19g (Saturated Fat 9g, Trans Fat 0g); Cholesterol 150mg; Sodium 880mg; Total Carbohydrate 28g (Dietary Fiber 2g, Sugars 7g); Protein 14g; EXCHANGES: 1 1/2 Starch; 1/2 Other Carbohydrate; 2 Fat; CARBOHYDRATE CHOICES: 2

Bacon-Cheese Pull-Aparts

1 egg

2 tablespoons milk

1 can (16.3 ounces) Pillsbury® Grands!® Flaky Layers refrigerated original biscuits

1 package (2.2 ounces) precooked bacon, cut into ½-inch pieces

¾ cup shredded Cheddar cheese (3 ounces)

4 medium green onions, finely chopped (¼ cup)

Heat oven to 350°F. Spray 11 × 7- or 12 × 8-inch (2-quart) glass baking dish with cooking spray. In large bowl, beat egg and milk with wire whisk until smooth.

Separate dough into 8 biscuits; cut each into quarters. Gently stir biscuit pieces into egg mixture to coat evenly. Fold in bacon, cheese and onions. Spoon mixture into baking dish; arrange biscuit pieces in single layer.

Bake 23 to 28 minutes or until golden brown. Cut into squares.

1 SERVING: Calories 290; Total Fat 17g (Saturated Fat 6g, Trans Fat 3½g); Cholesterol 45mg; Sodium 810mg; Total Carbohydrate 25g (Dietary Fiber 0g, Sugars 6g); Protein 11g; EXCHANGES: 1½ Starch; 1 High-Fat Meat; 1½ Fat; CARBOHYDRATE CHOICES: 1½

Expert Tips

■ Look for the precooked bacon near the packaged cooked meats at the supermarket.

■ This recipe was created by Terri Barton of Salt Lake City, Utah, and was a finalist in a national recipe contest.

Holiday Breakfast Bake

- 1 package (12 ounces) bulk pork sausage
- 1/3 cup chopped onion
- 1/3 cup chopped green bell pepper
- 1/3 cup chopped red bell pepper
- 10 eggs
- 1 cup shredded Cheddar cheese (4 ounces)
- 1 can (16.3 ounces) Pillsbury® Grands!® Flaky Layers refrigerated original biscuits

Heat oven to 375°F. Spray 13 × 9-inch (3-quart) baking dish with cooking spray. In 10-inch skillet, brown sausage, onion and bell peppers; drain well.

In large bowl, beat eggs. Stir in cheese and sausage mixture. Separate dough into 8 biscuits. Press biscuits into bottom of baking dish. Pour sausage mixture over biscuit crust.

Bake 25 to 30 minutes or until egg mixture is set and crust is deep golden brown. Cool 5 minutes before serving.

1 SERVING: Calories 410; Total Fat 26g (Saturated Fat 9g, Trans Fat 3½g); Cholesterol 295mg; Sodium 870mg; Total Carbohydrate 25g (Dietary Fiber 0g, Sugars 7g); Protein 19g; EXCHANGES: 1 Starch; ½ Other Carbohydrate; 2½ Fat; CARBOHYDRATE CHOICES: 1½

Expert Tip

A platter of mixed fresh fruits of the season is the perfect companion for this hearty breakfast dish.

Country Breakfast Pot Pie

3 tablespoons vegetable oil

1 bag (20 ounces) refrigerated shredded hash browns

1 cup shredded Swiss cheese (4 ounces)

8 eggs

1 tablespoon chopped fresh chives

½ teaspoon salt

¼ teaspoon freshly ground pepper

1½ cups cubed cooked ham (8 ounces)

1 package (3 ounces) cream cheese, cut into small cubes

1 can (12 ounces) Pillsbury® Big & Buttery refrigerated crescent dinner rolls

Heat oven to 375°F. Spray 11 × 7-inch (2-quart) glass baking dish with cooking spray. In 12-inch nonstick skillet, heat 2 tablespoons of the oil over medium-high heat. Spread potatoes in skillet; cook until golden brown on bottom.

Drizzle potatoes with remaining 1 tablespoon oil. Cut into quarters; turn sections over. Cook until golden brown. Remove hash browns from skillet; arrange in bottom and around side of baking dish. Sprinkle Swiss cheese over potatoes.

In bowl, beat eggs. Stir in chives, salt, pepper and ham. Pour into same skillet. Cook and stir over medium heat until partially cooked. Stir in cream cheese; cook and stir until eggs are cooked but moist. Spread over Swiss cheese.

Separate dough into triangles. Starting at short side of each triangle, roll up halfway. Arrange over hot egg mixture with tips toward center; do not overlap.

Bake 20 to 25 minutes or until crust is golden brown.

1 SERVING: Calories 650; Total Fat 36g (Saturated Fat 14g, Trans Fat 0g); Cholesterol 335mg; Sodium 1,320mg; Total Carbohydrate 54g (Dietary Fiber 3g, Sugars 8g); Protein 26g; EXCHANGES: 3 Starch; ½ Other Carbohydrate; 4 Fat; CARBOHYDRATE CHOICES: 3½

Puffed-Pancake Brunch Casserole

½ cup butter

2 cups Original Bisquick® mix

2 cups milk

8 eggs

1 cup shredded Swiss cheese (4 ounces)

1 pound cubed cooked ham (about 3 cups)

1 package (2.1 ounces) precooked bacon, chopped

2 cups shredded Cheddar cheese (8 ounces)

¼ teaspoon salt

¼ teaspoon ground mustard

Dash ground nutmeg

Heat oven to 375°F. Spray 13 × 9-inch (3-quart) glass baking dish with cooking spray. Place butter in dish; place in oven until melted, about 10 minutes.

In medium bowl, mix Bisquick, 1 cup of the milk and 2 of the eggs with whisk until tiny lumps remain. Pour over butter in baking dish. Layer with Swiss cheese, ham, bacon and Cheddar cheese. In large bowl, mix remaining 1 cup milk, remaining 6 eggs, the salt, mustard and nutmeg. Pour over casserole.

Bake uncovered 35 to 40 minutes or until golden brown. Let stand 10 minutes before serving.

1 SERVING: Calories 460; Total Fat 30g (Saturated Fat 15g, Trans Fat 1½g); Cholesterol 255mg; Sodium 1,430mg; Total Carbohydrate 19g (Dietary Fiber 0g, Sugars 4g); Protein 29g; EXCHANGES: 1 Starch; ½ Other Carbohydrate; ½ High-Fat Meat; 2 Fat; CARBOHYDRATE CHOICES: 1

Ham and Swiss Brunch Bake

PREP TIME: *25 minutes*
TOTAL TIME: *2 hours*
MAKES 10 SERVINGS

1 loaf (1 pound)
French bread, cut into
½-inch slices

2 tablespoons Dijon mustard

8 ounces thinly sliced
cooked ham

8 ounces thinly sliced
Swiss cheese

4 eggs

2 cups milk

¼ cup grated
Parmesan cheese

¼ cup Progresso®
plain bread crumbs

2 tablespoons chopped
fresh parsley

3 tablespoons butter or
margarine, melted

In ungreased 13 × 9-inch (3-quart) glass baking dish, arrange half of the bread slices, overlapping as needed. Brush bread in dish with mustard. Top evenly with ham and Swiss cheese, overlapping as needed. Top with remaining bread slices, arranging them over first layer of bread slices to make sandwiches.

In medium bowl, beat eggs and milk with wire whisk until well blended. Carefully pour over sandwiches. Cover; refrigerate at least 1 hour but no longer than 12 hours.

Meanwhile, in small bowl, mix Parmesan cheese, bread crumbs, parsley and butter. Set aside.

Heat oven to 375°F. Sprinkle crumb topping over casserole. Bake uncovered 30 to 35 minutes or until sandwiches are puffed and golden brown.

1 SERVING: Calories 360; Total Fat 16g (Saturated Fat 9g, Trans Fat 0g); Cholesterol 135mg; Sodium 810mg; Total Carbohydrate 32g (Dietary Fiber 1g, Sugars 7g); Protein 22g; EXCHANGES: 2 Starch; 2 High-Fat Meat; CARBOHYDRATE CHOICES: 2

Expert Tip

Prepare this dish the night before. Cover and refrigerate the sandwiches separately from the topping. Add the topping just before baking.

PREP TIME: *50 minutes*

TOTAL TIME: *3 hours 55 minutes*

MAKES 8 SERVINGS

Phyllo Egg Breakfast Torta

- 1 pound bulk ground Italian pork sausage
- 1 medium red bell pepper, chopped
- 1 medium onion, chopped (1/2 cup)
- 6 eggs
- 1/2 teaspoon black pepper
- 30 sheets frozen phyllo (filo) pastry (14 × 9 inch), thawed
- 3/4 cup butter or margarine, melted
- 2 cups shredded Swiss cheese (8 ounces)
- 1 box (9 ounces) Green Giant® frozen spinach, thawed and drained
- 2 tablespoons chopped fresh basil leaves
- 1/4 cup grated Parmesan cheese

In 10-inch nonstick skillet, cook sausage over medium-high heat 6 to 8 minutes or until no longer pink. Remove sausage to medium bowl. Reserve 1 tablespoon liquid in skillet. Reduce heat to medium. Add bell pepper and onion to skillet; cook 5 to 7 minutes, stirring occasionally, until tender. Remove from skillet; add to sausage in bowl.

In another medium bowl, beat eggs and pepper with wire whisk. Add to skillet; cook and stir over medium heat 3 to 5 minutes or until eggs are set.

Spray 13 × 9-inch (3-quart) baking dish with cooking spray. Unroll phyllo sheets; cover with plastic wrap and damp paper towel. Place 1 phyllo sheet in baking dish; brush with melted butter. Repeat 9 times.

Spread half of the sausage mixture over phyllo. Layer 10 more phyllo sheets and brush with butter. Sprinkle evenly with cooked eggs, Swiss cheese, spinach and basil. Layer 5 more phyllo sheets and brush with butter.

Top with remaining sausage mixture. Sprinkle with Parmesan cheese. Layer remaining 5 phyllo sheets and brush with butter.

Cover tightly; refrigerate 2 to 24 hours. Heat oven to 350°F. Uncover; bake 45 to 55 minutes or until top is golden brown. If desired, garnish with additional chopped fresh basil before serving.

1 SERVING: Calories 560; Total Fat 38g (Saturated Fat 20g, Trans Fat 1g); Cholesterol 255mg; Sodium 640mg; Total Carbohydrate 31g (Dietary Fiber 2g, Sugars 2g); Protein 23g; EXCHANGES: 2 Starch; 2½ High-Fat Meat; 3½ Fat; CARBOHYDRATE CHOICES: 2

Expert Tips

- Tomato pasta sauce makes a nice topping for this casserole.
- Serve with a tossed fruit salad.
- For a healthier version, try substituting the Italian sausage with lean turkey sausage.

Make–Ahead Alfredo Strata

PREP TIME: *10 minutes*
TOTAL TIME: *5 hours 5 minutes*
MAKES 8 SERVINGS

1 loaf (1 pound) unsliced rustic Italian bread, cut into 1-inch cubes (8 cups)

1 cup Green Giant® Valley Fresh Steamers® frozen chopped broccoli (from 12-ounce bag), thawed, drained

2 cups shredded Italian cheese blend (8 ounces)

5 eggs

2 cups milk

1 container (10 ounces) refrigerated Alfredo pasta sauce

Spray 13 × 9-inch (3-quart) glass baking dish with cooking spray. In baking dish, layer half of the bread cubes, the broccoli, 1 cup of the cheese and the remaining bread cubes.

In large bowl, beat eggs, milk and Alfredo sauce with wire whisk until well blended. Pour over ingredients in baking dish. Cover; refrigerate 4 hours or overnight.

Heat oven to 350°F. Uncover baking dish. Sprinkle remaining 1 cup cheese over strata. Bake 45 to 50 minutes or until knife inserted in center comes out clean and cheese is deep golden brown. Let stand 5 minutes before serving.

1 SERVING: Calories 450; Total Fat 25g (Saturated Fat 14g, Trans Fat 1g); Cholesterol 190mg; Sodium 780mg; Total Carbohydrate 35g (Dietary Fiber 2g, Sugars 5g); Protein 21g; EXCHANGES: 2½ Starch; 1 High-Fat Meat; 2 Fat; CARBOHYDRATE CHOICES: 2

Expert Tips

■ Alfredo sauce from a jar can be used in place of refrigerated sauce.

■ For a variation, make this an Alfredo Ham Strata by adding 1 cup diced cooked ham to the layers between the broccoli and cheese.

PREP TIME: *20 minutes*

TOTAL TIME: *5 hours 30 minutes*

MAKES 8 SERVINGS

Artichoke-Spinach Strata

- 2 teaspoons olive or vegetable oil
- 1 cup finely chopped red bell pepper (1 medium)
- ½ cup finely chopped onion (1 medium)
- 2 cloves garlic, finely chopped
- 1 can (14 ounces) quartered artichoke hearts, drained, coarsely chopped (1½ cups)
- 1 box (9 ounces) Green Giant® frozen spinach, thawed, squeezed to drain
- 8 cups cubed (1 inch) rustic round bread (about 1 pound)
- 1½ cups shredded Monterey Jack cheese (6 ounces)
- 6 eggs
- 2½ cups milk
- ½ teaspoon ground mustard
- 1 teaspoon salt
- ¼ teaspoon black pepper
- ½ cup shredded Parmesan cheese (2 ounces)

In 10-inch nonstick skillet, heat oil over medium heat. Add bell pepper, onion and garlic; cook about 6 minutes, stirring occasionally, until tender. Remove from heat. Stir in artichokes and spinach; set aside.

Spray 13 × 9-inch (3-quart) glass baking dish with cooking spray. Arrange bread cubes in dish. Spoon vegetable mixture evenly over bread cubes; sprinkle with Monterey Jack cheese.

In medium bowl, beat eggs, milk, mustard, salt and pepper with wire whisk until blended; pour evenly over bread, vegetables and cheese. Sprinkle with Parmesan cheese. Cover tightly with foil; refrigerate at least 4 hours but no longer than 24 hours.

Heat oven to 350°F. Bake covered 30 minutes. Uncover; bake 20 to 30 minutes longer or until top is golden brown and knife inserted in center comes out clean. Let stand 10 minutes before cutting.

1 SERVING: Calories 390; Total Fat 17g (Saturated Fat 8g, Trans Fat ½g); Cholesterol 190mg; Sodium 980mg; Total Carbohydrate 35g (Dietary Fiber 7g, Sugars 12g); Protein 24g; EXCHANGES: 1 Starch; 1 Other Carbohydrate; 1 Vegetable; 1 Fat; CARBOHYDRATE CHOICES: 2

Ham and Cheddar Strata

12 slices bread

2 cups cut-up cooked smoked ham (about 10 ounces)

2 cups shredded Cheddar cheese (8 ounces)

8 medium green onions with tops, peeled and thinly sliced ($\frac{1}{2}$ cup)

6 large eggs

2 cups milk

1 teaspoon ground mustard

$\frac{1}{4}$ teaspoon red pepper sauce

Paprika, if desired

Spray a 13 × 9-inch (3-quart) glass baking dish with cooking spray. Trim crusts from bread.

Arrange 6 bread slices in baking dish. Layer ham, cheese and onions on bread in dish. Cut remaining bread slices diagonally in half; arrange on onions.

In medium bowl, beat eggs, milk, mustard and pepper sauce with fork or wire whisk; pour evenly over bread. Cover with plastic wrap or foil and refrigerate up to 24 hours.

Heat oven to 300°F. Uncover strata and sprinkle with paprika. Bake uncovered 1 hour to 1 hour 10 minutes or until center is set and bread is golden brown. Let stand 10 minutes before cutting into serving pieces.

1 Serving: Calories 360; Total Fat 19g (Saturated Fat 9g, Trans Fat $\frac{1}{2}$g); Cholesterol 215mg; Sodium 1,010mg; Total Carbohydrate 24g (Dietary Fiber 1g, Sugars 6g); Protein 25g; EXCHANGES: 1 Starch; $\frac{1}{2}$ Other Carbohydrate; $\frac{1}{2}$ Fat; CARBOHYDRATE CHOICES: 1$\frac{1}{2}$

Expert Tips

- Use reduced-fat ham, reduced-fat Cheddar cheese and fat-free (skim) milk for 9 grams of fat and 280 calories per serving.
- Use 2 cups shredded Swiss cheese for the Cheddar cheese.
- The strata can be assembled and baked without refrigerating. After pouring the egg mixture over the bread, sprinkle with paprika and bake as directed in step 4.
- Slices of whole grain or whole wheat bread also make a good strata. And for a real flavor change, use slices of raisin-cinnamon bread.

Brunch Casserole

2 boxes Betty Crocker® Seasoned Skillets® hash brown potatoes

1½ pounds bulk spicy pork sausage

2 medium red bell peppers, chopped (2 cups)

8 medium green onions, chopped (½ cup)

1 cup shredded Cheddar cheese (4 ounces)

1 cup shredded pepper Jack cheese (4 ounces)

2 cups milk

½ teaspoon salt

½ teaspoon black pepper

6 eggs

Chopped fresh cilantro, if desired

Spray 3-quart casserole dish with cooking spray. In 4-quart bowl, cover potatoes with 10 cups boiling water. Let stand 3 minutes. Drain well; return potatoes to bowl.

In 12-inch skillet, cook sausage over medium heat 5 minutes. Add bell peppers; cook 4 minutes, stirring frequently, until sausage is no longer pink and peppers are tender. Drain. Add sausage mixture to potatoes in bowl; stir in onions and ½ cup of each of the cheeses. Spread in casserole dish.

In medium bowl, beat milk, salt, pepper and eggs until blended. Pour over sausage-potato mixture; sprinkle with remaining ½ cup of each cheese. Cover; refrigerate 8 hours or overnight.

Heat oven to 375°F. Uncover baking dish. Bake 50 minutes or until light golden brown and cheese is melted. Let stand 10 minutes before serving. Sprinkle with cilantro.

1 SERVING: Calories 606; Total Fat 38g (Saturated Fat 15g, Trans Fat 0g); Cholesterol 256mg; Sodium 1,558mg; Total Carbohydrate 36g (Dietary Fiber 4g, Sugars 4g); Protein 29g; EXCHANGES: 1½ Starch; ½ Vegetable; ½ Medium-Fat Meat; 3 High-Fat Meat; 2 Fat; CARBOHYDRATE CHOICES: 2½

Italian Pepperoni–Vegetable Quiche

1 box Pillsbury® refrigerated pie crusts, softened as directed on box

1 box (7 ounces) Green Giant® Immunity Blend frozen broccoli, carrots and pepper strips in an olive oil seasoning

1½ cups shredded mozzarella cheese (6 ounces)

½ cup chopped seeded tomato

½ cup sliced pepperoni, chopped

5 eggs

¾ cup milk

1 teaspoon Italian seasoning

Heat oven to 375°F. Place pie crust in ungreased 9-inch glass pie plate as directed on box for One-Crust Filled Pie.

Microwave broccoli, carrots and peppers as directed on box.

Sprinkle 1 cup of the cheese in crust. Top with tomato and pepperoni. Spoon broccoli, carrots and peppers over pepperoni. Sprinkle with remaining ½ cup cheese. In small bowl, beat eggs, milk and Italian seasoning. Pour egg mixture over cheese.

Bake 35 to 40 minutes or until crust is golden brown and knife inserted near center comes out clean. Cool 5 minutes before serving.

1 SERVING: Calories 380; Total Fat 25g (Saturated Fat 10g, Trans Fat 0g); Cholesterol 210mg; Sodium 540mg; Total Carbohydrate 23g (Dietary Fiber 1g, Sugars 4g); Protein 16g; EXCHANGES: 1 Starch; 1 Low-Fat Milk; 1½ Fat; CARBOHYDRATE CHOICES: 1½

Expert Tips

■ Top each serving with warm pizza sauce.

■ One-quarter pound of Italian sausage, cooked and drained, can be used in place of the pepperoni.

■ This quiche can also be served as a breakfast dish.

Loaded Potato Quiche

CRUST

2½ cups Original Bisquick® mix

6 tablespoons cold butter or margarine

¼ cup boiling water

FILLING

1½ cups chopped cooked ham

1½ cups frozen diced hash brown potatoes, thawed

1½ cups shredded sharp Cheddar cheese (6 ounces)

3 medium green onions, sliced (3 tablespoons)

5 eggs

¾ cup half-and-half

¼ teaspoon freshly ground pepper

3 slices bacon, crisply cooked, crumbled

Sour cream, if desired

Additional sliced green onions, if desired

Heat oven to 350°F. Spray 9½-inch glass deep-dish pie plate with cooking spray.

Place Bisquick mix in medium bowl. Cut in butter, using pastry blender (or pulling 2 table knives through mixture in opposite directions), until crumbly. Add boiling water; stir vigorously until soft dough forms. Using fingers dipped in Bisquick mix, press dough on bottom and up side of pie plate, forming edge on rim of plate.

Sprinkle ham, potatoes, cheese and 3 tablespoons onions in crust. In medium bowl, beat eggs, half-and-half and pepper until blended. Pour over ingredients in crust.

Bake 1 hour 5 minutes or until knife inserted in center comes out clean. Let stand 15 minutes before serving. Top with bacon, sour cream and additional onions.

1 SERVING: Calories 480; Total Fat 31g (Saturated Fat 14g, Trans Fat 2g); Cholesterol 203mg; Sodium 820mg; Total Carbohydrate 32g (Dietary Fiber 1g, Sugars 2g); Protein 21g; EXCHANGES: 2 Starch; 1 Lean Meat; 1 Medium-Fat Meat; 1 High-Fat Meat; 3 Fat; CARBOHYDRATE CHOICES: 2

Ragin' Cajun Quiche

1¼ cups Original Bisquick® mix

¼ cup butter or margarine, softened

2 tablespoons hot water

4 ounces pepper Jack cheese, shredded

1 cup diced smoked spicy andouille sausage (about 6 ounces)

⅓ cup thinly sliced green onions

1 cup half-and-half

1½ teaspoons Cajun seasoning

3 eggs

Heat oven to 400°F. Spray 9-inch glass pie plate with cooking spray.

In medium bowl, stir Bisquick mix and softened butter until mixed. (Mixture will be crumbly.) Add hot water; stir until soft dough forms. Press dough in bottom and up side of pie plate.

Layer cheese, sausage and green onions over crust in pie plate. In medium bowl, beat half-and-half, Cajun seasoning and eggs with whisk or fork until blended. Pour in pie plate.

Bake 32 to 38 minutes or until knife inserted in center comes out clean. Let stand 10 minutes before serving.

1 SERVING: Calories 500; Total Fat 32g (Saturated Fat 16g, Trans Fat 1½g); Cholesterol 240mg; Sodium 1,330mg; Total Carbohydrate 24g (Dietary Fiber 1g, Sugars 3g); Protein 29g; EXCHANGES: 1 Starch; ½ Low-Fat Milk; 3 Lean Meat; 4 Fat; CARBOHYDRATE CHOICES: 1½

Expert Tips

- Andouille is a heavily smoked and spicy sausage often used to flavor Cajun dishes.
- Cajun seasoning can be found in the herb and spice section of your grocery store.

Easy Cheese and Bacon Quiche

1¼ cups Original Bisquick® mix

¼ cup butter or margarine, softened

2 tablespoons boiling water

1 package (6 ounces) sliced Canadian bacon, chopped

1 cup shredded Swiss cheese (4 ounces)

4 medium green onions, thinly sliced (¼ cup)

1½ cups half-and-half

3 eggs

½ teaspoon salt

¼ teaspoon ground red pepper (cayenne)

Heat oven to 400°F. Grease bottom and side of 9-inch pie plate with shortening. Stir Bisquick and butter until blended. Add boiling water; stir vigorously until soft dough forms. Press dough in bottom and up side of pie plate, forming edge on rim of plate.

Sprinkle bacon, cheese and onions over crust. In medium bowl, beat half-and-half, eggs, salt and red pepper with spoon until blended. Pour into crust.

Bake 35 to 40 minutes or until edges are golden brown and center is set.

1 SERVING: Calories 300; Total Fat 21g (Saturated Fat 11g, Trans Fat 1g); Cholesterol 135mg; Sodium 790mg; Total Carbohydrate 15g (Dietary Fiber 0g, Sugars 4g); Protein 13g; EXCHANGES: 1 Starch; 1½ High-Fat Meat; 1½ Fat; CARBOHYDRATE CHOICES: 1

Expert Tip

Chop the Canadian bacon, shred the cheese and slice the onions the day before; store separately in refrigerator. Beat the half-and-half mixture; store covered in refrigerator.

Corn, Cheddar and Tomato Quiche

1 cup soymilk

4 eggs or 1 cup fat-free egg product

¼ cup chopped fresh cilantro

½ teaspoon chili powder

¼ teaspoon salt

¼ teaspoon pepper

1 cup Cascadian Farm® frozen organic sweet corn, thawed

¾ cup shredded reduced-fat Cheddar cheese (3 ounces)

1 medium tomato, seeded, chopped (¾ cup)

Heat oven to 350°F. Spray 9-inch glass pie plate with cooking spray.

In medium bowl, stir soymilk, eggs, cilantro, chili powder, salt and pepper until blended. Stir in corn, cheese and tomato; pour into pie plate.

Bake 30 to 35 minutes or until knife inserted in center comes out clean. Let stand 10 minutes before cutting.

1 SERVING: Calories 120; Total Fat 5g (Saturated Fat 2g, Trans Fat 0g); Cholesterol 145mg; Sodium 310mg; Total Carbohydrate 8g (Dietary Fiber 1g, Sugars 3g); Protein 10g; EXCHANGES: ½ Starch; CARBOHYDRATE CHOICES: ½

Chicken Enchilada Quiche

- 1 box Pillsbury® refrigerated pie crusts, softened as directed on box
- 4 eggs
- 1 cup half-and-half or milk
- 1 can (12.5 ounces) chunk chicken breast in water, drained (1½ cups)
- 1½ cups broken tortilla chips
- 2 cups shredded Monterey Jack cheese (8 ounces)
- 1 cup shredded Cheddar cheese (4 ounces)
- 1 cup Old El Paso® Thick 'n Chunky salsa
- 1 can (4.5 ounces) Old El Paso® chopped green chiles
- ½ teaspoon salt
- Pepper to taste, if desired
- Sour cream, if desired
- Old El Paso® Thick 'n Chunky salsa for serving, if desired

Heat oven to 350°F. Place pie crust in 9- or 9½-inch glass deep-dish pie pan as directed on box for One-Crust Filled Pie.

In medium bowl, beat eggs with wire whisk until blended. Beat in half-and-half. Stir in chicken, chips, both cheeses, 1 cup salsa, the green chiles and salt. Pour into crust-lined pan. Sprinkle pepper over top of filling.

Bake 55 to 65 minutes or until crust is light golden brown and knife inserted in center comes out clean. Let stand 10 minutes before serving. Cut into wedges. Serve with sour cream and/or salsa.

1 SERVING: Calories 480; Total Fat 31g (Saturated Fat 14g, Trans Fat ½g); Cholesterol 180mg; Sodium 1,260mg; Total Carbohydrate 28g (Dietary Fiber 1g, Sugars 5g); Protein 22g; EXCHANGES: 2 Starch; 2 Lean Meat; 5 Fat; CARBOHYDRATE CHOICES: 2

"Sausage" and Noodle Frittata

8 eggs

1 can (18.5 ounces) Progresso® Light vegetable and noodle soup

5 frozen soy-protein breakfast sausage links (4 ounces), thawed, cut into 1/4-inch pieces

1/2 medium red bell pepper, cut into bite-size strips

1 teaspoon Italian seasoning or dried basil

1/2 cup shredded reduced-fat Cheddar cheese (2 ounces)

Chopped fresh basil, if desired

Heat oven to 425°F. In medium bowl, beat eggs with wire whisk until blended. Stir in soup, sausage, bell pepper and Italian seasoning. Pour into 12-inch ovenproof nonstick skillet.

Bake 25 to 30 minutes or until set. Sprinkle cheese over top. Cover; let stand 5 minutes before serving. Cut into wedges to serve. Sprinkle basil over top.

1 SERVING: Calories 170; Total Fat 9g (Saturated Fat 2 1/2g, Trans Fat 0g); Cholesterol 285mg; Sodium 620mg; Total Carbohydrate 7g (Dietary Fiber 2g, Sugars 2g); Protein 15g; EXCHANGES: 1/2 Other Carbohydrate; CARBOHYDRATE CHOICES: 1/2

Sausage and Egg Breakfast Pizza

PREP TIME: *10 minutes*
TOTAL TIME: *30 minutes*
MAKES 4 SERVINGS

1 package (8 ounces) frozen brown-and-serve pork sausage links, cut into ½-inch pieces

6 eggs, beaten

4 ready-to-serve pizza crusts, 6 inches in diameter

1½ cups shredded Cheddar cheese (6 ounces)

Heat oven to 400°F. Spray 10-inch nonstick skillet with cooking spray; heat over medium heat. Cook sausage in skillet about 3 minutes, stirring occasionally, until brown; drain. Remove sausage from skillet; set aside.

Pour eggs into skillet. As mixture begins to set at bottom and side, gently lift cooked portions with spatula so that thin, uncooked portion can flow to bottom.

Do not stir. Cook 4 to 5 minutes or until eggs are thickened throughout but still moist.

Place pizza crusts on ungreased cookie sheets. Sprinkle with half of the cheese. Top each with eggs and sausage. Sprinkle with remaining cheese. Bake 10 to 12 minutes or until cheese is melted.

1 SERVING: Calories 889; Total Fat 49g (Saturated Fat 17g, Trans Fat 0g); Cholesterol 399mg; Sodium 1,520mg; Total Carbohydrate 72g (Dietary Fiber 2g, Sugars 1g); Protein 32g; EXCHANGES: 2 Starch; 1 Medium-Fat Meat; 2 High-Fat Meat; 3 Fat; CARBOHYDRATE CHOICES: 5

Expert Tips

- Sparkling apple cider or your favorite fruit juice goes well with this good morning goodie.
- For a veggie lift, add chopped tomato, green bell pepper and mushrooms before topping with the final cheese layer.

Bacon and Potato Breakfast Pizza

1 can (8 ounces) Pillsbury® refrigerated crescent dinner rolls

1 box (9 ounces) Green Giant® frozen roasted potatoes with garlic and herbs

4 eggs

1/3 cup milk

8 slices packaged precooked bacon, cut into 1-inch pieces

1 1/2 cups shredded Cheddar cheese (6 ounces)

Salt and pepper, if desired

2 tablespoons chopped fresh parsley

Heat oven to 350°F. Spray 13 × 9-inch pan with cooking spray. Unroll dough in pan. Press in bottom and 1/2 inch up sides to form crust; press perforations to seal. Bake 5 minutes.

Meanwhile, cut small slit in center of roasted potatoes pouch; microwave on High 2 to 3 minutes or until thawed. Remove potatoes from pouch; cut larger pieces in half.

In medium bowl, beat eggs. Stir in milk, bacon, 1 cup of the cheese, the thawed potatoes, salt and pepper.

Spoon potato mixture evenly over crust. Sprinkle remaining 1/2 cup cheese and the parsley over top.

Bake 20 to 25 minutes or until set and edges are golden brown. To serve, cut into squares.

1 SERVING: Calories 330; Total Fat 22g (Saturated Fat 9g, Trans Fat 1 1/2g); Cholesterol 140mg; Sodium 690mg; Total Carbohydrate 19g (Dietary Fiber 1g, Sugars 3g); Protein 14g; EXCHANGES: 1 Starch, 1 1/2 High-Fat Meat; 2 Fat; CARBOHYDRATE CHOICES: 1

Brunch Quiche Pizza

PAT-IN-PAN PIZZA CRUST

- 2 cups Gold Medal® all-purpose flour
- 1/4 teaspoon salt
- 1/2 cup vegetable oil
- 3 tablespoons cold water

FILLING

- 1 1/2 cups shredded Cheddar cheese (6 ounces)
- 1 package (3.5 ounces) sliced Canadian bacon, cut into strips
- 1/2 cup 1 1/2-inch pieces fresh asparagus
- 3 eggs
- 1 container (8 ounces) sour cream
- 2 medium green onions, chopped (2 tablespoons)

Heat oven to 425°F. In medium bowl, mix flour, salt and oil with fork until all flour is moistened. Sprinkle with cold water, 1 tablespoon at a time, tossing with fork until all water is absorbed. Gather pastry into a ball. Press in ungreased 12-inch pizza pan, building up edge. Bake 14 minutes.

Sprinkle cheese, bacon and asparagus evenly over baked crust. In medium bowl, beat eggs slightly with fork or wire whisk. Add sour cream and onions; beat until well blended. Spoon egg mixture evenly over pizza.

Bake 20 to 25 minutes or until knife inserted in center comes out clean and edges are golden brown. Serve warm.

1 SERVING: Calories 430; Total Fat 30g (Saturated Fat 11g, Trans Fat 0g); Cholesterol 130mg; Sodium 430mg; Total Carbohydrate 26g (Dietary Fiber 1g, Sugars 2g); Protein 15g; EXCHANGES: 1 1/2 Starch; 1 1/2 High-Fat Meat; 3 1/2 Fat; CARBOHYDRATE CHOICES: 2

Hawaiian Brunch Pizza

1½ cups Original Bisquick® mix

⅓ cup very hot water

¾ cup sour cream

½ teaspoon onion salt

3 eggs

1 package (6 ounces) sliced Canadian-style bacon, cut into thin strips

1 cup shredded Cheddar cheese (4 ounces)

1 can (20 ounces) pineapple chunks, well drained

¼ cup chopped green bell pepper

Heat oven to 425°F. Grease 12-inch pizza pan.

Mix Bisquick and hot water until soft dough forms. Press dough in pizza pan, using fingers dusted with Bisquick; pinch edge to form ½-inch rim. Bake 10 minutes.

Mix sour cream, onion salt and eggs; pour over crust. Layer bacon, cheese, pineapple and bell pepper on egg mixture. Bake about 25 minutes or until set. Cool slightly before serving.

1 SERVING: Calories 286; Total Fat 15g (Saturated Fat 7g, Trans Fat 1g); Cholesterol 114mg; Sodium 750mg; Total Carbohydrate 27g (Dietary Fiber 1g, Sugars 12); Protein 13g; EXCHANGES: 1 Starch; 1 Fruit; 1 Lean Meat; ½ Medium-Fat Meat; ½ High-Fat Meat; 1 Fat; CARBOHYDRATE CHOICES: 2½

Expert Tips

- If you don't have a pizza pan, press the dough into a 13-inch circle on a greased cookie sheet, using fingers dipped in Bisquick. Pinch the edge to form a ½-inch rim.
- After you grease the pizza pan, sprinkle it with cornmeal for an extra-crispy crust.

Smoky Brunch Pizza

PREP TIME: *30 minutes*
TOTAL TIME: *30 minutes*
MAKES 8 SERVINGS

1 can (13.8 ounces) Pillsbury® refrigerated classic pizza crust

2 tablespoons butter or margarine

1/4 cup chopped red bell pepper

4 green onions, sliced (1/4 cup)

8 eggs

1/4 cup milk

1/8 teaspoon black pepper

1 package (4 ounces) smoked salmon, flaked

1/2 cup chives-and-onion cream cheese (from 8-ounce container)

Heat oven to 425°F. Grease 12-inch pizza pan or 13 × 9-inch pan. Unroll dough; place in pan. Starting at center, press out dough with hands. Bake 6 to 7 minutes or until crust begins to brown.

Meanwhile, in 10-inch skillet, melt butter over medium heat. Add bell pepper and onions; cook and stir 3 to 4 minutes or until tender.

In medium bowl, beat eggs, milk and pepper. Add egg mixture to skillet. Cook 4 to 5 minutes, stirring occasionally, until thoroughly cooked but still moist. Fold in salmon. Remove from heat.

Spread cream cheese evenly over crust. Spoon cooked egg mixture over cream cheese.

Bake 9 to 12 minutes longer or until toppings are hot and crust is deep golden brown. If desired, garnish with additional green onions.

1 SERVING: Calories 290; Total Fat 15g (Saturated Fat 7g, Trans Fat 0g); Cholesterol 235mg; Sodium 650mg; Total Carbohydrate 25g (Dietary Fiber 0g, Sugars 5g); Protein 14g; EXCHANGES: 1 Starch, 1/2 Other Carbohydrate; 1/2 Fat; CARBOHYDRATE CHOICES: 1 1/2

Expert Tips

- Smoked salmon is similar to, but not the same as, lox. Lox is brine-cured and typically more salty than smoked salmon.
- To get a jump start on this pizza, cook the bell peppers and onions the day before and refrigerate until you're ready to complete the recipe.

Breakfast Calzones

PREP TIME: *15 minutes*
TOTAL TIME: *30 minutes*
MAKES 4 SERVINGS

4 eggs

¼ cup milk

Dash pepper

2 teaspoons butter or margarine

1 can (13.8 ounces) Pillsbury® refrigerated classic pizza crust

½ cup shredded mozzarella cheese (2 ounces)

16 slices pepperoni (about 2 ounces)

4 teaspoons grated Parmesan cheese

Heat oven to 400°F. Spray large cookie sheet with cooking spray.

In medium bowl, beat eggs, milk and pepper with whisk or fork until well blended. In 10-inch nonstick skillet, melt butter over medium heat. Add egg mixture; cook 3 to 5 minutes, stirring occasionally, until eggs are set but moist.

Unroll dough on large cutting board; pat into 14 × 10-inch rectangle. Cut dough into 4 (7 × 5-inch) rectangles. Sprinkle 2 table-spoons mozzarella cheese on half of each rectangle to within ½ inch of edges. Top evenly with pepperoni, Parmesan cheese and eggs. Fold plain half of dough over filling; press edges firmly with fork to seal. Place on cookie sheet.

Bake 11 to 13 minutes or until golden brown.

1 SERVING: Calories 449; Total Fat 21g (Saturated Fat 8g, Trans Fat 0g); Cholesterol 240mg; Sodium 1,150mg; Total Carbohydrate 36g (Dietary Fiber 1g, Sugars 1g); Protein 22g; EXCHANGES: 3 Starch; 1½ Medium-High Fat Meat; ½ High Fat Meat; 1 Fat; CARBOHYDRATE CHOICES: 3

Upside-Down Caramel Latte Bake

PREP TIME: *25 minutes*
TOTAL TIME: *9 hours 10 minutes*
MAKES 8 SERVINGS

CARAMEL BASE

¾ cup packed brown sugar

¼ cup granulated sugar

½ cup butter or margarine

¼ cup maple syrup

1 tablespoon instant espresso powder

½ cup chopped pecans

10 slices (½ inch thick) French bread

CARAMEL LAYER

¼ cup butter or margarine, melted

½ cup packed brown sugar

½ cup chopped pecans

10 slices (½ inch thick) French bread

CUSTARD

6 eggs

2 teaspoons vanilla

¾ cup whipping cream

¾ cup milk

¼ cup granulated sugar

WHIPPED TOPPING

½ cup whipping cream

1 tablespoon sugar

Heat oven to 350°F. Spray 13 × 9-inch (3-quart) baking dish with cooking spray.

In 2-quart saucepan, mix ¾ cup brown sugar, ¼ cup granulated sugar, ½ cup butter, the maple syrup and espresso. Cook 4 to 6 minutes over medium heat until sugars dissolve and mixture is smooth. Pour into baking dish. Sprinkle with ½ cup pecans. Top with 10 slices French bread, cutting slices in half if necessary to fit in baking dish in single layer.

Drizzle ¼ cup melted butter over bread in pan. Sprinkle with ½ cup brown sugar and ½ cup pecans. Top with 10 slices French bread.

In large bowl, beat custard ingredients with wire whisk. Slowly pour mixture over French bread. Press down on bread with spatula so all of bread absorbs egg mixture. Cover; refrigerate 8 to 24 hours.

Uncover; bake 35 to 40 minutes until puffed and lightly browned. Let stand 5 to 10 minutes before serving.

Meanwhile, in medium bowl, beat whipped topping ingredients with electric mixer on high speed until stiff peaks form. Serve each piece upside down with a dollop of whipped topping.

1 SERVING: Calories 760; Total Fat 44g (Saturated Fat 21g, Trans Fat 1g); Cholesterol 250mg; Sodium 440mg; Total Carbohydrate 79g (Dietary Fiber 2g, Sugars 59g); Protein 12g; EXCHANGES: 1 Starch; 4 Other Carbohydrate; 7 Fat; CARBOHYDRATE CHOICES: 5

Expert Tips

- Serve this dish with your favorite cup of coffee or tea.
- Top with a coffee bean.
- Walnuts can be substituted for the pecans.

Berry French Toast Bake

FRENCH TOAST BAKE

- ½ cup Gold Medal® all-purpose flour
- 1½ cups milk
- ¼ cup sugar
- 2 teaspoons vanilla
- ¼ teaspoon salt
- 6 eggs
- 1 loaf (1 pound) soft French bread, cut into 1-inch cubes (8 cups)
- 1½ cups Cascadian Farm® frozen organic harvest berries or blueberries (from two 10-ounce bags)

SAUCE

- ½ cup sugar
- 1½ teaspoons cornstarch
- 2 tablespoons orange juice
- 1 cup Cascadian Farm® frozen organic harvest berries or blueberries
- 1½ cups fresh strawberries, cut in half

Grease bottom and sides of 13 × 9-inch (3-quart) glass baking dish with butter. In large bowl, beat flour, milk, ¼ cup sugar, the vanilla, salt and eggs with wire whisk until smooth. Stir in bread and 1½ cups berries. Spoon into baking dish. Cover tightly and refrigerate at least 1 hour but no longer than 24 hours.

Heat oven to 400°F. Uncover bread mixture. Bake 25 to 35 minutes or until golden brown and knife inserted in center comes out clean.

Meanwhile, in 1½-quart saucepan, stir together ½ cup sugar and the cornstarch. Stir in orange juice until smooth. Stir in 1 cup harvest berries; heat to boiling over medium heat, stirring constantly. Cook about 4 minutes, stirring constantly, until slightly thickened; remove from heat. Just before serving, stir in strawberry halves. Serve warm over French toast bake.

1 SERVING: Calories 300; Total Fat 6g (Saturated Fat 2g, Trans Fat 0g); Cholesterol 130mg; Sodium 380mg; Total Carbohydrate 51g (Dietary Fiber 3g, Sugars 22g); Protein 10g; EXCHANGES: 1½ Starch, ½ Fruit, 1½ Other Carbohydrate; CARBOHYDRATE CHOICES: 3½

Bananas Foster French Toast

8 slices cinnamon bread, cut into ½-inch cubes (about 8 cups)

8 eggs

1 cup milk

2½ cups real maple syrup

1 teaspoon rum extract

6 ripe bananas, cut into ½-inch slices

1 cup chopped pecans

Spray bottom of 13 × 9-inch (3-quart) baking dish with cooking spray. Arrange bread cubes in baking dish. In large bowl, beat eggs, milk and ½ cup of the maple syrup with wire whisk. Pour over bread in baking dish. Cover and refrigerate 8 hours or overnight.

Heat oven to 350°F. Uncover; bake 35 to 40 minutes or until golden brown along edges. Let stand 7 to 10 minutes before serving.

Meanwhile, in medium microwavable bowl, microwave remaining 2 cups maple syrup uncovered on High 1 to 2 minutes, stirring every 30 seconds, until warm. Stir in rum extract.

Sprinkle banana slices and pecans evenly over bread; drizzle with 1 cup of the warmed syrup mixture. Serve immediately with remaining syrup.

1 SERVING: Calories 620; Total Fat 17g (Saturated Fat 3g, Trans Fat 0g); Cholesterol 215mg; Sodium 260mg; Total Carbohydrate 105g (Dietary Fiber 4g, Sugars 75g); Protein 11g; EXCHANGES: 2 Starch; 1 Fruit; 4 Other Carbohydrate; ½ High-Fat Meat; 2½ Fat; CARBOHYDRATE CHOICES: 7

Expert Tips

■ Serve with crisp bacon or sausage.

■ Rum extract can be found in the baking section of your local grocery store.

Blueberry–Orange French Toast

BLUEBERRY-ORANGE SYRUP*

$\frac{1}{3}$ cup sugar

1 teaspoon cornstarch

$\frac{1}{4}$ cup orange juice

2 cups fresh or Cascadian Farm® frozen organic blueberries

FRENCH TOAST

16 slices French bread, 1 inch thick

$\frac{1}{2}$ cup orange marmalade

6 eggs

$1\frac{1}{2}$ cups half-and-half

$\frac{1}{4}$ cup sugar

$\frac{1}{4}$ teaspoon ground nutmeg

2 teaspoons vanilla

$\frac{1}{4}$ cup margarine or butter, melted

*Makes about 3 cups
 = 3 tablespoons per slice.

In 1-quart saucepan, mix $\frac{1}{3}$ cup sugar, the cornstarch and orange juice until smooth; stir in blueberries. Heat to boiling over medium heat, stirring often. Boil 3 minutes, stirring often.

Spray jelly roll pan, $15\frac{1}{2} \times 10\frac{1}{2} \times 1$ inch, with cooking spray. Cut lengthwise slit in side of each bread slice, cutting to but not through other edge. Spread marmalade inside slit. Place in pan. In large bowl, beat eggs, half-and-half, $\frac{1}{4}$ cup sugar, the nutmeg and vanilla until well blended. Pour over bread; turn slices carefully to coat. Cover and refrigerate 8 hours or overnight.

Heat oven to 425°F. Uncover French toast. Drizzle with melted margarine. Bake 20 to 25 minutes or until golden brown. Serve with Blueberry-Orange Syrup.

1 SERVING: Calories 249; Total Fat 8g (Saturated Fat 3g, Trans Fat 1g); Cholesterol 88mg; Sodium 314mg; Total Carbohydrate 34g (Dietary Fiber 2g, Sugars 17g); Protein 6g; EXCHANGES: 2 Starch; 1 Other Carbohydrate; $\frac{1}{2}$ Medium-High-Fat Meat; 1 Fat; CARBOHYDRATE CHOICES: $2\frac{1}{2}$

Expert Tips

- Use day-old bread to make the French toast.
- Prepare the syrup up to 1 day ahead of time and store it covered in the refrigerator.

Best-Ever Banana Bread (Gluten Free)

PREP TIME: *15 minutes*
TOTAL TIME: *2 hours 40 minutes*
MAKES 16 SERVINGS

- 1 box Betty Crocker® Gluten Free yellow cake mix
- 1 cup mashed very ripe bananas (2 medium)
- ½ cup butter, softened
- 3 eggs
- ½ cup chopped nuts, if desired

Heat oven to 350°F. Grease bottom only of 9 × 5-inch or 8 × 4-inch loaf pan with shortening.

In large bowl, beat cake mix, mashed bananas, butter and eggs with electric mixer on low speed 30 seconds, then on medium speed 2 minutes, scraping bowl occasionally. Pour into pan.

Bake 9-inch loaf 55 to 60 minutes, 8-inch loaf 1 hour 5 minutes to 1 hour 15 minutes, or until toothpick inserted in center comes out clean. (Place sheet of foil over loaf to prevent overbrowning.) Cool 10 minutes. Loosen sides of loaf from pan; remove from pan to cooling rack. Cool about 1 hour before slicing.

1 SERVING: Calories 180; Total Fat 7g (Saturated Fat 4g, Trans Fat 0g); Cholesterol 55mg; Sodium 200mg; Total Carbohydrate 26g (Dietary Fiber 0g, Sugars 12g); Protein 2g; EXCHANGES: ½ Starch; 1 Other Carbohydrate; 1½ Fat; CARBOHYDRATE CHOICES: 2

Expert Tip

Cooking gluten free? Always read labels to make sure each recipe ingredient is gluten free. Products and ingredient sources can change.

PREP TIME: *20 minutes*

TOTAL TIME: *1 hour*

MAKES 12 SERVINGS

Caramel Pull-Apart Biscuits

2 cans (12 ounces each) Pillsbury® Grands!® Jr. Golden Layers® refrigerated buttermilk biscuits

1 cup packed brown sugar

½ cup whipping cream

1 teaspoon ground cinnamon

Heat oven to 350°F. Spray 12-cup star-shaped or regular fluted tube cake pan with cooking spray. Separate each can of biscuit dough into 10 biscuits; cut each biscuit into fourths. Layer biscuits in pan.

In small bowl, mix remaining ingredients; pour over biscuits.

Bake 30 to 35 minutes or until golden brown. Immediately turn pan upside down onto heatproof plate; let pan remain over biscuits 5 minutes. Serve warm.

1 SERVING: Calories 279; Total Fat 11g (Saturated Fat 4g, Trans Fat 2½g); Cholesterol 14mg; Sodium 609mg; Total Carbohydrate 42g (Dietary Fiber 1g, Sugars 21g); Protein 4g; EXCHANGES: 1½ Starch; 1 Other Carbohydrate; 2 Fat; CARBOHYDRATE CHOICES: 3

Expert Tips

- Using kitchen scissors makes quick work of cutting biscuits.
- Star-shaped fluted tube cake pans can be found at kitchen specialty stores.
- Spray the pan with cooking spray so the biscuits release easily.

Apple Breakfast Wedges

PREP TIME: *15 minutes*
TOTAL TIME: *40 minutes*
MAKES 6 SERVINGS

¼ cup packed brown sugar

¼ teaspoon ground cinnamon

2 medium cooking apples, peeled, thinly sliced (about 2 cups)

⅓ cup water

2 tablespoons butter or margarine

½ cup Original Bisquick® mix

2 eggs

Maple-flavored syrup, if desired

Heat oven to 400°F. Generously grease 9-inch glass pie plate with shortening or cooking spray. In medium bowl, mix brown sugar and cinnamon. Add apples; toss to coat. Set aside.

In 2-quart saucepan, heat water and butter to boiling. Reduce heat to low. Add Bisquick mix; stir vigorously until mixture forms a ball. Remove from heat. Beat in eggs, one at a time; continue beating until smooth.

Spread batter in bottom of pie plate. Arrange apples on top to within 1 inch of edge of pie plate.

Bake about 23 minutes or until puffed and edges are golden brown. Serve immediately. Drizzle with syrup.

1 SERVING: Calories 160; Total Fat 7g (Saturated Fat 3½g, Trans Fat ½g); Cholesterol 80mg; Sodium 170mg; Total Carbohydrate 20g (Dietary Fiber 0g, Sugars 13g); Protein 3g; EXCHANGES: 1 Starch; ½ Other Carbohydrate; 1 Fat; CARBOHYDRATE CHOICES: 1

Expert Tips

- Use slightly tart apples with a crisp texture, such as Haralson apples. If you like a sweeter apple, choose Fuji, Prairie Spy or Gala.
- Sprinkle with powdered sugar and serve with warm maple syrup.

Blueberry Fold-Over Coffee Cake

PREP TIME: *20 minutes*

TOTAL TIME: *1 hour 10 minutes*

MAKES 8 SERVINGS

2 cups Gold Medal® all-purpose flour

¼ cup sugar

⅓ cup butter or margarine, melted

⅔ cups milk

2 teaspoons baking powder

½ teaspoon salt

½ teaspoon grated lemon peel

2 cups fresh blueberries

⅓ cup sugar

1 tablespoon Gold Medal® all-purpose flour

2 teaspoons lemon juice

1 tablespoon butter or margarine, melted

1 tablespoon coarse white sparkling sugar or granulated sugar

Heat oven to 350°F. Grease cookie sheet with shortening.

In medium bowl, mix 2 cups flour, ¼ cup sugar, ⅓ cup butter, the milk, baking powder, salt and lemon peel with fork until dough leaves side of bowl and forms a ball.

Place dough on lightly floured surface; gently roll in flour to coat. Knead lightly 10 times. Roll into 12-inch circle. Fold circle into fourths. Carefully place on cookie sheet and unfold. Reshape if needed.

In small bowl, mix blueberries, ⅓ cup sugar, 1 tablespoon flour and the lemon juice. Spoon over dough to within 2 inches of edge, mounding fruit in center. Fold dough over fruit, making pleats to retain circle shape and leaving about 3-inch opening in center. Brush 1 tablespoon butter over dough; sprinkle with sparkling sugar.

Bake 35 to 40 minutes or until golden brown. Carefully remove from cookie sheet to serving plate. Let cool at least 10 minutes. Serve warm.

1 SERVING: Calories 300; Total Fat 10g (Saturated Fat 5g, Trans Fat ½g); Cholesterol 25mg; Sodium 340mg; Total Carbohydrate 47g (Dietary Fiber 2g, Sugars 20g); Protein 4g; EXCHANGES: 1 Starch; 2 Other Carbohydrate; 2 Fat; CARBOHYDRATE CHOICES: 3

Mixed–Berry Coffee Cake

COFFEE CAKE

- ¾ cup granulated sugar
- ¼ cup butter or margarine, softened
- 1 egg
- ½ cup milk
- 1½ cups all-purpose flour
- 2 teaspoons baking powder
- ½ teaspoon salt
- 2 tablespoons granulated sugar
- 1 teaspoon ground cinnamon
- 1½ cups mixed fresh berries (such as blueberries, raspberries and blackberries)
- ⅓ cup sliced almonds

GLAZE

- ½ cup powdered sugar
- ¼ teaspoon vanilla
- 2 to 3 teaspoons milk

Heat oven to 350°F. Grease and flour bottom and side of 9-inch round cake pan, or spray with baking spray with flour.

In large bowl, beat ¾ cup granulated sugar, the butter and egg with electric mixer on medium speed until fluffy. Beat in milk just until blended. Stir in flour, baking powder and salt. Spread batter in pan.

In medium bowl, stir together 2 tablespoons granulated sugar and the cinnamon. Add berries; toss with cinnamon-sugar mixture until well coated. Spoon berry mixture over batter. Sprinkle with almonds.

Bake 35 to 45 minutes or until toothpick inserted in center of cake comes out clean.

In small bowl, mix glaze ingredients until smooth and thin enough to drizzle. Drizzle glaze over warm coffee cake. Serve warm.

1 SERVING: Calories 310; Total Fat 9g (Saturated Fat 4½g, Trans Fat 0g); Cholesterol 45mg; Sodium 330mg; Total Carbohydrate 53g (Dietary Fiber 2g, Sugars 32g); Protein 5g; EXCHANGES: 1½ Starch; 2 Other Carbohydrate; 1½ Fat; CARBOHYDRATE CHOICES: 3½

Expert Tips

- Next time, try using sliced apples instead of the berries.
- Spice up this coffee cake by using apple pie spice or pumpkin pie spice instead of the cinnamon.

Orange Marmalade Coffee Cake

- $\frac{1}{2}$ cup orange marmalade
- $\frac{1}{4}$ cup sliced almonds
- 3 tablespoons butter or margarine, melted
- 2 tablespoons light corn syrup
- $2\frac{1}{4}$ cups Gold Medal® all-purpose flour
- $\frac{1}{4}$ cup sugar
- 1 tablespoon grated orange peel
- 3 teaspoons baking powder
- $\frac{1}{2}$ teaspoon salt
- About 1 cup half-and-half

Heat oven to 375°F. In 9-inch round cake pan or 8-inch square pan, mix marmalade, almonds, butter and corn syrup.

In medium bowl, mix flour, sugar, orange peel, baking powder and salt. Stir in just enough half-and-half so dough leaves side of bowl and forms a ball. Drop dough by 12 spoonfuls onto marmalade mixture; flatten slightly.

Bake 30 to 35 minutes or until golden brown. Immediately place heatproof serving plate upside down onto pan; turn plate and pan over. Let pan remain about 1 minute so marmalade mixture can drizzle over coffee cake. Serve warm or cool.

1 SERVING: Calories 320; Total Fat 10g (Saturated Fat $4\frac{1}{2}$g, Trans Fat 0g); Cholesterol 25mg; Sodium 380mg; Total Carbohydrate 53g (Dietary Fiber 2g, Sugars 20g); Protein 5g; EXCHANGES: $1\frac{1}{2}$ Starch; 2 Other Carbohydrate; 2 Fat; CARBOHYDRATE CHOICES: $3\frac{1}{2}$

Blueberry-Cherry Coffee Cake

PREP TIME: *20 minutes*

TOTAL TIME: *2 hours 30 minutes*

MAKES 16 SERVINGS

COFFEE CAKE

3 cups Original Bisquick® mix

¾ cup granulated sugar

¼ cup vegetable oil

1½ teaspoons vanilla

2 eggs

1 cup plain fat-free yogurt

2 cups fresh or Cascadian Farm® frozen organic blueberries

½ cup finely chopped almonds, if desired

¼ cup orange-flavored liqueur or orange juice

¾ cup dried cherries

GLAZE

1 cup powdered sugar

4 teaspoons orange juice

½ teaspoon vanilla

Heat oven to 350°F. Generously grease 12-cup fluted tube cake pan with shortening; lightly flour.

In large bowl, stir Bisquick mix, granulated sugar, oil, vanilla, eggs and yogurt until mixed. Stir in remaining coffee cake ingredients. Spread in pan.

Bake 50 to 55 minutes or until toothpick inserted near center comes out clean. Cool 15 minutes; remove from pan. Cool completely, about 1 hour.

In small bowl, stir glaze ingredients until smooth and thin enough to drizzle. Drizzle over coffee cake.

1 SERVING: Calories 240; Total Fat 7g (Saturated Fat 1½g, Trans Fat 1g); Cholesterol 25mg; Sodium 300mg; Total Carbohydrate 41g (Dietary Fiber 1g, Sugars 24g); Protein 4g; EXCHANGES: 1 Starch; 1½ Other Carbohydrate; 1½ Fat; CARBOHYDRATE CHOICES: 3

Expert Tip

For Cranberry Coffee Cake, use coarsely chopped cranberries instead of the blueberries, chopped dried apricots instead of the cherries and almond extract instead of the vanilla.

Mocha Streusel Coffee Cake

PREP TIME: *25 minutes*
TOTAL TIME: *2 hours 30 minutes*
MAKES 12 SERVINGS

STREUSEL

- 1/3 cup packed brown sugar
- 2 tablespoons all-purpose flour
- 1 tablespoon instant coffee granules or crystals
- 4 ounces semisweet baking chocolate, cut into 1-inch pieces
- 1/2 cup pecan pieces

COFFEE CAKE

- 1 cup granulated sugar
- 1 cup butter or margarine, softened
- 3 eggs
- 1/2 teaspoon almond extract
- 2 3/4 cups all-purpose flour
- 2 teaspoons baking powder
- 1 teaspoon ground cinnamon
- 1/4 teaspoon baking soda
- 1/4 teaspoon salt
- 1 container (8 ounces) plain yogurt

Heat oven to 350°F. Spray angel food (tube cake) pan with cooking spray. In food processor bowl with metal blade, place brown sugar, 2 tablespoons flour and the instant coffee. Cover; process with on-and-off pulses until mixed. Add chocolate; pulse to finely chop. Add pecans; pulse to chop. Set aside.

In large bowl, beat granulated sugar and butter with electric mixer on medium speed until fluffy. Beat in 1 egg at a time until well blended. Add almond extract; mix well.

In small bowl, mix 2 3/4 cups flour, the baking powder, cinnamon, baking soda and salt. Add half of the flour mixture to sugar-egg mixture; beat with electric mixer on low speed just until combined. Add yogurt; blend well. Add remaining flour mixture; mix well.

Spoon half of the batter into pan, spreading evenly. Sprinkle with half of the streusel mixture. Top with remaining batter and remaining streusel mixture.

Bake 55 to 65 minutes or until toothpick inserted in center comes out clean. Cool upright in pan on cooling rack 1 hour. Remove cake from pan. Serve warm or cool.

1 SERVING: Calories 450; Total Fat 23g (Saturated Fat 12g, Trans Fat 1g); Cholesterol 95mg; Sodium 300mg; Total Carbohydrate 54g (Dietary Fiber 2g, Sugars 29g); Protein 7g; EXCHANGES: 2 Starch; 1 1/2 Other Carbohydrate; 4 1/2 Fat; CARBOHYDRATE CHOICES: 3 1/2

Expert Tip

Make a date to meet for coffee or tea with friends, and bring along this warm coffee cake—what a nice surprise. Remember to take a plastic knife and some paper plates or napkins, too.

Almond Coffee Cake

¾ cup butter or margarine, softened

1 cup granulated sugar

3 ounces almond paste (⅓ cup)

½ teaspoon almond extract

2 eggs

1½ cups Gold Medal® all-purpose flour

½ teaspoon baking powder

⅛ teaspoon salt

½ cup sliced almonds

Powdered sugar, if desired

Fresh berries, if desired

Heat oven to 350°F. Line 8-inch square pan with foil, leaving 1 inch of foil overhanging at 2 opposite sides of pan; spray foil with cooking spray.

In large bowl, beat butter, granulated sugar and almond paste with electric mixer on medium speed until light and fluffy. Beat in almond extract and eggs until well blended. On low speed, beat in flour, baking powder and salt just until blended. Spread batter in pan; sprinkle with almonds.

Bake 45 minutes or until toothpick inserted in center comes out clean. Cool completely in pan on cooling rack, about 1 hour. Use foil to lift cake out of pan; cut into squares. Sprinkle with powdered sugar. Garnish with berries.

1 SERVING: Calories 374; Total Fat 21g (Saturated Fat 11g, Trans Fat ½g); Cholesterol 88; Sodium 189mg; Total Carbohydrate 42g (Dietary Fiber 1g, Sugars 26g); Protein 5g; EXCHANGES: 1 Starch; 1½ Other Carbohydrate; 4 Fat; CARBOHYDRATE CHOICES: 3

Expert Tip

This rich, dense coffee cake is a sweet addition to any breakfast or brunch menu.

Apple Cinnamon Coffee Cake

STREUSEL

- ¼ cup packed brown sugar
- ¼ cup old-fashioned oats
- 2 tablespoons chopped walnuts
- 1 tablespoon butter

COFFEE CAKE

- 1 box (15.3 ounces) Betty Crocker® Fiber One™ apple cinnamon muffin mix
- ¾ cup water
- 2 tablespoons vegetable oil
- 2 eggs

GLAZE

- ¼ cup powdered sugar
- 1 teaspoon water

Heat oven to 400°F. Spray bottom only of 9-inch round cake pan with cooking spray. In small bowl, mix brown sugar, oats and walnuts. Cut in butter with fork until mixture is crumbly; set aside.

In medium bowl, stir muffin mix, water, oil and eggs just until blended (batter may be lumpy). Spread in pan. Sprinkle with streusel.

Bake 24 to 28 minutes or until toothpick inserted in center comes out clean. Cool 30 minutes.

In small bowl, mix glaze ingredients until smooth; drizzle over coffee cake. Serve warm or cooled.

1 SERVING: Calories 240; Total Fat 9g (Saturated Fat 3g, Trans Fat 0g); Cholesterol 40mg; Sodium 240mg; Total Carbohydrate 37g (Dietary Fiber 5g, Sugars 22g); Protein 3g; EXCHANGES: 1 Starch; 1½ Other Carbohydrate; 1½ Fat; CARBOHYDRATE CHOICES: 2½

Expert Tip

Reduce the Carbohydrate Choices to 2 when you skip the powdered sugar glaze.

Apple-Honey Breakfast Bars

PREP TIME: *20 minutes*

TOTAL TIME: *1 hour 20 minutes*

MAKES 16 SERVINGS

3 cups Fiber One® Honey Clusters® cereal

¼ cup roasted sunflower nuts

2 cups corn syrup or honey

¼ cup packed brown sugar

1 cup dried apple slices, coarsely chopped

½ teaspoon ground cinnamon

½ cup peanut butter

Butter bottom and sides of 8-inch square pan, or spray with cooking spray. Place cereal in resealable food-storage plastic bag; seal bag and slightly crush with rolling pin or meat mallet (or slightly crush in food processor).

In large bowl, mix cereal and sunflower nuts; set aside.

In 3-quart saucepan, heat corn syrup, brown sugar, apples and cinnamon just to boiling over medium-high heat, stirring occasionally. Remove from heat; stir in peanut butter. Pour over cereal mixture; stir gently until evenly coated.

Press mixture evenly into pan with back of wooden spoon. Refrigerate about 1 hour or until set. For bars, cut into 4 rows by 4 rows. Store covered at room temperature.

1 SERVING: Calories 160; Total Fat 5g (Saturated Fat 1g, Trans Fat 0g); Cholesterol 0mg; Sodium 110mg; Total Carbohydrate 25g (Dietary Fiber 3g, Sugars 13g); Protein 3g; EXCHANGES: 1 Starch; ½ Other Carbohydrate; 1 Fat; CARBOHYDRATE CHOICES: 1½

Expert Tips

- Honey will slide easily out of the measuring cup if you first spray the cup with cooking spray.

- Apples are loaded with soluble fiber that helps to lower blood cholesterol. Start slowly so you have time to get used to more fiber in your diet.

Beef and Pork

Wild Rice and Mushroom Pot Pie

FILLING

1 pound lean (at least 80%) ground beef

1 small yellow onion, chopped (¼ cup)

1 package (8 ounces) fresh white mushrooms, chopped

2 cloves garlic, finely chopped

1 can (15 ounces) cooked wild rice (2 cups)

1 bag (12 ounces) Green Giant® Valley Fresh Steamers™ frozen mixed vegetables

1 can (10¾ ounces) condensed 98% fat-free cream of mushroom soup

¼ cup milk

½ teaspoon salt

¼ teaspoon pepper

TOPPING

1½ cups Original Bisquick® mix

¾ cup milk

1 egg

Heat oven to 400°F. Heat 12-inch nonstick skillet over medium-high heat. Cook beef, onion and mushrooms in skillet 7 to 9 minutes, stirring occasionally, until beef is thoroughly cooked and liquid is absorbed. Add garlic; cook and stir 30 seconds. Remove from heat.

Reserve ½ cup wild rice; set aside. Add remaining wild rice, the frozen vegetables, soup, ¼ cup milk, the salt and pepper to beef mixture; stir to combine. Spoon into ungreased 2-quart casserole.

In medium bowl, mix topping ingredients and reserved ½ cup wild rice with fork. Pour over beef mixture.

Bake uncovered 28 to 32 minutes or until crust is golden brown.

1 SERVING: Calories 590; Total Fat 16g (Saturated Fat 6g, Trans Fat 2g); Cholesterol 85mg; Sodium 1,750mg; Total Carbohydrate 82g (Dietary Fiber 6g, Sugars 9g); Protein 29g; EXCHANGES: 4½ Starch; ½ Other Carbohydrate; 1 Vegetable; 2 Lean Meat; 1½ Fat; CARBOHYDRATE CHOICES: 5½

Expert Tips

▪ If canned wild rice is hard to find, use the pouch variety or cook your own according to package directions.

▪ Add ⅓ cup toasted almonds to the beef mixture before spooning it into the 2-quart casserole.

▪ Round out the meal with a crisp green salad.

Burger 'n Fries Pot Pie

1½ pounds lean (at least 80%) ground beef

1 large onion, chopped (about 1 cup)

2 tablespoons all-purpose flour

1 can (14.5 ounces) diced tomatoes, undrained

1 cup shredded Cheddar cheese (4 ounces)

2 cups frozen crispy French-fried potatoes (from 20-ounce bag)

Heat oven to 450°F. In 12-inch nonstick skillet, cook beef and onion over medium-high heat about 8 minutes, stirring occasionally, until beef is thoroughly cooked; drain well. Sprinkle flour over beef mixture. Cook 1 minute, stirring constantly. Stir in tomatoes; heat to boiling. Remove from heat.

In ungreased 1½-quart casserole, spread beef mixture. Sprinkle with cheese. Arrange frozen potatoes evenly in single layer on top.

Bake uncovered about 20 minutes or until potatoes are golden brown. Let stand 5 minutes before serving.

1 SERVING: Calories 340; Total Fat 20g (Saturated Fat 9g, Trans Fat 1½g); Cholesterol 90mg; Sodium 340mg; Total Carbohydrate 13g (Dietary Fiber 2g, Sugars 3g); Protein 26g; EXCHANGES: 1 Starch; 1 Fat; CARBOHYDRATE CHOICES: 1

Expert Tips

■ Be sure to drain the cooked ground beef really well. Any extra juices will make the pot pie too watery.

■ When it's too cold outside to grill those burgers, comfort food calls and this pot pie will surely hit the spot!

■ Serve this pot pie with ketchup, if desired.

Mongolian Steak & String Beans Pot Pie

MARINADE

¼ cup reduced-sodium soy sauce

3 tablespoons sweet rice wine

1 tablespoon sesame oil

1 teaspoon hoisin sauce

2 tablespoons packed brown sugar

1 tablespoon cornstarch

2 teaspoons grated gingerroot

2 cloves garlic, finely chopped

STEAK AND VEGETABLES

1 pound boneless beef top sirloin steak (¾ inch thick), trimmed of fat, cut into 2 × ¼-inch strips

1 tablespoon butter or margarine

1 clove garlic, finely chopped

4 ounces fresh button or beech mushrooms, sliced

2 medium green onions, sliced (2 tablespoons)

1 can (13.8 ounces) Pillsbury® refrigerated classic pizza crust

½ pound fresh green beans, trimmed, cut into 2-inch pieces

1 tablespoon black or regular sesame seeds

1 egg

1 tablespoon water

In large bowl, mix marinade ingredients. Add steak strips; stir to coat. Cover and refrigerate 1 hour to marinate.

Meanwhile, in 10-inch skillet, melt butter over medium heat. Cook garlic and mushrooms in butter 2 to 3 minutes, stirring occasionally, until mushrooms are soft. Remove from heat; stir in onions.

Unroll pizza dough; cut into 4 rectangles. Spoon 2 tablespoons mushroom mixture onto center of each rectangle. Pull 4 corners of dough to center; twist firmly to seal. Allow side edges to remain open to vent. Place bundles on tray, cover and refrigerate until ready to top meat mixture.

Heat oven to 350°F. In 2-quart saucepan, heat 1 cup water to boiling. Add green beans; cover and cook over medium heat 3 to 4 minutes to blanch. Drain.

Drain steak, reserving marinade. In 10-inch skillet, heat reserved marinade to boiling over medium-high heat; cook about 2 minutes or until sauce is thickened. Remove from heat; stir in steak, green beans and sesame seeds.

Divide mixture evenly among 4 ungreased 10-ounce ramekins or custard cups. Place a filled bundle on top of steak mixture in each ramekin, gently shaping to fit inside. In small bowl, beat egg and water with fork. Brush over tops of bundles.

Place ramekins on cookie sheet with sides. Bake 30 to 35 minutes or until dough is golden brown and mixture is bubbly.

1 SERVING: Calories 560; Total Fat 16g (Saturated Fat 5g, Trans Fat 0g); Cholesterol 125mg; Sodium 1,330mg; Total Carbohydrate 64g (Dietary Fiber 2g, Sugars 15g); Protein 38g; EXCHANGES: 3 Starch; 1 Other Carbohydrate; 1 Vegetable; 4 Lean Meat; CARBOHYDRATE CHOICES: 4

Expert Tip

Green beans can be cooked 6 to 8 minutes or until crisp-tender if very tender beans are desired.

Tamale Pot Pie

- 1 pound lean (at least 80%) ground beef
- 1 box (9 ounces) Green Giant® Niblets® frozen corn, thawed, drained
- 1 can (14.5 ounces) diced tomatoes, undrained
- 1 can (2¼ ounces) sliced ripe olives, drained
- 2 tablespoons Original Bisquick® mix
- 1 tablespoon chili powder
- 2 teaspoons ground cumin
- ½ teaspoon salt
- 1 cup Original Bisquick® mix
- ½ cup cornmeal
- ½ cup milk
- 1 egg

Heat oven to 400°F. In 10-inch skillet, cook beef over medium heat, stirring occasionally, until thoroughly cooked; drain. Stir in corn, tomatoes, olives, 2 tablespoons Bisquick mix, the chili powder, cumin and salt. Heat to boiling, stirring frequently; boil and stir 1 minute. Keep warm over low heat.

In medium bowl, stir remaining ingredients until blended. Pour beef mixture into ungreased 9-inch square pan. Spread cornmeal mixture over beef mixture.

Bake uncovered about 25 minutes or until crust is light brown.

1 SERVING: Calories 360; Total Fat 14g (Saturated Fat 5g, Trans Fat 1½g); Cholesterol 85mg; Sodium 690mg; Total Carbohydrate 38g (Dietary Fiber 3g, Sugars 5g); Protein 19g; EXCHANGES: 1½ Starch; 1 Other Carbohydrate; ½ Fat; CARBOHYDRATE CHOICES: 2½

Expert Tips

- A 15.25-ounce can of Green Giant® whole kernel corn, drained, can be used instead of the frozen corn.
- Serve a salad of fresh greens and avocado and orange slices tossed with your favorite vinaigrette dressing.

Ground Beef and Twice-Baked Potato Pie

PREP TIME: *15 minutes*

TOTAL TIME: *1 hour 5 minutes*

MAKES 4 SERVINGS

1 pound lean (at least 80%) ground beef

¼ cup chopped onion

¼ cup Progresso® plain bread crumbs

½ teaspoon dried sage

½ teaspoon salt

1 egg

1 package (1 pound 8 ounces) refrigerated garlic mashed potatoes

1 cup shredded Cheddar cheese (4 ounces)

¼ cup chopped fresh tomato, if desired

2 slices precooked bacon, chopped, if desired

2 medium green onions, chopped (2 tablespoons), if desired

Heat oven to 350°F. In large bowl, mix beef, onion, bread crumbs, sage, salt and egg until well blended. Press in bottom of ungreased 8-inch square (2-quart) glass baking dish. Spread mashed potatoes evenly over top. Sprinkle evenly with cheese.

Bake uncovered about 50 minutes or until meat thermometer inserted in center of beef mixture reads 160°F. Sprinkle with tomato, bacon and green onions.

1 SERVING: Calories 570; Total Fat 36g (Saturated Fat 17g, Trans Fat 2½g); Cholesterol 175mg; Sodium 1,220mg; Total Carbohydrate 28g (Dietary Fiber 1g, Sugars 2g); Protein 33g; EXCHANGES: 2 Starch; 2½ Fat; CARBOHYDRATE CHOICES: 2

Expert Tips

- Regular flavor mashed potatoes can be used instead of garlic mashed potatoes.
- If you have fresh sage on hand, use 2 teaspoons fresh instead of the dried sage.

PREP TIME: *50 minutes*

TOTAL TIME: *1 hour 25 minutes*

MAKES 6 SERVINGS

Meatball Sandwich Pot Pie

- 1 box Pillsbury® refrigerated pie crusts, softened as directed on box
- 1 medium onion, halved, sliced (about 1 cup)
- 1 medium green bell pepper, coarsely chopped (1 cup)
- 1 package (14 to 16 ounces) frozen cooked Italian meatballs (about 32), thawed, halved
- 1½ cups tomato pasta sauce
- 1½ cups shredded mozzarella cheese (6 ounces)
- 1 egg yolk
- 2 teaspoons water

Heat oven to 425°F. Prepare pie crust as directed on package for two-crust pie using 9-inch glass pie pan.

Spray large skillet with nonstick cooking spray. Heat over medium-high heat until hot. Add onion and bell pepper; cook 3 to 4 minutes or until crisp-tender, stirring frequently. Add meatballs, pasta sauce and ¾ cup of the cheese. Reduce heat to low; simmer 5 minutes or until thoroughly heated, stirring occasionally. Spoon meatball mixture into crust-lined pan. Sprinkle with remaining ¾ cup cheese.

With sharp knife, cut small shapes, such as half moons, from remaining pie crust; reserve shapes. Place cut-out crust on top of pie; seal edges and flute. Brush small shapes with water; attach to top crust.

In small bowl, beat egg yolk and 2 teaspoons water until well blended. Brush top crust with egg yolk mixture.

Bake at 425°F for 25 to 35 minutes or until crust is golden brown and filling is bubbly. Cover edge of crust with strips of foil after 15 to 20 minutes of baking to prevent excessive browning. Let stand 10 minutes before serving.

1 SERVING: Calories 640; Total Fat 35g (Saturated Fat 15g, Trans Fat ½g); Cholesterol 135mg; Sodium 1,230mg; Total Carbohydrate 56g (Dietary Fiber 2g, Sugars 9g); Protein 26g; EXCHANGES: 3 Starch; ½ Other Carbohydrate; 4 Fat; CARBOHYDRATE CHOICES: 4

Deep-Dish Lasagna Pie

- 1 pound bulk Italian pork sausage
- 1 large onion, chopped (about 1 cup)
- 2 cups tomato pasta sauce
- ½ teaspoon dried oregano
- 1 egg
- 1 container (15 ounces) part-skim ricotta cheese
- ½ cup grated Parmesan cheese
- 2 cups shredded mozzarella cheese (8 ounces)
- 2 cans (13.8 ounces each) Pillsbury® refrigerated classic pizza crust

Heat oven to 425°F. Spray 13 × 9-inch (3-quart) glass baking dish with cooking spray. In 12-inch nonstick skillet, cook sausage and onion over medium-high heat 5 to 7 minutes, stirring occasionally, until sausage is no longer pink; drain well. Stir in pasta sauce and oregano; cook until thoroughly heated.

In medium bowl, beat egg. Stir in ricotta cheese, Parmesan cheese and 1½ cups of the mozzarella cheese.

Unroll dough for 1 pizza crust. Press in bottom and 1 inch up sides of dish. Spread cheese mixture over dough in bottom of dish. Spread sausage mixture over cheese mixture. Unroll dough for second pizza crust; place over sausage mixture and press edges to seal. Cut 4 slits in top crust.

Bake uncovered 15 minutes. Cover dish with sheet of foil to prevent excessive browning. Bake 9 to 11 minutes longer or until crust is golden brown. Top with remaining ½ cup mozzarella cheese. Let stand 5 minutes before serving.

1 SERVING: Calories 600; Total Fat 25g (Saturated Fat 11g, Trans Fat 0g); Cholesterol 85mg; Sodium 1,530mg; Total Carbohydrate 64g (Dietary Fiber 3g, Sugars 14g); Protein 30g; EXCHANGES: 2 Starch; 2½ Other Carbohydrate; 3 High-Fat Meat; CARBOHYDRATE CHOICES: 4

Expert Tip

This pot pie has all of your favorite lasagna flavors without all of the time-consuming assembly!

Mexican Shepherd's Pie

PREP TIME: *20 minutes*

TOTAL TIME: *30 minutes*

MAKES 4 SERVINGS

1 pound extra lean (at least 93%) ground beef

½ cup sliced green onions

1 cup Old El Paso® Thick 'n Chunky Salsa

1½ teaspoons chili powder

¾ teaspoon cumin

1 can (11 ounces) Green Giant® SteamCrisp® Mexicorn® corn, drained

1⅓ cups water

2 tablespoons butter or margarine

1 cup milk

1 pouch Betty Crocker® loaded mashed potatoes (from 6.1-ounce box)

½ cup shredded Cheddar cheese (2 ounces)

1 medium tomato, sliced into thin wedges

Tortilla chips, if desired

In 10-inch skillet, cook ground beef and ¼ cup of the green onions over medium-high heat 5 to 7 minutes, stirring occasionally until beef is thoroughly cooked; drain. Stir in salsa, chili powder and cumin. Spoon corn evenly over beef mixture in skillet. Cover and cook over low heat until mixture is thoroughly heated.

Meanwhile, in 2-quart saucepan, heat water and butter to boiling. Remove from heat. Stir in milk and 1 pouch potatoes with seasoning just until blended. Let stand about 1 minute or until liquid is absorbed; beat with fork until smooth.

Spoon potatoes over corn in skillet; spread evenly. Sprinkle with cheese and remaining ¼ cup green onions. Cover; cook over low heat about 5 minutes or until cheese is melted. Arrange tomato wedges in spoke fashion over potatoes.

Garnish with tortilla chips around outside edge of skillet.

1 SERVING: Calories 470; Total Fat 19g (Saturated Fat 10g, Trans Fat ½g); Cholesterol 100mg; Sodium 1,360mg; Total Carbohydrate 42g (Dietary Fiber 3g, Sugars 11g); Protein 32g; EXCHANGES: 1½ Starch; ½ Other Carbohydrate; ½ Low-Fat Milk; ½ Vegetable; 3 Lean Meat; 1½ Fat; CARBOHYDRATE CHOICES: 3

Expert Tips

■ Replace ground beef with ground turkey breast and use reduced-fat cheese.

■ To save time, cook the ground beef and onions ahead of time; refrigerate until you prepare the recipe.

Greek Spanakopita Pie

1 pound lean ground beef

1 cup chopped onion (1 large)

1 box (9 ounces) Green Giant® frozen spinach, thawed and squeezed dry

1/4 cup chopped fresh Italian (flat-leaf) parsley

1/2 teaspoon salt

1/4 teaspoon pepper

1 can (15 ounces) diced tomatoes with Italian-style herbs, undrained

12 sheets frozen phyllo (filo) (14 × 9 inch), thawed

6 tablespoons butter or margarine, melted

1/4 cup Progresso® Italian style bread crumbs

1 cup crumbled feta cheese (4 ounces)

Heat oven to 350°F. Spray 9-inch pie plate with cooking spray.

In 10-inch skillet, cook beef and onion over medium-high heat, stirring frequently; drain. Stir in spinach, parsley, salt, pepper and all but 1/2 cup of the tomatoes. Cook and stir until hot; set aside.

Cover phyllo sheets with damp paper towel. Arrange sheets, layering 3 at a time, in an × shape and then in a + shape to create a spoke pattern on work surface, brushing each with butter and sprinkling with 1 teaspoon of the bread crumbs as it is added.

Transfer all layers of phyllo to pie plate, gently easing dough down sides of pie plate and allowing excess dough to hang over edge. Place beef mixture in pie plate; top with feta cheese. Fold overhanging phyllo up and over filling, leaving 2- to 3-inch center of filling uncovered. Spoon remaining 1/2 cup tomatoes in center. Brush phyllo with butter.

Bake 40 to 50 minutes or until golden brown. Let stand 5 minutes before serving.

1 SERVING: Calories 400; Total Fat 25g (Saturated Fat 13g, Trans Fat 1½g); Cholesterol 95mg; Sodium 810mg; Total Carbohydrate 24g (Dietary Fiber 3g, Sugars 4g); Protein 20g; EXCHANGES: 1 Starch; 1 Vegetable; 3 Fat; CARBOHYDRATE CHOICES: 1½

Expert Tips

- For a more authentic flavor, substitute ground lamb for the ground beef.
- Serve this pie with a Greek salad and retsina, an up-and-coming wine from the Nemea region of Greece.

Spicy Pork Chimichurri-Style Casserole

PREP TIME: *30 minutes*

TOTAL TIME: *1 hour 30 minutes*

MAKES 5 SERVINGS

2 tablespoons olive oil

2 tablespoons all-purpose flour

1 teaspoon salt

½ teaspoon paprika

¼ teaspoon black pepper

1 pork tenderloin (about 1 pound), cut into ¾-inch cubes

1 large onion, halved, cut into ½-inch-thick wedges

1 pound unpeeled small red potatoes, quartered (2½ cups)

¾ to 1 pound sweet potatoes (about 2 medium), peeled, cut into 1½-inch pieces (3 cups)

1 cup chopped fresh parsley

2 tablespoons chopped fresh oregano leaves

2 tablespoons fresh lime juice

½ teaspoon crushed red pepper flakes

2 cloves garlic, finely chopped

1¾ cups Progresso® chicken broth (from 32-ounce carton)

1 can (12 ounces) Pillsbury® Grands!® Jr. Golden Layers® refrigerated biscuits (10 biscuits)

¼ cup finely chopped fresh cilantro

Heat oven to 350°F. In 3- or 4-quart ovenproof Dutch oven, heat oil over medium-high heat. In large shallow bowl, mix flour, salt, paprika and black pepper. Stir in pork until evenly coated. Add to hot oil; cook and stir until evenly browned. Add remaining ingredients except biscuits and cilantro, including any unused flour mixture; mix well.

If handles of Dutch oven are not ovenproof, wrap them in foil. Cover Dutch oven; bake 40 minutes. Remove Dutch oven from oven; increase oven temperature to 375°F.

Separate dough into 10 biscuits; arrange on top of hot pork mixture. Bake uncovered 14 to 18 minutes longer or until biscuits are golden brown. Sprinkle with cilantro before serving.

1 SERVING: Calories 550; Total Fat 19g (Saturated Fat 4g, Trans Fat 3g); Cholesterol 40mg; Sodium 1,630mg; Total Carbohydrate 66g (Dietary Fiber 5g, Sugars 11g); Protein 28g; EXCHANGES: 3 Starch; 1½ Other Carbohydrate; 2½ Lean Meat; 2 Fat; CARBOHYDRATE CHOICES: 4½

Expert Tips

■ One pound of boneless pork shoulder can be substituted for the pork tenderloin.

■ Chimichurri originated in Argentina as a sauce or marinade for grilled meats. It is typically served as an accompaniment, but we've used the ingredients to flavor this casserole.

PREP TIME: *25 minutes*

TOTAL TIME: *45 minutes*

MAKES 6 SERVINGS

Two-Bean Burger Casserole

6 slices bacon

1 pound lean (at least 80%) ground beef

1 cup chopped onions (2 medium)

1 can (16 ounces) baked beans with bacon and brown sugar, undrained

1 can (15 ounces) Progresso® red kidney beans, drained, ¼ cup liquid reserved

¼ cup packed brown sugar

¼ cup ketchup

3 tablespoons white vinegar

1 can (11 ounces) Pillsbury® refrigerated original breadsticks (12 breadsticks)

1 tablespoon milk

2 teaspoons sesame seeds

Heat oven to 400°F. In 12-inch nonstick skillet, cook bacon over medium heat, turning once, until crisp. Drain on paper towels; crumble bacon. Drain drippings from skillet.

In skillet, cook beef and onions over medium-high heat, stirring occasionally, until thoroughly cooked; drain. Stir in bacon, baked beans, kidney beans with reserved ¼ cup liquid, brown sugar, ketchup and vinegar. Reduce heat to medium-low; cook until bubbly, stirring occasionally. Pour into ungreased 11 × 7-inch (2-quart) glass baking dish.

Unroll dough; separate into 12 strips. Arrange strips in lattice design over bean mixture, overlapping as necessary to fit. Brush dough with milk; sprinkle with sesame seeds.

Bake 15 to 20 minutes or until breadsticks are golden brown and filling is bubbly.

1 SERVING: Calories 590; Total Fat 19g (Saturated Fat 7g, Trans Fat ½g); Cholesterol 65mg; Sodium 1,040mg; Total Carbohydrate 74g (Dietary Fiber 7g, Sugars 29g); Protein 31g; EXCHANGES: 3 Starch; 2 Other Carbohydrate; CARBOHYDRATE CHOICES: 5

Cheesy Biscuit Bean 'n Beef Casserole

½ pound lean (at least 80%) ground beef

½ cup chopped onion

1 can (21 ounces) baked beans with bacon and brown sugar sauce, undrained

1 can (16 ounces) kidney beans, drained, rinsed

1 can (15.8 ounces) great northern beans, drained, rinsed

½ cup barbecue sauce

1 can (10.2 ounces) Pillsbury® Grands!® Homestyle refrigerated buttermilk biscuits, separated and each cut into 6 pieces

½ cup finely shredded Cheddar cheese (2 ounces)

Heat oven to 350°F. Spray 11 × 7-inch (2-quart) glass baking dish with cooking spray.

In 12-inch nonstick skillet, cook beef and onion over medium heat 4 to 6 minutes, stirring occasionally, until beef is thoroughly cooked; drain. Stir in baked beans, kidney beans, great northern beans and barbecue sauce. Heat to boiling, stirring occasionally. Pour into baking dish. Immediately top hot mixture with biscuit pieces. Sprinkle with cheese.

Bake 18 to 20 minutes or until biscuits are golden brown and baked through.

1 SERVING: Calories 700; Total Fat 20g (Saturated Fat 8g, Trans Fat 3g); Cholesterol 45mg; Sodium 1,490mg; Total Carbohydrate 96g (Dietary Fiber 14g, Sugars 28g); Protein 34g; EXCHANGES: 4 Starch; 3 Vegetable; 3 Lean Meat; 2½ Fat; CARBOHYDRATE CHOICES: 6½

Expert Tips

- For extra flavor, stir in ½ cup cooked bacon bits.
- Finely shredded cheese is a great way to extend the cheese in a recipe, although regular shredded cheese can be used.

Crusty-Topped Beef in Beer

BEEF MIXTURE

2 tablespoons olive or vegetable oil

1½ pounds boneless beef stew meat, cut into 1-inch pieces

½ teaspoon salt

¼ teaspoon freshly ground pepper

3 medium carrots, sliced (1½ cups)

1 onion, halved, cut into ½-inch-thick wedges (about 3 cups)

3 tablespoons all-purpose flour

3 cups cubed unpeeled potatoes

¼ cup chopped fresh parsley

1 tablespoon packed brown sugar

1 teaspoon beef bouillon granules

1 teaspoon dried thyme

1 can (14.5 ounces) diced tomatoes with basil, garlic and oregano, undrained

1 can (12 ounces) beer

TOPPING

1 cup small pretzel twists

1 can (12 ounces) Pillsbury® Grands!® Jr. Golden Layers® refrigerated biscuits (10 biscuits)

2 tablespoons spicy brown mustard

Heat oven to 350°F. In 4-quart Dutch oven, heat oil over medium-high heat. Add beef in batches; cook and stir until browned. With slotted spoon, remove beef to bowl; sprinkle with salt and pepper.

When all beef is browned and removed from Dutch oven, add carrots and onion to drippings. Cook and stir over medium-high heat 3 to 4 minutes, scraping up browned bits. Sprinkle with flour; stir to mix well. Stir in beef and remaining beef mixture ingredients. Pour into ungreased 13 × 9-inch (3-quart) glass baking dish.

Cover dish with foil. Bake about 1 hour 30 minutes or until beef is tender and sauce is thickened. Remove from oven; stir. Increase oven temperature to 375°F.

Place pretzels in 1-gallon food-storage plastic bag; crush with rolling pin to make about ¾ cup. Separate dough into 10 biscuits; cut each into 4 pieces. Brush mustard over dough pieces. Drop handful of dough pieces at a time into bag; shake to coat. Place biscuit pieces evenly on beef mixture, leaving space between pieces.

Bake uncovered 14 to 18 minutes longer or until biscuits are golden brown.

1 SERVING: Calories 420; Total Fat 19g (Saturated Fat 5g, Trans Fat 2½g); Cholesterol 45mg; Sodium 950mg; Total Carbohydrate 42g (Dietary Fiber 3g, Sugars 8g); Protein 20g; EXCHANGES: 1½ Starch; 1 Other Carbohydrate; 1 Vegetable; 1½ Fat; CARBOHYDRATE CHOICES: 3

Expert Tips

- You can choose to purchase the refrigerated cubed potatoes instead of peeling and cubing fresh potatoes.
- If you love garlic, spear a couple cloves of garlic on toothpicks and add to beef mixture. Remove the garlic after the first bake time.
- When browning meat, it is a must to use a heavy aluminum-based Dutch oven. The stainless steel or lighter-weight varieties tend to get hotter and burn the food, so they need careful attention during cooking.

Philly Cheese and Ground Beef Casserole

PREP TIME: *20 minutes*
TOTAL TIME: *1 hour*
MAKES 8 SERVINGS

1½ pounds lean (at least 80%) ground beef

1 package (8 ounces) sliced mushrooms

1 teaspoon salt

½ teaspoon pepper

8 slices (1 ounce each) provolone cheese

2 tablespoons butter or margarine

2 large onions, halved and thinly sliced into wedges

2 medium red bell peppers, cut into strips

2 cloves garlic, finely chopped

1 can (16.3 ounces) Pillsbury® Grands!® Homestyle original biscuits

Heat oven to 350°F. Spray 13 × 9-inch (3-quart) baking dish with cooking spray.

In 12-inch skillet, cook beef, mushrooms, salt and pepper over medium-high heat 7 to 9 minutes, stirring frequently, until beef is thoroughly cooked; drain. Place in baking dish. Arrange cheese over beef mixture, overlapping slices if needed.

In same skillet, melt butter over medium-high heat. Add onions and bell peppers. Cook over medium-high heat 3 to 5 minutes, stirring frequently, until peppers are crisp-tender. Stir in garlic; cook 1 to 2 minutes longer. Spoon over cheese in baking dish.

Separate dough into 8 biscuits. On lightly floured surface, pat biscuits into 5-inch circles. Arrange biscuits over vegetable mixture.

Bake 35 to 40 minutes or until biscuits are golden brown on top.

1 SERVING: Calories 490; Total Fat 28g (Saturated Fat 13g, Trans Fat 4g); Cholesterol 80mg; Sodium 1,200mg; Total Carbohydrate 31g (Dietary Fiber 1g, Sugars 9g); Protein 27g; EXCHANGES: 1½ Starch; 1½ Vegetable; 3 Fat; CARBOHYDRATE CHOICES: 2

Expert Tip

To easily cut peppers, cut a thin slice off bottom of pepper. Set pepper on cutting board, cut side down. Cut strips of pepper from stem down to board, cutting just the flesh and leaving seeds and core attached to stem.

Quick Sausage Supper

¾ pound bulk pork sausage

½ cup chopped onion (1 medium)

2 tablespoons Gold Medal® all-purpose flour

1 can (14.5 ounces) diced tomatoes, undrained

1 can (4 ounces) Green Giant® mushroom pieces and stems, undrained

1 teaspoon dried oregano leaves

½ teaspoon dried basil leaves

¼ teaspoon garlic powder

⅛ teaspoon pepper

1 can (12 ounces) Pillsbury® Golden Layers® refrigerated buttermilk flaky biscuits

1 cup shredded mozzarella cheese (4 ounces)

Heat oven to 375°F. In 10-inch ovenproof skillet with 2-inch-deep sides, cook sausage and onion over medium heat 5 to 7 minutes, stirring occasionally, until sausage is no longer pink.

Sprinkle flour over sausage mixture in skillet. Add tomatoes, mushrooms, oregano, basil, garlic powder and pepper; mix well. Cook until slightly thickened, stirring occasionally. Reduce heat; simmer uncovered while preparing biscuits.

Separate dough into 10 biscuits; cut each into quarters. Arrange biscuit pieces over hot sausage mixture. Sprinkle with cheese.

Bake uncovered 16 to 20 minutes or until biscuits are golden brown.

1 SERVING: Calories 360; Total Fat 19g (Saturated Fat 7g, Trans Fat 2½g); Cholesterol 35mg; Sodium 1,070mg; Total Carbohydrate 31g; (Dietary Fiber 1g, Sugars 6g); Protein 15g; EXCHANGES: 1½ Starch; ½ Other Carbohydrate; 1½ High-Fat Meat; 1½ Fat; CARBOHYDRATE CHOICES: 2

Expert Tips

- Not sure if your skillet is ovenproof? Wrap the handle in a double layer of heavy-duty foil.
- The filling must be piping hot when the biscuits are arranged over it.
- Try a combination of shredded Italian cheeses in this recipe.
- You can use Asiago, fontina and provolone cheese instead of the mozzarella. All of these cheeses melt nicely.

PREP TIME: *15 minutes*
TOTAL TIME: *35 minutes*

MAKES 6 SERVINGS

Chow Mein Dinner

1 pound ground beef

2 cups water

3 tablespoons soy sauce

1 tablespoon mild-flavor molasses

½ teaspoon ground ginger

¼ teaspoon garlic powder

3 tablespoons Original Bisquick® mix

2 cups frozen stir-fry vegetables (from 1-pound bag)

2 cups Original Bisquick® mix

⅔ cup water

Cook beef in 10-inch skillet over medium heat, stirring occasionally, until brown; drain.

Mix 2 cups water, the soy sauce, molasses, ginger, garlic powder and 3 tablespoons Bisquick; stir into beef mixture. Stir in frozen vegetables. Cook about 1 minute, stirring frequently, until boiling.

Stir remaining ingredients until soft dough forms. Drop by 6 spoonfuls onto boiling beef mixture; reduce heat.

Cook uncovered 10 minutes. Cover and cook 10 minutes longer.

1 SERVING: Calories 363; Total Fat 18g (Saturated Fat 6g, Trans Fat 2g); Cholesterol 51mg; Sodium 1,062mg; Total Carbohydrate 33g (Dietary Fiber 2g, Sugars 4g); Protein 19g; EXCHANGES: 2 Starch; ½ Vegetable; ½ Medium-High-Fat Meat; 1 Fat; CARBOHYDRATE CHOICES: 2½

Expert Tips

- Use a 20-ounce package of a frozen meat and vegetable combination instead of the ground beef and frozen stir-fry vegetables.
- Chill one or two 15¼-ounce cans of tropical fruit salad. Serve the fruit in individual small glass dishes and, for an added touch, sprinkle with shredded coconut.
- Garnish this flavorful dinner with crushed red pepper. It adds a touch of color and an extra spark of flavor.

Biscuit-Topped Beef and Corn Casserole

2¼ cups Original Bisquick® mix

⅔ cup milk

2 tablespoons sliced pimiento-stuffed green olives

1 pound lean (at least 80%) ground beef

1 medium onion, chopped (½ cup)

1½ teaspoons minced garlic (from 4.5-ounce jar)

1 can (14.5 ounces) diced tomatoes with roasted garlic and onion, undrained

1 can (14.75 ounces) Green Giant® cream-style corn, undrained

1 teaspoon chili powder

½ cup shredded Mexican cheese blend or Cheddar cheese (2 ounces)

Heat oven to 400°F. In large bowl, stir Bisquick mix, milk and olives until soft dough forms.

In 12-inch skillet, cook beef, onion and garlic over medium heat 8 to 10 minutes, stirring occasionally, until beef is thoroughly cooked; drain. Stir in tomatoes, corn and chili powder. Heat to boiling. Pour in ungreased 11 × 7-inch (2-quart) glass baking dish. Drop biscuit dough by tablespoonfuls over mixture.

Bake 20 minutes. Sprinkle cheese over biscuits; bake 5 to 10 minutes longer or until biscuits are lightly browned and cheese is melted.

1 SERVING: Calories 450; Total Fat 19g (Saturated Fat 7g, Trans Fat 1½g); Cholesterol 60mg; Sodium 1,040mg; Total Carbohydrate 46g (Dietary Fiber 3g, Sugars 10g); Protein 22g; EXCHANGES: 2 Starch; 1 Other Carbohydrate; 1 Fat; CARBOHYDRATE CHOICES: 3

Expert Tips

■ If tomatoes with garlic and onion are not available, substitute a can of plain diced tomatoes and increase minced garlic to 2 teaspoons and chopped onion to ¾ cup.

■ Serve with a mixed-greens salad and, for dessert, rainbow sherbet topped with fresh fruit.

Taco Beef Bake with Cheddar Biscuit Topping

PREP TIME: *15 minutes*
TOTAL TIME: *50 minutes*

MAKES 6 SERVINGS

- 1 pound lean (at least 80%) ground beef
- 1 package (1.25 ounces) Old El Paso® 40% less sodium taco seasoning mix
- 1 cup Old El Paso® Thick 'n Chunky salsa
- 2 cups Green Giant® Valley Fresh Steamers™ Niblets® frozen corn
- 2 cups Original Bisquick® mix
- 1 cup shredded Cheddar cheese (4 ounces)
- ⅔ cup milk

Heat oven to 425°F. In 10-inch skillet, cook beef over medium-high heat 5 to 7 minutes, stirring occasionally, until thoroughly cooked; drain.

Stir taco seasoning mix, salsa and corn into beef. Heat to boiling, stirring occasionally. Pour into ungreased 8-inch square pan or 8-inch square (2-quart) glass baking dish.

Meanwhile, in medium bowl, stir Bisquick mix, cheese and milk until soft dough forms.

Drop dough by 12 spoonfuls onto beef mixture.

Bake uncovered 20 to 25 minutes or until topping is golden brown.

1 SERVING: Calories 460; Total Fat 21g (Saturated Fat 9g, Trans Fat 1½g), Cholesterol 70mg; Sodium 1,370mg; Total Carbohydrate 44g (Dietary Fiber 2g, Sugars 7g); Protein 23g; EXCHANGES: 2½ Starch; ½ Other Carbohydrate; 2 Fat; CARBOHYDRATE CHOICES: 3

Expert Tip

Serve with a mixed-greens salad and fresh fruit.

Popover Pizza Casserole

1 pound ground beef

1 jar or can (14 to 15 ounces) pizza sauce

2 eggs

1 cup milk

1 tablespoon vegetable oil

1 cup Gold Medal® all-purpose flour

½ teaspoon salt

2 cups shredded Cheddar cheese (8 ounces)

2 medium green onions, chopped (2 tablespoons), if desired

Heat oven to 425°. Cook beef in 10-inch skillet over medium heat 8 to 10 minutes, stirring occasionally, until brown; drain. Stir in pizza sauce. Heat to boiling; reduce heat to low and keep warm.

Beat eggs, milk, oil, flour and salt with wire whisk until foamy. Spoon beef mixture into ungreased rectangular baking dish, 13 × 9 × 2 inches. Sprinkle with cheese. Pour egg mixture over cheese. Sprinkle with onions.

Bake uncovered 25 to 30 minutes or until puffy and golden brown. Serve immediately.

1 SERVING: Calories 502; Total Fat 31g (Saturated Fat 14g, Trans Fat 1g); Cholesterol 166mg; Sodium 829mg; Total Carbohydrate 25g (Dietary Fiber 2g, Sugars 6g); Protein 30g; EXCHANGES: ½ Starch; 1½ Other Carbohydrate; 2½ Medium-Fat Meat; 1½ High-Fat Meat; 1½ Fat CARBOHYDRATE CHOICES: 2

Expert Tips

■ If you like, use spaghetti sauce instead of the pizza sauce.

■ The entire green onion, both white and green parts, is edible. The white portion of a green onion has a slightly stronger flavor than the green stems.

Italian Crescent Casserole

1 pound ground beef, cooked, drained

1 cup basil and garlic tomato pasta sauce (from 16-ounce jar)

1 can (8 ounces) Pillsbury® refrigerated crescent dinner rolls

1½ cups shredded Italian cheese blend (6 ounces)

¼ teaspoon dried basil

Heat oven to 375°F. In 10-inch skillet, mix beef and pasta sauce. Heat to boiling over medium-high heat, stirring occasionally.

Separate dough into 8 triangles. Place dough in ungreased 9-inch glass pie plate in spoke pattern, with narrow tips overlapping rim of plate about 3 inches. Press dough in side and bottom to form crust; sprinkle with 1 cup of the cheese.

Spoon meat mixture evenly over cheese. Bring tips of dough over filling to meet in center; do not overlap. Sprinkle with remaining ½ cup cheese and the basil.

Bake 15 to 20 minutes.

1 SERVING: Calories 390; Total Fat 23g (Saturated Fat 9g, Trans Fat 2½g); Cholesterol 65mg; Sodium 830mg; Total Carbohydrate 22g (Dietary Fiber 1g, Sugars 9g); Protein 24g; EXCHANGES: 1 Starch; ½ Other Carbohydrate; 1½ Fat; CARBOHYDRATE CHOICES: 1½

Barbecue Beef and Potato Bake

PREP TIME: *15 minutes*

TOTAL TIME: *49 minutes*

MAKES 6 SERVINGS

1 package (7.2 ounces) Betty Crocker® roasted garlic mashed potatoes

2 cups hot water

1⅓ cups milk

¼ cup butter or margarine

1 container (18 or 20 ounces) refrigerated original barbecue sauce with shredded beef

1½ cups shredded Cheddar cheese (6 ounces)

1 cup French-fried onions (from 2.8-ounce can)

Heat oven to 350°F. Spray rectangular baking dish, 11 × 7 × 1½ inches, with cooking spray.

Make potatoes as directed on package for 8 servings, using 2 pouches potatoes and seasoning, hot water, milk and butter. Spread half of the potatoes over bottom of baking dish. Layer with beef, 1 cup of the cheese and remaining potatoes.

Cover with foil and bake about 30 minutes or until hot. Sprinkle with remaining ½ cup cheese. Sprinkle onions around edges of baking dish. Bake uncovered 3 to 4 minutes longer or until cheese is melted and onions are brown.

1 SERVING: Calories 558; Total Fat 30g (Saturated Fat 16g, Trans Fat 1g); Cholesterol 78mg; Sodium 680mg; Total Carbohydrate 50g (Dietary Fiber 3g, Sugars 18g); Protein 22g; EXCHANGES: 2 Starch; 1 Other Carbohydrate; 1 Medium-High Fat; 1 High-Fat Meat; 2½ Fat; CARBOHYDRATE CHOICES: 3

Expert Tips

- As well as barbecue beef, cooked barbecue chicken and barbecue pork can be used in this recipe if you'd like to try something different.
- This casserole can easily be cut into squares; serve it with a spatula rather than with a spoon.
- The mashed potatoes can be made ahead and refrigerated until you're ready to make dinner.

Potato-Topped Meat Loaf Casserole

PREP TIME: *20 minutes*
TOTAL TIME: *55 minutes*
MAKES 6 SERVINGS

MEAT LOAF

1 pound extra-lean (at least 90%) ground beef

3 tablespoons Progresso® plain bread crumbs

3 tablespoons steak sauce

1 tablespoon instant minced onion

1/2 teaspoon salt

1/4 teaspoon pepper

1 egg

FILLING

2 2/3 cups water

1/4 cup butter or margarine

1 teaspoon salt

2/3 cup milk

2 cups Betty Crocker® Potato Buds® mashed potatoes (dry)

1 1/2 cups Green Giant® Valley Fresh Steamers® frozen chopped broccoli, thawed

1/2 cup shredded sharp Cheddar cheese (2 ounces)

Heat oven to 350°F. Spray 8-inch square (2-quart) glass baking dish with cooking spray. In medium bowl, mix meat loaf ingredients. Press in bottom and up sides of baking dish to within 1/2 inch of top.

In 2-quart saucepan, heat water, butter and 1 teaspoon salt to boiling. Remove from heat. Stir in milk and dry potatoes just until moistened. Let stand about 30 seconds or until liquid is absorbed. Stir in broccoli and cheese. Spoon over meat shell.

Bake 30 to 35 minutes or until meat loaf is thoroughly cooked and meat thermometer inserted in center of meat reads 160°F. Let stand 5 minutes; drain liquid along edges.

1 SERVING: Calories 230; Total Fat 15g (Saturated Fat 8g, Trans Fat 1/2g); Cholesterol 105mg; Sodium 840mg; Total Carbohydrate 6g (Dietary Fiber 0g, Sugars 3g); Protein 17g; EXCHANGES: 1/2 Starch; 1 1/2 Lean Meat; 1 1/2 Fat; CARBOHYDRATE CHOICES: 1/2

Expert Tips

■ You can use 1 1/2 cups of your favorite vegetable in this recipe. Try frozen mixed vegetables, frozen peas or green beans.

■ Use cheese-flavored potatoes.

■ To save a little time, purchase refrigerated mashed potatoes for this recipe.

■ Substitute your favorite meat (ground chicken, turkey, pork).

Potato-Topped Oven Swiss Steak

PREP TIME: *20 minutes*
TOTAL TIME: *2 hours 35 minutes*
MAKES 8 SERVINGS

SWISS STEAK

1½ pounds boneless beef round steak (½ inch thick), cut into pieces

3 medium carrots, sliced (1½ cups)

1 large onion, cut into thin wedges (2 cups)

1 can (14.5 ounces) diced tomatoes with Italian herbs, undrained

1 jar (12 ounces) beef gravy

TOPPING

1 box (7.2 ounces) Betty Crocker® butter and herb seasoned mashed potatoes (2 pouches)

2½ cups water

1⅓ cups milk

¼ cup butter or margarine

1 egg, beaten

Heat oven to 325°F. In ungreased 13 × 9-inch (3-quart) glass baking dish, arrange beef in single layer. Top with carrots and onion.

In medium bowl, mix tomatoes and gravy; spoon over beef and vegetables. Cover with foil; bake 2 hours.

In 3-quart saucepan, make both pouches of potatoes as directed on box using water, milk and butter. Stir in egg until well blended.

Remove baking dish from oven. Uncover; spoon or pipe potato mixture over hot mixture. Return to oven; bake uncovered 15 to 20 minutes longer or until potatoes are set and light golden brown.

1 SERVING: Calories 342; Total Fat 14g (Saturated Fat 7g, Trans Fat 1); Cholesterol 98mg; Sodium 911mg; Total Carbohydrate 29g (Dietary Fiber 4g, Sugars 7g); Protein 24g; EXCHANGES: 1 Starch; 1 Vegetable; 2½ Lean Meat; 1 Fat; CARBOHYDRATE CHOICES: 2

Expert Tip

Enjoy this casserole with a crisp salad. Toss purchased salad greens, sliced fresh strawberries and slivered almonds with a balsamic vinaigrette.

Potato and Ground Beef Gratin

PREP TIME: *30 minutes*

TOTAL TIME: *1 hour 45 minutes*

MAKES 6 SERVINGS

- 1 pound lean (at least 80%) ground beef
- 1 teaspoon salt
- ½ teaspoon pepper
- 3 tablespoons butter or margarine
- 1 small onion, chopped (¼ cup)
- 3 tablespoons all-purpose flour
- 2 teaspoons chopped fresh thyme
- 3 cups milk
- 3 cups shredded mild Cheddar cheese (12 ounces)
- 6 medium white potatoes (2½ pounds), peeled, thinly sliced (6 cups)

Heat oven to 375°F. Spray 13 × 9-inch (3-quart) glass baking dish with cooking spray.

In 10-inch skillet, cook beef, salt and pepper over medium-high heat 5 to 7 minutes, stirring frequently, until beef is thoroughly cooked; drain.

Meanwhile, in 3-quart saucepan, melt butter over medium-low heat. Add onion; cook about 2 minutes, stirring occasionally, until tender. Stir in flour. Cook 1 to 2 minutes, stirring constantly, until bubbly; remove from heat. Stir in thyme.

Stir milk into onion mixture. Heat to boiling, stirring constantly. Boil and stir 1 minute; remove from heat. Stir in 2 cups of the cheese until melted.

Spread half of the potatoes in baking dish. Top with beef; spread remaining potatoes over beef. Pour cheese sauce over potatoes.

Cover with foil; bake 45 minutes. Sprinkle remaining 1 cup cheese over potatoes. Bake uncovered 15 to 20 minutes longer or until top is brown and bubbly and potatoes are tender. Let stand 5 minutes before serving.

1 SERVING: Calories 640; Total Fat 36g (Saturated Fat 20g, Trans Fat 1½g); Cholesterol 130mg; Sodium 880mg; Total Carbohydrate 45g (Dietary Fiber 4g, Sugars 9g); Protein 35g; EXCHANGES: 2½ Starch; ½ Other Carbohydrate; 4 High-Fat Meat; ½ Fat; CARBOHYDRATE CHOICES: 3

Cheesy Polenta and Ham Gratin

1 tablespoon butter

¼ cup finely chopped onion

¾ cup whipping cream

¼ cup shredded fresh Parmesan cheese (1 ounce)

1 package (1-pound) prepared polenta, cut into ½-inch slices

1 cup cooked ham strips (2 × ¼ × ¼ inch)

1 cup shredded Swiss cheese (4 ounces)

1 tablespoon chopped fresh parsley

Heat oven to 425°F. Spray 8-inch square (2-quart) glass baking dish with cooking spray. Melt butter in small saucepan over medium-high heat. Add onion; cook 2 to 3 minutes or until softened but not browned, stirring frequently.

Add whipping cream and Parmesan cheese; mix well. Bring to a boil. Reduce heat to medium; cook 2 to 4 minutes or until slightly thickened, stirring occasionally.

Arrange polenta slices, overlapping and layering if necessary, in bottom of baking dish. Top with ham and Swiss cheese. Pour sauce over top.

Bake 20 to 25 minutes or until sauce is bubbly and cheese is lightly browned. Sprinkle with parsley.

1 SERVING: Calories 432; Total Fat 32g (Saturated Fat 19g, Trans Fat 1g); Cholesterol 132mg; Sodium 399mg; Total Carbohydrate 15g (Dietary Fiber 1g, Sugars 3g); Protein 20g; EXCHANGES: 1½ Starch; 1 Lean Meat; 1 Medium-Fat Meat; 1 High-Fat Meat; 5 Fat; CARBOHYDRATE CHOICES: 1

Expert Tips

- The French word gratin refers to recipes that are topped with cheese or buttered bread crumbs before being browned in the oven. Gratin dishes are shallow, producing a broad surface area for the best part—the crispy topping.

- Polenta is a mush made from cornmeal. It is available ready-to-eat and packaged in a plastic wrapper in the refrigerated section of the grocery store. It can also be found in the shelf-stable section of the store.

- Assemble this recipe in four oval ramekins, evenly distributing the polenta slices, ham, cheese and sauce. Bake the gratins as directed until the cheese is lightly browned.

Creamy Ham and Potato Casserole

3 cups frozen potatoes O'Brien with onions and peppers (from 28-ounce bag)

1½ cups Green Giant® frozen cut green beans

1½ cups finely chopped cooked ham

¾ cup milk

½ cup shredded American cheese (2 ounces)

1 can (10¾ ounces) condensed 98% fat-free cream of chicken soup with 30% less sodium

Heat oven to 375°F. Spray 8-inch square (2-quart) glass baking dish with cooking spray.

In large bowl, mix all ingredients; spoon into baking dish.

Bake about 1 hour or until bubbly and hot. Let stand 5 minutes before serving.

1 SERVING: Calories 280; Total Fat 11g (Saturated Fat 5g, Trans Fat 0g); Cholesterol 50mg; Sodium 1,300mg; Total Carbohydrate 26g (Dietary Fiber 2g, Sugars 5g); Protein 19g; EXCHANGES: 1 Starch; ½ Other Carbohydrate; 1 Vegetable; CARBOHYDRATE CHOICES: 2

Expert Tips

■ Instead of the frozen green beans, you can substitute any Green Giant® frozen vegetable.

■ Change the flavor of this casserole and use diced cooked turkey instead of the ham.

Spicy Southwestern Potatoes and Ham

½ cup gourmet spreadable cheese with garlic and herbs (from 4- to 6.5-ounce package)

1 cup half-and-half

1 tablespoon finely chopped chipotle chiles in adobo sauce, if desired

1 package (1 pound 4 ounces) refrigerated sliced home fries

1 package (1 pound) Green Giant® frozen broccoli cuts, thawed

1 cup cooked ham strips (2 × ¼ × ¼ inch)

1 cup shredded Cheddar cheese (4 ounces)

Heat oven to 350°F. Spray 13 × 9-inch (3-quart) glass baking dish with cooking spray. Place spreadable cheese in medium bowl. Gradually stir in half-and-half and chiles; blend well. Set aside.

In baking dish, layer potatoes, broccoli and ham. Pour spreadable cheese mixture over top; sprinkle with Cheddar cheese. Cover with foil.

Bake 45 minutes. Uncover; bake an additional 15 minutes or until bubbly around edges.

1 SERVING: Calories 366; Total Fat 23g (Saturated Fat 14g, Trans Fat 1g); Cholesterol 79mg; Sodium 377mg; Total Carbohydrate 23g (Dietary Fiber 3g, Sugars 2g); Protein 16g; EXCHANGES: 1 Starch; 1 Vegetable; 1 Medium-Fat Meat; 1½ High-Fat Meat; 1½ Fat; CARBOHYDRATE CHOICES: 1½

Expert Tips

■ Chipotle peppers are smoked jalapeño chiles, available dry or canned in adobo sauce. For a mild casserole without the distinctive smoky flavor of these chiles, simply omit them.

■ To reduce the fat in each serving of this recipe by about 10 grams, use light garlic and herb cheese spread in place of the regular spread.

■ Freeze remaining chipotle chiles in small, recipe-size quantities. Place the chiles in ice cube trays until they are frozen solid, then transfer them to a resealable plastic freezer bag.

Beef and Bean Taco Casserole

1 pound lean (at least 80%) ground beef

1 can (16 ounces) Old El Paso® refried beans

1 jar (16 ounces) Old El Paso® Thick 'n Chunky salsa

1 package (1 ounce) Old El Paso® 40% less sodium taco seasoning mix

2½ cups coarsely broken tortilla chips

½ medium green bell pepper, chopped (¾ cup)

4 medium green onions, sliced (¼ cup)

2 medium tomatoes, chopped (1½ cups)

1 cup shredded Cheddar or Monterey Jack cheese (4 ounces)

¼ cup sliced ripe olives

1 cup shredded lettuce

Heat oven to 350°F. In 12-inch skillet, cook beef over medium-high heat 5 to 7 minutes, stirring occasionally, until thoroughly cooked; drain. Stir in refried beans, salsa and taco seasoning mix. Reduce heat to medium. Heat to boiling, stirring occasionally.

In ungreased 2-quart casserole, place 2 cups of the broken tortilla chips. Top evenly with beef mixture. Sprinkle with bell pepper, onions, 1 cup of the tomatoes, the cheese and olives.

Bake uncovered 20 to 30 minutes or until hot and bubbly and cheese is melted.

Top baked casserole with lettuce, remaining ½ cup tomatoes and remaining ½ cup tortilla chips.

1 SERVING: Calories 510; Total Fat 24g (Saturated Fat 10g, Trans Fat 1g); Cholesterol 85mg; Sodium 1,720mg; Total Carbohydrate 44g (Dietary Fiber 7g, Sugars 6g); Protein 29g; EXCHANGES: 2 Starch; ½ Other Carbohydrate; 1 Vegetable; 1½ Fat; CARBOHYDRATE CHOICES: 3

Expert Tips

■ This is an easy recipe to take and bake. Just save the toppings to take and serve with the hot casserole.

■ In place of the Cheddar cheese, try using a taco-flavored cheese.

Beef and Green Chile Enchiladas

- 1 pound lean (at least 80%) ground beef
- ½ cup chopped onion (1 medium)
- 1 cup Green Giant® Niblets® frozen corn
- ½ cup sour cream
- 1 can (4.5 ounces) Old El Paso® chopped green chiles
- 2 cups shredded colby-Monterey Jack cheese (8 ounces)
- 1 can (10 ounces) Old El Paso® enchilada sauce
- 6 flour tortillas (8 inch)

  Shredded lettuce, chopped tomatoes and additional sour cream, if desired

Heat oven to 350°F. In 10-inch nonstick skillet, cook ground beef and onion over medium-high heat until beef is thoroughly cooked, stirring frequently. Drain. Add corn; cook and stir about 3 minutes or until corn is thawed. Stir in sour cream, green chiles and 1 cup of the cheese.

Spread about ¼ cup of the enchilada sauce in 13 × 9-inch (3-quart) glass baking dish. Spread about 2 teaspoons enchilada sauce on each tortilla. Top each with ⅔ cup beef mixture. Roll up tortillas; place seam side down over enchilada sauce in baking dish.

Drizzle remaining enchilada sauce evenly over filled tortillas. Sprinkle with remaining 1 cup cheese. Spray sheet of foil with cooking spray; place sprayed side down on baking dish and seal tightly.

Bake 45 to 50 minutes or until thoroughly heated. Serve garnished with lettuce, tomato and additional sour cream.

1 SERVING: Calories 551; Total Fat 34g (Saturated Fat 15g, Trans Fat 1g); Cholesterol 97mg; Sodium 926mg; Total Carbohydrate 34g (Dietary Fiber 3g, Sugars 3g); Protein 27g; EXCHANGES: 2 Starch; ½ Vegetable; 3 High-Fat Meat; 1½ Fat; CARBOHYDRATE CHOICES: 2

Expert Tip

You can use Cheddar, colby or Monterey Jack cheese instead of the blend. If you want to add extra spice, use hot pepper Monterey Jack cheese in place of some of the blend.

Beef Tortilla Casserole

- 1 pound lean (at least 80%) ground beef
- ½ cup chopped onion
- 1 box (14.2 ounces) Old El Paso® enchilada dinner kit
- ½ cup water
- 1 can (4.5 ounces) Old El Paso® chopped green chiles
- 1 cup sour cream
- 1 cup shredded Cheddar cheese (4 ounces)

Heat oven to 350°F. In 10-inch skillet, cook beef and onion, stirring occasionally, until beef is thoroughly cooked; drain. Stir in both pouches enchilada sauce (from dinner kit), the seasoning mix (from dinner kit), water and chiles; heat until hot.

In ungreased 11 × 7-inch baking dish, spread 1 cup of the beef mixture. Cut tortillas (from dinner kit) in half. Place 6 tortilla halves on beef; spread with ½ cup of the sour cream. Top with ½ cup of the cheese, 1 cup of the beef mixture and remaining 6 tortilla halves. Top with remaining sour cream, beef mixture and cheese.

Bake 30 minutes. If desired, serve with additional sour cream, diced red bell pepper and chopped fresh cilantro.

1 SERVING: Calories 410; Total Fat 25g (Saturated Fat 13g, Trans Fat 1½g); Cholesterol 90mg; Sodium 1,000mg; Total Carbohydrate 24g (Dietary Fiber 2g, Sugars 5g); Protein 22g; EXCHANGES: 1 Starch, ½ Other Carbohydrate; 2½ Fat; CARBOHYDRATE CHOICES: 1½

Expert Tip

Serve with a tossed salad with fruity chunks of pineapple, mango or oranges.

Enchilada Lasagna

PREP TIME: *20 minutes*
TOTAL TIME: *1 hour 35 minutes*

MAKES 8 SERVINGS

1½ pounds lean (at least 80%) ground beef

1 medium onion, chopped (½ cup)

3 cloves garlic, chopped

2 cans (10 ounces each) Old El Paso® enchilada sauce

2 teaspoons ground cumin

1 teaspoon salt

1 egg, beaten

1½ cups cottage cheese

1 can (4 ounces) Old El Paso® whole green chiles, drained, chopped

12 no-boil lasagna noodles

4 cups shredded Mexican cheese blend (16 ounces)

1 can (14.5 ounces) Muir Glen® organic diced tomatoes, drained

Heat oven to 350°F. Spray 13 × 9-inch (3-quart) glass baking dish with cooking spray.

In 12-inch nonstick skillet, cook beef, onion and garlic over medium-high heat 5 to 7 minutes, stirring occasionally, until beef is thoroughly cooked; drain. Stir in 1 can of enchilada sauce, the cumin and salt; set aside. In small bowl, mix egg, cottage cheese and chiles; set aside.

Using remaining can of enchilada sauce, ladle ⅓ cup of the sauce into baking dish. Top with 4 noodles, half of the beef mixture (about 1¾ cups), half of the cottage cheese mixture (about 1 cup) and 1 cup of the shredded cheese. Repeat layers. Top with remaining 4 noodles. Pour remaining enchilada sauce over noodles. Spoon tomatoes over sauce.

Cover; bake 45 minutes. Uncover; sprinkle with remaining 2 cups shredded cheese. Bake 10 to 15 minutes longer or until edges are bubbly. Let stand 10 minutes before cutting.

1 SERVING: Calories 570; Total Fat 30g (Saturated Fat 15g, Trans Fat 1g); Cholesterol 145mg; Sodium 1,520mg; Total Carbohydrate 36g (Dietary Fiber 2g, Sugars 6g); Protein 38g; EXCHANGES: 2 Starch; ½ Other Carbohydrate; 2½ Lean Meat; 2 High-Fat Meat; 1 Fat; CARBOHYDRATE CHOICES: 2½

Expert Tips

■ For a smoother cheese layer, process cottage cheese in a food processor. Add egg and chiles and proceed as directed.

■ Dry lasagna noodles can be used in place of no-boil noodles, but they need to be cooked and well drained before assembling the lasagna.

Slow Cooker Couscous-Stuffed Peppers

4 large bell peppers

½ pound 85% lean ground beef

½ cup chopped onion

1 large clove garlic, finely chopped

1 can (15 ounces) tomato sauce

½ teaspoon ground cumin

¼ teaspoon salt

¼ teaspoon ground cinnamon

⅛ teaspoon ground red pepper (cayenne)

⅔ cup uncooked couscous

½ cup water

Pine nuts, if desired

Fresh cilantro, if desired

Cut thin slice from stem end of each bell pepper to remove top of pepper. Remove seeds and membranes; rinse peppers.

In 10-inch skillet, cook beef, onion and garlic over medium-high heat about 5 minutes, stirring occasionally, until beef is brown; drain. Stir in tomato sauce, cumin, salt, cinnamon and red pepper. Stir in couscous. Divide beef mixture evenly among peppers.

Pour water into 4½- to 6-quart slow cooker; stand peppers upright in cooker.

Cover and cook on Low heat setting 5 to 7 hours or until peppers are tender. Garnish with pine nuts and cilantro.

1 SERVING: Calories 300; Total Fat 9g (Saturated Fat 3g, Trans Fat ½g); Cholesterol 39mg; Sodium 750mg; Total Carbohydrate 38g (Dietary Fiber 6g, Sugars 9g); Protein 17g; EXCHANGES: 1½ Starch; 3 Vegetable; 1½ Medium-Fat Meat; CARBOHYDRATE CHOICES: 2½

Expert Tip

Couscous is available in regular, precooked (which cooks in just 5 minutes) and flavored varieties.

Spicy BEERbacoa Tacos

BEEF

1 fresh beef brisket (not corned beef), 2 to 3 pounds, trimmed of fat

½ teaspoon salt

¼ teaspoon pepper

2 teaspoons vegetable oil

3 cloves garlic, cut in half

CHIPOTLE SALSA

1 can (14.5 ounces) Muir Glen® organic fire roasted diced tomatoes, undrained

½ cup Mexican beer

2 canned chipotle chiles in adobo sauce

CARAMELIZED ONIONS

1 teaspoon vegetable oil

1 large onion, sliced (3 cups)

TACO SHELLS AND TOPPINGS

16 Old El Paso® Stand 'N Stuff® taco shells, heated as directed on box

1 cup crumbled queso fresco cheese

1 medium avocado, pitted, peeled and sliced

Spray 5-quart slow cooker with cooking spray. Heat 12-inch non-stick skillet over high heat. Season brisket with salt and pepper on both sides. Add 2 teaspoons oil to skillet. Cook brisket in oil about 3 minutes on each side or until brown.

Carefully transfer brisket to slow cooker and add garlic.

Meanwhile, place chipotle salsa ingredients in blender. Cover; blend on medium speed until smooth. Pour half of the salsa into slow cooker (about 1 cup). Cover and refrigerate remaining salsa. Cover slow cooker; cook on High heat setting 4 to 4½ hours or until brisket is very tender.

Meanwhile, in same skillet, add 1 teaspoon oil; heat over high heat. Stir in onion slices. Reduce heat to medium-low, and continue cooking and stirring until onions are caramelized, about 15 minutes. Remove from skillet; cover and refrigerate until serving time.

Remove brisket from slow cooker and shred with fork. Reheat caramelized onions. Spoon brisket into each taco shell and top with caramelized onions.

Spoon 1 tablespoon reserved salsa over each. Top with queso fresco and avocado.

1 SERVING: Calories 230; Total Fat 12g (Saturated Fat 4½g, Trans Fat 0g); Cholesterol 40mg; Sodium 300mg; Total Carbohydrate 13g (Dietary Fiber 1g, Sugars 2g); Protein 15g; EXCHANGES: ½ Starch; ½ Other Carbohydrate; ½ Fat; CARBOHYDRATE CHOICES: 1

Expert Tip

To make a perfect accompanying cocktail, pour a shot of aged tequila. Open a bottle of Mexican beer. Serve with a lime wedge and a pile of coarse salt.

BBQ Beef with Creamy Slaw on Cheese-Garlic Biscuits

BBQ BEEF

1 boneless beef rump roast (4 pounds)

2 cups barbecue sauce

1 bottle (12 ounces) dark beer

CREAMY COLESLAW

1 container (6 ounces) Yoplait® Greek fat-free plain yogurt

1/4 cup mayonnaise

1 tablespoon sugar

3 tablespoons apple cider vinegar

1/4 teaspoon salt

4 cups thinly sliced cabbage

2 tablespoons chopped green onions (2 medium)

CHEESE-GARLIC BISCUITS

2 pouches (7.75 ounces each) Bisquick® Complete cheese-garlic biscuits

Spray 4- to 5-quart slow cooker with cooking spray. Place beef into slow cooker.

In small bowl, mix barbecue sauce and beer; pour over beef. Cover; cook on Low heat setting 8 to 10 hours or until beef is tender.

Meanwhile, in large bowl, mix yogurt, mayonnaise, sugar, vinegar and salt until smooth. Stir in cabbage and green onions. Cover; refrigerate until ready to serve.

About 30 minutes before serving, remove beef from slow cooker; place on cutting board. Shred beef with 2 forks; return to slow cooker to keep warm.

Heat oven to 450°F. Make and bake biscuits as directed on pouches, making 8 biscuits per package.

To serve, split biscuits in half. Spoon about 1/2 cup beef mixture over each biscuit; top with about 3 tablespoons coleslaw.

1 SERVING: Calories 340; Total Fat 11g (Saturated Fat 31/2g, Trans Fat 2g); Cholesterol 65mg; Sodium 690mg; Total Carbohydrate 32g (Dietary Fiber 0g, Sugars 14g); Protein 27g; EXCHANGES: 11/2 Starch; 1/2 Other Carbohydrate; 1/2 Vegetable; 2 Lean Meat; CARBOHYDRATE CHOICES: 2

Harvest Beef Stew

PREP TIME: *35 minutes*

TOTAL TIME: *4 hours 45 minutes*

MAKES 8 SERVINGS

2 pounds beef stew meat, cut into 1-inch cubes

4 medium carrots, cut into 1-inch pieces

2 medium onions, cut into eighths

4 cloves garlic, finely chopped

1 can (28 ounces) Muir Glen® organic diced tomatoes, undrained

⅓ cup uncooked quick-cooking tapioca

1 tablespoon chopped fresh basil or 1 teaspoon dried basil

1 tablespoon cumin seeds

1 teaspoon salt

8 ears Green Giant® Nibblers® frozen corn-on-the-cob or 1 box (9 ounces) Green Giant® Niblets® frozen whole kernel corn

8 small red potatoes, cut in half (1 pound)

2 small zucchini, thinly sliced

Heat oven to 325°F. In Dutch oven, mix all ingredients except corn, potatoes and zucchini. Cover; bake 2 hours 30 minutes, stirring 2 or 3 times during the first 1 hour 30 minutes.

Stir in corn and potatoes. Cover; bake 1 hour to 1 hour 30 minutes longer or until beef and vegetables are tender.

Stir in zucchini. Cover; let stand 10 minutes before serving.

1 SERVING: Calories 350; Total Fat 12g (Saturated Fat 4g, Trans Fat 0g); Cholesterol 72mg; Sodium 649mg; Total Carbohydrate 34g (Dietary Fiber 4g, Sugars 8g); Protein 27g; EXCHANGES: 1 Starch; 3 Lean Meat; 2 Vegetable; 1 Fat; CARBOHYDRATE CHOICES: 2½

Expert Tips

■ Tapioca's not just for pudding! Tapioca is used to thicken this hearty stew because it doesn't need to be stirred and won't break down during the long baking process.

■ Use an ovenproof Dutch oven and cover. Check the manufacturer's information of your Dutch oven to be sure. Don't use one with plastic handles on the pot or cover if you're not certain it's ovenproof.

Greek Beef Stew

2 pounds lean beef boneless round roast

$1/3$ cup Gold Medal® all-purpose flour

$3/4$ teaspoon ground cinnamon

2 cups frozen small whole onions (from 1-pound bag)

$1\frac{1}{2}$ cups water

$3/4$ cup Italian-style tomato paste (from two 6-ounce cans)

$3/4$ cup dry red wine or apple juice

1 tablespoon red wine vinegar or vinegar

1 tablespoon honey

3 cups hot cooked bulgur wheat pilaf, rice, or pasta

$1/2$ cup crumbled feta cheese, if desired

Remove excess fat from beef. Cut beef into 1-inch pieces. Toss beef, flour and cinnamon. Rinse frozen onions in cold water to separate; drain. Place beef and onions in $3\frac{1}{2}$- to 4-quart slow cooker.

Mix water, tomato paste, wine, vinegar and honey. Pour over beef mixture.

Cover and cook on Low heat setting 9 to 10 hours or until beef is tender. Serve over pasta. Sprinkle with cheese.

1 SERVING: Calories 388; Total Fat 8g (Saturated Fat 3g, Trans Fat 0g); Cholesterol 101mg; Sodium 355mg; Total Carbohydrate 35g (Dietary Fiber 6g, Sugars 8g); Protein 38g; EXCHANGES: 1 Starch; 2 Vegetable; 5 Very Lean Meat; CARBOHYDRATE CHOICES: 2

Expert Tips

- Skim the fat from stews or soups with a spoon, or place a slice of bread on the top of the mixture for a few minutes to absorb the fat.

- Lamb is a frequently served meat in Mediterranean countries. You can use a small lamb roast in place of the beef if you'd like.

- Feta cheese can be purchased in a variety of flavors, including herb-and-garlic and sun-dried tomato.

Slow-Cooked Korean Beef Stew

PREP TIME: *10 minutes*

TOTAL TIME: *9 hours 30 minutes*

MAKES 6 SERVINGS

2 pounds beef stew meat, cut into 1-inch pieces

1 bag (16 ounces) ready-to-eat baby-cut carrots

6 green onions, cut into 1-inch pieces

2 cloves garlic, chopped

½ cup tomato juice

¼ cup soy sauce

3 tablespoons sugar

2 tablespoons sesame or vegetable oil

¼ teaspoon pepper

2 teaspoons cornstarch

4 teaspoons cold water

3 cups hot cooked rice

Spray 3- to 4-quart slow cooker with cooking spray. In slow cooker, mix beef, carrots, onions, garlic, tomato juice, soy sauce, sugar, oil and pepper.

Cover; cook on Low heat setting 9 to 11 hours (or on High setting 4 hours 30 minutes to 5 hours 30 minutes).

In small bowl, mix cornstarch and cold water until blended; stir into beef mixture in slow cooker. If cooking on Low heat setting, increase to High. Cover; cook about 20 minutes longer or until mixture is slightly thickened. Serve with rice.

1 SERVING: Calories 470; Total Fat 21g (Saturated Fat 7g, Trans Fat ½g); Cholesterol 80mg; Sodium 1,070mg; Total Carbohydrate 39g (Dietary Fiber 3g, Sugars 11g); Protein 31g; EXCHANGES: 1½ Starch; 1 Other Carbohydrate; ½ Vegetable; ½ Fat; CARBOHYDRATE CHOICES: 2½

Slow Cooker Beef Stew with Shiitake Mushrooms

PREP TIME: *20 minutes*

TOTAL TIME: *8 hours 20 minutes*

MAKES 8 SERVINGS

12 new potatoes, cut into fourths (1½ pounds)

1 medium onion, chopped (½ cup)

1 bag (8 ounces) ready-to-eat baby-cut carrots

1 package (3.4 ounces) fresh shiitake mushrooms, sliced

1 can (14.5 ounces) Muir Glen® organic diced tomatoes, undrained

1 can (10.5 ounces) condensed beef broth

½ cup Gold Medal® all-purpose flour

1 tablespoon Worcestershire sauce

1 teaspoon salt

1 teaspoon sugar

1 teaspoon dried marjoram

¼ teaspoon pepper

1 pound beef stew meat, cut into ½-inch pieces

In 3½- to 4-quart slow cooker, mix all ingredients except beef. Add beef.

Cover; cook on Low heat setting 8 to 9 hours. Stir well before serving.

Note: This recipe was tested in slow cookers with heating elements in the side and bottom of the cooker, not in cookers that stand only on a heated base. For slow cookers with just a heated base, follow the manufacturer's directions for layering ingredients and choosing a temperature.

1 SERVING: Calories 225; Total Fat 6g (Saturated Fat 2g, Trans Fat 0g); Cholesterol 36mg; Sodium 775mg; Total Carbohydrate 25g (Dietary Fiber 3g, Sugars 6g); Protein 16g; EXCHANGES: 1 Starch; 1½ Vegetable; 2 Lean Meat; ½ Fat; CARBOHYDRATE CHOICES: 2

Expert Tips

▪ Shiitake mushrooms add a wonderful, rich flavor to this easy beef stew. If they aren't available, you can use 2 cups of sliced regular white mushrooms.

▪ To make sure everything is done at the same time, cut the meat and vegetables into the sizes specified in the recipe.

Slow Cooker Burgundy Stew with Herb Dumplings

PREP TIME: *20 minutes*

TOTAL TIME: *9 hours*

MAKES 8 SERVINGS

STEW

- 2 pounds boneless beef bottom or top round, cut into 1-inch pieces
- 4 medium carrots, cut into ¼-inch slices (2 cups)
- 2 medium stalks celery, sliced (1 cup)
- 2 medium onions, sliced
- 1 can (14.5 ounces) diced tomatoes, undrained
- 2 jars (4.5 ounces each) Green Giant® sliced mushrooms, drained
- ¾ cup dry red wine or Progresso® beef flavored broth (from 32-ounce carton)
- 1½ teaspoons salt
- 1 teaspoon dried thyme
- 1 teaspoon ground mustard
- ¼ teaspoon pepper
- ¼ cup water
- 3 tablespoons Gold Medal® all-purpose flour

DUMPLINGS

- 1½ cups Original Bisquick® mix
- ½ teaspoon dried thyme
- ¼ teaspoon dried sage, crushed
- ½ cup milk

In 4- to 5-quart slow cooker, mix all stew ingredients except water and flour.

Cover; cook on Low heat setting 8 to 10 hours (or High heat setting 4 to 5 hours).

In small bowl, mix water and flour; gradually stir into beef mixture.

In small bowl, mix Bisquick, ½ teaspoon thyme and the sage. Stir in milk just until Bisquick mix is moistened. Drop dough by spoonfuls onto hot beef mixture.

Increase heat setting to High. Cover; cook 25 to 35 minutes or until toothpick inserted in center of dumplings comes out clean. Serve immediately.

1 SERVING: Calories 300; Total Fat 7g (Saturated Fat 2½g, Trans Fat 1g); Cholesterol 65mg; Sodium 990mg; Total Carbohydrate 28g (Dietary Fiber 3g, Sugars 6g); Protein 30g; EXCHANGES: 1½ Starch; 1½ Vegetable; 3 Very Lean Meat; 1 Fat; CARBOHYDRATE CHOICES: 2

Expert Tips

- Save time cleaning and slicing carrots by using 2 cups of ready-to-eat baby-cut carrots instead.
- To make fluffy dumplings, drop the dumpling dough onto the stew pieces rather than directly into the liquid. The dumplings will steam rather than settle into the liquid and become soggy. Also, be sure the stew is piping hot, so the dumplings will start to cook from the steam right away.

Chunky Beef Ragu

- 3 ounces thinly sliced prosciutto or pancetta, chopped
- 1½ pounds beef stew meat, cut into 1-inch pieces
- 2 jars (7 ounces each) sun-dried tomatoes in oil, drained, chopped (1¼ cups)
- 2 medium carrots, sliced (1 cup)
- 1 cup chopped celery
- 1 medium onion, chopped (½ cup)
- 2 cloves garlic, finely chopped
- 1 can (14.5 ounces) diced tomatoes, undrained
- ½ cup dry red wine
- 1½ teaspoons dried basil
- 1½ teaspoons dried oregano
- ½ teaspoon salt
- ¼ teaspoon crushed red pepper flakes

In 10-inch nonstick skillet, cook prosciutto over medium-high heat about 5 minutes, stirring frequently, until crisp. Drain on paper towels.

Spray 5- to 6-quart slow cooker with cooking spray. In cooker, mix all ingredients.

Cover; cook on Low heat setting 8 to 9 hours (or on High heat setting 4 hours to 4 hours 30 minutes).

1 SERVING: Calories 300; Total Fat 16g (Saturated Fat 6g, Trans Fat ½g); Cholesterol 70mg; Sodium 640mg; Total Carbohydrate 13g (Dietary Fiber 3g, Sugars 7g); Protein 26g; EXCHANGES: ½ Other Carbohydrate; 1 Vegetable; 3½ Lean Meat; 1 Fat; CARBOHYDRATE CHOICES: 1

Everyday Cassoulet

PREP TIME: *20 minutes*

TOTAL TIME: *2 hours 20 minutes*

MAKES 6 SERVINGS

4 strips bacon, chopped

½ pound bulk pork sausage

½ pound boneless pork tenderloin, cubed

⅓ cup diced onion

2 cloves garlic, finely chopped

2 cans (15 ounces each) cannellini beans, drained

1 can (14.5 ounces) diced tomatoes, undrained

½ cup Progresso® chicken broth (from 32-ounce carton)

¼ cup white wine or chicken broth

1 teaspoon dried sage leaves

1 teaspoon dried thyme leaves

¼ teaspoon pepper

1 dried bay leaf

Heat oven to 350°F. In 12-inch skillet, cook bacon over medium-high heat, stirring occasionally, until crisp. Remove from skillet. Add sausage, cubed pork, onion and garlic to skillet. Cook until pork is browned, stirring occasionally. Stir in bacon and remaining ingredients. Pour into ungreased 2½-quart casserole.

Cover casserole. Bake 1 hour 45 minutes. Uncover; bake 15 minutes longer or until pork is fork-tender and flavors are blended. Remove bay leaf; spoon into decorative soup bowls to serve.

1 SERVING: Calories 330; Total Fat 9g (Saturated Fat 3g, Trans Fat 0g); Cholesterol 45mg; Sodium 820mg; Total Carbohydrate 34g (Dietary Fiber 8g, Sugars 3g); Protein 26g; EXCHANGES: 2 Starch; 3 Lean Meat; CARBOHYDRATE CHOICES: 2

Expert Tips

■ You can substitute canned great northern beans for the cannellini beans, if you prefer.

■ Serve with toasted French bread/baguette slices on the side.

Slow Cooker Picadillo

PREP TIME: *20 minutes*

TOTAL TIME: *3 hours 20 minutes*

MAKES 12 SERVINGS

- 2 pounds ground beef
- 1 large onion, chopped (1 cup)
- 1 cup raisins
- 2 teaspoons chili powder
- 1 teaspoon salt
- ¾ teaspoon ground cinnamon
- ½ teaspoon ground cumin
- ½ teaspoon pepper
- 2 cloves garlic, finely chopped
- 2 medium apples, peeled and chopped
- 2 cans (10 ounces each) diced tomatoes and green chiles, undrained
- ½ cup slivered almonds, toasted

Cook beef and onion in 12-inch skillet over medium heat, stirring occasionally, until beef is brown; drain.

Mix beef mixture and remaining ingredients except almonds in 3½- to 6-quart slow cooker.

Cover and cook on Low heat setting 3 to 4 hours or until most of the liquid is absorbed. Stir in almonds.

1 SERVING: Calories 235; Total Fat 10g (Saturated Fat 3g, Trans Fat ½g); Cholesterol 49mg; Sodium 270mg; Total Carbohydrate 19g (Dietary Fiber 3g, Sugars 15g); Protein 17g; EXCHANGES: 1 Fruit; 1 Vegetable; 2 Lean Meat; 1 Fat; CARBOHYDRATE CHOICES: 1

Expert Tip

Place 2 cups Picadillo in freezer or refrigerator containers. Cover and refrigerate up to 4 days or freeze up to 4 months. To thaw frozen Picadillo, place container in the refrigerator about 8 hours.

Skillet Ground Beef Stew

PREP TIME: *15 minutes*

TOTAL TIME: *30 minutes*

MAKES 4 SERVINGS

1 pound lean (at least 80%) ground beef

½ teaspoon salt

½ teaspoon pepper

2 tablespoons Gold Medal® all-purpose flour

1 package (8 ounces) sliced fresh mushrooms (about 3 cups)

1½ cups Progresso® beef flavored broth (from 32-ounce carton)

⅓ cup heavy whipping cream

4 teaspoons Dijon mustard

1 pound unpeeled Yukon Gold or red potatoes, cut into ½-inch cubes (3 medium)

2 medium carrots, thinly sliced (1 cup)

2 tablespoons chopped fresh parsley

In 12-inch nonstick skillet, cook beef over medium-high heat 5 to 7 minutes, stirring occasionally, until thoroughly cooked; drain. Stir in salt, pepper and flour.

Add mushrooms; cook 3 minutes, stirring occasionally.

In small bowl, mix broth, whipping cream and mustard with wire whisk. Add to beef mixture. Stir in potatoes and carrots.

Reduce heat to medium-low. Cover; cook 15 minutes until vegetables are tender and sauce is slightly thickened. Sprinkle with parsley.

1 SERVING: Calories 410; Total Fat 21g (Saturated Fat 9g, Trans Fat 1g); Cholesterol 100mg; Sodium 830mg; Total Carbohydrate 30g (Dietary Fiber 4g, Sugars 4g); Protein 25g; EXCHANGES: 2 Starch; 2½ High-Fat Meat; CARBOHYDRATE CHOICES: 2

Expert Tips

- If the sauce is too thin at the end of the cooking process, increase the heat to medium-high and cook uncovered another few minutes until the liquid reduces and is slightly thickened.

- Purchase presliced carrots in the refrigerated case of the produce department to shave a few minutes off prep time.

Beef, Summer Squash and Sweet Potato Curry

PREP TIME: *20 minutes*

TOTAL TIME: *30 minutes*

MAKES 6 SERVINGS

1 cup uncooked regular long-grain white rice

2 cups water

1 pound lean (at least 80%) ground beef

1 medium onion, chopped (½ cup)

1 tablespoon grated gingerroot

2 tablespoons curry powder

1 teaspoon ground cumin

1 teaspoon salt

1 large sweet potato, peeled, cut into ½-inch cubes (3 cups)

1 can (14.5 ounces) diced tomatoes, undrained

1 cup Progresso® reduced-sodium chicken broth (from 32-ounce carton)

2 medium zucchini, cut in half lengthwise, then cut crosswise into ½-inch slices (2 cups)

½ cup plain yogurt

Cook rice in water as directed on package.

Meanwhile, in 12-inch skillet, cook beef and onion over medium-high heat 5 to 7 minutes, stirring occasionally, until beef is thoroughly cooked and onion is tender; drain.

Add gingerroot, curry powder, cumin and salt to skillet; cook 1 minute, stirring occasionally. Stir in sweet potato, tomatoes and broth. Heat to boiling; reduce heat. Cover; simmer 10 minutes or until potato is almost tender. Stir in zucchini. Cover; cook 5 to 10 minutes longer or until potato and zucchini are just tender.

Serve beef mixture over rice. Top each serving with about 1 tablespoon yogurt.

1 SERVING: Calories 420; Total Fat 10g (Saturated Fat 4g, Trans Fat ½g); Cholesterol 50mg; Sodium 1,030mg; Total Carbohydrate 58g (Dietary Fiber 4g, Sugars 11g); Protein 22g; EXCHANGES: 3½ Starch; 1 Vegetable; 1 High-Fat Meat; CARBOHYDRATE CHOICES: 4

Expert Tips

■ Fresh unpeeled gingerroot, tightly wrapped, can be frozen up to 6 months. To use, slice off a piece of frozen ginger and return the rest to the freezer.

■ Curry powder is a blend of several spices, such as turmeric, coriander, cumin and fenugreek. To ensure maximum freshness and flavor, keep ground spices for only 1 year.

Ground Beef Curry

PREP TIME: *50 minutes*

TOTAL TIME: *50 minutes*

MAKES 6 SERVINGS

1½ cups uncooked regular long-grain white rice

1 pound lean (at least 80%) ground beef

1 small onion, chopped (¼ cup)

1 clove garlic, finely chopped

2 tablespoons grated gingerroot (about 3 inches)

1 tablespoon tomato paste

1 teaspoon salt

2 teaspoons ground cumin

2 teaspoons chili powder

1 teaspoon garam masala

2 cans (14.5 ounces each) diced tomatoes, undrained

3 tablespoons chopped fresh cilantro

Cook rice in water as directed on package.

Meanwhile, in 12-inch skillet, cook beef, onion, garlic and gingerroot over medium-high heat 5 to 7 minutes, stirring occasionally, until beef is thoroughly cooked; drain if desired.

Stir remaining ingredients except cilantro into beef mixture. Reduce heat to medium. Simmer uncovered 8 to 10 minutes, stirring occasionally, until slightly thickened.

Serve beef mixture over rice. Garnish with cilantro.

1 SERVING: Calories 360; Total Fat 9g (Saturated Fat 3½g, Trans Fat ½g); Cholesterol 45mg; Sodium 1,200mg; Total Carbohydrate 50g (Dietary Fiber 3g, Sugars 4g); Protein 18g; EXCHANGES: 2 Starch; 1½ Other Carbohydrate; CARBOHYDRATE CHOICES: 3

Expert Tips

- From India, garam masala is a blend of up to 12 dry-roasted ground spices, including black pepper, cinnamon, cloves, coriander, cumin, cardamom, dried chiles, fennel, mace and nutmeg. It can be found at Indian stores and in the spice aisle of gourmet grocery stores.
- Serve with flatbread crackers.

Slow Cooker Cuban Flank Steak

PREP TIME: *15 minutes*
TOTAL TIME: *8 hours 30 minutes*
MAKES 8 SERVINGS

1 large onion, thinly sliced

1 medium red bell pepper, cut into strips (1½ cups)

1 medium green bell pepper, cut into strips (1½ cups)

1 beef flank steak (2 pounds), cut into 8 pieces

2 tablespoons chili powder

1 teaspoon dried oregano

2 teaspoons dried minced garlic

1 teaspoon salt

2 tablespoons lime juice

1 cup Progresso® beef flavored broth (from 32-ounce carton)

2 cups uncooked regular long-grain white rice

1 can (15 ounces) Progresso® black beans, drained, rinsed

Spray 3½- to 4-quart slow cooker with cooking spray. In cooker, place onion and peppers. Top with beef. Sprinkle with chili powder, oregano, garlic and salt. Drizzle with lime juice. Add broth.

Cover; cook on Low heat setting 8 to 10 hours.

About 20 minutes before serving, cook rice as directed on package.

Remove beef from cooker; place on cutting board. Shred beef with 2 forks; return to cooker and mix well. Stir in black beans. Increase heat setting to High. Cover; cook about 15 minutes longer or until thoroughly heated. Serve beef and sauce over rice.

1 SERVING: Calories 420; Total Fat 6g (Saturated Fat 2g, Trans Fat 0g); Cholesterol 85mg; Sodium 640mg, Total Carbohydrate 53g (Dietary Fiber 4g, Sugars 2g); Protein 40g; EXCHANGES: 2½ Starch; ½ Other Carbohydrate; 1 Vegetable; CARBOHYDRATE CHOICES: 3½

Expert Tip

The sauce that collects is packed with flavor, but if you prefer, drain excess sauce before serving.

Kentucky Burgoo

PREP TIME: *20 minutes*

TOTAL TIME: *3 hours 15 minutes*

MAKES 12 SERVINGS

3 tablespoons vegetable oil

Salt

3 to 4 pounds pork shoulder or country ribs, cut into large pieces (3 to 4 inches wide)

2 to 3 pounds chuck roast, stew meat, or inexpensive cut of beef, cut into large pieces (3 to 4 inches wide)

3 to 4 chicken legs or thighs

1 green pepper, chopped

1 large onion, chopped

2 carrots, chopped

2 stalks celery, chopped

5 cloves garlic, chopped

1 carton (32 ounces) chicken broth

1 carton (32 ounces) beef broth

1 can (28 ounces) crushed tomatoes

2 large russet potatoes

4 to 8 tablespoons Worcestershire sauce

1 bag (16 ounces) frozen corn

1 bag (14 ounces) frozen lima beans

Tabasco or other hot sauce on the side

Heat vegetable oil on medium-high heat in a large soup pot (at least 8-quart size). Salt meats well on all sides. When oil is shimmering hot, working in batches, brown all meats. Do not crowd pan or meat will steam and not brown well. Do not move meat while browning a side. Let meat pieces get well seared. Remove browned meats to a bowl.

Add green pepper, onion, carrots and celery to pot and brown them. If necessary, add a little more oil. After a few minutes of cooking, sprinkle salt over vegetables.

When vegetables are well browned, add garlic and cook 30 seconds more, until fragrant. Add browned meats, chicken and beef broths and tomatoes; stir to combine. Bring to a simmer, cover, reduce heat and simmer gently 2 hours.

Uncover and remove meat pieces. Strip chicken off bone and discard skin if you want. Break larger pieces of meat into smaller, more manageable pieces. (The reason you did not do this at first is because meats stay juicier when they cook in larger pieces.) Return all meat pieces to pot and bring to a strong simmer.

Peel and cut potatoes into chunks about the size of meat pieces (if using new potatoes, you can skip peeling). Add to stew and cook until done, about 45 minutes.

When potatoes are done, add Worcestershire sauce, mix well and taste for salt. Add more Worcestershire sauce to taste if needed. Add corn and lima beans. Mix well and cook at least 10 minutes, or longer if you'd like.

Here is where you decide whether you want a burgoo that's been hammered into a thick mass or a stew with bright colors in it. It's your call.

Taste one more time for salt, and add either Worcestershire or salt if you want. Serve with crusty bread or cornbread and a bottle of hot sauce on the side.

1 SERVING: Calories 547; Total Fat 21 (Saturated Fat 6, Trans Fat 0g); Cholesterol 151; Sodium 1,155; Total Carbohydrate 34 (Dietary Fiber 5, Sugars 7g); Protein 53; EXCHANGES: 1½ Starch; 1½ Vegetable; 5½ Lean Meat; 1 Medium-Fat Meat; 1½ Fat; CARBOHYDRATE CHOICES: 2

Expert Tip

As with most stews, burgoo is even better the second day. It's excellent as a Sunday dinner when you want lunches for the coming week.

Beef 'n Veggie Soup with Mozzarella

PREP TIME: *30 minutes*

TOTAL TIME: *30 minutes*

MAKES 8 SERVINGS

1 pound lean (at least 80%) ground beef

1 large onion, chopped (1 cup)

2 cups Green Giant® Valley Fresh Steamers™ frozen mixed vegetables

1 can (14.5 ounces) diced tomatoes with green pepper, celery and onions (or other variety), undrained

4 cups water

5 teaspoons beef bouillon granules

1½ teaspoons Italian seasoning

¼ teaspoon pepper

1 cup shredded mozzarella cheese (4 ounces)

In 4-quart Dutch oven, cook beef and onion over medium-high heat 5 to 7 minutes, stirring occasionally, until beef is thoroughly cooked; drain.

Stir in remaining ingredients except cheese. Heat to boiling; reduce heat. Simmer uncovered 6 to 8 minutes, stirring occasionally, until vegetables are tender.

Sprinkle 2 tablespoons cheese in each of 8 soup bowls; fill bowls with soup.

1 SERVING: Calories 200; Total Fat 9g (Saturated Fat 4½g, Trans Fat ½g); Cholesterol 45mg; Sodium 790mg; Total Carbohydrate 13g (Dietary Fiber 3g, Sugars 5g); Protein 15g; EXCHANGES: ½ Other Carbohydrate; 1 Vegetable; CARBOHYDRATE CHOICES: 1

Expert Tip

Make this soup your way with what's on hand. Use any frozen veggie, your favorite cheese and the herbs you like best.

Asian Beef and Noodle Soup

3 ounces uncooked cellophane noodles

1 tablespoon dark sesame oil

1½ pounds beef boneless top sirloin steak, cut into bite-size strips

2 teaspoons finely chopped garlic

2 packages (3.5 ounces each) fresh shiitake mushrooms or button mushrooms, sliced

6 cups Progresso® beef flavored broth (from two 32-ounce cartons)

2 cups finely sliced bok choy

1 cup julienne strips (matchstick-size) carrots

½ teaspoon salt

½ teaspoon ground ginger

⅛ teaspoon pepper

2 medium green onions, chopped (2 tablespoons)

Soak bundle of cellophane noodles in warm water in medium bowl 10 to 15 minutes or until softened; drain. Cut noodle bundle into thirds. Cover and set aside.

Heat oil in 5- to 6-quart Dutch oven over medium-high heat. Cook beef, garlic and mushrooms in oil 5 to 6 minutes, stirring occasionally, just until beef is no longer pink.

Stir in remaining ingredients except noodles and onions. Heat to boiling; reduce heat to medium-low. Cover and cook 14 to 15 minutes, stirring occasionally, until beef is tender.

Stir in noodles. Cover and cook 2 to 3 minutes or until noodles are hot. Sprinkle with onions.

1 SERVING: Calories 249; Total Fat 8g (Saturated Fat 2g, Trans Fat 0g); Cholesterol 48mg; Sodium 1,172mg; Total Carbohydrate 15g (Dietary Fiber 2g, Sugars 1g); Protein 28g; EXCHANGES: 1 Starch; ½ Vegetable; 3½ Very Lean Meat; ½ Fat; CARBOHYDRATE CHOICES: 1

Expert Tips

■ If you can't find cellophane noodles, you can use vermicelli instead. Simply cook and drain 3 ounces vermicelli as directed on package, and stir into soup in step 4.

■ Sesame oil comes in two varieties. One is light in color and has a light, nutty flavor. The darker sesame oil has a stronger flavor and aroma. Feel free to use either one in this recipe.

■ A salad of pink grapefruit sections, sliced seeded cucumbers and sliced celery tossed with your favorite Asian dressing goes great with this noodle soup dinner. Try topping the salad with rice crackers for extra crunch.

Tomato, Beef and Barley Soup

1 pound lean (at least 80%) ground beef

2 cans (19 ounces each) Progresso® Vegetable Classics hearty tomato soup

2 cups water

½ cup uncooked quick-cooking barley

1 cup sliced celery

1 cup Green Giant® frozen mixed vegetables (from 1-pound bag)

6 tablespoons shredded fresh Parmesan cheese

In 4-quart saucepan or Dutch oven, cook beef over medium-high heat 5 to 7 minutes, stirring occasionally, until thoroughly cooked; drain.

Stir in soup, water, barley and celery. Heat to boiling, stirring occasionally.

Reduce heat to low; simmer uncovered about 15 minutes, stirring occasionally, until barley is tender.

Stir in frozen mixed vegetables. Cook 6 to 7 minutes, stirring occasionally, until mixture is hot. Sprinkle each serving with 1 tablespoon cheese.

1 SERVING: Calories 320; Total Fat 11g (Saturated Fat 4½g, Trans Fat ½g); Cholesterol 50mg; Sodium 890mg; Total Carbohydrate 35g (Dietary Fiber 6g, Sugars 8g); Protein 20g; EXCHANGES: 1½ Starch; ½ Other Carbohydrate; 1 Vegetable; CARBOHYDRATE CHOICES: 2

Expert Tips

■ In place of the hearty tomato soup, use Progresso® Vegetable Classics tomato basil soup.

■ Serve this soup with crusty French rolls.

Slow Cooker Beefy French Onion Soup

7 small onions, cut in half and thinly sliced (about 7 cups)

1 tablespoon butter or margarine, melted

2 tablespoons sugar

2 dried bay leaves

1½ pounds beef stew meat

3 cans (10.5 ounces each) condensed beef consommé

¼ cup dry sherry or apple juice

1 cup apple juice

¼ teaspoon dried thyme

8 slices (½ inch thick) French bread, toasted

2 cups shredded Swiss cheese (8 ounces)

Toss onions, butter and sugar in 5- to 6-quart slow cooker. Top with bay leaves and beef.

Cover and cook on Low heat setting 9 to 10 hours or until onions are deep brown.

Stir in beef consommé, sherry, apple juice and thyme. Increase heat setting to High. Cover and cook 10 minutes or until hot. Remove bay leaves.

To serve, spoon into ovenproof soup bowls and top each serving with slice of toast and ¼ cup cheese. If desired, broil with tops 6 inches from heat 3 to 5 minutes or until cheese is bubbly and begins to brown.

1 SERVING: Calories 440; Total Fat 19g (Saturated Fat 9g, Trans Fat 0g); Cholesterol 84mg; Sodium 1,133mg; Total Carbohydrate 34g (Dietary Fiber 2g, Sugars 10g); Protein 31g; EXCHANGES: 1 Vegetable; 2½ Lean Meat; 1 Medium-Fat Meat; 1 High-Fat Meat; 2 Fat; CARBOHYDRATE CHOICES: 2

Expert Tips

■ For best results, don't double this recipe. If the onions are packed too deeply in the slow cooker, they steam and stay pale and boiled tasting instead of caramelizing. They would eventually caramelize, but not before the beef would become dried out and overcooked.

■ A fresh tossed salad with a vinaigrette would taste great with this rich soup. Spoil your family with a small fancy French pastry from the bakery for dessert.

■ If you broil the soup with cheese on top, place the soup bowls on pretty plates to protect fingers and your table from the hot bowls.

Poultry

Herbed Chicken Lattice Pot Pie

- 1 cup uncooked instant white rice
- 1 cup water
- 2 tablespoons olive oil
- 1¼ pounds boneless skinless chicken breasts, cut into ¾-inch pieces
- 1 large red bell pepper, chopped (about 1½ cups)
- 1 large onion, chopped (about 1 cup)
- 1 medium zucchini, chopped (about 1 cup)
- 2 tablespoons savory herb with garlic soup mix (from packet in 2.4-ounce box)
- ¾ cup milk
- 1 can (8 ounces) Pillsbury® Crescent Recipe Creations® refrigerated seamless dough sheet

Heat oven to 375°F. Spray 9-inch glass pie plate with cooking spray. Cook rice in water as directed on package. Pat cooked rice evenly in bottom of pie plate. In 12-inch nonstick skillet, heat 1 tablespoon of the oil over medium-high heat. Add chicken; cook and stir until no longer pink in center. Remove chicken from skillet.

Heat remaining 1 tablespoon oil in skillet. Add bell pepper, onion and zucchini; cook and stir until crisp-tender. In small bowl, mix soup mix and milk; stir into vegetable mixture. Heat to boiling over high heat. Remove from heat; stir in chicken (discard chicken juices). Spoon over rice in pie plate.

Unroll dough on work surface; cut lengthwise into 8 strips. Arrange 4 strips evenly in same direction over filling. Top with remaining strips in opposite direction. Fold overhanging ends of strips at an angle around edge of pie plate to form rim.

Bake about 20 minutes. Let stand 5 minutes before serving.

1 SERVING: Calories 390; Total Fat 15g (Saturated Fat 4½g, Trans Fat 0g); Cholesterol 60mg; Sodium 570mg; Total Carbohydrate 38g (Dietary Fiber 2g, Sugars 7g); Protein 26g; EXCHANGES: 2 Starch; ½ Other Carbohydrate; 3 Lean Meat; 1 Fat; CARBOHYDRATE CHOICES: 2½

Expert Tip

All you need to complete this meal is a simple green salad!

Garden Vegetable Chicken Pot Pie

PREP TIME: *10 minutes*

TOTAL TIME: *45 minutes*

MAKES 4 SERVINGS

1 Pillsbury® refrigerated pie crust

1 tablespoon butter or margarine

1 tablespoon all-purpose flour

1 can (18.5 ounces) Progresso® Vegetable Classics garden vegetable soup

1 bag (12 ounces) Green Giant® Valley Fresh Steamers™ frozen mixed vegetables, thawed, drained

2 cups cubed cooked chicken

½ teaspoon dried thyme

Heat oven to 400°F. Remove pie crust from box; set aside.

In 3-quart saucepan, melt butter, stirring constantly. Stir in flour. Cook, stirring constantly, until smooth and bubbly. Stir in soup, vegetables, chicken and thyme. Heat over high heat, stirring frequently, until mixture is hot and bubbly. Pour into ungreased 2-quart casserole.

Unroll pie crust and place over top of casserole. Roll up outer 1-inch edge of crust so rolled crust edge fits inside edge of casserole; press crust lightly onto soup mixture. Cut several slits in crust to allow steam to escape.

Bake 30 to 35 minutes or until crust is golden brown. Let stand 10 minutes before serving.

1 SERVING: Calories 500; Total Fat 22g (Saturated Fat 8g, Trans Fat 0g); Cholesterol 75mg; Sodium 850mg; Total Carbohydrate 50g (Dietary Fiber 6g, Sugars 5g); Protein 24g; EXCHANGES: 3 Starch; 1 Vegetable; 2 Lean Meat; 3 Fat; CARBOHYDRATE CHOICES: 3

Expert Tip

Turkey, ham and beef make great stand-ins for the chicken.

Chicken Souvlaki Pot Pie

- 2 tablespoons olive or vegetable oil
- 1¼ pounds boneless skinless chicken breasts, cut into bite-size strips
- 1 medium red onion, chopped (about 1¼ cups)
- 2 small zucchini, cut in half lengthwise, then cut crosswise into slices (about 2⅓ cups)
- 2 cloves garlic, finely chopped
- 2 teaspoons chili powder
- 1½ teaspoons dried oregano
- ½ teaspoon salt
- 1 can (14.5 ounces) diced tomatoes, undrained
- ½ cup plain yogurt
- 2 tablespoons all-purpose flour
- 1 box Pillsbury® refrigerated pie crusts, softened as directed on box

Heat oven to 400°F. In 12-inch nonstick skillet, heat 1 tablespoon of the oil over medium-high heat. Add chicken; cook about 8 minutes, stirring occasionally, until no longer pink in center. Remove chicken from skillet.

Heat remaining 1 tablespoon oil in skillet. Add onion and zucchini; cook and stir about 6 minutes or until zucchini is crisp-tender. Return chicken to skillet (discard chicken juices). Stir in garlic, chili powder, oregano and salt. Cook and stir 2 minutes. Stir in tomatoes; cook until thoroughly heated. Remove from heat.

In small bowl, beat yogurt and flour with wire whisk until blended; stir into chicken mixture. Spoon into ungreased 9-inch glass pie plate.

Unroll pie crust over hot chicken mixture. Fold excess crust under and press to form thick crust edge; flute. Cut slits in several places in crust. Place pie plate on cookie sheet with sides.

Bake 25 to 30 minutes or until crust is golden brown (sauce may bubble slightly over crust). Let stand 5 minutes before serving.

1 SERVING: Calories 490; Total Fat 24g (Saturated Fat 8g, Trans Fat 0g); Cholesterol 70mg; Sodium 720mg; Total Carbohydrate 42g (Dietary Fiber 2g, Sugars 4g); Protein 26g; EXCHANGES: 2 Starch; ½ Other Carbohydrate; 1½ Vegetable; 2½ Lean Meat; 3 Fat; CARBOHYDRATE CHOICES: 3

Expert Tips

- Stirring flour into the yogurt before the mixture is added to the chicken filling allows the sauce to thicken when heated without separating.
- The chili powder and oregano are cooked in the skillet because heat helps bring out their aromatic flavors.

Chicken Pot Pie with Flaky Crust

1 sheet frozen puff pastry (from 17.3-ounce package), thawed

1 tablespoon olive or vegetable oil

3/4 pound boneless skinless chicken breasts, cut into 1/2-inch pieces

1 large onion, coarsely chopped (1 cup)

1 cup quartered ready-to-eat baby-cut carrots (5 to 6 ounces)

3/4 cup Green Giant® frozen sweet peas (from 1-pound bag)

1/2 cup sour cream

1 jar (12 ounces) chicken gravy

2 tablespoons cornstarch

1/4 teaspoon dried thyme leaves

1/4 teaspoon pepper

1 egg, beaten, if desired

Heat oven to 375°F. On lightly floured surface, unroll puff pastry. With rolling pin, roll out into 11-inch square. Cut off corners to make an 11-inch round. Cut slits or small designs in several places in pastry; set aside.

In 10-inch skillet, heat oil over medium-high heat. Add chicken; cook about 4 minutes, stirring frequently, until no longer pink in center. Add onion and carrots; cook 5 minutes, stirring frequently, until vegetables are crisp-tender. Remove from heat; stir in peas.

In medium bowl, beat remaining ingredients except egg with wire whisk until well blended. Stir into chicken mixture in skillet. Spoon into 9-inch deep-dish glass pie plate. Place pastry over filling, allowing to hang over edge.

Bake 20 minutes. Brush crust with beaten egg. Cover edge of crust with strips of foil to prevent excessive browning.

Bake 20 to 25 minutes longer or until crust is golden brown. Let stand 10 minutes before serving.

1 SERVING: Calories 610; Total Fat 37g (Saturated Fat 13g, Trans Fat 2 1/2g); Cholesterol 135mg; Sodium 720mg; Total Carbohydrate 44g (Dietary Fiber 3g, Sugars 7g); Protein 27g; EXCHANGES: 1 Starch; 1 1/2 Other Carbohydrate; 1 Vegetable; 3 Very Lean Meat; 7 Fat; CARBOHYDRATE CHOICES: 3

Expert Tips

- You can use 2 3/4 cups Green Giant® frozen mixed vegetables instead of the onion, carrots and frozen peas. Just stir them into the cooked chicken before adding the gravy mixture.

- Use a miniature cookie or canapé cutter to make steam holes in the pastry. Save the pastry cutouts and place on top of the pastry after brushing it with egg. Bake as directed.

PREP TIME: *35 minutes*

TOTAL TIME: *1 hour 20 minutes*

MAKES 6 SERVINGS

Chicken Paprikash Pot Pie

1 box Pillsbury® refrigerated pie crusts

4 slices bacon, cut into ½-inch pieces

¾ pound boneless skinless chicken breast halves, cut into ½-inch pieces

1 cup coarsely chopped onions

1 cup coarsely chopped red or green bell pepper

1 cup sliced carrots

1 cup Green Giant® frozen sweet peas

½ cup sour cream

1 jar (12 ounces) home-style chicken gravy

3 tablespoons cornstarch

3 teaspoons paprika

Heat oven to 425°F. Prepare pie crust as directed on package for two-crust pie using 9-inch pie pan.

In large skillet over medium heat, cook bacon until crisp. Reserve 1 tablespoon drippings with bacon in skillet.

Add chicken to skillet; cook and stir until no longer pink. Add onions, bell pepper and carrots; cook and stir until vegetables are tender. Stir in peas.

In small bowl, combine all remaining ingredients; mix well. Stir into chicken mixture in skillet. Spoon into crust-lined pan. Top with second crust and flute edges; cut slits or small designs in several places on top of crust.

Bake 30 to 35 minutes or until crust is golden brown. Cover edge of crust with strips of foil after 10 to 15 minutes of baking to prevent excessive browning. Let stand 10 minutes before serving.

1 SERVING: Calories 520; Total Fat 27g (Saturated Fat 11g, Trans Fat 0g); Cholesterol 60mg; Sodium 880mg; Total Carbohydrate 49g (Dietary Fiber 3g, Sugars 5g); Protein 20g; EXCHANGES: 3 Starch; 1 Vegetable; 1½ Lean Meat; 4 Fat; CARBOHYDRATE CHOICES: 3

Cornbread-Topped Chicken Pot Pie

PREP TIME: *30 minutes*

TOTAL TIME: *1 hour*

MAKES 4 SERVINGS

1 pound boneless skinless chicken breasts, cut into ½-inch pieces

½ teaspoon peppered seasoned salt

1 large onion, chopped (1 cup)

1 jar (12 ounces) chicken gravy

1 bag (1 pound) frozen broccoli, carrots and cauliflower

½ cup sour cream

1 pouch (6.5 ounces) Betty Crocker® cornbread and muffin mix

⅓ cup milk

2 tablespoons butter or margarine, melted

1 egg

2 tablespoons shredded Parmesan cheese

Heat oven to 400°F. Spray 13 × 9-inch (3-quart) glass baking dish with cooking spray. Sprinkle chicken with seasoned salt. In 12-inch nonstick skillet, cook chicken and onion over medium-high heat 4 to 6 minutes, stirring occasionally, until chicken is brown.

Stir in gravy. Heat to boiling. Reduce heat to medium-low; cover and cook about 5 minutes, stirring occasionally, until chicken is no longer pink in center. Meanwhile, place vegetables in colander. Rinse with hot water until thawed. Remove chicken mixture from heat. Stir in vegetables and sour cream; keep warm.

In medium bowl, mix cornbread and muffin mix, milk, butter and egg with spoon just until moistened (batter will be lumpy). Spoon chicken mixture into baking dish. Drop batter by spoonfuls around edges of warm chicken mixture. Sprinkle cheese over batter.

Bake uncovered 20 to 22 minutes or until cornbread is deep golden brown. Let stand 5 minutes before serving.

1 SERVING: Calories 570; Total Fat 24g (Saturated Fat 11g, Trans Fat ½g); Cholesterol 160mg; Sodium 1,190mg; Total Carbohydrate 53g (Dietary Fiber 4g, Sugars 15g); Protein 37g; EXCHANGES: 2 Starch; 1 Other Carbohydrate; 1 Vegetable; 4 Very Lean Meat; 4 Fat; CARBOHYDRATE CHOICES: 3½

Expert Tips

- Make sure that the chicken filling is still hot before dropping the cornbread batter on top, to ensure that the cornbread will bake throughout.

- This recipe will work with lots of other vegetable combinations. Let your family pick their favorite, or you can substitute leftover cooked vegetables for the frozen vegetables.

- Enjoy grapes and apple wedges with this family-pleasin' meal.

Buffalo Chicken Pie

2 cups cooked chicken strips

$\frac{1}{2}$ cup Buffalo wing sauce

1 cup shredded Cheddar cheese (4 ounces)

$\frac{1}{2}$ cup crumbled blue cheese (2 ounces)

1 cup chopped celery (about 2$\frac{1}{2}$ stalks)

1 cup Original Bisquick® mix

$\frac{1}{2}$ cup cornmeal

$\frac{1}{2}$ cup milk

1 egg

$\frac{2}{3}$ cup blue cheese dressing

Heat oven to 400°F. In large bowl, toss chicken and Buffalo wing sauce until well coated. Stir in cheeses and celery. Pour into ungreased 9-inch glass pie plate.

In medium bowl, mix Bisquick, cornmeal, milk and egg. Pour over chicken mixture; spread to cover.

Bake 25 to 30 minutes or until topping is golden brown. Cut into wedges; drizzle with blue cheese dressing.

1 SERVING: Calories 510; Total Fat 30g (Saturated Fat 10g, Trans Fat 1g); Cholesterol 110mg; Sodium 1,180mg; Total Carbohydrate 36g (Dietary Fiber 1g, Sugars 10g); Protein 25g; EXCHANGES: 2 Starch; $\frac{1}{2}$ Other Carbohydrate; 2$\frac{1}{2}$ Lean Meat; 4 Fat; CARBOHYDRATE CHOICES: 2$\frac{1}{2}$

Expert Tips

■ Use refrigerated cooked chicken strips (from two 6-ounce packages) or any cooked chicken for this recipe.

■ Look for bottled Buffalo wing sauce in the condiment aisle of the grocery store.

Chicken Pot Pie Cupcakes

PREP TIME: *15 minutes*
TOTAL TIME: *45 minutes*
MAKES 12 SERVINGS

1 can (18.5 ounces) Progresso® Rich & Hearty chicken pot pie–style soup

⅓ cup Betty Crocker® Potato Buds® mashed potatoes (dry)

½ cup Green Giant® frozen mixed vegetables, cooked

¼ teaspoon dried thyme

¼ teaspoon pepper

2 cans (8 ounces each) Pillsbury® Crescent Recipe Creations® refrigerated flaky dough sheet

1 tablespoon butter, melted

Heat oven to 375°F. Spray 12 regular-size muffin cups with cooking spray.

In medium bowl, mix soup, potatoes (dry), cooked vegetables, thyme and pepper.

Unroll 1 can of dough; spread with half of the soup mixture. Starting at shortest side, roll up; pinch edges to seal. Cut into 6 slices. Place 1 slice in each of 6 muffin cups. Repeat with remaining dough and soup mixture.

Bake 25 to 30 minutes or until golden brown. Brush top of each with melted butter; remove from pan. Serve immediately.

1 SERVING: Calories 170; Total Fat 8g (Saturated Fat 3½g, Trans Fat 0g); Cholesterol 5mg; Sodium 470mg; Total Carbohydrate 22g (Dietary Fiber 0g, Sugars 4g); Protein 3g; EXCHANGES: 1 Starch; ½ Other Carbohydrate; 1½ Fat; CARBOHYDRATE CHOICES: 1½

Expert Tip

If substituting crescent rolls for the dough sheet, be sure to firmly press perforations to seal before spreading with soup mixture.

Alfredo Chicken Pot Puff Pies

- 1 sheet frozen puff pastry (from 17.3-ounce package), thawed as directed on package
- 1 tablespoon butter or margarine
- 2 tablespoons finely chopped shallots
- 2 cups chopped cooked chicken
- 2 cups frozen peas and carrots
- 1 jar (16 ounces) Alfredo pasta sauce
- 1 teaspoon dried thyme
- 1 egg

Heat oven to 400°F. Lightly spray 4 (10-ounce) custard cups or ramekins with cooking spray. On lightly floured surface, roll puff pastry to 13-inch square. Cut into 4 squares. Lightly press 1 square in bottom and up sides of each custard cup, letting corners hang over sides.

In 10-inch skillet, melt butter over medium heat. Add shallots. Cook about 3 minutes, stirring occasionally, until shallots are softened. Add chicken, frozen peas and carrots, and Alfredo sauce. Cook 3 to 4 minutes longer, stirring occasionally, until peas are thawed and mixture is hot. Sprinkle with thyme; stir well.

Spoon mixture into pastry-lined custard cups. Fold corners over filling, pinching to almost close tops. In small bowl, beat egg with fork or wire whisk; brush pastry tops with egg.

Bake 25 to 30 minutes or until pastry is deep golden brown. Let stand 5 minutes. Serve in cups, or remove to individual serving plates.

1 SERVING: Calories 730; Total Fat 50g (Saturated Fat 21g, Trans Fat 2½g); Cholesterol 285mg; Sodium 1,070mg; Total Carbohydrate 42g (Dietary Fiber 3g, Sugars 6g); Protein 28g; EXCHANGES: 1½ Starch; 1 Other Carbohydrate; 1 Vegetable; 8 Fat; CARBOHYDRATE CHOICES: 3

Expert Tips

- If you don't have 10-ounce custard cups, look for them in any kitchen or department store. Many grocery stores also carry them in the baking aisle. They are inexpensive and have a multitude of uses in the kitchen.
- Look for the puff pastry in the dessert section of the frozen food aisle in the grocery store.

Mini Chicken Alfredo Pot Pies

PREP TIME: *20 minutes*
TOTAL TIME: *50 minutes*
MAKES 8 SERVINGS

4 cups chopped cooked chicken

4 cups Green Giant® Valley Fresh Steamers™ frozen mixed vegetables (from two 12-ounce bags), thawed, well drained

1 jar (16 ounces) Alfredo pasta sauce

½ cup milk

¼ cup grated Parmesan cheese

1 can (8 ounces) Pillsbury® refrigerated garlic bread-sticks (8 breadsticks)

Heat oven to 400°F. Place 8 (10-ounce) ramekins or custard cups on large cookie sheet with sides. In 3-quart saucepan, heat chicken, thawed vegetables, pasta sauce and milk over medium heat, stirring occasionally, until thoroughly heated. Spoon mixture into ramekins.

Sprinkle cheese on plate. Unroll dough. Separate 1 strip at a time; press both sides into cheese. Twist strip; arrange on mixture in ramekin in loose spiral shape, beginning at outside and coiling toward center. Repeat with remaining strips of dough and cheese. Sprinkle any remaining cheese over dough.

Bake 15 minutes. Cover ramekins loosely with sheet of foil; bake about 12 minutes longer or until filling is hot and bubbly.

1 SERVING: Calories 520; Total Fat 33g (Saturated Fat 16g, Trans Fat 2g); Cholesterol 120mg; Sodium 630mg; Total Carbohydrate 28g (Dietary Fiber 4g, Sugars 6g); Protein 29g; EXCHANGES: 1 Starch; ½ Other Carbohydrate; 1 Vegetable; 3 Lean Meat; 5 Fat; CARBOHYDRATE CHOICES: 2

Expert Tips

- The frozen vegetables called for in this recipe work well because the pieces are about the same size and cook in the same amount of time.

- The ramekins are covered with foil after baking 15 minutes so the breadsticks don't get too golden brown.

Burrito Pot Pies

- 1¼ cups Bisquick® Heart Smart mix
- ¾ cup shredded reduced-fat Cheddar cheese (3 ounces)
- ¼ cup water
- 1 egg
- 2 cups cut-up cooked chicken
- 1 jar (16 ounces) Old El Paso® Thick 'n Chunky salsa
- 1 can (15 ounces) Progresso® black beans, drained, rinsed
- 1 can (11 ounces) Green Giant® Niblets® whole kernel corn, drained
- 1 teaspoon ground cumin
- 1 ripe avocado, pitted, peeled and chopped
- Reduced-fat sour cream, if desired
- Lime wedges, if desired

Heat oven to 400°F. Spray 6 (10-ounce) ramekins or custard cups with cooking spray; place on 15 × 10 × 1-inch pan.

In medium bowl, stir Bisquick mix, ½ cup of the cheese, water and egg until soft dough forms. Set aside.

In 3-quart saucepan, heat chicken, salsa, beans, corn and cumin to boiling. Remove from heat; fold in avocado. Divide chicken mixture evenly among ramekins. Spoon dollop of Bisquick mixture over each (dough will not cover entire top).

Bake 15 to 20 minutes or until crust is golden brown and filling is bubbly. Sprinkle with remaining ¼ cup cheese. Serve with sour cream and lime wedges.

1 SERVING: Calories 380; Total Fat 12g (Saturated Fat 2½g, Trans Fat 0g); Cholesterol 80mg; Sodium 1,330mg; Total Carbohydrate 42g (Dietary Fiber 5g, Sugars 6g); Protein 24g; EXCHANGES: 2½ Starch; ½ Vegetable; 2 Lean Meat; 1 Fat; CARBOHYDRATE CHOICES: 3

Expert Tips

- Do you have frozen corn on hand? It will work just as well as the canned corn. Just thaw 1¼ cups corn and drain before using.

- These individual pot pies are the perfect way to help control portions. Ramekins are also ideal for making individual desserts.

French Onion–Chicken Pot Pies

- ¼ cup butter or margarine
- 2½ pounds boneless skinless chicken thighs, cut into ½-inch pieces
- 2 large onions, halved, then thinly sliced (about 1½ cups)
- 2 packages (8 ounces each) sliced fresh mushrooms (6 cups)
- ¼ cup all-purpose flour
- 4 cups water
- ¼ cup dry sherry or water
- 1 box (2 ounces) onion soup mix (2 envelopes)
- ¼ teaspoon pepper
- 1 can (16.3 ounces) Pillsbury® Grands!® Flaky Layers refrigerated original biscuits (8 biscuits)
- 6 ounces Gruyère cheese, shredded (1½ cups)

Heat oven to 350°F. Spray 8 (10-ounce) ramekins or custard cups with cooking spray. Place ramekins on large cookie sheet with sides. In 12-inch nonstick skillet, melt 2 tablespoons of the butter over medium-high heat. Add chicken; cook about 10 minutes, stirring occasionally, until no longer pink in center. Remove chicken from skillet; discard chicken juices.

Melt remaining 2 tablespoons butter in skillet. Add onions and mushrooms; cook and stir about 8 minutes or until golden brown. Sprinkle flour over vegetables. Cook and stir 1 minute. Stir in water, sherry and soup mix; heat to boiling. Boil about 3 minutes, stirring occasionally, until slightly thickened.

Spoon chicken into ramekins (about ½ cup each). Spoon onion mixture over chicken (about ⅔ cup each). Sprinkle with pepper. Separate dough into 8 biscuits. Place 1 biscuit in each ramekin.

Bake about 20 minutes or until biscuits are golden. Carefully remove from oven. Sprinkle 3 tablespoons cheese over each biscuit. Bake 4 to 5 minutes longer or until cheese is melted.

1 SERVING: Calories 630; Total Fat 33g (Saturated Fat 13g, Trans Fat 4g); Cholesterol 125mg; Sodium 1,360mg; Total Carbohydrate 38g (Dietary Fiber 2g, Sugars 10g); Protein 42g; EXCHANGES: 2 Starch; 1 Vegetable; 1½ Fat; CARBOHYDRATE CHOICES: 2½

Expert Tip

A cookie sheet measuring 17½ x 13½ inches is large enough to hold all of the ramekins.

Chicken Paprika Shepherd's Pie

1 pouch Betty Crocker® roasted garlic mashed potatoes (from 7.2-ounce box)

1 cup hot water

½ cup milk

3 tablespoons butter or margarine

1 pound boneless skinless chicken breasts, cut into ½-inch pieces

1 medium onion, chopped (½ cup)

1½ cups Green Giant ® Valley Fresh Steamers™ frozen mixed vegetables

1 jar (12 ounces) home-style chicken gravy

2¼ teaspoons paprika

½ cup sour cream

Heat oven to 350°F. Spray 2-quart shallow casserole or 8-inch square glass baking dish with cooking spray. Make mashed potatoes as directed on box for 4 servings—except use 1 cup hot water, ½ cup milk and 2 tablespoons of the butter.

Meanwhile, in 12-inch nonstick skillet, melt remaining 1 tablespoon butter over medium-high heat. Add chicken and onion; cook 4 to 6 minutes, stirring frequently, until chicken is no longer pink in center. Stir in mixed vegetables, gravy and 2 teaspoons of the paprika. Cover; cook over medium-low heat 5 minutes, stirring frequently to prevent sticking.

Stir sour cream into chicken mixture. Spoon into casserole. Spoon or pipe potatoes in 8 mounds around edge of casserole. Sprinkle potatoes with remaining ¼ teaspoon paprika.

Bake uncovered 25 to 35 minutes or until mixture bubbles around edge of casserole.

1 SERVING: Calories 490; Total Fat 24g (Saturated Fat 12g, Trans Fat ½g); Cholesterol 115mg; Sodium 930mg; Total Carbohydrate 37g (Dietary Fiber 5g, Sugars 7g); Protein 32g; EXCHANGES: 1½ Starch; ½ Other Carbohydrate; 1 Vegetable; 3½ Lean Meat; 2½ Fat; CARBOHYDRATE CHOICES: 2½

Expert Tip

To add a slightly smoky flavor to the casserole, add about ¼ pound sliced smoked kielbasa sausage when you stir in the vegetables.

Country Chicken and Biscuits

6 cups cut-up cooked chicken

1¼ cups chopped onions

1¼ cups chopped celery

1 bag (12 ounces) Green Giant® Valley Fresh Steamers™ frozen mixed vegetables

3½ cups Progresso® chicken broth (from 32-ounce carton)

⅓ cup cornstarch

¾ cup cold water

2 tablespoons chopped fresh parsley

3⅓ cups Original Bisquick® mix

1 cup milk

Heat oven to 400°F. Heat chicken, onions, celery, mixed vegetables and chicken broth to boiling in 5-quart Dutch oven. Stir cornstarch into cold water until dissolved; stir into chicken mixture. Heat to boiling, stirring constantly. Boil and stir 1 minute; remove from heat. Stir in parsley. Pour into ungreased rectangular pan, 13 × 9 × 2 inches.

Stir Bisquick mix and milk until soft dough forms. Drop by 30 teaspoonfuls onto chicken mixture.

Bake 25 to 30 minutes or until biscuits are golden brown.

1 SERVING: Calories 309; Total Fat 8g (Saturated Fat 2g, Trans Fat 1g); Cholesterol 63mg; Sodium 770mg; Total Carbohydrate 32g (Dietary Fiber 1g, Sugars 4g); Protein 26g; EXCHANGES: 2 Starch; ½ Vegetable; 3 Lean Meat; ½ Fat; CARBOHYDRATE CHOICES: 2

Expert Tips

■ Complete this comfort meal with homemade cinnamon applesauce. Just stir ground cinnamon into applesauce to taste and serve warm if desired.

■ For Parmesan-garlic biscuits, stir ¼ cup grated Parmesan cheese and ½ teaspoon garlic powder into the dough before dropping it onto chicken mixture.

■ Replace parsley with fresh basil or oregano for a touch of Italy.

Puff Pastry–Topped Chicken Pie

1 package (17.3 ounces) frozen puff pastry sheets, thawed

1 egg, beaten

6 tablespoons butter or margarine

4 medium stalks celery, thinly sliced (2 cups)

2 medium onions, chopped (1 cup)

1 cup Gold Medal® all-purpose flour

1 carton (32 ounces) Progresso® chicken broth (4 cups)

3 cups half-and-half

½ cup dry white wine, if desired

2 bags (12 ounces) Green Giant® Valley Fresh Steamers™ frozen mixed vegetables, thawed, drained

6 cups bite-size pieces cooked chicken

2 teaspoons dried tarragon leaves

1 teaspoon salt

¼ teaspoon pepper

Heat oven to 400°F. On lightly floured surface, unfold pastry sheets, pressing fold marks flat and sealing any tears. Measure diameter of soup plate or bowl to be used as serving dishes. Using small sharp knife, cut 12 tree shapes from pastry, about 4 to 5 inches tall and wide, to fit in soup plate. Reroll cut dough to ¼-inch thickness as necessary to cut all trees.

On ungreased cookie sheets, arrange pastry trees ½ inch apart. Brush with egg. Bake about 8 minutes or until puffed and golden brown.

Meanwhile, in 4-quart Dutch oven, melt butter over medium heat. Add celery and onions; cook 5 to 7 minutes, stirring occasionally, until crisp-tender but not browned. Stir in flour until no lumps remain. Slowly add broth, half-and-half and wine, stirring constantly. Heat to boiling, stirring constantly; cook 2 to 3 minutes or until slightly thickened.

Stir in mixed vegetables, chicken, tarragon, salt and pepper; cook 2 to 3 minutes longer or until hot. Remove from heat. Spoon about 1¼ cups chicken mixture into each soup plate. Top with pastry tree.

1 SERVING: Calories 590; Total Fat 34g (Saturated Fat 15g, Trans Fat 2g); Cholesterol 165mg; Sodium 750mg; Total Carbohydrate 41g (Dietary Fiber 5g, Sugars 7g); Protein 29g; EXCHANGES: 2 Starch; ½ Other Carbohydrate; 1 Vegetable; 3 Lean Meat; 5 Fat; CARBOHYDRATE CHOICES: 3

Expert Tips

- To make a day ahead, refrigerate the chicken mixture and store pastry trees in an airtight container. To serve, heat chicken mixture in microwave until hot.
- Cut the pastry toppers in any shape.

Southwestern Cornbread Casserole

- 2 teaspoons vegetable oil
- 3 medium onions, chopped (1½ cups)
- 1 can (15 ounces) Progresso® black beans, drained, rinsed
- 1 can (11 ounces) Green Giant® SteamCrisp® Mexicorn® whole kernel corn with red and green bell peppers, drained
- 1 can (10 ounces) diced tomatoes with green chiles, drained
- 1 can (10 ounces) Old El Paso® enchilada sauce
- ½ cup Old El Paso® Thick 'n Chunky salsa
- 2 cups chopped cooked chicken
- ¼ cup chopped fresh cilantro
- 2 pouches (6.5 ounces each) Betty Crocker® cornbread and muffin mix
- ⅓ cup milk
- 4 eggs
- 1½ cups shredded Mexican cheese blend (6 ounces)

  Sliced fresh jalapeño chiles, if desired

Heat oven to 350°F. Spray 8 (8-ounce) individual baking dishes with cooking spray. In 10-inch skillet, heat oil over medium heat. Cook onions in oil 5 minutes, stirring occasionally, until tender.

In large bowl, mix beans, corn, tomatoes, enchilada sauce and salsa. Stir in chicken, cilantro and onions. Spoon mixture into baking dishes.

In medium bowl, stir muffin mix, milk and eggs just until moistened. Spoon topping by heaping spoonfuls over chicken mixture.

Bake uncovered 20 to 25 minutes or until filling is bubbly and topping is golden brown. Sprinkle with cheese blend. Bake 5 minutes longer or until cheese is melted. Garnish with jalapeños.

1 SERVING: Calories 449; Total Fat 14g (Saturated Fat 5g, Trans Fat 0g); Cholesterol 156; Sodium 1,015mg; Total Carbohydrate 55g (Dietary Fiber 4g, Sugars 16g); Protein 25g; EXCHANGES: 3 Starch; 1 Vegetable; 1 Very Lean Meat; ½ Medium-Fat Meat; 1 High-Fat Meat; 1 Fat; CARBOHYDRATE CHOICES: 4

Expert Tip

Use rotisserie chicken from the deli for this hearty one-dish meal.

Moroccan-Style Chicken-Crescent Casserole

PREP TIME: *25 minutes*

TOTAL TIME: *50 minutes*

MAKES 6 SERVINGS

1 tablespoon olive or vegetable oil

6 boneless skinless chicken breasts (about 1½ pounds), cut into bite-size pieces

½ cup chopped onion

½ cup sliced carrot

1 can (14.5 ounces) diced fire-roasted or regular tomatoes, undrained

1 tablespoon tomato paste

3 tablespoons chopped fresh parsley

3 tablespoons chopped fresh cilantro

1½ teaspoons paprika

½ teaspoon salt

½ teaspoon ground cumin

¼ to ½ teaspoon ground cinnamon

⅛ teaspoon ground red pepper (cayenne)

1 can (8 ounces) Pillsbury® refrigerated crescent dinner rolls (8 rolls)

1 egg, beaten

1 tablespoon sliced almonds

Fresh cilantro, for garnish

Heat oven to 375°F. In 12-inch skillet, heat oil over medium-high heat. Add chicken, onion and carrot; cook and stir about 7 minutes or until chicken is browned and no longer pink in center. Stir in tomatoes, tomato paste, parsley, cilantro, paprika, salt, cumin, cinnamon and red pepper. Cook and stir about 5 minutes or until thoroughly heated.

Into ungreased 11 × 7-inch (2-quart) glass baking dish or 9½- or 10-inch deep-dish pie plate, pour hot chicken mixture. Immediately unroll dough over chicken mixture; pinch edges and perforations to seal. Brush dough with beaten egg; sprinkle with almonds.

Bake 18 to 25 minutes or until deep golden brown. If desired, garnish with fresh cilantro.

1 SERVING: Calories 320; Total Fat 13g (Saturated Fat 4g, Trans Fat 0g); Cholesterol 70mg; Sodium 690mg; Total Carbohydrate 23g (Dietary Fiber 2g, Sugars 6g); Protein 29g; EXCHANGES: 1 Starch; 1 Vegetable; 3½ Lean Meat; ½ Fat; CARBOHYDRATE CHOICES: 1½

Expert Tip

We offer two amounts of cinnamon. Ease into Moroccan flavor with ¼ teaspoon, or use ½ teaspoon for authentic taste.

Grilled Chicken and Tortellini with Roasted Red Pepper Cream

PREP TIME: *30 minutes*

TOTAL TIME: *30 minutes*

MAKES 4 SERVINGS

- 1 package (9 ounces) refrigerated cheese-filled tortellini
- 2 cups Green Giant Select® Frozen 100% broccoli florets, large pieces cut up
- ⅓ cup drained roasted red bell peppers (from a jar)
- 1 container (10 ounces) refrigerated Alfredo sauce
- 1 package (6 ounces) refrigerated grilled chicken breast strips
- 2 tablespoons diced roasted red bell peppers (from a jar)
- 2 tablespoons butter, melted
- ¼ cup Progresso® Italian style bread crumbs

Cook tortellini and broccoli as directed on tortellini package. Drain; return tortellini and broccoli to saucepan.

Meanwhile, puree ⅓ cup roasted peppers in blender. Add Alfredo sauce; blend until mixed.

Add Alfredo sauce mixture, chicken and 2 tablespoons roasted peppers to tortellini and broccoli in saucepan; mix well. Cook and stir over medium heat for 2 to 3 minutes or until thoroughly heated, stirring occasionally. Spoon into ungreased shallow 1- to 1½-quart casserole. In small bowl, combine butter and bread crumbs; mix well. Sprinkle over top.

Broil 4 to 6 inches from heat for 1 to 2 minutes or until topping is golden brown.

1 SERVING: Calories 490; Total Fat 25g (Saturated Fat 14g, Trans Fat 0g) Cholesterol 105mg; Sodium 1,153mg; Total Carbohydrate 43g (Dietary Fiber 2g, Sugars 5g); Protein 25g; EXCHANGES: 2½ Starch; 2½ Other Carbohydrate; 1 Vegetable; 2 Medium-Fat Meat; 4 Fat; CARBOHYDRATE CHOICES: 3

Expert Tips

- Instead of the blender, use a food processor with the metal blade to puree roasted red peppers; combine them with the Alfredo sauce.
- This recipe is easily doubled; use a shallow 2- or 3-quart baking dish.

Buffalo Chicken and Potatoes

1¼ pounds boneless skinless chicken breasts, cut into 1-inch strips

⅓ cup Buffalo wing sauce

6 cups frozen (thawed) southern-style hash brown potatoes

1 cup ranch or blue cheese dressing

½ cup shredded Cheddar cheese (2 ounces)

1 can (10 ounces) condensed cream of celery soup

½ cup cornflake crumbs

2 tablespoons butter or margarine, melted

¼ cup chopped green onions (3 to 4 medium)

Heat oven to 350°F. Spray 13 × 9-inch (3-quart) baking dish with cooking spray.

In medium bowl, stir together chicken strips and wing sauce.

In large bowl, stir together potatoes, dressing, cheese and soup. Spoon into baking dish. Place chicken strips in single layer over potato mixture.

In small bowl, stir together crumbs and butter. Sprinkle over chicken. Cover with foil. Bake 30 minutes; uncover and bake 20 to 25 minutes longer or until potatoes are tender and juice of chicken is no longer pink when centers of thickest pieces are cut. Sprinkle with green onions.

1 SERVING: Calories 620; Total Fat 33g (Saturated Fat 9g, Trans Fat 0g); Cholesterol 90mg; Sodium 1,240mg; Total Carbohydrate 51g (Dietary Fiber 5g, Sugars 5g); Protein 28g; EXCHANGES: 2½ Starch; 1 Other Carbohydrate; 3 Lean Meat; 4½ Fat; CARBOHYDRATE CHOICES: 3½

Expert Tips

■ For authentic flavor, go with red hot Buffalo wing sauce. Other flavors to try include teriyaki, sweet and sour or barbecue.

■ For a cheesy hash brown side dish, omit the chicken and wing sauce. Serve casserole with barbecued chicken or baked ham.

■ Try using precut chicken tenders to make prep time shorter.

■ Serve with additional blue cheese dressing.

Baked Chicken Panzanella

2 cups chopped cooked chicken

1 can (14.5 ounces) diced tomatoes with garlic, onion and oregano, drained

4 medium green onions, sliced (¼ cup)

1 package (5 ounces) Italian-seasoned croutons

¼ cup Italian dressing

¾ cup shredded Parmesan cheese

¼ cup sliced fresh basil

Heat oven to 350°F. In ungreased 11 × 7-inch (2-quart) baking dish, layer chicken, tomatoes, green onions and croutons. Drizzle with Italian dressing.

Cover with foil. Bake 20 minutes. Uncover; top with cheese. Bake about 10 minutes longer or until hot and cheese is melted. Sprinkle with basil.

1 SERVING: Calories 290; Total Fat 14g (Saturated Fat 4½g; Trans Fat 1½g); Cholesterol 50mg; Sodium 830mg; Total Carbohydrate 20g (Dietary Fiber 2g, Sugars 4g); Protein 21g; EXCHANGES: 1 Starch; ½ Other Carbohydrate; CARBOHYDRATE CHOICES: 1

Expert Tips

- Any cooked chicken will work in this recipe. Use rotisserie chicken or refrigerated cubed cooked chicken. Or use leftover grilled chicken, which would give a slightly smoky flavor to the casserole.

- This casserole is a hot version of the Italian bread salad panzanella.

Chicken Divan

CASSEROLE

- 2 tablespoons butter or margarine

- 3 tablespoons Gold Medal® all-purpose flour

- 2 teaspoons chicken bouillon granules

- 2 cups milk

- ½ cup mayonnaise or salad dressing

- 1 tablespoon Dijon mustard

- 2 boxes (9 ounces each) Green Giant® frozen broccoli spears, thawed, drained

- 3 cups cubed cooked chicken or turkey

- ½ cup shredded Cheddar cheese (2 ounces)

TOPPING

- ⅓ cup Progresso® plain bread crumbs

- 1 tablespoon butter or margarine, melted

Heat oven to 350°F. In 2-quart saucepan, melt 2 tablespoons butter over medium heat. Stir in flour and bouillon granules. Gradually stir in milk, cooking and stirring constantly with wire whisk, until mixture boils and thickens. Stir in mayonnaise and mustard until well blended.

In ungreased 12 × 8-inch (2-quart) glass baking dish, arrange broccoli spears. Top with chicken. Spoon sauce over chicken. Sprinkle with cheese.

In small bowl, mix topping ingredients; sprinkle over top. Bake about 30 minutes or until thoroughly heated.

1 SERVING: Calories 460; Total Fat 30g (Saturated Fat 10g, Trans Fat ½g); Cholesterol 100mg; Sodium 690mg; Total Carbohydrate 17g (Dietary Fiber 2g, Sugars 7g); Protein 28g; EXCHANGES: 1 Starch; 1 Vegetable; 3 Lean Meat; 4 Fat; CARBOHYDRATE CHOICES: 1

Expert Tip

Chopped cooked ham makes a delicious stand-in for the chicken or turkey.

Green Bean and Chicken Casserole

1 can (10¾ ounces) condensed cream of chicken soup

¼ cup milk

1 cup herb-seasoned stuffing crumbs

¼ cup butter or margarine, melted

4 boneless skinless chicken breasts (about 1¼ pounds), cut into 1-inch-wide strips

2 cups Green Giant® frozen cut green beans, thawed

Heat oven to 350°F. Lightly spray 11 × 7-inch glass baking dish with cooking spray. In small bowl, mix soup and milk until well blended. In another small bowl, mix stuffing crumbs and melted butter.

In baking dish, layer chicken, green beans, soup mixture and stuffing mixture.

Bake uncovered about 45 minutes or until chicken is no longer pink in center and mixture is hot and bubbly.

1 SERVING: Calories 450; Total Fat 23g (Saturated Fat 11g, Trans Fat 1g); Cholesterol 125mg; Sodium 1,000mg; Total Carbohydrate 25g (Dietary Fiber 2g, Sugars 4g); Protein 37g; EXCHANGES: 1½ Starch; 1 Vegetable; 4 Very Lean Meat; 4 Fat; CARBOHYDRATE CHOICES: 1½

Expert Tips

■ For a taste of Thanksgiving, add ½ teaspoon ground sage to the soup mixture.

■ A fruit salad with poppy seed dressing would complement this casserole.

Chicken Artichoke Casserole

1 tablespoon olive oil

1 cup chopped red bell pepper

¼ cup sliced green onions (4 medium)

3 cups chopped cooked chicken

1 can (14 ounces) artichoke hearts in water, drained, chopped

1 container (10 ounces) refrigerated reduced-fat Alfredo pasta sauce

1 cup shredded Asiago cheese (4 ounces)

½ cup reduced-fat mayonnaise

1½ cups Romano cheese croutons (from 5-ounce bag), coarsely crushed

Sliced green onions, for garnish

Heat oven to 350°F. Spray 11 × 7-inch (2-quart) baking dish with cooking spray. In 6-inch skillet, heat olive oil over medium heat. Add bell pepper and onions; cook 2 to 3 minutes, stirring occasionally, until they start to soften. In large bowl, mix bell pepper mixture and all remaining ingredients except croutons and green onions for garnish. Spoon into baking dish. Top with croutons.

Bake 30 to 35 minutes or until hot and bubbly. If desired, sprinkle with additional sliced green onions.

1 SERVING: Calories 460; Total Fat 28g (Saturated Fat 11g, Trans Fat 1g); Cholesterol 105mg; Sodium 890mg; Total Carbohydrate 20g (Dietary Fiber 4g, Sugars 5g); Protein 30g; EXCHANGES: 1 Starch; 1 Vegetable; 2 Fat; CARBOHYDRATE CHOICES: 1

Expert Tips

- If refrigerated Alfredo sauce is not available, use about 1 cup Alfredo sauce from a jar.

- Use regular canned artichoke hearts for this recipe, not the marinated ones. Artichoke hearts are available in several sizes. Choose the least expensive, as they are chopped in this recipe.

Chicken and Vegetable Alfredo

- 1 bag (19 ounces) Green Giant® frozen broccoli and carrots with garlic and herbs
- 1 cup all-purpose flour
- ¼ cup grated Parmesan cheese
- ⅓ cup cold butter or margarine, cut into small pieces
- 1 egg, slightly beaten
- 1½ cups cubed cooked chicken
- 1 jar (16 ounces) four-cheese Alfredo pasta sauce
- 1 can (15.25 ounces) Green Giant® whole kernel sweet corn, drained

Heat oven to 375°F. In large microwavable bowl, microwave broccoli and carrot mixture as directed on package, using minimum cook time.

Meanwhile, in small bowl, mix flour, Parmesan cheese, butter and egg with pastry blender or fork until crumbly. Set aside.

To hot vegetables in large bowl, add chicken, pasta sauce and corn. Stir gently to combine. Pour into ungreased 2-quart casserole or 9-inch deep-dish glass pie plate. Sprinkle with crumbly mixture.

Bake 20 to 25 minutes or until topping is golden brown.

1 SERVING: Calories 610; Total Fat 39g (Saturated Fat 23g, Trans Fat 1½g); Cholesterol 170mg; Sodium 830mg; Total Carbohydrate 40g (Dietary Fiber 3g, Sugars 6g); Protein 24g; EXCHANGES: 2½ Starch; 2 Vegetable; 3 Lean Meat; 4½ Fat; CARBOHYDRATE CHOICES: 2½

Expert Tips

- Two cans (5 ounces each) tuna in water, drained and flaked, can be used in place of the chicken.
- Alfredo sauce comes in different flavor varieties. Experiment to find your favorite.

Zesty Chicken and Rice Casserole with Roasted Red Peppers

PREP TIME: *30 minutes*

TOTAL TIME: *30 minutes*

MAKES 4 SERVINGS

2 cups uncooked instant rice

1 can (14 ounces) ready-to-serve chicken broth

1 package (9 ounces) refrigerated grilled chicken strips

1 jar (7 or 7.25 ounces) roasted red bell peppers, chopped

1/4 cup halved pitted kalamata olives

1/3 cup purchased Italian salad dressing

1 ounce (1/4 cup) shredded fresh Parmesan cheese

2 tablespoons chopped fresh parsley

Cook rice in large saucepan as directed on package using chicken broth instead of water and salt.

Add chicken, roasted peppers, olives and salad dressing; mix well. Cover; cook over low heat for 5 to 10 minutes or until thoroughly heated, stirring occasionally. Pour mixture into ungreased 2½-quart casserole. Sprinkle with Parmesan cheese.

Broil 4 to 6 inches from heat for 1 to 2 minutes or until cheese is melted. Sprinkle with parsley.

1 SERVING: Calories 407; Total Fat 15g (Saturated Fat 3g, Trans Fat 0g); Cholesterol 41mg; Sodium 1,674mg; Total Carbohydrate 47g (Dietary Fiber 2g, Sugars 4g); Protein 22g; EXCHANGES: 3 Starch; 3 Other Carbohydrate; ½ Vegetable; 2 Very Lean Meat; 2½ Fat; CARBOHYDRATE CHOICES: 3

Expert Tips

■ Kalamata olives are Greek olives marinated in wine vinegar. Each deep purple, almond-shaped olive is slit lengthwise so that it soaks up lots of marinade. Kalamata olives are packed in olive oil or vinegar. Look for them next to other olives at the grocery store.

■ To reduce the fat in each serving of this recipe by about 7 grams, use light Italian salad dressing in place of regular dressing.

■ Try roasting a fresh red bell pepper for this recipe. Broil the whole pepper until its skin chars and blackens, then immediately place it in a small brown paper bag. Fold the bag to seal it and set it aside for 10 minutes. Peel the pepper under cool running water, then seed and chop it.

Cheesy Chicken and Rice Casserole

1 can (18.5 ounces) Progresso® chicken cheese enchilada soup

¾ cup water

¾ cup uncooked regular long-grain white rice

½ teaspoon ground cumin

¼ teaspoon pepper

1 can (15 ounces) Progresso® black beans, drained, rinsed

1 box (9 ounces) Green Giant® Niblets® frozen corn

1 package (1 pound) boneless skinless chicken breast halves

1 cup shredded Colby-Monterey Jack cheese blend (4 ounces)

Heat the oven to 375°F. In ungreased 2-quart glass baking dish, mix soup, water, rice, cumin, pepper, beans and corn. Top with chicken.

Cover; bake about 30 minutes or until juice of chicken is clear when center of thickest part is cut (170°F) and rice is tender. Stir rice around chicken. Top with cheese. Bake uncovered 5 to 10 minutes or until cheese is melted.

1 SERVING: Calories 531; Total Fat 16g (Saturated Fat 7g, Trans Fat 0g); Cholesterol 106mg; Sodium 1,058mg; Total Carbohydrate 55g; (Dietary Fiber 4g, Sugars 5g); Protein 40g, EXCHANGES: 3 Starch; 3 Lean Meat; 1 High-Fat Meat; 1 Fat; CARBOHYDRATE CHOICES:4

Swiss Chicken Casserole

PREP TIME: *15 minutes*
TOTAL TIME: *1 hour 5 minutes*
MAKES 8 SERVINGS

4 cups boiling water

2 boxes (6 ounces each) sun-dried tomato Florentine long grain and wild rice mix

4 large boneless skinless chicken breasts

8 slices thick-sliced fully cooked deli ham (about 10 ounces)

¼ cup diced red bell pepper

4 slices (1 ounce each) Swiss cheese, cut in half

Heat oven to 350°F. Spray 13 × 9-inch (3-quart) baking dish with cooking spray.

Stir boiling water, rice and rice seasoning mixes in baking dish.

Cut chicken breasts in half lengthwise; wrap ham slice around each chicken piece. Stir bell pepper into rice. Place wrapped chicken over rice. Cover with foil.

Bake 40 to 45 minutes; uncover and bake about 10 minutes longer or until liquid is absorbed and juice of chicken is clear when thickest part is cut.

Top each chicken breast with cheese. Bake uncovered 3 to 4 minutes or until cheese is melted.

1 SERVING: Calories 240; Total Fat 8g (Saturated Fat 4g, Trans Fat 0g); Cholesterol 75mg; Sodium 660mg; Total Carbohydrate 13g (Dietary Fiber 0g, Sugars 0g); Protein 28g; EXCHANGES: 1 Starch; 3½ Very Lean Meat; 1 Fat; CARBOHYDRATE CHOICES: 1

Expert Tips

■ Use other varieties of rice mixtures, such as chicken or mushroom.

■ Serve with steamed whole green beans.

Salsa Chicken and Rice Casserole

1 can (10 ounces) Old El Paso® enchilada sauce

1 cup uncooked converted white rice

1 cup Old El Paso® Thick 'n Chunky salsa

2 cans (10¾ ounces each) condensed cream of celery soup

1 can (15 ounces) black beans, drained, rinsed

5 bone-in chicken breast halves with skin

Heat oven to 325°F. Spray 13 × 9-inch (3-quart) glass baking dish with cooking spray. Reserve 2 tablespoons enchilada sauce for brushing on chicken. In large bowl, mix remaining enchilada sauce, the uncooked rice, salsa, soup and beans; pour into baking dish.

Arrange chicken, skin side up, over rice mixture. Cover tightly with foil.

Bake 1 hour. Uncover; brush chicken with reserved 2 tablespoons enchilada sauce. Bake uncovered 1 hour longer or until chicken is fork-tender, its juices run clear and skin is slightly crisp.

1 SERVING: Calories 555; Total Fat 20g (Saturated Fat 5g, Trans Fat 0g); Cholesterol 106mg; Sodium 1,750mg; Total Carbohydrate 54g (Dietary Fiber 4g, Sugars 5g); Protein 38g; EXCHANGES: 3 Starch; 4 Lean Meat; 2½ Fat; CARBOHYDRATE CHOICES: 4

Expert Tip

Be sure to use converted rice in this recipe and not regular white rice. The acidity in the salsa and enchilada sauce prevents the nonconverted rice from becoming tender.

Jerk Chicken Casserole

PREP TIME: *15 minutes*

TOTAL TIME: *1 hour*

MAKES 6 SERVINGS

1¼ teaspoons salt

½ teaspoon pumpkin pie spice

¾ teaspoon ground allspice

¾ teaspoon dried thyme

¼ teaspoon ground red pepper (cayenne)

6 boneless skinless chicken thighs

1 tablespoon vegetable oil

1 can (15 ounces) Progresso® black beans, drained, rinsed

1 large sweet potato (1 pound), peeled, cubed (3 cups)

¼ cup honey

¼ cup lime juice

2 teaspoons cornstarch

2 tablespoons sliced green onions (2 medium)

Heat oven to 375°F. Spray 8-inch square (2-quart) baking dish with cooking spray. In small bowl, mix salt, pumpkin pie spice, allspice, thyme and red pepper. Rub mixture on all sides of chicken. In 12-inch nonstick skillet, heat oil over medium-high heat. Cook chicken in oil 2 to 3 minutes per side, until brown.

In baking dish, layer beans and sweet potato. Top with browned chicken. In small bowl, mix honey, lime juice and cornstarch; add to skillet. Heat to boiling, stirring constantly. Pour over chicken in baking dish.

Bake 35 to 45 minutes or until juice of chicken is clear when center of thickest part is cut (165°F) and sweet potatoes are fork-tender. Sprinkle with green onions.

1 SERVING: Calories 320; Total Fat 8g (Saturated Fat 2g, Trans Fat 0g); Cholesterol 45mg; Sodium 550mg; Total Carbohydrate 41g (Dietary Fiber 8g, Sugars 16g); Protein 20g; EXCHANGES: 1½ Starch; 1 Other Carbohydrate; 2 Lean Meat; ½ Fat; CARBOHYDRATE CHOICES: 3

Expert Tips

■ If a dry jerk seasoning or rub is available, use it to save a few minutes. This is a mild jerk seasoning rub; an authentic jerk rub will be spicier.

■ You can substitute ¼ teaspoon ground cinnamon, ⅛ teaspoon ground ginger and ⅛ teaspoon ground nutmeg for the pumpkin pie spice.

■ Small boneless skinless chicken breasts can be substituted for the thighs, if you prefer, or use bone-in thighs.

Sausage and Chicken Cassoulet

PREP TIME: *30 minutes*
TOTAL TIME: *1 hour 15 minutes*
MAKES 6 SERVINGS

- 4 slices bacon, cut into 1-inch pieces
- 6 bone-in chicken thighs (about 2 pounds), skin removed if desired
- 1 cup ready-to-eat baby-cut carrots
- 1 medium onion, chopped (½ cup)
- 1 teaspoon dried thyme
- ½ teaspoon salt
- ¼ teaspoon pepper
- 4 ounces Polish sausage links, cut into ½-inch pieces
- 2 cans (15 ounces each) navy beans, drained, rinsed
- 1 can (14.5 ounces) diced tomatoes with roasted garlic, undrained

Heat oven to 350°F. In 12-inch nonstick skillet, cook bacon over medium-high heat until crisp. Remove from skillet; drain on paper towels. Reserve 1 tablespoon drippings in skillet.

Add chicken to skillet; cook over medium-high heat about 4 minutes, turning once, until golden brown. Stir in carrots, onion, thyme, salt and pepper; cook 4 to 5 minutes or until chicken and vegetables are browned. Drain well. Remove chicken from skillet.

In ungreased 13 × 9-inch (3-quart) glass baking dish, mix sausage, beans, tomatoes, bacon, carrots and onion. Top with chicken thighs; cover with foil.

Bake about 45 minutes or until juice of chicken is clear when thickest part is cut to bone (165°F) and vegetables are tender.

1 SERVING: Calories 440; Total Fat 18g (Saturated Fat 6g, Trans Fat 0g); Cholesterol 75mg; Sodium 650mg; Total Carbohydrate 38g (Dietary Fiber 14g, Sugars 4g); Protein 33g; EXCHANGES: 2 Starch; 1 Vegetable; 3½ Lean Meat; 1½ Fat; CARBOHYDRATE CHOICES: 2½

Expert Tip

Great northern beans can be used instead of the navy beans.

Sausage-Stuffed Shells

PREP TIME: *30 minutes*

TOTAL TIME: *1 hour 20 minutes*

MAKES 12 SERVINGS

24 jumbo pasta shells (from 12-ounce box)

1 pound lean Italian turkey sausage, casings removed

1 container (15 ounces) light ricotta cheese

2 cups shredded reduced-fat Italian cheese blend (8 ounces)

1 box (9 ounces) Green Giant® frozen spinach, thawed, squeezed to drain

½ teaspoon dried basil

¾ cup finely shredded carrots (1 medium)

1 jar (25.5 ounces) Muir Glen® organic Italian herb pasta sauce

Heat oven to 350°F. Spray 13 × 9-inch (3-quart) glass baking dish with cooking spray. Cook and drain pasta as directed on package, omitting salt.

In 10-inch nonstick skillet, crumble sausage. Cook over medium heat, stirring frequently, until no longer pink; drain.

In medium bowl, stir ricotta cheese, 1 cup of the Italian cheese blend, the spinach and basil until well mixed. Stir in carrots and sausage.

Spread about ½ cup of the pasta sauce over bottom of baking dish. Spoon about 3 tablespoons sausage mixture into each pasta shell. Arrange shells, filled sides up, on sauce in baking dish. Pour remaining pasta sauce over stuffed shells. Spray 15-inch piece of foil with cooking spray; cover shells with foil.

Bake 40 minutes. Uncover; sprinkle with remaining 1 cup Italian cheese blend. Bake uncovered 5 to 10 minutes longer or until cheese is melted.

1 SERVING: Calories 290; Total Fat 9g (Saturated Fat 3g, Trans Fat 0g); Cholesterol 40mg; Sodium 720mg; Total Carbohydrate 33g (Dietary Fiber 2g, Sugars 7g); Protein 19g; EXCHANGES: 2 Starch; ½ Vegetable; 1½ Lean Meat; ½ Fat; CARBOHYDRATE CHOICES: 2

Make-Ahead White Chicken Lasagna

PREP TIME: *40 minutes*
TOTAL TIME: *10 hours 15 minutes*
MAKES 12 SERVINGS

1 tablespoon butter or margarine

1 pound boneless skinless chicken breasts, cut into 1/2-inch pieces

1 1/2 cups coarsely chopped red bell pepper (2 medium)

1 cup finely chopped celery

1/2 cup chopped onion

2 cloves garlic, finely chopped

1 pint (2 cups) half-and-half

1/2 cup Progresso® chicken broth

4 ounces cream cheese

2 cups Gouda cheese, shredded (7 ounces)

1 container (12 ounces) small-curd cottage cheese

1/4 cup fresh basil, cut into thin strips

1 egg, beaten

9 uncooked lasagna noodles

1 package (16 ounces) sliced mozzarella cheese

1/2 cup grated Parmesan cheese

Fresh basil sprigs or chopped basil, if desired

Spray 13 × 9-inch (3-quart) glass baking dish with cooking spray. In 4-quart Dutch oven, melt butter over medium-high heat. Add chicken; cook 3 minutes, stirring occasionally. Stir in bell pepper, celery, onion and garlic; cook about 2 minutes, stirring occasionally, until chicken is no longer pink in center.

Reduce heat to low. Add half-and-half, broth and cream cheese; cook and stir until cream cheese is melted. Gradually add Gouda cheese, stirring until cheese is melted. Remove from heat; set aside. In bowl, mix cottage cheese, 1/4 cup fresh basil and the egg until blended.

Spread 1 cup chicken mixture in baking dish. Top with 3 noodles, 1 1/2 cups chicken mixture, half of the cottage cheese mixture and half of the mozzarella cheese. Repeat layers once, starting with noodles. Top with remaining 3 noodles and remaining chicken mixture. Sprinkle with Parmesan cheese. Cover with foil; refrigerate at least 8 hours or overnight.

Heat oven to 350°F. Bake lasagna covered 45 minutes. Uncover; bake 30 to 35 minutes longer or until noodles are tender and casserole is bubbly. Cover; let stand 15 minutes before serving. Garnish with basil sprigs.

1 SERVING: Calories 440; Total Fat 26g (Saturated Fat 15g, Trans Fat 1/2g); Cholesterol 115mg; Sodium 640mg; Total Carbohydrate 20g (Dietary Fiber 1g, Sugars 5g); Protein 33g; EXCHANGES: 1 Starch; 1/2 Other Carbohydrate; 4 Lean Meat; 2 1/2 Fat; CARBOHYDRATE CHOICES: 1

Expert Tips

■ Add 1 1/2 cups julienne-cut cooked ham to lasagna layers for a flavor twist.

■ No-cook lasagna noodles are available and can be used in this recipe for immediate baking.

Thyme-Roasted Chicken with Vegetables

PREP TIME: *25 minutes*

TOTAL TIME: *2 hours 10 minutes*

MAKES 6 SERVINGS

1 whole chicken (3 to 3½ pounds)

6 medium carrots

4 medium stalks celery

3 large baking potatoes (russet or Idaho), about 8 ounces each

3 medium onions

2 tablespoons butter or margarine

1 tablespoon chopped fresh or 1 teaspoon dried thyme

Heat oven to 375°F. Fold wings of chicken across back so tips are touching. There may be a little resistance, but once in this position, they will stay. Tie legs to tail with string or use skewers; if tail is missing, tie legs together.

In shallow roasting pan, place chicken breast side up. Insert ovenproof meat thermometer with tip in thickest part of inside thigh and not touching bone. Roast chicken uncovered 45 minutes.

While chicken is roasting, peel carrots and cut into 1-inch pieces. Cut celery into 1-inch pieces. Scrub potatoes thoroughly with vegetable brush or peel them, and cut into 1½-inch pieces. Peel onions and cut into wedges.

Remove chicken from oven. Arrange carrots, celery, potatoes and onions around chicken. In 1-quart saucepan, heat butter over low heat just until melted. (Or place butter in small microwavable bowl; cover with microwavable paper towel and microwave on High 10 to 20 seconds or until melted.) Stir thyme into butter, then drizzle over chicken and vegetables.

Cover chicken and vegetables with foil. Roast 45 to 60 minutes longer or until thermometer reads 165°F and vegetables are tender when pierced with fork. Or check for doneness by wiggling the legs; if they move easily, chicken is done.

Remove vegetables from pan and cover with foil to keep warm while carving chicken.

To carve, place chicken, breast up and with its legs to your right if you're right-handed or to the left if left-handed, on cutting board; remove ties from legs.

1 SERVING: Calories 400; Total Fat 17g (Saturated Fat 6g, Trans Fat ½g); Cholesterol 95mg; Sodium 180mg; Total Carbohydrate 32g (Dietary Fiber 5g, Sugars 7g); Protein 30g; EXCHANGES: 1 Starch; ½ Other Carbohydrate; 1½ Vegetable; 3½ Lean Meat; 1 Fat; CARBOHYDRATE CHOICES: 2

Expert Tip

If you have an ovenproof platter, place the vegetables on the platter, cover with foil and place in the oven, which has been turned off, while you carve the chicken.

Country French Chicken and Rice

¼ cup chopped oil-packed sun-dried tomatoes, drained

2 tablespoons herbes de Provence

2 tablespoons olive oil

2 tablespoons lemon juice

1 tablespoon finely chopped garlic

1 teaspoon salt

8 bone-in chicken thighs, skin and fat removed (about 2 pounds)

1½ cups sliced mushrooms

1 cup uncooked regular long-grain white rice

1 medium carrot, shredded (¾ cup)

2 cups boiling water

1 tablespoon chopped fresh Italian (flat-leaf) parsley

2 teaspoons grated lemon peel

In heavy-duty 1-gallon resealable food-storage plastic bag, mix tomatoes, herbes de Provence, oil, lemon juice, garlic and ½ teaspoon of the salt. Add chicken thighs and mushrooms; seal bag. Turn to coat thighs and mushrooms in marinade. Refrigerate 2 to 24 hours.

Heat oven to 375°F. Spray 13 × 9-inch (3-quart) baking dish with cooking spray.

Place rice, carrot and remaining ½ teaspoon salt in baking dish; stir in boiling water. Place chicken thighs, mushrooms and marinade evenly over rice mixture.

Cover with foil. Bake 50 to 60 minutes or until liquid is absorbed and juice of chicken is no longer pink when centers of thickest pieces are cut. Sprinkle with parsley and lemon peel.

1 SERVING: Calories 260; Total Fat 10g (Saturated Fat 2½g, Trans Fat 0g); Cholesterol 45mg; Sodium 360mg; Total Carbohydrate 23g (Dietary Fiber 1g, Sugars 1g); Protein 18g; EXCHANGES: 1½ Starch; 2 Lean Meat; ½ Fat; CARBOHYDRATE CHOICES: 1½

Expert Tip

If herbes de Provence is not available, use any combination of dried basil, fennel seed, lavender, marjoram, rosemary, sage, summer savory, tarragon or thyme.

Chicken Mole Enchiladas Supreme

PREP TIME: *5 minutes*

TOTAL TIME: *15 minutes*

MAKES 6 SERVINGS

- 2 tablespoons mole sauce (from 8.25-ounce jar), stirred
- 1 cup Progresso® reduced-sodium chicken broth (from 32-ounce carton)
- 2 cups chopped deli rotisserie chicken (from 2-pound chicken)
- 6 low-carb flour tortillas (6 inch)
- 3 cups shredded lettuce
- 1½ cups refrigerated prechopped tomato
- ¼ cup crumbled queso fresco cheese (1 ounce)
- 6 medium green onions, chopped (6 tablespoons)

Heat oven to 425°F. Place mole sauce in medium saucepan. Gradually add broth, stirring with wire whisk until smooth. Cook over medium-high heat, stirring often, until thoroughly heated.

Meanwhile, place chicken in small microwavable bowl. Cover with microwavable plastic wrap, folding back one edge or corner ¼ inch to vent steam. Microwave on High 1 to 2 minutes or until thoroughly heated.

Spray 11 × 7-inch (2-quart) glass baking dish with cooking spray. Spoon ⅓ cup chicken down center of each tortilla. Spoon 1 tablespoon sauce over chicken on each tortilla; fold 2 sides toward center. Place enchiladas, seam sides down, in baking dish. Pour remaining sauce over enchiladas.

Bake uncovered 9 to 10 minutes or until thoroughly heated.

Place 1 enchilada on each serving plate; top with lettuce, tomato, cheese and onions.

1 SERVING: Calories 212; Total Fat 6g (Saturated Fat 1g, Trans Fat 0g); Cholesterol 44; Sodium 889mg; Total Carbohydrate 23g (Dietary Fiber 11g, Sugars 3g); Protein 28g; EXCHANGES: 1 Starch; ½ Vegetable; 2 Lean Meat; ½ Fat; CARBOHYDRATE CHOICES: 1½

Indian-Style Curry Chicken

4 cups frozen potatoes O'Brien with onions and peppers (from 28-ounce bag), thawed

1 bag (12 ounces) Green Giant® Valley Fresh Steamers™ frozen sweet peas, thawed

1 can (14.5 ounces) diced tomatoes with green chiles, undrained

4 teaspoons curry powder

½ teaspoon salt

3 tablespoons all-purpose flour

1 teaspoon paprika

1 teaspoon garlic salt

12 chicken drumsticks

1 tablespoon vegetable oil

Heat oven to 350°F. Spray 13 × 9-inch (3-quart) glass baking dish with cooking spray. In large bowl, stir together potatoes, peas, tomatoes, 2 teaspoons of the curry powder and the salt. Spread evenly in baking dish.

In large resealable food-storage plastic bag, mix remaining 2 teaspoons curry powder, the flour, paprika and garlic salt; shake to mix. Add drumsticks; seal bag and shake to coat.

In 12-inch skillet, heat oil over medium-high heat. Cook drumsticks in oil 8 to 10 minutes, turning frequently, until skin is brown (cook 6 drumsticks at a time if all don't fit in skillet). Place drumsticks in 2 rows lengthwise over potato mixture, alternating direction of drumsticks to cover potato mixture. Cover tightly with foil.

Bake 30 minutes. Remove foil; bake about 10 minutes longer or until juice of chicken is clear when thickest part is cut to bone (165°F).

1 SERVING: Calories 510; Total Fat 21g (Saturated Fat 5g, Trans Fat 0g); Cholesterol 85mg; Sodium 990mg; Total Carbohydrate 46g (Dietary Fiber 6g, Sugars 8g); Protein 35g; EXCHANGES: 2 Starch; 2½ Vegetable; 1 Fat; CARBOHYDRATE CHOICES: 3

Expert Tips

■ If canned vegetables are on sale, use 2 cans (15 ounces each) Green Giant® sweet peas, drained, instead of the frozen peas.

■ Curry powder can be found in the spice and herb section of your local grocery store. Curry powder is actually a blend of herbs, spices and seeds. The blend can vary dramatically. The type most often found in grocery stores resembles the blends of southern India. The "Madras" variety will be hotter than the standard variety.

Fast and Easy Jambalaya

- ½ teaspoon lemon-pepper seasoning
- ½ teaspoon garlic powder
- 1¼ pounds boneless skinless chicken breasts, cut into ½-inch cubes
- 3 tablespoons vegetable oil
- 1 cup chopped onion
- 1 package (12 ounces) smoked Polish or kielbasa sausage, cut into ½-inch slices
- 1 jar (16 ounces) Old El Paso® Thick 'n Chunky picante sauce (any variety)
- 1 can (14.5 ounces) Italian stewed tomatoes, undrained
- 1¼ cups Green Giant® Valley Fresh Steamers™ frozen sweet peas
- 2⅔ cups hot cooked instant rice

Sprinkle lemon-pepper seasoning and garlic powder over chicken cubes. In 12-inch skillet or 3-quart saucepan, heat oil over medium-high heat. Add chicken; cook 5 minutes, stirring frequently, until no longer pink in center.

Stir in onions and sausage; cook 5 minutes, stirring occasionally. Stir in picante sauce and tomatoes. Reduce heat to medium; cook 12 minutes, stirring occasionally.

Stir in peas; cook 5 to 7 minutes, stirring occasionally, until peas are tender. Serve over hot cooked rice.

1 SERVING: Calories 780; Total Fat 39g (Saturated Fat 12g, Trans Fat 1g); Cholesterol 135mg; Sodium 2,340mg; Total Carbohydrate 58g (Dietary Fiber 5g, Sugars 15g); Protein 48g; EXCHANGES: 2 Starch; 1½ Other Carbohydrate; 1 Vegetable; 5 High-Fat Meat; CARBOHYDRATE CHOICES: 4

Expert Tips

- Jambalaya, a Creole classic, varies widely depending on the cook. Some say this dish got its name from the French word for ham (jambon), which was the main ingredient in many of the first jambalayas.

- This recipe was created by Sharon Nank of Granger, Indiana, and was a finalist in a national recipe contest.

Easy Chicken and Rice

1 cup uncooked regular long-grain white rice

2¼ cups water

2 tablespoons olive oil

1 package (8 ounces) sliced fresh mushrooms (about 3 cups)

2 small red or yellow bell peppers, cut into bite-size strips (about 2 cups)

8 medium green onions with tops, finely chopped (½ cup)

3 cloves garlic, finely chopped

1 cup tomato pasta sauce

½ cup Progresso® chicken broth (from 32-ounce carton)

2 cups shredded deli rotisserie chicken (from 2-pound chicken)

1 cup shredded Parmesan cheese (4 ounces)

3 tablespoons chopped fresh parsley

Cook rice in water as directed on package.

Meanwhile, in deep 12-inch skillet, heat oil over medium-high heat. Cook mushrooms, bell peppers, onions and garlic in oil 2 to 3 minutes, stirring frequently, until vegetables are tender. Remove from heat until rice is cooked.

Stir rice, pasta sauce, broth, chicken and ½ cup of the cheese into vegetable mixture; cook over medium-low heat about 3 to 5 minutes, stirring occasionally, until mixture is hot. Sprinkle with remaining ½ cup cheese and the parsley.

1 SERVING: Calories 360; Total Fat 13g (Saturated Fat 5g, Trans Fat 0g); Cholesterol 55mg; Sodium 840mg; Total Carbohydrate 35g (Dietary Fiber 2g, Sugars 5g); Protein 25g; EXCHANGES: 1½ Starch; 2 Vegetable; CARBOHYDRATE CHOICES: 2

Expert Tips

■ You can use either curly-leaf or flat-leaf parsley for this recipe. When purchasing parsley, look for a bunch with bright-green leaves that show no sign of wilting.

■ Make this dish extra colorful by using 1 red bell pepper and 1 yellow bell pepper.

Chicken Tagine

- 1 tablespoon vegetable oil
- 3 - to 3½-pound cut-up whole chicken
- 1 medium onion, sliced
- 2 cloves garlic, finely chopped
- ¼ cup chopped fresh cilantro
- 1 teaspoon ground cumin
- 1 teaspoon ground turmeric
- 1 teaspoon ground ginger
- 1 teaspoon salt
- 1 cinnamon stick (2 inches long)
- 1 cup Progresso® chicken broth (from 32-ounce carton)
- 1 can (14.5 ounces) diced tomatoes, undrained
- 1 cup dried plums, cut into bite-size pieces
- ½ cup pitted whole green olives
- 1 small lemon, cut into fourths

Chopped fresh cilantro for garnish

Hot cooked couscous or rice, if desired

In 4-quart Dutch oven, heat oil over medium-high heat. Place chicken, skin sides down, in hot oil; add onion and garlic. Cook 6 to 10 minutes, turning chicken occasionally, until chicken is brown on all sides.

Reduce heat to medium. Sprinkle cilantro, cumin, turmeric, ginger and salt over chicken. Add cinnamon stick; pour broth and tomatoes over chicken. Turn chicken several times to coat evenly. Add plums, olives and lemon, pressing into liquid around chicken. Reduce heat to low. Cover and simmer about 30 minutes or until juice of chicken is clear when thickest part is cut to bone (165°F).

Remove chicken to deep serving platter; cover to keep warm. Increase heat to high; boil sauce uncovered about 5 minutes, stirring occasionally, until thickened. Pour sauce over chicken. Garnish with additional chopped fresh cilantro if desired. Serve over couscous.

1 SERVING: Calories 370; Total Fat 18g (Saturated Fat 4½g, Trans Fat 0g); Cholesterol 85mg; Sodium 920mg; Total Carbohydrate 23g (Dietary Fiber 4g, Sugars 13g); Protein 29g; EXCHANGES: ½ Fruit; 2 Vegetable; ½ Fat; CARBOHYDRATE CHOICES: 1½

Expert Tip

Cooking chicken with the skin on adds to the flavor, not the fat. Research has found that the fat doesn't transfer to the meat during cooking. So go ahead and leave the skin on—it helps keep juices in, creates more moist, and tender meat and boosts the flavor. Then, once the chicken is cooked, remove the skin and throw it away to save on fat, calories and cholesterol.

Chicken Cacciatore

1 tablespoon butter or margarine

1 pound boneless skinless chicken breasts, cut into 1-inch pieces

1 medium green bell pepper, cut into small bite-size strips

1 box Hamburger Helper® Italian four cheese lasagna

1½ cups hot water

1 can (14.5 ounces) diced tomatoes, undrained

1 can (4 ounces) Green Giant® mushroom stems and pieces, drained

¼ cup grated Parmesan cheese

In 10-inch skillet, melt butter over medium heat. Cook chicken and bell pepper in butter, stirring occasionally, until outside of chicken turns white.

Stir in uncooked pasta and sauce mix (from Hamburger Helper box), water, tomatoes and mushrooms. Heat to boiling, stirring occasionally. Reduce heat; cover and simmer about 10 minutes, stirring occasionally, until pasta is tender. Remove from heat; sprinkle with cheese.

Cover; let stand 5 minutes (sauce will thicken as it stands).

1 SERVING: Calories 250; Total Fat 6g (Saturated Fat 2½g, Trans Fat 0g); Cholesterol 55mg; Sodium 1,090mg; Total Carbohydrate 27g (Dietary Fiber 1g, Sugars 7g); Protein 22g; EXCHANGES: 1½ Starch; ½ Vegetable; 2 Very Lean Meat; 1 Fat; CARBOHYDRATE CHOICES: 2

Expert Tip

Shredded Parmesan cheese will make this cacciatore look more special and can be found in your grocer's dairy case.

Chicken with Savory Sauce

2 tablespoons olive oil

4 medium green onions, sliced (¼ cup)

2 tablespoons chopped fresh rosemary

2 tablespoons chopped fresh parsley

2 teaspoons chopped fresh thyme

2 cloves garlic, finely chopped

1 red jalapeño chile, seeded and finely chopped

6 boneless skinless chicken thighs or 4 chicken breast halves (about 1¼ pounds)

1 cup sliced shiitake or regular white mushrooms (3 ounces)

1 cup dry white wine or chicken broth

1 tablespoon balsamic vinegar

1 tablespoon currants

½ teaspoon salt

Heat oil in 12-inch skillet over medium heat. Cook onions, rosemary, parsley, thyme, garlic and chile in oil 5 minutes, stirring frequently.

Add chicken to skillet. Cook about 15 minutes, turning occasionally, until chicken is brown. Add mushrooms, ½ cup of the wine and the vinegar. Heat to boiling; reduce heat. Simmer uncovered about 5 minutes or until about half of the liquid has evaporated.

Pour remaining ½ cup wine over chicken; sprinkle with currants and salt. Cover and simmer about 20 minutes or until juice of chicken is no longer pink when centers of thickest pieces are cut. Uncover and cook 5 minutes longer to crisp chicken.

1 SERVING: Calories 260; Total Fat 11g (Saturated Fat 2g, Trans Fat 0); Cholesterol 85mg; Sodium 387mg; Total Carbohydrate 8g (Dietary Fiber 2g, Sugars 3); Protein 22g; EXCHANGES: 1 Vegetable; 3 Lean Meat; 1½ Fat; CARBOHYDRATE CHOICES: ½

Expert Tip

This interesting recipe is also known as *pollo ubriaco* (drunken chicken); sometimes 2 full cups of wine (one white and one red) are added. In this case, the vinegar offers the contrast of flavor in place of red wine, and the currants bring an interesting sweet effect to the peppery undertone. Dip slices of toasted rustic bread in the juices for a delicious treat.

Arroz con Pollo

- 1 tablespoon olive or vegetable oil
- 4 boneless skinless chicken breasts
- 1 large onion, coarsely chopped
- 1 cup uncooked converted or regular long-grain white rice
- 1 teaspoon ground cumin
- 1/8 teaspoon saffron threads, crushed
- 2 cups chicken broth
- 1/2 cup Old El Paso® Thick 'n Chunky salsa
- 1 red bell pepper, coarsely chopped
- 1/2 cup Green Giant® Valley Fresh Steamers™ frozen sweet peas

In 12-inch skillet, heat oil over medium-high heat until hot. Add chicken; cook 4 to 5 minutes or until browned, turning once. Remove chicken from skillet; cover to keep warm.

Add onion to skillet; cook and stir 3 to 4 minutes or until tender. Add rice, cumin and saffron; stir to mix well. Stir in broth and salsa. Heat to boiling; cook 5 minutes. Return chicken to skillet. Reduce heat; cover and simmer 15 minutes.

Stir in bell pepper and peas; cook about 5 minutes longer or until liquid is absorbed, chicken is fork-tender and juice is clear when center of thickest part is cut (165°F).

1 SERVING: Calories 420; Total Fat 9g (Saturated Fat 2g, Trans Fat 0g); Cholesterol 75mg; Sodium 1,390mg; Total Carbohydrate 49g (Dietary Fiber 3g, Sugars 5g); Protein 35g; EXCHANGES: 3 Starch; 3 1/2 Lean Meat; CARBOHYDRATE CHOICES: 3

Expert Tips

- The rice in this casserole is flavored and colored with saffron. Considered to be the world's most expensive spice, saffron "threads" are dried stigmas of a crocus that grows in Europe and Asia.
- Arroz con pollo is Spanish for "rice with chicken."

Slow Cooker Green Chile–Chicken Enchilada Casserole

PREP TIME: *15 minutes*

TOTAL TIME: *6 hours 20 minutes*

MAKES 6 SERVINGS

2 cans (4.5 ounces each) Old El Paso® chopped green chiles

1 can (10¾ ounces) condensed cream of chicken soup

1 can (10 ounces) Old El Paso® green enchilada sauce or other green chile enchilada sauce

¼ cup mayonnaise or salad dressing

12 corn tortillas (6 inch), cut into ¾-inch strips

3 cups shredded cooked chicken

1 can (15 ounces) Progresso® black beans, drained, rinsed

2 cups shredded Mexican cheese blend (8 ounces)

2 large tomatoes, chopped (about 2 cups)

2 cups chopped lettuce

½ cup sour cream

Spray 3- to 4-quart slow cooker with cooking spray. In cooker, spread 1 can of the green chiles. In medium bowl, mix remaining can of green chiles, the soup, enchilada sauce and mayonnaise.

Arrange one-third of the tortilla strips over chiles in cooker. Top with 1 cup of the chicken, ½ cup of the beans, ½ cup of the cheese and 1 cup of the enchilada sauce mixture, spreading to edges of cooker to completely cover tortilla strips. Repeat layers twice, reserving last ½ cup of cheese.

Cover; cook on Low heat setting 6 to 7 hours. Top with remaining ½ cup cheese. Cover; cook about 5 minutes longer or until cheese is melted. Serve with tomatoes, lettuce and sour cream.

1 SERVING: Calories 630; Total Fat 32g (Saturated Fat 13g, Trans Fat ½g); Cholesterol 115mg; Sodium 1,240mg; Total Carbohydrate 48g (Dietary Fiber 9g, Sugars 6g); Protein 39g; EXCHANGES: 2 Starch; 0 Fruit; 1½ Other Carbohydrate; 4½ Lean Meat; 0 High-Fat Meat; 3 Fat; CARBOHYDRATE CHOICES: 3

Expert Tips

■ Rotisserie chicken works well for this recipe. Just remove the skin and bones, and shred the meat with 2 forks. One average rotisserie chicken yields about 3½ to 4 cups cooked chicken.

■ Red enchilada sauce can be used. It will give a pink tint to the finished recipe.

■ You could serve this recipe with tortilla chips as an appetizer.

Slow Cooker Greek Chicken Stew

- 2 cups baby-cut carrots, halved lengthwise if large

- 1 bag (1 pound) frozen small whole onions

- 6 bone-in chicken thighs (from two 1.5-pound packages), skin removed

- 1 teaspoon ground cinnamon

- 1/2 teaspoon salt

- 1/2 teaspoon pepper

- 2 cloves garlic, finely chopped

- 2 cans (14 1/2 ounces each) diced tomatoes, undrained

- 1/3 cup tomato paste

- 2 teaspoons grated lemon peel

- 1/2 teaspoon dried oregano

- 1/4 cup chopped parsley

Spray 4- to 5-quart slow cooker with cooking spray. Place carrots and onions in slow cooker. Top with chicken thighs. Sprinkle with cinnamon, salt, pepper and garlic; top with tomatoes. Cover; cook on Low heat setting 7 to 9 hours or until vegetables are tender and chicken pulls apart easily with a fork.

Remove chicken with slotted spoon; cover to keep warm. Stir tomato paste, lemon peel and oregano into liquid in slow cooker. Cover; cook about 15 minutes longer or until thickened and hot. Meanwhile, remove chicken from bones. Stir chicken into mixture in slow cooker, breaking up larger pieces.

To serve, spoon stew in shallow bowls and top with parsley.

1 SERVING: Calories 200; Total Fat 6g (Saturated Fat 2g, Trans Fat 0g); Cholesterol 45mg; Sodium 580mg; Total Carbohydrate 20g (Dietary Fiber 5g, Sugars 10g); Protein 17g; EXCHANGES: 1/2 Other Carbohydrate; 2 Vegetable; 2 Lean Meat; CARBOHYDRATE CHOICES: 1

Expert Tips

- Since either chicken thighs or turkey thighs would work well in this recipe, purchase whichever one is priced less per pound for the best savings.

- For added flavor, substitute a flavored diced tomato such as one with roasted garlic or one with added Italian seasoning.

Slow Cooker Chicken Marsala

PREP TIME: *10 minutes*
TOTAL TIME: *5 hours 25 minutes*
MAKES 8 SERVINGS

- 2 cloves garlic, finely chopped
- 1 tablespoon vegetable oil
- 8 boneless skinless chicken breasts
- ½ teaspoon salt
- ½ teaspoon pepper
- 2 jars (6 ounces each) Green Giant® sliced mushrooms, drained
- 1 cup sweet Marsala wine or Progresso® chicken broth (from 32-ounce carton)
- ½ cup water
- ¼ cup cornstarch
- 3 tablespoons chopped fresh parsley

Spray 4- to 5-quart slow cooker with cooking spray. In cooker, place garlic and oil. Sprinkle chicken with salt and pepper; place in cooker over garlic. Place mushrooms over chicken; pour wine over all. Cover; cook on Low heat setting 5 to 6 hours.

Remove chicken from cooker; place on plate and cover to keep warm. In small bowl, mix water and cornstarch until smooth; stir into liquid in cooker. Increase heat setting to High; cover and cook about 10 minutes or until sauce is slightly thickened.

Return chicken to cooker. Cover; cook on High heat setting 5 minutes longer or until chicken is hot.

To serve, spoon mushroom mixture over chicken breasts; sprinkle with parsley.

1 SERVING: Calories 190; Total Fat 6g (Saturated Fat 1½g, Trans Fat 0g); Cholesterol 70mg; Sodium 360mg; Total Carbohydrate 7g (Dietary Fiber 1g, Sugars 1g); Protein 26g; EXCHANGES: ½ Other Carbohydrate; 3½ Very Lean Meat; 1 Fat; CARBOHYDRATE CHOICES: ½

Expert Tips

- Serve on a bed of white rice with a green salad.
- Make sure to use sweet Marsala wine. Dry Marsala makes this dish taste too acidic.

West African Peanut-Chicken Stew

1 pound boneless skinless chicken breasts (about 4)

1 box Betty Crocker® Chicken Helper® jambalaya

2 tablespoons vegetable oil

2½ cups hot water

1 can (14.5 ounces) diced tomatoes with onion and pepper, undrained

½ pound sliced fully cooked Polish or kielbasa sausage, if desired

2 tablespoons peanut butter

Cut chicken into strips, about 2 × ¼ inch. In 3- to 4-quart saucepan, stir chicken and chicken seasoning (from jambalaya mix) until chicken is evenly coated; stir in oil. (For best results, use saucepan with nonstick finish.)

Cook chicken uncovered over medium-high heat about 8 minutes, turning chicken over after 5 minutes, until dark brown on both sides. Stir in hot water, sauce mix and uncooked rice (from jambalaya mix), tomatoes and sausage. Heat to boiling, stirring occasionally. Reduce heat; cover and simmer about 25 minutes, stirring once, until rice is tender.

Stir in peanut butter. Cook about 2 minutes longer or until mixture is thickened. Cover; let stand about 5 minutes or until most of liquid is absorbed.

1 SERVING: Calories 350; Total Fat 12g (Saturated Fat 2½g, Trans Fat 0g); Cholesterol 55mg; Sodium 1,080mg; Total Carbohydrate 34g (Dietary Fiber 2g, Sugars 5g); Protein 25g; EXCHANGES: 1½ Starch; ½ Other Carbohydrate; 1 Vegetable; 2½ Very Lean Meat; 2 Fat; CARBOHYDRATE CHOICES: 2

Expert Tip

Freeze chicken breasts for up to 30 minutes, and they'll be much easier to cut.

Chicken–Vegetable–Barley Soup

PREP TIME: *25 minutes*

TOTAL TIME: *30 minutes*

MAKES 8 SERVINGS

5 cups Progresso® reduced-sodium chicken broth (from two 32-ounce cartons)

2 cups shredded deli rotisserie chicken breast (from 2-pound chicken)

1/2 teaspoon kosher (coarse) salt

1/2 teaspoon pepper

1 bag (16 ounces) frozen vegetables for soup with tomatoes

3/4 cup uncooked quick-cooking barley

2 cups chopped fresh baby spinach leaves

In 5-quart Dutch oven, stir together broth, chicken, salt, pepper and frozen vegetables. Heat to boiling. Stir in barley; reduce heat. Cover; simmer 10 minutes, stirring occasionally.

Remove from heat; stir in spinach. Let stand 5 minutes before serving.

1 SERVING: Calories 151; Total Fat 1g (Saturated Fat 1/2g, Trans Fat 0g); Cholesterol 22; Sodium 620mg; Total Carbohydrate 20g (Dietary Fiber 5g, Sugars 3g); Protein 13g; EXCHANGES: 1 Starch; 1 Vegetable; 1 Lean Meat; CARBOHYDRATE CHOICES: 1

Expert Tip

This simple soup is rich in fiber, potassium and magnesium—all of which protect against heart disease.

Italian Chicken Noodle Soup

- 1 tablespoon olive or vegetable oil
- 2 boneless skinless chicken breasts (about ½ pound), cut into ½-inch pieces
- 1 medium onion, chopped (½ cup)
- 1 carton (32 ounces) Progresso® chicken broth (4 cups)
- 2 cups water
- 3 medium carrots, sliced (1½ cups)
- 2 cups broccoli florets
- 1½ cups uncooked medium egg noodles
- 1 teaspoon dried basil
- ½ teaspoon garlic-pepper blend
- ¼ cup shredded Parmesan cheese

In 4-quart saucepan, heat oil over medium heat. Add chicken. Cook 4 to 6 minutes, stirring occasionally, until no longer pink in center. Stir in onion. Cook 2 to 3 minutes, stirring occasionally, until onion is tender.

Stir in broth, water and carrots. Heat to boiling. Cook 5 minutes over medium heat. Stir in broccoli, noodles, basil and garlic-pepper blend. Heat to boiling; reduce heat. Simmer uncovered 8 to 10 minutes, stirring occasionally, until vegetables and noodles are tender.

Top each serving with cheese.

1 SERVING: Calories 170; Total Fat 6g (Saturated Fat 2g, Trans Fat 0g); Cholesterol 35mg; Sodium 710mg, Total Carbohydrate 13g (Dietary Fiber 2g, Sugars 3g); Protein 15g; EXCHANGES: 1 Starch; 1½ Very Lean Meat; 1 Fat; CARBOHYDRATE CHOICES: 1

Expert Tips

- You can substitute chicken thighs for part or all of the chicken breasts. Usually, two boneless thighs will equal one breast half.
- Fresh vegetables are used to make this colorful soup, but you could use frozen vegetables if you like.

Chicken Vegetable Pot Pie Soup

PREP TIME: *20 minutes*
TOTAL TIME: *1 hour*
MAKES 6 SERVINGS

1 sheet frozen puff pastry (from 17.3-ounce package), thawed

2 tablespoons butter or margarine

6 small red potatoes, cut into eighths

1 medium stalk celery, coarsely chopped (½ cup)

1 medium carrot, coarsely chopped (½ cup)

1 small onion, coarsely chopped (¼ cup)

5 cups Progresso® chicken broth (from two 32-ounce cartons)

¼ cup Gold Medal® Wondra® quick-mixing flour

1 teaspoon poultry seasoning

¼ teaspoon salt

⅛ teaspoon pepper

2½ cups 1-inch pieces cooked chicken

1 cup Green Giant® Valley Fresh Steamers™ frozen sweet peas

¼ cup whipping cream

Heat oven to 400°F. Cut 6 rounds from puff pastry with 3-inch round cutter. Place on ungreased cookie sheet. Bake 12 to 15 minutes or until puffed and golden brown. Keep warm.

While pastry is baking, melt butter in 4½- to 5-quart Dutch oven over medium-high heat. Add potatoes, celery, carrot and onion; cook 5 to 6 minutes, stirring frequently, until onion is softened.

Beat broth, flour, poultry seasoning, salt and pepper into potato mixture with wire whisk. Heat to boiling; reduce heat to medium-low. Cover; cook 15 to 20 minutes, stirring occasionally, until potatoes are tender and soup is slightly thickened.

Stir remaining ingredients into soup. Cover; cook 5 to 6 minutes, stirring occasionally, until chicken and peas are hot. Ladle soup into bowls; top each serving with pastry.

1 SERVING: Calories 600; Total Fat 28g (Saturated Fat 11g, Trans Fat 2g); Cholesterol 120mg; Sodium 1,170mg; Total Carbohydrate 57g (Dietary Fiber 6g, Sugars 4g); Protein 28g; EXCHANGES: 3 Starch; 1 Other Carbohydrate; 2½ Lean Meat; 3½ Fat; CARBOHYDRATE CHOICES: 4

Expert Tips

- Look for puff pastry in the freezer section of the supermarket with the frozen pie shells. What do you do with the leftover cut pastry pieces? Sprinkle them with some cinnamon and sugar, and bake for a special snack-time treat.

- Wondering what to serve with this soup? A fresh green salad with sliced tomatoes and roasted garlic dressing is the perfect answer to this puzzling question.

- An easy way to add layers of flavor is to use poultry seasoning. A blend of sage, thyme, marjoram, rosemary, black pepper and nutmeg, this seasoning lends a subtle savory note to chicken and turkey dishes.

Seafood

Seafood Chowder Pot Pie

1 teaspoon salt

2 cups peeled and diced russet potatoes (2 medium)

4 slices bacon, cut in half

⅓ cup Gold Medal® all-purpose flour

2 bottles (8 ounces each) clam juice

¼ cup whipping cream

½ teaspoon onion salt

1 cup frozen peas and carrots, thawed

1 cup Green Giant® Niblets® frozen corn, thawed

1 tablespoon chopped fresh thyme

1 cup cooked peeled deveined medium shrimp, tail shells removed (about 6 ounces)

1 can (6 ounces) crabmeat, drained, flaked (about 1 cup)

1 sheet frozen (thawed) puff pastry (from 17.3-ounce package)

In 2-quart saucepan, heat 2 cups water and the salt to boiling over high heat. Add potatoes; heat to boiling. Reduce heat to medium. Cover and simmer 5 to 7 minutes or until tender; drain.

Heat oven to 400°F. Spray 11 × 7-inch (2-quart) baking dish with cooking spray.

Meanwhile, in heavy 3-quart saucepan, cook bacon over medium heat, turning occasionally, until crisp. Remove bacon; crumble and set aside. Using wire whisk, stir flour into bacon drippings. Gradually stir in clam juice, whipping cream and onion salt. Heat until thickened and bubbly, stirring constantly. Stir in potatoes, bacon, peas and carrots, corn and thyme. Cook 3 to 4 minutes longer or until hot.

Stir in shrimp and crabmeat. Spoon mixture into baking dish.

On lightly floured surface, unfold pastry. Roll into 12 × 8-inch rectangle. With sharp knife, cut slits in pastry to allow steam to escape. Place pastry in baking dish over hot seafood mixture. Roll outer edges of pastry over edges of baking dish and press onto edges.

Bake 30 to 40 minutes or until crust is deep golden brown. Let stand 10 minutes before serving.

1 SERVING: Calories 440; Total Fat 22g (Saturated Fat 8g, Trans Fat 1½g); Cholesterol 145mg; Sodium 1,090mg; Total Carbohydrate 42g (Dietary Fiber 3g, Sugars 3g); Protein 19g; EXCHANGES: 2½ Starch; ½ Other Carbohydrate; 1½ Lean Meat; 3 Fat; CARBOHYDRATE CHOICES: 3

Expert Tips

■ Cut shell or fish shapes out of excess dough, brush with beaten egg and attach to unbaked crust.

■ Taste before adding salt to the chowder mixture. Salt levels vary in the clam juice, bacon and seafood, which will affect the desired amount of salt.

Not-Your-Mother's Tuna Pot Pie

PREP TIME: *25 minutes*
TOTAL TIME: *50 minutes*
MAKES 5 SERVINGS

1 cup uncooked ditalini (short tubes) pasta

4 slices bacon

1 large onion, chopped (about 1 cup)

1 teaspoon dried thyme

2 tablespoons all-purpose flour

1 cup Progresso® chicken broth (from 32-ounce carton)

²⁄₃ cup milk

2 cups frozen crinkle-cut carrots, thawed, well drained

1 can (12 ounces) solid white tuna in water, drained, flaked

1 can (7 ounces) Green Giant® Niblets® whole kernel corn, drained

2 tablespoons Dijon mustard

2 slices white bread

2 tablespoons butter or margarine, melted

Heat oven to 375°F. Cook pasta as directed on package, using minimum cook time; drain. In 12-inch nonstick skillet, cook bacon over medium-high heat until crisp. Reserving drippings in skillet, remove bacon to drain on paper towels. Crumble bacon; set aside.

Add onion and thyme to drippings. Cook over medium-high heat, stirring occasionally, until onion is golden brown. Stir in flour; cook 1 minute, stirring constantly. Stir in broth and milk; heat to boiling. Boil, stirring constantly, until thickened. Stir in carrots, tuna, corn, pasta and mustard; heat to boiling. Fold in bacon. Spoon into ungreased 2-quart casserole.

Place bread in food processor. Cover; process with on-and-off pulses several times to make bread crumbs. In small bowl, mix bread crumbs and butter. Sprinkle over tuna mixture.

Bake uncovered 20 to 25 minutes or until mixture is bubbly and topping is golden brown.

1 SERVING: Calories 380; Total Fat 11g (Saturated Fat 5g, Trans Fat 0g); Cholesterol 40mg; Sodium 940mg; Total Carbohydrate 43g (Dietary Fiber 4g, Sugars 7g); Protein 27g; EXCHANGES: 2½ Starch; 1 Vegetable; 2½ Lean Meat; ½ Fat; CARBOHYDRATE CHOICES: 3

Expert Tips

- If you don't have sliced bacon on hand but you do have real bacon bits, you can sauté the onion and thyme in 1 tablespoon olive oil, then just sprinkle the pot pie with about ¼ cup bacon bits before you add the bread crumbs.

- This recipe takes a few pantry items and turns them into a delicious, one-dish meal.

PREP TIME: *20 minutes*
TOTAL TIME: *50 minutes*
MAKES 4 SERVINGS

Louisiana-Style Shrimp Casserole

- 2 tablespoons butter or margarine
- 1 clove garlic, finely chopped
- 2 cups frozen bell pepper and onion stir-fry (from 1-pound bag)
- ¼ cup finely chopped celery
- 2 tablespoons Original Bisquick® mix
- 1 can (14.5 ounces) diced tomatoes, undrained
- ¼ teaspoon salt
- ¼ teaspoon red pepper sauce
- 12 ounces cooked peeled deveined medium shrimp, thawed if frozen, tail shells removed
- ¾ cup Original Bisquick® mix
- ¼ cup milk
- 1 egg

Heat oven to 400°F. In 10-inch skillet, melt butter over medium-high heat. Add garlic; stir-fry vegetables and celery. Cook about 5 minutes, stirring frequently, until vegetables are crisp-tender.

Stir 2 tablespoons Bisquick mix into vegetable mixture until blended. Stir in tomatoes, salt, pepper sauce and shrimp. Reduce heat to medium-low. Cook about 7 minutes, stirring occasionally, until bubbling and thickened. Pour shrimp mixture into ungreased 8-inch square (2-quart) glass baking dish.

In small bowl, stir ¾ cup Bisquick mix, the milk and egg with fork until smooth.

Pour over shrimp mixture. Bake 20 to 30 minutes or until crust is golden brown.

1 SERVING: Calories 320; Total Fat 12g (Saturated Fat 6g, Trans Fat 1½g); Cholesterol 235mg; Sodium 870mg; Total Carbohydrate 29g (Dietary Fiber 2g, Sugars 7g); Protein 24g; EXCHANGES: 1½ Starch; 1 Vegetable; 2½ Very Lean Meat; 2 Fat; CARBOHYDRATE CHOICES: 2

Expert Tips

- Make the shrimp filling ahead, spoon into the baking dish, cover and refrigerate. When ready to bake, just stir up the Bisquick mix topping and bake as directed.
- Jazz up the look of this seafood sensation by sprinkling the top of the unbaked casserole with a tablespoon of chopped fresh parsley and a teaspoon of Cajun seasoning.
- This southern favorite tastes just as delicious with 2 cups diced cooked chicken in place of the shrimp.

Smoked Salmon– Potato Gratin

PREP TIME: *35 minutes*

TOTAL TIME: *1 hour 15 minutes*

MAKES 8 SERVINGS

2½ pounds golden potatoes, peeled and thinly sliced (6 medium), about 8 cups

2 tablespoons butter

1 cup thinly sliced leeks

2 tablespoons Gold Medal® all-purpose flour

3 cups half-and-half

1 cup shredded Gruyère or Swiss cheese

2 tablespoons chopped fresh dill weed

½ teaspoon salt

¼ teaspoon pepper

12 ounces smoked salmon (not lox), cut or flaked into ½-inch pieces

TOPPING

1 cup Progresso® plain bread crumbs

3 tablespoons butter or margarine, melted

Fill 4-quart saucepan two-thirds with water; heat to boiling over high heat. Cook sliced potatoes in water 6 to 9 minutes or until almost tender; drain and return to saucepan.

Heat oven to 350°F. Spray 3-quart casserole with cooking spray.

In 12-inch nonstick skillet, melt 2 tablespoons butter over medium heat. Cook and stir leeks in butter about 5 minutes or until softened. Stir in flour. Gradually stir in half-and-half. Heat to boiling. Remove from heat. Stir in cheese, dill, salt and pepper until cheese is melted.

Pour sauce over potatoes in saucepan. Spoon half of potato mixture into casserole. Top with half the salmon. Repeat layers.

Stir together bread crumbs and melted butter; sprinkle over potato mixture. Bake uncovered 30 to 40 minutes or until potatoes are tender and topping is golden brown.

1 SERVING: Calories 490; Total Fat 25g (Saturated Fat 14g, Trans Fat 1g); Cholesterol 75mg; Sodium 720mg; Total Carbohydrate 47g (Dietary Fiber 4g, Sugars 6g); Protein 19g; EXCHANGES: 2 Starch; 1 Other Carbohydrate; 2 Lean Meat; 3½ Fat; CARBOHYDRATE CHOICES: 3

Expert Tips

- Substitute 1 can (14¾ ounces) red salmon, skinned and boned, for the smoked salmon.
- Serve with steamed asparagus and a crisp chardonnay.
- This is a new rendition of scalloped potatoes and ham, great to serve at a brunch.

Seafood Scalloped Potatoes

1 bag (28 ounces) frozen potatoes with onions and peppers

1 bag (7 ounces) frozen cooked salad shrimp

1 cup shredded Cheddar cheese (4 ounces)

1 can (18.5 ounces) Progresso® Traditional New England clam chowder

2 tablespoons butter or margarine, melted

½ cup Progresso® plain bread crumbs

Heat oven to 350°F. Spray 13 × 9-inch (3-quart) glass baking dish with cooking spray. Layer potatoes, shrimp and cheese in baking dish. Pour soup evenly over top.

In small bowl, mix butter and bread crumbs; sprinkle over potato mixture.

Bake 50 to 60 minutes or until bubbly around edges and bread crumbs are golden brown on top.

1 SERVING: Calories 350; Total Fat 15g (Saturated Fat 8g, Trans Fat 0g); Cholesterol 100mg; Sodium 660mg; Total Carbohydrate 37g (Dietary Fiber 3g, Sugars 2g); Protein 18g; EXCHANGES: 2½ Starch; 1½ Very Lean Meat; 2½ Fat; CARBOHYDRATE CHOICES: 2½

Tuna with Cheese–Garlic Biscuits

2 cans (5 ounces each) tuna in water, drained, flaked

1 can (10¾ ounces) condensed cream of chicken and mushroom soup

1½ cups Green Giant® Valley Fresh Steamers™ frozen mixed vegetables, thawed, drained

⅔ cup milk

1¼ cups Original Bisquick® mix

⅓ cup shredded Cheddar cheese

½ cup milk

2 tablespoons butter or margarine, melted

⅛ teaspoon garlic powder

Heat oven to 425°F. In ungreased 2-quart casserole, mix tuna, soup, vegetables and ⅔ cup milk. Bake uncovered 20 minutes.

In medium bowl, stir Bisquick mix, cheese and ½ cup milk until soft dough forms.

Drop dough by 6 spoonfuls onto hot tuna mixture.

Bake uncovered 10 to 12 minutes longer or until biscuits are golden brown. Mix butter and garlic powder; brush over warm biscuits.

1 SERVING: Calories 320; Total Fat 14g (Saturated Fat 6g, Trans Fat 1g); Cholesterol 40mg; Sodium 930mg; Total Carbohydrate 29g (Dietary Fiber 3g, Sugars 5g); Protein 20g; EXCHANGES: 1½ Starch; ½ Other Carbohydrate; 2 Very Lean Meat; 2½ Fat; CARBOHYDRATE CHOICES: 2

Expert Tips

- You can use two 5-ounce cans of chunk chicken instead of the tuna.
- Be sure to use canned tuna packed in water for this recipe. Per serving, it reduces the fat by 3 grams and yields 30 fewer calories than if you'd used oil-packed tuna.
- You can substitute condensed cream of celery or cream of chicken soup for the chicken and mushroom soup.

Tuna and Broccoli Bake

PREP TIME: *10 minutes*

TOTAL TIME: *55 minutes*

MAKES 6 SERVINGS

2 cups fresh broccoli florets

2 cans (5 ounces each) tuna in water, drained

2 cups shredded Cheddar cheese (8 ounces)

¾ cup Original Bisquick® mix

¾ cup sour cream

¾ cup milk

3 eggs

Heat oven to 350°F. Spray 8-inch square (2-quart) baking dish with cooking spray.

Sprinkle broccoli, tuna and 1½ cups of the cheese in baking dish.

In large bowl, stir Bisquick mix, sour cream, milk and eggs with wire whisk or fork until blended. Pour into baking dish.

Bake 30 to 40 minutes or until knife inserted in center comes out clean. Sprinkle with remaining ½ cup cheese. Let stand 5 minutes before serving.

1 SERVING: Calories 380; Total Fat 24g (Saturated Fat 13g, Trans Fat 1g); Cholesterol 180mg; Sodium 610mg; Total Carbohydrate 15g (Dietary Fiber 1g, Sugars 4g); Protein 26g; EXCHANGES: 1 Starch; 1½ Fat; CARBOHYDRATE CHOICES: 1

Tuna–Vegetable Casserole

2 cups Corn Chex® cereal

1 box (7 ounces) elbow macaroni (2½ cups)

1 can (10¾ ounces) condensed cream of mushroom soup

1 can (5 ounces) tuna in water, drained

1 bag (12 ounces) Green Giant® Valley Fresh Steamers™ frozen mixed vegetables, thawed, drained

1 cup milk

½ teaspoon salt

¼ teaspoon pepper

1 tablespoon butter or margarine, melted

½ cup shredded Cheddar cheese (2 ounces)

Heat oven to 400°F. Place cereal in food-storage plastic bag or between sheets of waxed paper; crush with rolling pin. Set aside.

Cook and drain macaroni as directed on box. In ungreased 2-quart casserole, stir soup, tuna, vegetables, milk, salt and pepper until blended. Stir in macaroni. In small bowl, mix crushed cereal and melted butter with fork; sprinkle over mixture in casserole.

Bake uncovered about 30 minutes or until bubbly around edges and hot. Sprinkle with cheese; let stand 5 minutes before serving.

1 SERVING: Calories 430; Total Fat 12g (Saturated Fat 6g, Trans Fat 0g); Cholesterol 30mg; Sodium 1,150mg; Total Carbohydrate 58g (Dietary Fiber 4g, Sugars 7g); Protein 21g; EXCHANGES: 3 Starch; ½ Other Carbohydrate; 1 Vegetable; 1½ Lean Meat; 1 Fat; CARBOHYDRATE CHOICES: 4

Expert Tips

■ Serve this family-style casserole with a tossed green salad, topped with your favorite dressing—Italian or ranch would be yummy!

■ Don't want to use mixed veggies? Use another vegetable such as green beans or peas instead.

Contemporary Tuna–Noodle Casserole

PREP TIME: *20 minutes*

TOTAL TIME: *50 minutes*

MAKES 6 SERVINGS

2 cups uncooked fusilli pasta (6 ounces)

1 jar (16 ounces) Alfredo pasta sauce

1/3 cup dry white wine or chicken broth

1 teaspoon Italian seasoning

1 teaspoon grated lemon peel

2 cans (5 ounces each) solid white albacore tuna in water, drained

1 box (9 ounces) Green Giant® frozen sugar snap peas, thawed, drained

1 jar (4.5 ounces) Green Giant® whole mushrooms, drained

1/2 cup Progresso® plain bread crumbs

2 tablespoons butter or margarine, melted

Heat oven to 375°F. Spray 2-quart baking dish with cooking spray.

Cook and drain pasta as directed on package using minimum cook time. In large bowl, stir Alfredo sauce, wine, Italian seasoning, lemon peel, tuna, peas, mushrooms and pasta. Spoon into baking dish.

In small bowl, stir together bread crumbs and butter; sprinkle in baking dish.

Bake 25 to 30 minutes or until topping is golden brown.

1 SERVING: Calories 530; Total Fat 29g (Saturated Fat 18g, Trans Fat 1g); Cholesterol 100mg; Sodium 730mg; Total Carbohydrate 41g (Dietary Fiber 3g, Sugars 4g); Protein 24g; EXCHANGES: 2½ Starch; 2½ Lean Meat; 4 Fat; CARBOHYDRATE CHOICES: 3

Expert Tips

■ Land lovers can substitute 2 cups cut-up cooked chicken for the tuna.

■ For a retro topping, omit the buttered bread crumbs and substitute ½ cup crushed potato chips.

Creamy Blue Cheese–Salmon Casserole

PREP TIME: *10 minutes*

TOTAL TIME: *6 hours 25 minutes*

MAKES 8 SERVINGS

10 to 12 small red potatoes (1½ pounds), cut in half

1 pound fresh green beans, trimmed, cut into 1-inch pieces

1 can (15.25 ounces) Green Giant® whole kernel sweet corn, drained

1 can (10¾ ounces) condensed cream of potato soup

½ cup water

½ teaspoon pepper

½ cup half-and-half

3 tablespoons Gold Medal® all-purpose flour

1½ pounds salmon fillets, skin removed, cut into bite-size pieces

1 cup crumbled blue cheese (4 ounces)

2 tablespoons chopped fresh chives

Spray 3- to 4-quart slow cooker with cooking spray. In slow cooker, mix potatoes, beans, corn, soup, water and pepper.

Cover; cook on Low heat setting 6 to 7 hours (or on High heat setting 3 hours to 3 hours 30 minutes).

In 1-cup measuring cup, mix half-and-half and flour with whisk until well blended. Stir into potato mixture. Stir in salmon.

If using Low heat setting, increase to High. Cover; cook 15 to 20 minutes longer or until salmon flakes easily with fork. Stir in cheese and chives.

1 SERVING: Calories 460; Total Fat 12g (Saturated Fat 6g, Trans Fat 0g); Cholesterol 75mg; Sodium 580mg; Total Carbohydrate 57g (Dietary Fiber 7g, Sugars 7g); Protein 29g; EXCHANGES: 2½ Starch; ½ Other Carbohydrate; ½ Low-Fat Milk; 1½ Vegetable; 2 Very Lean Meat; 1½ Fat; CARBOHYDRATE CHOICES: 1

Expert Tips

- Look for salmon fillets that already have the skin removed, if possible, to save time from having to remove it.

- For an economical alternative, 2 cans (7½ ounces each) water-packed chunk-style boneless skinless salmon, drained, can be used instead of the fresh salmon. Since it's already cooked, stir it into the potato mixture about 10 minutes before the total cooking time is done, and cook just until thoroughly heated.

Parmesan-Shrimp Pasta Bake

1 package (16 ounces) uncooked farfalle (bow-tie) pasta

6 tablespoons butter or margarine

3 cloves garlic, finely chopped

6 tablespoons Gold Medal® all-purpose flour

1/3 cup dry vermouth or chicken broth

2 3/4 cups half-and-half

1/2 cup clam juice

1 tablespoon tomato paste or ketchup

3/4 teaspoon salt

1/4 teaspoon pepper

1 pound uncooked peeled deveined medium shrimp, thawed if frozen

2 tablespoons chopped fresh or 2 teaspoons dried dill weed

3/4 cup freshly grated Parmesan cheese

Heat oven to 350°F. Grease shallow 2-quart casserole with shortening or spray with cooking spray. Cook and drain pasta as directed on package.

Melt butter in 2-quart saucepan over medium heat. Cook garlic in butter 1 minute, stirring constantly. Stir in flour. Cook, stirring constantly with wire whisk, until smooth and bubbly.

Stir in vermouth. Stir in half-and-half, clam juice, tomato paste, salt and pepper. Cook over medium heat, stirring constantly, until thickened. Stir in shrimp, dill weed and 1/4 cup of the cheese.

Stir pasta into shrimp mixture. Pour into casserole. Sprinkle with remaining 1/2 cup cheese. Bake uncovered 35 to 40 minutes or until light brown and hot.

1 SERVING: Calories 531; Total Fat 23g (Saturated Fat 13g, Trans Fat 1/2g); Cholesterol 148mg; Sodium 637mg; Total Carbohydrate 52g (Dietary Fiber 2g, Sugars 3g); Protein 27g; EXCHANGES: 3 Starch; 2 Lean Meat; 4 Fat; CARBOHYDRATE CHOICES: 3

Expert Tip

Organize a holiday progressive dinner with friends or neighbors. Start with appetizers and cocktails at the first house; have soup, salad and bread at the second stop; the main course and perhaps a vegetable at the next; and dessert and coffee at the last. It's an easy way to share the cooking, plus you get to see everyone's holiday decorations.

Shrimp and Pea Pod Casserole

PREP TIME: *5 minutes*
TOTAL TIME: *45 minutes*
MAKES 6 SERVINGS

3 cups uncooked penne pasta (9 ounces uncooked)

½ cup butter or margarine

2 cups sliced fresh mushrooms

2 cloves garlic, finely chopped

½ cup Gold Medal® all-purpose flour

½ teaspoon salt

¼ teaspoon pepper

2 cups milk

2 tablespoons sherry or dry white wine, if desired

1¾ cups Progresso® chicken broth (from 32-ounce carton)

¾ cup shredded Fontina or Swiss cheese (3 ounces)

1 pound cooked peeled deveined medium shrimp, thawed if frozen

2 cups frozen sugar snap pea pods (from 1-pound bag), thawed and drained

¼ cup finely shredded Parmesan cheese

¼ cup sliced almonds

Heat oven to 350°F. Spray 13 × 9-inch glass baking dish with cooking spray.

Cook and drain pasta as directed on package.

Meanwhile, in 4-quart saucepan or Dutch oven, melt butter over low heat. Cook mushrooms and garlic in butter, stirring occasionally, until mushrooms are tender. Stir in flour, salt and pepper. Cook over medium heat, stirring constantly, until mixture is smooth and bubbly. Gradually stir in milk, sherry and broth until smooth. Heat to boiling, stirring constantly. Stir in Fontina cheese until melted; remove from heat.

Stir pasta, shrimp and pea pods into mushroom mixture. Pour into baking dish. Sprinkle with Parmesan cheese and almonds.

Bake uncovered 20 to 25 minutes or until cheese is golden brown.

1 SERVING: Calories 590; Total Fat 27g (Saturated Fat 13g, Trans Fat 1g); Cholesterol 215mg; Sodium 980mg; Total Carbohydrate 51g (Dietary Fiber 5g, Sugars 7g); Protein 35g; EXCHANGES: 3 Starch; 1 Vegetable; 1½ Fat; CARBOHYDRATE CHOICES: 3½

Salmon Paella Bake

PREP TIME: *15 minutes*

TOTAL TIME: *1 hour*

MAKES 6 SERVINGS

- 1½ cups uncooked Arborio rice
- 1 medium onion, chopped (½ cup)
- 1 large red bell pepper, chopped (about 1¾ cups)
- 1 teaspoon grated lemon peel
- ¾ teaspoon salt
- ½ teaspoon crushed saffron threads
- 4 cups chicken broth
- ½ pound smoked turkey kielbasa sausage, cut into ¾-inch slices
- 1 salmon fillet (1½ pounds), skin removed and cut into 6 pieces
- 1 tablespoon vegetable oil
- 2 tablespoons chopped fresh Italian (flat-leaf) parsley

Heat oven to 350°F. Spray 13 × 9-inch (3-quart) baking dish with cooking spray. Place rice, onion, bell pepper, lemon peel, ½ teaspoon of the salt and the saffron in baking dish.

Heat chicken broth to boiling. Stir broth into rice mixture. Arrange kielbasa slices over rice. Cover with foil. Bake 20 minutes.

Arrange salmon over rice; brush fillets with vegetable oil. Sprinkle with remaining ¼ teaspoon salt. Bake uncovered 20 to 25 minutes longer or until fish flakes easily with fork, rice is tender and broth is absorbed. Sprinkle with parsley.

1 SERVING: Calories 450; Total Fat 14g (Saturated Fat 3½g, Trans Fat 0g); Cholesterol 95mg; Sodium 1,430mg; Total Carbohydrate 44g (Dietary Fiber 1g, Sugars 2g); Protein 37g; EXCHANGES: 3 Starch; 4 Lean Meat; CARBOHYDRATE CHOICES: 3

Expert Tips

- When shopping for the fish, look for a salmon fillet with uniform thickness so fish cooks evenly. Ask the butcher to remove the skin.
- For a kick of spice, add a chopped jalapeño chile with the rice and substitute chopped fresh cilantro for the parsley.
- Serve with fresh lemon slices or wedges.

Salmon and Couscous Bake

1 pound salmon fillets, about ¾ inch thick

1 package (5.6 ounces) toasted pine nut couscous mix

1½ cups hot water

1 tablespoon olive or vegetable oil

1 tablespoon lemon juice

½ teaspoon dried dill weed

1 small zucchini, coarsely chopped

1 small yellow summer squash, coarsely chopped

¼ teaspoon dried dill weed

Toasted pine nuts, if desired

Heat oven to 350°. Spray square baking dish, 8 × 8 × 2 inches, with cooking spray. Cut fish into 4 serving pieces.

Stir couscous, seasoning packet from couscous mix, water, oil, lemon juice, ½ teaspoon dill weed, the zucchini and summer squash in baking dish. Place fish on couscous mixture. Sprinkle fish with ¼ teaspoon dill weed.

Cover and bake 20 to 25 minutes or until liquid is absorbed and fish flakes easily with fork. Sprinkle with pine nuts.

1 SERVING: Calories 419; Total Fat 21g (Saturated Fat 4½g, Trans Fats 0g); Cholesterol 62mg; Sodium 437mg; Total Carbohydrate 29g (Dietary Fiber 2g, Sugars 3g); Protein 30g; EXCHANGES: 2 Starch; ½ Vegetable; 3 Lean Meat; 2½ Fat; CARBOHYDRATE CHOICES: 2

Expert Tips

■ Many kinds of fresh fish can be substituted for the salmon. We recommend sea bass, snapper, grouper or haddock.

■ Packed with omega-3 fatty acids, salmon is low in fat and high in poly-unsaturated oils.

Impossibly Easy Salmon Asparagus Bake

PREP TIME: *15 minutes*

TOTAL TIME: *1 hour 5 minutes*

MAKES 12 SERVINGS

- 2 packages (10 ounces each) frozen cut asparagus, thawed and well drained
- 8 medium green onions, sliced (½ cup)
- 3 cups shredded Swiss cheese (12 ounces)
- 2 cans (6 to 7½ ounces each) salmon or tuna, drained and flaked
- 1½ cups Original Bisquick® mix
- 1½ cups milk
- 1 tablespoon chopped fresh or 1 teaspoon dried basil
- ¼ teaspoon pepper
- 4 eggs

Heat oven to 400°F. Spray rectangular 13 × 9 × 2-inch baking dish with cooking spray. Sprinkle asparagus, onions, 1½ cups of the cheese and the salmon in baking dish.

In medium bowl, stir remaining ingredients except cheese until blended. Pour into baking dish.

Bake 40 to 45 minutes or until knife inserted in center comes out clean. Sprinkle with remaining 1½ cups cheese. Bake about 2 minutes or until cheese is melted. Cool 5 minutes before cutting.

1 SERVING: Calories 261; Total Fat 13g (Saturated Fat 7g, Trans Fats ½); Cholesterol 122mg; Sodium 435mg; Total Carbohydrate 16g (Dietary Fiber 1g, Sugars 3); Protein 19g; EXCHANGES: 1 Starch; 2 Vegetable; 1 High-fat Meat; 1 Lean Meat; CARBOHYDRATE CHOICES: 1

Expert Tip

Cover the assembled dish and refrigerate overnight. To serve, uncover and bake 50 to 55 minutes.

Shrimp and Artichoke Quiche

PREP TIME: *10 minutes*

TOTAL TIME: *55 minutes*

MAKES 6 SERVINGS

¾ pound frozen cooked shrimp, thawed, coarsely chopped (1½ cups)

3 medium green onions, sliced (3 tablespoons)

1 cup shredded Swiss cheese (4 ounces)

1 cup shredded Parmesan cheese (4 ounces)

1 cup Original Bisquick® mix

2 eggs

1 cup milk

1½ teaspoons Cajun seasoning

1 can (14 ounces) Progresso® artichoke hearts, drained, cut lengthwise in half

Heat oven to 400°F. Lightly spray 9-inch glass pie plate with cooking spray. Sprinkle shrimp and onions in pie plate.

In small bowl, mix cheeses. Sprinkle 1 cup of the cheese mixture over shrimp and onions. In medium bowl, stir Bisquick mix, eggs, milk and Cajun seasoning with fork or whisk until blended. Pour evenly over cheeses. Top with artichoke heart halves, cut sides down, and remaining 1 cup cheese mixture.

Bake 30 to 35 minutes or until knife inserted in center comes out clean. Let stand 10 minutes before serving.

1 SERVING: Calories 332; Total Fat 15g (Saturated Fat 8g, Trans Fat 1g); Cholesterol 215; Sodium 971mg; Total Carbohydrate 19g (Dietary Fiber 1g, Sugars 4g); Protein 29g; EXCHANGES: 1 Starch; ½ Vegetable; 2 Lean Meat; 1 Medium-High-Fat Meat; 1 High-Fat Meat; 1 Fat; CARBOHYDRATE CHOICES: 1

Easy Salmon Puff

1 cup Original Bisquick® mix

1 cup milk

½ cup sour cream

1 teaspoon dried dill weed

4 eggs

2 cans (6 ounces each) boneless skinless salmon, drained, flaked

1 cup shredded Havarti or Swiss cheese (4 ounces)

Heat oven to 375°F. Spray 9-inch glass pie plate with cooking spray. In small bowl, stir Bisquick mix, milk, sour cream, dill weed and eggs with wire whisk until blended. Gently stir in salmon and cheese. Pour into pie plate.

Bake uncovered 35 to 40 minutes or until knife inserted in center comes out clean.

1 SERVING: Calories 340; Total Fat 20g (Saturated Fat 10g, Trans Fat 1g); Cholesterol 215mg; Sodium 630mg; Total Carbohydrate 17g (Dietary Fiber 0g, Sugars 5g); Protein 22g; EXCHANGES: 1 Starch; 2½ Lean Meat; 2½ Fat; CARBOHYDRATE CHOICES: 1

Expert Tips

■ Give this rich quiche-like pie a leaner look by using fat-free (skim) milk, reduced-fat sour cream and Bisquick Heart Smart® mix. You'll save 4 grams of fat and 25 calories per serving.

■ Havarti cheese, a rich Danish cheese, comes in a variety of flavors including dill. If you like, you can use dill Havarti in this recipe and delete the dill weed.

Crab and Spinach Strata

PREP TIME: *20 minutes*
TOTAL TIME: *9 hours 25 minutes*
MAKES 8 SERVINGS

- 9 or 10 slices (½ inch thick) French bread
- ½ cup basil pesto
- 2 cups finely shredded Swiss cheese (8 ounces)
- 1 package (12 ounces) refrigerated chunk-style imitation crabmeat
- 1 box (9 ounces) Green Giant® frozen spinach, thawed, squeezed to drain
- 1 medium red bell pepper, chopped (1 cup)
- 1 medium onion, chopped (½ cup)
- 8 eggs
- 1½ cups milk
- ½ teaspoon salt

Spray 13 × 9-inch (3-quart) glass baking dish with cooking spray. Arrange bread slices in single layer in bottom of baking dish. Cut remaining bread into cubes to fill in empty spaces.

Spread pesto over bread. Sprinkle with 1 cup of the cheese. Layer crabmeat, spinach, bell pepper, onion and remaining 1 cup cheese over bread.

In large bowl, beat eggs, milk and salt until well blended. Pour over mixture in baking dish. Cover; refrigerate 8 hours or overnight.

Heat oven to 350°F. Bake uncovered 45 to 55 minutes or until set and knife inserted in center comes out clean. Let stand 10 minutes before serving.

1 SERVING: Calories 380; Total Fat 23g (Saturated Fat 9g, Trans Fat 0g); Cholesterol 255mg; Sodium 860mg; Total Carbohydrate 17g (Dietary Fiber 2g, Sugars 5g); Protein 25g; EXCHANGES: ½ Starch; ½ Other Carbohydrate; 1 Fat; CARBOHYDRATE CHOICES: 1

Expert Tips

- Serve this strata with green grapes.
- Freeze any leftover pesto in small quantities and use later in soups or sauces.

Seafood-Spinach Lasagna

PREP TIME: *40 minutes*

TOTAL TIME: *1 hour 40 minutes*

MAKES 12 SERVINGS

9 uncooked lasagna noodles

1 tablespoon butter or margarine

10 ounces bay scallops (about 1 cup), cut into bite-size pieces

1 can (6 ounces) cooked crabmeat (about 1 cup)

6 ounces cooked peeled deveined medium shrimp, tail shells removed (about 1 cup)

1 large onion, chopped (1 cup)

3 cloves garlic, finely chopped

1 container (8 ounces) cream cheese with chives and onion

1 container (10 ounces) refrigerated reduced-fat Alfredo pasta sauce

⅓ cup dry white wine or chicken broth

1 container (16 ounces) ricotta cheese

3 cups shredded Italian cheese blend (12 ounces)

1 box (9 ounces) Green Giant® frozen spinach, thawed and squeezed dry

¼ cup chopped fresh basil

1 egg, slightly beaten

Heat oven to 350°F. Spray 13 × 9-inch (3-quart) baking dish with cooking spray.

Cook and drain noodles as directed on package using minimum cook time.

Meanwhile, in 10-inch skillet, melt butter over medium heat. Add scallops; cook 2 minutes, stirring constantly until firm and opaque. With slotted spoon, remove to medium bowl. Add crabmeat and shrimp to bowl; cover and refrigerate. In same skillet, cook onion and garlic 4 to 5 minutes, stirring occasionally, until onion is softened.

Reduce heat to low; stir in cream cheese until softened. Beat in Alfredo sauce and wine with wire whisk; remove from heat.

In medium bowl, stir together ricotta cheese, 2 cups of the cheese blend, the spinach, basil and egg; set aside.

Spread ½ cup of the cream cheese sauce in baking dish. Top with 3 noodles.

Spread half the ricotta mixture (about 1½ cups) and one-third of the seafood mixture (about 1 cup) over noodles; spread with ⅔ cup of the cream cheese sauce. Top with 3 noodles, remaining ricotta mixture, half the remaining seafood mixture and ⅔ cup of the cream cheese sauce. Top with remaining noodles, seafood and cream cheese sauce.

Cover with foil. Bake 40 minutes; uncover and sprinkle with remaining 1 cup cheese blend. Bake uncovered about 10 minutes longer or until cheese is melted. Let stand 10 minutes before cutting.

1 SERVING: Calories 370; Total Fat 20g (Saturated Fat 12g, Trans Fat ½g); Cholesterol 125mg; Sodium 860mg; Total Carbohydrate 20g (Dietary Fiber 1g, Sugars 3g); Protein 26g; EXCHANGES: 1½ Starch; 3 Lean Meat; 2 Fat; CARBOHYDRATE CHOICES: 1

Cajun Lasagna

PREP TIME: *30 minutes*

TOTAL TIME: *1 hour 35 minutes*

MAKES 8 SERVINGS

- 10 uncooked lasagna noodles
- 2 cans (14.5 ounces each) diced tomatoes with green chiles, drained
- 1 bag (12 ounces) frozen cooked peeled deveined miniature/tiny shrimp (tails off), thawed, rinsed and drained
- ½ pound smoked spicy sausage (andouille or kielbasa), cut into ¼-inch slices
- 1 jar (16 ounces) Alfredo pasta sauce
- 2 cups shredded mozzarella cheese (8 ounces)
- ½ cup shredded Parmesan cheese (2 ounces)
- 2 tablespoons chopped fresh parsley, if desired

Heat oven to 350°F. Cook and drain noodles as directed on package.

Spread 1 cup of the tomatoes in ungreased 13 × 9-inch (3-quart) glass baking dish.

Top with 5 noodles, overlapping slightly as needed. Layer with half each of the remaining tomatoes, the shrimp, sausage, Alfredo sauce and mozzarella cheese.

Repeat layers. Sprinkle Parmesan cheese over top.

Cover dish with foil. Bake about 30 minutes or until center is hot and bubbly. Uncover; bake 15 to 20 minutes longer or until cheese is melted. Let stand 15 minutes before cutting. Sprinkle with parsley.

1 SERVING: Calories 510; Total Fat 29g (Saturated Fat 17g, Trans Fat 1g); Cholesterol 175mg; Sodium 1,370mg; Total Carbohydrate 31g (Dietary Fiber 3g, Sugars 6g); Protein 32g; EXCHANGES: 1½ Starch; 1 Vegetable; 2 Fat; CARBOHYDRATE CHOICES: 2

Expert Tips

- To reduce the spiciness, swap the sausage with 2 cups of cut-up cooked chicken instead.
- Save preparation time by using mini lasagna (mafalda) noodles and stirring all of the ingredients together to make an oven casserole.

Seafood Manicotti

PREP TIME: *50 minutes*

TOTAL TIME: *1 hour 20 minutes*

MAKES 4 SERVINGS

- 8 uncooked manicotti
- 1 cup whole-milk ricotta cheese
- 1 package (3 ounces) cream cheese, softened
- ¼ cup chopped green onions
- 6 ounces (about 25) frozen cooked small shrimp, thawed, tails removed and shrimp cut in half crosswise
- 1 can (6 ounces) crabmeat, drained, flaked
- 1½ cups meatless tomato pasta sauce
- 2 ounces (½ cup) shredded mozzarella cheese

Cook manicotti as directed on package. Drain; rinse with cold water to cool.

Meanwhile, heat oven to 375°F. In medium bowl, combine ricotta cheese and cream cheese; mix well. Gently stir in onions, shrimp and crabmeat.

Spread ½ cup of the pasta sauce in ungreased 11 × 7-inch (2-quart) glass baking dish. Fill each cooked manicotti with seafood mixture; place over sauce. Spoon remaining 1 cup pasta sauce over manicotti. Cover tightly with foil.

Bake 25 to 30 minutes or until bubbly. Uncover baking dish; sprinkle with mozzarella cheese. Bake uncovered an additional 5 to 8 minutes or until cheese is melted. Let stand 5 minutes before serving.

1 SERVING: Calories 494; Total Fat 21g (Saturated Fat 12g, Trans Fats 0g); Cholesterol 185mg; Sodium 1,020mg; Total Carbohydrate 46g (Dietary Fiber 2g, Sugars 10g); Protein 36g; EXCHANGES: 3 Starch; 4 Lean Meat; 2 Fat; CARBOHYDRATE CHOICES: 3

Expert Tips

- Shrimp count is the number of shrimp in 1 pound. The larger and heavier the shrimp, the fewer it takes to weigh 1 pound and, therefore, the lower the count. If you try to substitute one count for another, your recipe, which was developed by weight and volume, may not be successful.
- For the creamiest texture, use whole-milk ricotta.
- Garnish the casserole with chopped parsley.

Seafood and Asparagus Manicotti

PREP TIME: *30 minutes*

TOTAL TIME: *1 hour 10 minutes*

MAKES 6 SERVINGS

12 uncooked manicotti pasta shells (from 8-ounce package)

1 jar (26 ounces) tomato pasta sauce

¼ cup dry white wine or nonalcoholic white wine

¾ cup half-and-half

1 package (6 ounces) frozen cooked salad shrimp, thawed

6 ounces refrigerated imitation crabmeat sticks (from 12-ounce package), cut into ¼-inch pieces

1 box (9 ounces) Green Giant® frozen asparagus cuts, thawed, coarsely chopped

½ cup chopped sun-dried tomatoes in oil, drained

⅓ cup cream cheese, softened

2 cups shredded mozzarella cheese (8 ounces)

¼ cup lightly packed cut-up strips fresh basil leaves

Heat oven to 350°F. Cook and drain pasta as directed on package.

Meanwhile, in 2-quart saucepan, heat tomato sauce and wine to boiling over medium heat. Reduce heat to low; simmer 4 minutes. Remove from heat; stir in half-and-half. In ungreased 13 × 9-inch (3-quart) glass baking dish, spread 1 cup of the tomato sauce mixture.

In medium bowl, mix shrimp, crabmeat, asparagus, tomatoes, cream cheese and ½ cup of the mozzarella cheese. Spoon about ¼ cup seafood mixture into each pasta shell. Arrange in baking dish. Pour remaining tomato sauce mixture evenly over shells.

Cover dish with foil. Bake 25 to 30 minutes or until hot. Top with remaining 1½ cups mozzarella cheese. Bake uncovered 5 to 10 minutes longer or until cheese is melted. Sprinkle with basil before serving.

1 SERVING: Calories 550; Total Fat 23g (Saturated Fat 11g, Trans Fat 0g); Cholesterol 95mg; Sodium 1,290mg; Total Carbohydrate 58g (Dietary Fiber 4g, Sugars 16g); Protein 29g; EXCHANGES: 2½ Starch; 1 Other Carbohydrate; 1 Vegetable; 2½ Very Lean Meat; 4 Fat; CARBOHYDRATE CHOICES: 4

Expert Tips

■ This recipe can be assembled the night before and refrigerated. Increase first bake time to 35 minutes.

■ To cut basil into strips, stack several basil leaves, roll them up tight and slice across the vein with a sharp knife. Fluff with fingertips to separate.

Fish Sticks Marinara

PREP TIME: *10 minutes*
TOTAL TIME: *40 minutes*
MAKES 6 SERVINGS

2 boxes (9 ounces each) Green Giant® frozen broccoli spears, thawed, drained

1 tablespoon olive or vegetable oil

$\frac{1}{2}$ teaspoon dried basil leaves

1 clove garlic, chopped ($\frac{1}{2}$ teaspoon)

12 frozen breaded fish sticks

1 container (15 ounces) marinara sauce or 2 cups tomato pasta sauce (any variety)

$\frac{1}{4}$ cup shredded Parmesan cheese (1 ounce)

6 slices (1 ounce each) mozzarella cheese

Heat oven to 350°F. In ungreased 8-inch square (2-quart) glass baking dish, arrange broccoli. Drizzle with oil; sprinkle with basil and garlic.

Place fish sticks on broccoli. Spoon marinara sauce over fish. Sprinkle with Parmesan cheese. Arrange mozzarella cheese on top.

Bake uncovered about 30 minutes or until thoroughly heated.

1 SERVING: Calories 330; Total Fat 17g (Saturated Fat 6g, Trans Fat 1g); Cholesterol 30mg; Sodium 700mg; Total Carbohydrate 26g (Dietary Fiber 3g, Sugars 10g); Protein 17g; EXCHANGES: 1½ Other Carbohydrate; 1 Vegetable; 1½ Fat; CARBOHYDRATE CHOICES: 2

Expert Tips

- With no cutting and just a bit of chopping, this casserole is easy enough for the kids to prepare!

- For a fun "kid-rific" presentation, cut shapes from the mozzarella cheese with small cookie cutters. Arrange on the casserole during the last 5 minutes of baking.

Seafood Crepes

PREP TIME: *45 minutes*

TOTAL TIME: *45 minutes*

MAKES 4 SERVINGS

CREPES

- $2/3$ cup Gold Medal® all-purpose flour
- 1 cup milk
- 1 tablespoon vegetable oil
- 1 teaspoon sugar
- $1/4$ teaspoon baking powder
- $1/4$ teaspoon salt
- 1 egg

FILLING

- 2 tablespoons butter or margarine
- $1/4$ cup chopped fresh mushrooms
- 4 medium green onions, chopped ($1/4$ cup)
- $2/3$ cup small cooked shrimp
- 1 package (6 ounces) frozen cooked crabmeat, thawed, drained
- $1/2$ cup half-and-half
- 2 packages (3 ounces each) cream cheese, cubed
- 1 cup shredded Swiss cheese (4 ounces)

In medium bowl, beat all crepe ingredients with wire whisk or hand beater until smooth. For each crepe, lightly butter 7- or 8-inch skillet; heat over medium heat until bubbly. Pour slightly less than $1/4$ cup batter into skillet; rotate skillet until batter covers bottom. Cook until light brown; turn and cook other side until light brown. Stack crepes, placing waxed paper between each. Keep crepes covered to prevent them from drying out.

In 2-quart saucepan, melt butter over medium heat. Cook mushrooms and 2 tablespoons of the onions in butter, stirring occasionally, until onions are tender.

Stir in shrimp, crabmeat, half-and-half and cream cheese. Cook over medium heat, stirring constantly, until cheese is melted.

Spoon about $1/4$ cup seafood mixture down center of each crepe; roll up. Place in 11 × 7-inch (2-quart) glass baking dish. Sprinkle with Swiss cheese.

Microwave uncovered on High 4 to 6 minutes or until cheese is melted and crepes are heated through. Sprinkle with remaining 2 tablespoons onions.

1 SERVING: Calories 606; Total Fat 40g (Saturated Fat 22g, Trans Fats 1g); Cholesterol 275mg; Sodium 746mg; Total Carbohydrate 26g (Dietary Fiber 1g, Sugars 6g); Protein 37g EXCHANGES: 1 Starch; 2 Lean Meat; 1 Medium-Fat Meat; 1 High-Fat Meat; 5 Fat; CARBOHYDRATE CHOICES: 2

Expert Tips

- Freeze cooked crepes, layered between waxed paper, up to 3 months. Thaw uncovered at room temperature about 15 minutes or until soft.
- Instead of microwaving the filled crepes, they can be baked at 350°F about 15 minutes or until warm and bubbly.

Roasted Tilapia and Vegetables

½ pound fresh asparagus spears, cut in half

2 small zucchini, halved lengthwise, cut into ½-inch pieces

1 red bell pepper, cut into ½-inch strips

1 large onion, cut into ½-inch wedges, separated

2 tablespoons olive oil

2 teaspoons Montreal steak seasoning

4 tilapia fillets (about 1½ pounds)

1 tablespoon butter or margarine, melted

½ teaspoon paprika

Heat oven to 450°F. In large bowl, mix asparagus, zucchini, bell pepper, onion and oil. Sprinkle with 1 teaspoon of the steak seasoning; toss to coat. Spread vegetables in ungreased 15 × 10 × 1-inch pan. Place on lower oven rack; bake 5 minutes.

Meanwhile, spray 13 × 9-inch (3-quart) glass baking dish with cooking spray. Pat tilapia fillets dry with paper towels. Brush with butter; sprinkle with remaining 1 teaspoon steak seasoning and the paprika. Place in baking dish.

Place baking dish on middle oven rack in oven. Bake fish and vegetables 17 to 18 minutes longer or until fish flakes easily with fork and vegetables are tender.

1 SERVING: Calories 290; Total Fat 12g (Saturated Fat 3½g, Trans Fat 0g); Cholesterol 100mg; Sodium 520mg; Total Carbohydrate 11g (Dietary Fiber 3g, Sugars 5g); Protein 35g; EXCHANGES: 2 Vegetable; 4 Lean Meat; ½ Fat; CARBOHYDRATE CHOICES: 1

Expert Tip

Any firm white fish fillets can be used. Baking time will vary depending on the thickness of the fillets.

Baked Fish Packets with Chinese Parsley Paste

PREP TIME: *30 minutes*

TOTAL TIME: *30 minutes*

MAKES 4 SERVINGS

FISH

1 pound cod, flounder or red snapper fillets

½ pound daikon radish, peeled, thinly sliced

1 pound fresh asparagus spears, cut into 1-inch pieces

¼ cup dry sherry or Progresso® chicken broth (from 32-ounce carton)

½ teaspoon salt

PARSLEY PASTE

1 cup fresh cilantro leaves

1 cup fresh parsley sprigs

2 tablespoons lemon juice

1 tablespoon canola oil

½ teaspoon grated gingerroot

¼ teaspoon grated lemon peel

1 green onion, cut into 1-inch pieces

3 cloves garlic, cut in half

Dash salt, if desired

GARNISH, IF DESIRED

Pine nuts, toasted

Heat oven to 425°F. Cut fish into 4 serving pieces. Cut 4 (18 × 12-inch) sheets of heavy-duty foil. Divide radish and asparagus evenly among and on center of each sheet. Sprinkle each with 1 tablespoon of the sherry and ⅛ teaspoon of the salt. Top with fish. Bring up 2 sides of foil so edges meet. Seal edges, making tight ½-inch fold; fold again, allowing space for heat circulation and expansion. Fold other sides to seal.

Place packets on ungreased cookie sheet. Bake about 15 minutes or until fish flakes easily with fork.

Meanwhile, place all parsley paste ingredients in blender. Cover; blend on medium to high speed, stopping blender frequently to scrape sides, until smooth.

To serve, cut large × across top of each packet; carefully fold back foil to allow steam to escape. Spoon about 2 tablespoons parsley paste over each serving. Garnish with pine nuts.

1 SERVING: Calories 170; Total Fat 5g (Saturated Fat ½g, Trans Fat 0g); Cholesterol 60mg; Sodium 410mg; Total Carbohydrate 7g (Dietary Fiber 3g, Sugars 3g); Protein 24g; EXCHANGES: 1½ Vegetable; 3 Very Lean Meat; ½ Fat; CARBOHYDRATE CHOICES: ½

Expert Tips

■ To toast pine nuts, sprinkle in ungreased heavy skillet. Cook over medium heat 5 to 7 minutes, stirring frequently until nuts begin to brown, then stirring constantly until nuts are light brown.

■ Serve this flavorful fish on a bed of whole wheat pasta or brown rice.

Shrimp, Sweet Corn and New Potato Boil

6 cups water

1 teaspoon salt

1 package (3 ounces) shrimp and crab boil mixture

1 pound small red potatoes

4 medium ears sweet corn, cut in half

1 pound uncooked peeled deveined medium shrimp, thawed if frozen

3 tablespoons butter or margarine, melted

1 lemon, cut into wedges

Fresh ground pepper, if desired

Chopped fresh parsley, if desired

Cocktail sauce, if desired

Mix water, salt and bag of crab boil mixture in 4-quart Dutch oven. Cover and heat to boiling. Add potatoes and corn. Heat to boiling; reduce heat to medium. Cover and cook 10 to 15 minutes or just until potatoes are tender and corn is bright yellow.

Remove Dutch oven from heat. Add shrimp; let stand 3 to 5 minutes or until shrimp are pink and firm.

Drain potatoes, corn and shrimp; discard crab boil bag. Place corn and potatoes on serving platter; drizzle with melted butter. Arrange shrimp on platter; squeeze juice from lemon wedges over shrimp. Sprinkle with pepper and parsley; serve with cocktail sauce.

1 SERVING: Calories 408; Total Fat 13g (Saturated Fat 6g, Trans Fats 0g); Cholesterol 206mg; Sodium 418mg; Total Carbohydrate 50g (Dietary Fiber 7g, Sugars 10g); Protein 23g; EXCHANGES: 2 Starch; 1/2 Fruit; 3 Very Lean Meat; 2 Fat; CARBOHYDRATE CHOICES: 3

Expert Tips

- If crab boil package contains two bags, use both bags.

- The crab boil mixture can be found in the spice section of the supermarket. If unavailable, use a combination of 3 teaspoons crushed red pepper flakes, 6 dried bay leaves and 12 whole cloves. Place seasonings on a square of cheesecloth; bring corners up and tie with string.

- Warm breadsticks and a tossed salad or coleslaw would nicely accompany this easy meal. Top it off with a chocolate dessert.

Skillet Fish and Veggies

PREP TIME: *25 minutes*

TOTAL TIME: *25 minutes*

MAKES 4 SERVINGS

2 tablespoons butter or margarine

1 cup sliced leeks

1 cup shredded carrots (from 10-ounce bag)

1 pound cod fillets, cut into 4 serving pieces

1 can (11 ounces) Green Giant® SteamCrisp® Niblets® vacuum-packed whole kernel corn or Mexicorn® SteamCrisp® whole kernel corn with red and green bell peppers, drained

Lemon wedges, if desired

In 10-inch skillet, melt butter over medium-high heat. Cook leeks and carrots in butter 3 minutes, stirring frequently, until softened.

Mound vegetable mixture into 4 piles in skillet. Place 1 piece of fish on each mound. Pour corn over fish. Reduce heat to medium-low. Cover; cook 10 minutes or until fish flakes easily with fork. Serve with lemon wedges.

1 SERVING: Calories 200; Total Fat 7g (Saturated Fat 4g, Trans Fat 0g); Cholesterol 75mg; Sodium 550mg; Total Carbohydrate 10g (Dietary Fiber 2g, Sugars 4g); Protein 23g; EXCHANGES: ½ Starch; 3 Very Lean Meat; 1 Fat; CARBOHYDRATE CHOICES: ½

Expert Tip

Snapper, grouper or any fish with mild flavor and medium-firm to firm texture can be used instead of cod.

Potato-Crusted Salmon

PREP TIME: *10 minutes*
TOTAL TIME: *20 minutes*
MAKES 4 SERVINGS

- 1 pound wild salmon, swordfish or arctic char fillets, ¾ inch thick
- 1 egg white, slightly beaten
- 2 tablespoons water
- ⅓ cup Betty Crocker® Potato Buds® mashed potatoes (dry)
- 2 teaspoons cornstarch
- 1 teaspoon paprika
- 1 teaspoon lemon pepper seasoning
- 1 teaspoon olive or vegetable oil

Remove and discard skin from fish. Cut fish into 4 serving pieces. In one bowl, mix egg white and water with fork. In a separate bowl, mix dry potatoes, cornstarch, paprika and lemon-pepper seasoning. Dip just the top sides of fish into egg white mixture, then press into potato mixture.

In 12-inch nonstick skillet, heat oil over high heat. Cook fish, potato sides down, in oil 3 minutes. Carefully turn fish, using wide slotted spatula. Reduce heat to medium. Cook about 3 minutes longer or until fish flakes easily with fork.

1 SERVING: Calories 230; Total Fat 9g (Saturated Fat 2g, Trans Fats 0g); Cholesterol 62mg; Sodium 95mg; Total Carbohydrate 6g (Dietary Fiber 0g, Sugars ½g); Protein 22g; EXCHANGES: 3 Lean Meat; ½ Fat; CARBOHYDRATE CHOICES: 0

Expert Tips

- Salmon is familiar to most of us, but arctic char may be new to you. Arctic char is related to both trout and salmon and tastes like a combination of the two.
- Carefully turn over frying fish so that it falls in the pan away from you. This will send any hot oil away from you instead of toward you.
- Are you an herb lover? Add 2 teaspoons dried basil leaves to the potato mixture to make Basil Potato-Crusted Salmon.

Spicy Shrimp and Broccoli

PREP TIME: *20 minutes*
TOTAL TIME: *30 minutes*
MAKES 4 SERVINGS

½ cup water

¼ cup sake, rice wine or Progresso® chicken broth (from 32-ounce carton)

1 tablespoon cornstarch

2 tablespoons hoisin sauce

1 tablespoon oyster sauce

2 teaspoons soy sauce

2 teaspoons chili puree with garlic

1 tablespoon vegetable oil

12 ounces medium shrimp, peeled and deveined

1 clove garlic, finely chopped

2 teaspoons finely chopped gingerroot

1½ cups broccoli florets

1 medium bell pepper, cut into strips

4 medium green onions, cut into 1-inch pieces

⅓ cup peanuts, roasted and unsalted

4 cups hot cooked rice

Mix water, sake, cornstarch, hoisin sauce, oyster sauce, soy sauce and chili puree.

Heat wok or 12-inch skillet over high heat. Add oil; rotate wok to coat sides. Add shrimp, garlic and gingerroot; stir-fry 1 minute. Add broccoli, bell pepper and onions; stir-fry until shrimp are pink and firm.

Stir in sake mixture. Heat to boiling, stirring constantly. Boil and stir 1 minute. Sprinkle with peanuts. Serve over rice.

1 SERVING: Calories 459; Total Fat 12g (Saturated Fat 2g, Trans Fat 0g); Cholesterol 120mg; Sodium 640mg; Total Carbohydrate 58g (Dietary Fiber 4g, Sugars 4g); Protein 35g; EXCHANGES: 3 Starch; 2 Vegetable; 2 Lean Meat; 2 Fat; CARBOHYDRATE CHOICES: 4

Expert Tips

■ A hot 'n spicy sauce, chili puree is made from chiles, soybeans, salt, oil and garlic. It is used both as a seasoning and a condiment.

■ Shrimp are generally sold by number or "count" per pound, and that can be confusing because counts vary among suppliers and markets. Don't hesitate to ask your grocery store for clarification.

Fire-Roasted Shrimp Veracruz

PREP TIME: *15 minutes*
TOTAL TIME: *15 minutes*
MAKES 4 SERVINGS

1 tablespoon olive or vegetable oil

1 pound uncooked peeled deveined medium shrimp, thawed if frozen, tail shells removed

1/4 cup sliced green onions (4 medium)

1 fresh jalapeño or serrano chile, seeded, finely chopped

1 teaspoon grated orange peel

1 teaspoon chopped fresh thyme leaves or 1/2 teaspoon dried thyme leaves

1 can (14.5 ounces) Muir Glen® organic fire roasted diced tomatoes, undrained

In 12-inch skillet, heat oil over medium-high heat. Add shrimp, onions, chile, orange peel and thyme; cook 1 minute, stirring frequently.

Stir in tomatoes. Heat to boiling. Reduce heat; simmer uncovered about 5 minutes, stirring occasionally, until shrimp are pink and sauce is slightly thickened.

1 SERVING: Calories 140; Total Fat 4 1/2 g (Saturated Fat 1/2 g, Trans Fat 0g); Cholesterol 160mg; Sodium 320mg; Total Carbohydrate 6g (Dietary Fiber 1g, Sugars 3g); Protein 18g; EXCHANGES: 1 Vegetable; 2 1/2 Very Lean Meat; 1/2 Fat; CARBOHYDRATE CHOICES: 1/2

Expert Tip

Serve this saucy shrimp mixture over rice or couscous, or with crusty French bread. Add a tossed salad to complete the meal.

Sesame–Ginger Shrimp and Vegetable Stir-Fry

PREP TIME: *20 minutes*
TOTAL TIME: *20 minutes*
MAKES 4 SERVINGS

2 cups uncooked instant rice

2 cups water

1 tablespoon vegetable oil

1 package (16 ounces) fresh stir-fry vegetables, cut into bite-size pieces (4 cups)

12 ounces uncooked peeled deveined medium shrimp, tails removed

½ cup sesame-ginger stir-fry seasoning sauce (from 12-ounce bottle)

Cook rice in water as directed on package.

Meanwhile, heat oil in 12-inch nonstick skillet or wok over medium-high heat until hot. Add vegetables; cook and stir 3 minutes. Add shrimp; cook and stir an additional 3 to 4 minutes or until shrimp turn pink and vegetables are crisp-tender.

Add seasoning sauce to shrimp and vegetables. Cook and stir 1 to 2 minutes or until thoroughly heated. Serve over rice.

1 SERVING: Calories 386; Total Fat 8g (Saturated Fat 1g, Trans Fats 0g); Cholesterol 129mg; Sodium 2,432mg; Total Carbohydrate 46g (Dietary Fiber 1g, Sugars 5g); Protein 22g; EXCHANGES: 2½ Starch; 1 Vegetable; 1 Very Lean Meat; 1½ Fat; CARBOHYDRATE CHOICES: 3

Expert Tips

■ Look for sesame-ginger stir-fry seasoning sauce in the grocery store's Asian foods or sauces and marinades section. Brands vary by sweetness and spice level.

■ Look for precut stir-fry vegetables in the grocery store's produce department.

■ Use your favorite vegetables in place of prepared stir-fry vegetables. Try bean sprouts and shredded napa cabbage with bite-size pieces of green onion, broccoli, carrots, mushrooms and pea pods; measure 4 cups. Or swing by the salad bar and choose 4 cups of cut vegetables.

Sweet-and-Sour Shrimp

PREP TIME: *30 minutes*

TOTAL TIME: *30 minutes*

MAKES 4 SERVINGS

1 cup uncooked converted white rice

3 cups water

2 cups fresh broccoli florets

1 small red bell pepper, cut into 1/4 x 2-inch strips

1 egg white

1 tablespoon water

1 cup Original Bisquick® mix

1 tablespoon cornstarch

1 teaspoon paprika

1/2 teaspoon ground red pepper (cayenne)

1/2 teaspoon salt

1 pound uncooked peeled deveined medium shrimp, thawed if frozen, tail shells removed

4 tablespoons vegetable oil

1/2 cup sliced almonds, toasted

1 cup sweet-and-sour sauce (from 10-ounce jar), warmed

Cook rice in 2 1/2 cups of the water according to package directions.

Meanwhile, in 12-inch nonstick skillet or wok, heat 1/4 cup of the water over medium-high heat. Add broccoli; cook about 3 minutes, stirring frequently, until water evaporates. Add bell pepper and remaining 1/4 cup water; cook 3 minutes longer, stirring frequently, until vegetables are crisp-tender. Remove vegetables to bowl; cover to keep warm.

In small bowl, beat egg white and 1 tablespoon water with whisk. In large resealable food-storage plastic bag, place Bisquick mix, cornstarch, paprika, red pepper and salt. Working in 2 batches, dip shrimp in egg white mixture; remove with slotted spoon and place in bag. Shake bag to coat shrimp with Bisquick mixture.

Wipe same skillet with paper towel. In skillet, heat 2 tablespoons of the oil over medium heat. Cook half of the shrimp in oil 2 minutes on each side or until pink. Drain on paper towels. Wipe skillet again. Repeat with remaining oil and shrimp.

Return vegetables to skillet; cook and stir until heated. Add shrimp; gently toss to combine.

Serve shrimp mixture over cooked rice; top with almonds and sweet-and-sour sauce.

1 SERVING: Calories 710; Total Fat 25g (Saturated Fat 4g, Trans Fat 1g); Cholesterol 160mg; Sodium 1,140mg; Total Carbohydrate 93g (Dietary Fiber 5g, Sugars 27g); Protein 28g; EXCHANGES: 4 1/2 Starch; 1 1/2 Other Carbohydrate; 1 Vegetable; 2 Lean Meat; 3 Fat; CARBOHYDRATE CHOICES: 6

Expert Tips

■ For a spicier dish, add chopped jalapeño chile, seeded if desired, with the vegetables.

■ To toast almonds, sprinkle in ungreased heavy skillet. Cook over medium heat 5 to 7 minutes, stirring frequently until nuts begin to brown, then stirring constantly until nuts are light brown.

■ To pack in more nutrition and whole grains, try using instant brown rice instead of white rice. Cook according to package directions.

Thai Seared Shrimp with Tomato, Basil and Coconut

PREP TIME: *15 minutes*
TOTAL TIME: *25 minutes*
MAKES 4 SERVINGS

- 1 tablespoon peanut or vegetable oil
- 1 pound uncooked peeled deveined medium shrimp, thawed if frozen, tail shells removed
- 1 cup sliced red onion
- 1 to 2 teaspoons green or red Thai curry paste
- 1 can (14.5 ounces) Muir Glen® organic diced or fire roasted diced tomatoes, drained
- 1 tablespoon lime juice
- 2 teaspoons packed brown sugar
- ½ cup coconut milk (not cream of coconut)
- ¼ cup chopped fresh Thai basil or basil
- Hot cooked rice, if desired

In 10-inch skillet, heat oil over medium-high heat. Cook shrimp and onion in oil 2 minutes, stirring constantly. Stir in curry paste; cook 1 minute.

Stir in tomatoes, lime juice and brown sugar. Heat to boiling. Reduce heat; simmer 1 minute. Stir in coconut milk and basil. Heat over low heat until hot.

Serve over rice.

1 SERVING: Calories 200; Total Fat 9g (Saturated Fat 5g, Trans Fat 0g); Cholesterol 160mg; Sodium 310mg; Total Carbohydrate 11g (Dietary Fiber 2g, Sugars 7g); Protein 19g; EXCHANGES: ½ Other Carbohydrate; 1 Vegetable; 2½ Very Lean Meat; 1½ Fat; CARBOHYDRATE CHOICES: 1

Expert Tip

Add an authentic Thai flavor with a drizzle of *nam pla*, a pungent Asian fish sauce. Look for it, along with the curry paste, at Asian grocery stores.

Mediterranean Shrimp with Bulgur

PREP TIME: *25 minutes*
TOTAL TIME: *25 minutes*
MAKES 6 SERVINGS

2 cups water

1 cup uncooked bulgur wheat

2 teaspoons olive oil

1 medium onion, chopped (½ cup)

¼ cup dry white wine or nonalcoholic wine

2 cans (14.5 ounces each) diced tomatoes with basil, oregano and garlic, undrained

3 tablespoons chopped fresh parsley

1 tablespoon capers, drained

¼ teaspoon freshly ground black pepper

⅛ teaspoon crushed red pepper flakes

1 pound uncooked peeled deveined small shrimp (30 to 40 count)

½ cup crumbled reduced-fat feta cheese (2 ounces)

In 2-quart saucepan, heat water to boiling. Add bulgur; reduce heat to low. Cover; simmer about 12 minutes or until water is absorbed.

Meanwhile, in 12-inch skillet, heat oil over medium heat. Add onion; cook about 4 minutes, stirring occasionally, until tender. Stir in wine; cook 1 minute, stirring frequently.

Stir tomatoes, 1½ tablespoons of the parsley, the capers, black pepper and red pepper flakes into onion. Cook 3 minutes. Stir in shrimp. Cover; cook 4 to 5 minutes or until shrimp are pink.

Stir cooked bulgur into shrimp mixture. Sprinkle with cheese. Cover; cook 2 minutes. Sprinkle with remaining 1½ tablespoons parsley.

1 SERVING: Calories 210; Total Fat 4g (Saturated Fat 1½g, Trans Fat 0g); Cholesterol 110mg; Sodium 480mg; Total Carbohydrate 25g (Dietary Fiber 6g, Sugars 4g); Protein 18g; EXCHANGES: 1 Starch; 1 Vegetable; 2 Very Lean Meat; ½ Fat; CARBOHYDRATE CHOICES: 1½

Expert Tip

If you cannot find diced tomatoes with basil, oregano and garlic, use plain diced tomatoes and add 1 teaspoon each of finely chopped fresh garlic, dried oregano and dried basil.

Champagne Shrimp Risotto

2 tablespoons butter or margarine

1 medium onion, thinly sliced

1 pound uncooked peeled deveined medium shrimp, thawed if frozen

$\frac{1}{2}$ cup brut champagne, dry white wine or Progresso® chicken broth

1$\frac{1}{2}$ cups uncooked Arborio or other short-grain white rice

2 cups Progresso® chicken broth (from 32-ounce carton), warmed

1 cup clam juice or water, warmed

2 cups chopped arugula, watercress or spinach

$\frac{1}{3}$ cup grated Parmesan cheese

$\frac{1}{2}$ teaspoon ground pepper

Chopped fresh parsley, if desired

In 12-inch skillet or 4-quart Dutch oven, melt butter over medium-high heat. Add onion; cook, stirring frequently, until tender. Reduce heat to medium. Add shrimp; cook uncovered about 8 minutes, turning once, until shrimp are pink. Remove shrimp from skillet; keep warm.

Add champagne to onion in skillet; cook until liquid has evaporated. Stir in rice. Cook uncovered over medium heat about 5 minutes, stirring frequently, until edges of rice kernels are translucent.

In 4-cup glass measuring cup, mix chicken broth and clam juice; pour $\frac{1}{2}$ cup of the mixture over rice. Cook uncovered, stirring occasionally, until liquid is absorbed. Repeat with remaining broth mixture, $\frac{1}{2}$ cup at a time, until rice is tender and creamy.

About 5 minutes before risotto is done, stir in shrimp, arugula, cheese and pepper. Sprinkle with parsley before serving.

1 SERVING: Calories 320; Total Fat 6g (Saturated Fat 3$\frac{1}{2}$g, Trans Fat 0g); Cholesterol 125mg; Sodium 610mg; Total Carbohydrate 43g (Dietary Fiber 1g, Sugars 1g); Protein 19g; EXCHANGES: 2$\frac{1}{2}$ Starch; 1 Vegetable; 1$\frac{1}{2}$ Lean Meat; CARBOHYDRATE CHOICES: 3

Expert Tips

- Even though you may be tempted, don't rush the process! When making risotto, adding the broth a little at a time ensures that the dish will be creamy while allowing the grains to remain separate.

- Leave out the shrimp and serve this as a lovely main course for your vegetarian friends.

Slow Cooker Thai Chicken and Shrimp

1 package (1 pound 4 ounces) bone-in skinless chicken thighs

1 can (14 ounces) coconut milk (not cream of coconut)

1 package (3.5 ounces) Thai peanut sauce mix (2 envelopes)

2 medium carrots, sliced (1 cup)

1 medium onion, chopped ($\frac{1}{2}$ cup)

3 cups water

3 cups uncooked instant rice

1 pound uncooked peeled deveined medium shrimp, thawed if frozen and tails removed

1 cup Green Giant® frozen sweet peas (from 1-pound bag)

1 tablespoon cornstarch

$\frac{1}{3}$ cup chopped peanuts, if desired

3 tablespoons chopped fresh cilantro, if desired

Place chicken in $3\frac{1}{2}$- to 4-quart slow cooker. Add coconut milk. Stir in both envelopes of sauce mix, the carrots and onion. Cover and cook on Low heat setting 8 to 10 hours.

About 30 minutes before serving, heat water to boiling in 2-quart saucepan over high heat. Remove from heat and stir in rice. Cover and let stand about 5 minutes or until water is absorbed. Fluff rice with fork before serving.

Remove chicken from cooker; keep warm. Add shrimp and peas to cooker.

Increase heat setting to High. Mix $\frac{1}{4}$ cup sauce from cooker and the cornstarch in small bowl; stir into mixture in cooker. Cover and cook 5 to 10 minutes, stirring frequently, until shrimp are pink and firm and sauce has thickened slightly.

Meanwhile, remove chicken from bones; coarsely chop chicken and return to cooker. Serve chicken mixture over rice. Garnish with peanuts and cilantro.

1 SERVING: Calories 566; Total Fat 21g (Saturated Fat 15g, Trans Fat 0g); Cholesterol 193mg; Sodium 359mg; Total Carbohydrate 52g (Dietary Fiber 3g, Sugars 5g); Protein 41g; EXCHANGES: 3 Starch; 4 Lean Meat; 3 Fat; 1 Vegetable; CARBOHYDRATE CHOICES: $3\frac{1}{2}$

Expert Tips

■ If you're not a shrimp lover, just omit it for a tasty Thai Chicken.

■ Look for Thai peanut sauce mix in the ethnic foods section of your grocery store.

■ Bone-in chicken is used because the bones help keep the chicken from shredding during the long cooking time.

■ Reduced-fat ("lite") coconut milk can be used in place of the regular coconut milk.

■ For a change of pace, serve over cooked jasmine rice.

Slow Cooker Jambalaya

PREP TIME: *15 minutes*
TOTAL TIME: *8 hours 15 minutes*
MAKES 8 SERVINGS

1 large onion, chopped (1 cup)

1 medium green bell pepper, chopped (1 cup)

2 medium stalks celery, chopped (1 cup)

3 cloves garlic, finely chopped

1 can (28 ounces) Muir Glen® organic diced tomatoes, undrained

2 cups chopped fully cooked smoked sausage

1 tablespoon parsley flakes

$\frac{1}{2}$ teaspoon dried thyme

$\frac{1}{2}$ teaspoon salt

$\frac{1}{4}$ teaspoon pepper

$\frac{1}{4}$ teaspoon red pepper sauce

$\frac{3}{4}$ pound uncooked peeled deveined medium shrimp, thawed if frozen

4 cups hot cooked rice

In $3\frac{1}{2}$- to 6-quart slow cooker, mix all ingredients except shrimp and rice.

Cover; cook on Low heat setting 7 to 8 hours (or High heat setting 3 to 4 hours).

Stir in shrimp. If needed, reduce heat setting to Low; cover and cook on Low heat setting about 1 hour longer or until shrimp are pink and firm. Serve jambalaya with rice.

Note: This recipe was tested in slow cookers with heating elements in the side and bottom of the cooker, not in cookers that stand only on a heated base. For slow cookers with just a heated base, follow the manufacturer's directions for layering ingredients and choosing a temperature.

1 SERVING: Calories 287; Total Fat 9g (Saturated Fat 3g, Trans Fats 0g); Cholesterol 89mg; Sodium 793mg; Total Carbohydrate 30g (Dietary Fiber 2g, Sugars 4g); Protein 12g; EXCHANGES: 1 Starch; 1½ Lean Meat; 1 High-Fat Meat; CARBOHYDRATE CHOICES: 2

Expert Tips

- Heat up this Cajun favorite by sprinkling with more red pepper sauce just before serving. If you want to use fresh parsley and thyme, add them with the shrimp so the flavor isn't lost during the long cooking.

- Spicy and smoky, andouille sausage is traditionally used for this dish. If you're in a more mellow mode, leftover ham works just as well.

- To serve, spray the inside of a $\frac{1}{2}$-cup measuring cup with cooking spray. For each serving, press the hot rice into the cup. Place the cup upside down in the bottom of a bowl and unmold the rice. Spoon the jambalaya around the mound of rice. Serve with warm crusty French bread.

Slow Cooker Cioppino

- 2 large onions, chopped (2 cups)
- 2 medium stalks celery, finely chopped (about 1 cup)
- 5 cloves garlic, finely chopped (about 2½ teaspoons)
- 1 can (28 ounces) diced tomatoes, undrained
- 1 bottle (8 ounces) clam juice
- 1 can (6 ounces) tomato paste
- ½ cup dry white wine or water
- 1 tablespoon red wine vinegar
- 1 tablespoon olive or vegetable oil
- 2½ teaspoons Italian seasoning
- ¼ teaspoon sugar
- ¼ teaspoon crushed red pepper flakes
- 1 dried bay leaf
- 1 pound firm-textured white fish, cut into 1-inch pieces
- ¾ pound uncooked peeled deveined medium shrimp
- 1 can (6½ ounces) chopped clams with juice, undrained
- 1 can (6 ounces) crabmeat, drained
- ¼ cup chopped fresh parsley

In 5- to 6-quart slow cooker, mix all ingredients except fish, shrimp, clams, crabmeat and parsley.

Cover. Cook on High heat setting 3 to 4 hours.

Stir in fish, shrimp, clams and crabmeat. Reduce heat setting to Low. Cover; cook 30 to 45 minutes longer or until fish flakes easily with fork. Remove bay leaf. Stir in parsley.

1 SERVING: Calories 210; Total Fat 3½g (Saturated Fat ½g, Trans Fat 0g); Cholesterol 120mg; Sodium 570mg; Total Carbohydrate 14g (Dietary Fiber 3g, Sugars 7g); Protein 28g; EXCHANGES: 1 Starch; 3½ Very Lean Meat; CARBOHYDRATE CHOICES: 1

Expert Tip

Be sure to serve plenty of hearty bread with this fish stew so everyone can soak up every last drop of the wonderful broth in the bottom of the bowl.

New Orleans "Best" Gumbo

PREP TIME: *1 hour*
TOTAL TIME: *3 hours 10 minutes*
MAKES 15 SERVINGS

6 cups water

1 package (1 pound) chicken gizzards, chopped

2 tablespoons seasoned salt

2 teaspoons parsley flakes

1 tablespoon garlic powder

1 tablespoon onion powder

1 teaspoon dried thyme

1 teaspoon black pepper

1 teaspoon paprika

Dash of ground red pepper (cayenne)

1 large green bell pepper, chopped (1½ cups)

1 large onion, chopped (1 cup)

5 cloves garlic, finely chopped

2 pounds uncooked turkey or beef sausage links, cut into 1-inch slices

½ cup vegetable oil

1 cup Gold Medal® all-purpose flour

4 cups hot water

1 bag (1 pound) frozen chopped okra

1 package (6 ounces) frozen ready-to-serve crabmeat, thawed and drained

2 pounds uncooked peeled deveined shrimp

1 can (8 ounces) regular or smoked oysters, drained

Hot cooked rice, if desired

In 8-quart pot, heat 6 cups water to boiling. Add gizzards, seasoned salt, parsley, garlic powder, onion powder, thyme, black pepper, paprika, red pepper, bell pepper, onion and garlic. Heat to boiling; reduce heat. Simmer uncovered 1 hour, stirring occasionally. Stir in sausage. Cover and simmer 1 hour, stirring occasionally.

Meanwhile, in heavy 2-quart saucepan, heat oil over high heat. Stir in flour; reduce heat to medium. Cook 15 to 20 minutes, stirring constantly, until mixture is dark brown; remove from heat.

Stir flour mixture into gizzard mixture until blended. Stir in 4 cups hot water, 1 cup at a time, stirring constantly. Stir in okra, crabmeat, shrimp and oysters. Heat to boiling; reduce heat to low. Simmer uncovered 5 to 10 minutes or until shrimp are pink and firm. Serve over rice.

1 SERVING: Calories 318; Total Fat 16g (Saturated Fat 1½g, Trans Fat 0g); Cholesterol 203mg; Sodium 1,181mg; Total Carbohydrate 13g (Dietary Fiber 1g, Sugars 2g); Protein 31g; EXCHANGES: ½ Starch; 1 Vegetable; 2½ Lean Meat; 2 Fat; CARBOHYDRATE CHOICES: 1

Expert Tip

Gumbo is the African name for "okra." One of the three important ingredients (along with onions and bell peppers) in gumbo, okra is used to thicken and flavor many southern dishes.

Italian Seafood Stew with Garlic–Herb Croutons

PREP TIME: *1 hour*

TOTAL TIME: *1 hour 30 minutes*

MAKES 8 SERVINGS

12 fresh clams in shells

2 tablespoons white vinegar

12 fresh mussels in shells

2 bottles (8 ounces each) clam juice

2 cans (14.5 ounces each) diced tomatoes, undrained

2 cans (15 ounces each) tomato sauce

1 cup dry white wine or water

1 container (7 ounces) refrigerated pesto

1 pound cod fillets, cut into bite-size pieces

1/2 pound uncooked peeled deveined medium shrimp (about 16), thawed if frozen, tail shells removed

1/2 pound uncooked sea scallops (about 16), thawed if frozen

3 tablespoons butter or margarine, softened

16 slices (1/2 inch thick) French bread

Discard any broken-shell or open (dead) clams. Place remaining clams in large container. Cover with 1½ cups water and the vinegar. Let stand 30 minutes; drain. Scrub clams in cold water.

Meanwhile, discard any broken-shell or open (dead) mussels. Scrub remaining mussels in cold water, removing any barnacles with a dull paring knife. Pull beard by giving it a tug (using a kitchen towel may help). If you have trouble removing it, use a pliers to grip and pull gently. Place mussels in large container. Cover with cool water. Agitate water with hand, then drain and discard water. Repeat several times until water runs clear; drain.

Heat oven to 350°F. In 4-quart Dutch oven, mix clam juice, tomatoes, tomato sauce, wine and 1/2 cup of the pesto. Layer cod, shrimp, scallops, mussels and clams in Dutch oven. Heat to boiling over medium-high heat; reduce heat. Cover and simmer 15 to 20 minutes or until mussel and clam shells have opened.

Meanwhile, in small bowl, mix butter and remaining pesto until well blended. Spread on both sides of bread. On ungreased cookie sheet, place bread in single layer. Bake 10 to 15 minutes, turning once, until toasted on both sides.

Discard any mussels or clams that don't open. Spoon stew into soup bowls; top with croutons.

1 SERVING: Calories 450; Total Fat 21g (Saturated Fat 5g, Trans Fat 1/2g); Cholesterol 110mg; Sodium 1,590mg; Total Carbohydrate 33g (Dietary Fiber 4g, Sugars 7g); Protein 32g; EXCHANGES: 2 Starch; 1 Vegetable; 3½ Very Lean Meat; 3½ Fat; CARBOHYDRATE CHOICES: 2

Expert Tips

■ Double up on frozen seafood and fish if fresh is hard to come by.

■ Have all the ingredients assembled on a tray or cookie sheet in your refrigerator so you can whip this up in minutes on Christmas Eve.

Catfish Stew in Biscuit Bowls

1 can (16.3 ounces) Pillsbury® Grands!® Flaky Layers refrigerated original or buttermilk biscuits

2 slices bacon

½ cup chopped onion (1 medium)

1 bag (12 ounces) Green Giant® Valley Fresh Steamers™ frozen mixed vegetables

1 jar (2.5 ounces) Green Giant® sliced mushrooms, drained

½ cup milk

1 can (10¾ ounces) condensed cream of celery soup

½ teaspoon garlic powder

¼ teaspoon dried thyme

¼ teaspoon pepper

¼ teaspoon hot pepper sauce

1 pound catfish or other white fish fillets, cut into 1-inch pieces

Heat oven to 350°F. On ungreased large cookie sheet, turn 8 (6-ounce) custard cups upside down; spray outsides of cups with cooking spray. Separate dough into 8 biscuits; press each to form 6-inch circle. Press each biscuit over bottom and around side of each cup. Using fingers, press dough around each cup, forming bowl.

Bake 15 to 18 minutes or until golden brown. Carefully remove custard cups. Set aside.

Meanwhile, in 3-quart saucepan, cook bacon until crisp; drain on paper towel. Crumble bacon; set aside. Reserve 1 tablespoon drippings in saucepan.

Cook onion in drippings 2 to 3 minutes, stirring occasionally, until tender. Stir in all remaining ingredients except catfish and cooked bacon. Heat to boiling.

Reduce heat to medium; stir in catfish. Cook uncovered, about 10 minutes, stirring occasionally, until fish flakes easily with fork. Spoon stew into biscuit bowls. Garnish with crumbled bacon.

1 SERVING: Calories 370; Total Fat 16g (Saturated Fat 3½g, Trans Fat 3½g); Cholesterol 45mg; Sodium 970mg; Total Carbohydrate 37g (Dietary Fiber 3g, Sugars 9g); Protein 19g; EXCHANGES: 1½ Starch; ½ Other Carbohydrate; 1 Vegetable; 1 Fat; CARBOHYDRATE CHOICES: 2½

Potato–Clam Chowder

PREP TIME: *10 minutes*

TOTAL TIME: *50 minutes*

MAKES 4 SERVINGS

4 cups hot water

1 box (4.7 ounces) Betty Crocker® au gratin potatoes

½ teaspoon salt, if desired

1 cup Green Giant® Valley Fresh Steamers™ Niblets® frozen corn

1 cup Green Giant® Select® frozen broccoli florets

3 cups milk

1 small onion, chopped (¼ cup)

2 cans (6½ ounces each) minced clams, undrained

Heat water, potatoes and salt to boiling in 3-quart saucepan. Boil 20 minutes; drain.

Stir in sauce mix from box and remaining ingredients. Heat to boiling over medium-high heat, stirring occasionally.

Reduce heat; simmer uncovered about 10 minutes, stirring occasionally, until potatoes are tender.

1 SERVING: Calories 360; Total Fat 5g (Saturated Fat 2½g, Trans Fat 0g); Cholesterol 60mg; Sodium 900mg; Total Carbohydrate 50g (Dietary Fiber 3g, Sugars 11g); Protein 28g; EXCHANGES: 2½ Starch; ½ Low-Fat Milk; 1 Vegetable; 2 Very Lean Meat; CARBOHYDRATE CHOICES: 3

Expert Tips

■ From clam to ham—use 1 cup chopped fully cooked ham in place of the canned clams.

■ Bags of frozen diced onions are available with the other vegetables in the freezer case. No more tears!

Fire-Roasted Tomato-Basil Crab Bisque

PREP TIME: *30 minutes*
TOTAL TIME: *1 hour*
MAKES 6 SERVINGS

- 1 can (14.5 ounces) Muir Glen® organic fire roasted crushed or diced tomatoes, undrained
- 2 cups organic chicken broth
- ½ cup finely chopped celery
- ¼ cup finely sliced green onions (white part only)
- 6 tablespoons unsalted butter
- 2 tablespoons Gold Medal® all-purpose flour
- 2½ cups half-and-half
- ¼ cup dry white wine
- ½ teaspoon salt
- ¼ teaspoon pepper
- ¾ pound fresh lump crabmeat or 2 packages (6 ounces each) pasteurized refrigerated lump crabmeat
- 2 tablespoons chopped fresh basil

In 2-quart saucepan, combine tomatoes, broth, celery and onions. Cook over medium-high heat 10 to 12 minutes, stirring occasionally, until celery is softened.

In 4-quart saucepan, melt butter over low heat. Using wire whisk, stir flour into butter. Cook 1 minute, stirring constantly. Slowly add half-and-half, stirring constantly. Stir in tomato mixture, 1 cup at a time.

Stir in wine, salt and pepper. Bring to a boil over medium-high heat. Reduce heat to low; stir in crabmeat and basil. Cover and simmer 30 minutes, stirring occasionally.

1 SERVING: Calories 330; Total Fat 24g (Saturated Fat 15g, Trans Fat 1g); Cholesterol 120mg; Sodium 940mg; Total Carbohydrate 10g (Dietary Fiber 1g, Sugars 7g); Protein 17g; EXCHANGES: ½ Other Carbohydrate; 2½ Lean Meat; 3½ Fat; CARBOHYDRATE CHOICES: ½

Pasta

Italian Meatball Pie

1 package (9 ounces) refrigerated fettuccine

1 egg

1 tablespoon butter or margarine, melted

1½ cups shredded Italian-style cheese blend (6 ounces)

1¼ cups spaghetti sauce

1 package (16 ounces) frozen Italian-style or regular meatballs, 1 inch in diameter (32 meatballs), thawed

1 medium bell pepper, cut into thin strips

Chopped fresh parsley, if desired

Heat oven to 350°F. Spray pie plate, 9 × 1¼ inches, with cooking spray. Cook and drain fettuccine as directed on package.

Beat egg and butter in large bowl with fork or wire whisk. Stir in fettuccine and 1 cup of the cheese. Spoon mixture into pie plate; press evenly on bottom and up side of pie plate using back of wooden spoon or rubber spatula.

Toss spaghetti sauce, meatballs and bell pepper in large bowl. Spoon meatball mixture into fettuccine crust.

Cover with foil and bake 45 minutes. Sprinkle with remaining ½ cup cheese. Bake uncovered about 5 minutes longer or until cheese is melted. Sprinkle with parsley.

1 SERVING: Calories 443; Total Fat 19g (Saturated Fat 9g, Trans Fat 0g); Cholesterol 109mg; Sodium 776mg; Total Carbohydrate 41g (Dietary Fiber 3g, Sugars 6g); Protein 27g; EXCHANGES: 1½ Starch; 1 Fat; CARBOHYDRATE CHOICES: 2½

Expert Tips

■ What used to be called "spaghetti sauce" is now most often called "marinara sauce" because its uses stretch far beyond spaghetti. Either sauce will work, and the flavor choices are endless!

■ The pie is covered with foil to keep the edge of the crust moist, not dry and chewy.

Italian Fettuccine Pie

½ pound lean (at least 80%) ground beef

1 small onion, finely chopped (¼ cup)

1 can (8 ounces) stewed tomatoes, undrained

1 can (8 ounces) tomato sauce

½ teaspoon Italian seasoning

6 ounces uncooked fettuccine

2 eggs

1 tablespoon butter or margarine, melted

1 cup shredded mozzarella cheese (4 ounces)

1 cup small-curd cottage cheese

1 cup Green Giant® Valley Fresh Steamers™ frozen chopped broccoli, thawed, or chopped fresh broccoli

¼ cup grated Parmesan cheese

Heat oven to 350°F. In 10-inch skillet, cook beef and onion over medium heat, stirring occasionally, until beef is brown; drain. Stir in tomatoes, tomato sauce and Italian seasoning. Heat to boiling, stirring occasionally. Reduce heat. Cover; simmer 10 minutes, stirring occasionally.

Meanwhile, cook and drain fettuccine as directed on package.

In medium bowl, beat one of the eggs and the butter. Stir in fettuccine and mozzarella cheese. In ungreased 9-inch quiche dish or pie plate, spoon and press mixture evenly in bottom and up side of dish.

In small bowl, mix cottage cheese and remaining egg; spread over fettuccine mixture in dish. Sprinkle with broccoli. Spoon beef mixture evenly over top.

Sprinkle with Parmesan cheese.

Bake uncovered about 30 minutes or until hot in center. Let stand 10 minutes before cutting.

1 SERVING: Calories 350; Total Fat 15g (Saturated Fat 7g, Trans Fat ½g); Cholesterol 140mg; Sodium 800mg; Total Carbohydrate 28g (Dietary Fiber 2g, Sugars 6g); Protein 25g; EXCHANGES: 1 Starch; ½ Other Carbohydrate; 1 Vegetable; CARBOHYDRATE CHOICES: 2

Expert Tips

■ An easy way to form the pasta shell is to spoon the fettuccine mixture into the pie plate and then press firmly with another pie plate.

■ Wrap unbaked pie tightly and label. Freeze no longer than 1 month. About 2 hours 15 minutes before serving, heat oven to 400°F. Unwrap pie and re-cover with foil. Bake about 2 hours or until hot in center. Let stand 10 minutes before cutting.

Cheesy Rigatoni with Eggplant Sauce

PREP TIME: *20 minutes*
TOTAL TIME: *50 minutes*
MAKES 4 SERVINGS

2½ cups uncooked rigatoni pasta (7 ounces)

2 tablespoons olive oil

1 medium onion, chopped (½ cup)

1 small unpeeled eggplant, cut into ½-inch cubes (3 cups)

1 medium zucchini, halved lengthwise, cut into ¼-inch slices (1½ cups)

1 can (14.5 ounces) diced tomatoes with basil, garlic and oregano, undrained

1 can (8 ounces) Muir Glen® organic tomato sauce

1½ cups shredded mozzarella cheese (6 ounces)

Heat oven to 350°F. Spray 12 × 8-inch (2-quart) glass baking dish with cooking spray. Cook and drain pasta as directed on package, using minimum cook time.

Meanwhile, in 12-inch nonstick skillet, heat oil over medium-high heat. Cook onion, eggplant and zucchini in oil 5 to 7 minutes, stirring frequently, until crisp-tender. Stir in tomatoes and tomato sauce.

Spoon cooked pasta into baking dish. Spoon vegetable sauce over pasta.

Cover tightly with foil; bake 20 minutes. Uncover; sprinkle with cheese. Bake uncovered 5 to 7 minutes longer or until cheese is melted.

1 SERVING: Calories 540; Total Fat 17g (Saturated Fat 6g, Trans Fat 0g); Cholesterol 25mg; Sodium 1,000mg; Total Carbohydrate 71g (Dietary Fiber 8g, Sugars 11g); Protein 25g; EXCHANGES: 4 Starch; 2 Vegetable; 2 Fat; CARBOHYDRATE CHOICES: 5

Expert Tip

Put this together the night before. Then, bake it the next night for dinner. Since it will be cold, bake it about 10 minutes longer before topping with the cheese.

Overnight Rotini Bake

PREP TIME: *20 minutes*

TOTAL TIME: *9 hours 15 minutes*

MAKES 8 SERVINGS

1½ pounds 90% lean ground beef

1 large onion, chopped (1 cup)

1 large bell pepper, chopped (1 cup)

2 large cloves garlic, finely chopped

1 can (28 ounces) crushed tomatoes, undrained

2 cups hot water

1 envelope (1 ounce) onion soup mix (from 2-ounce package)

1 teaspoon Italian seasoning

3 cups uncooked rotini or fusilli (corkscrew) pasta (9 ounces)

1½ cups shredded Italian cheese blend or mozzarella cheese (6 ounces)

Spray rectangular baking dish, 13 × 9 × 2 inches, with cooking spray.

Cook beef, onion, bell pepper and garlic in 4-quart Dutch oven over medium-high heat, stirring occasionally, until beef is brown; drain. Stir in tomatoes, water, soup mix (dry), Italian seasoning and pasta. Spoon into baking dish.

Cover tightly with foil and refrigerate at least 8 hours but no longer than 24 hours.

Heat oven to 375°. Bake covered 45 minutes. Sprinkle with cheese. Bake uncovered about 10 minutes or until cheese is melted and casserole is bubbly.

1 SERVING: Calories 403; Total Fat 15g (Saturated Fat 7g, Trans Fat ½g); Cholesterol 70mg; Sodium 935mg; Total Carbohydrate 39g (Dietary Fiber 4g, Sugars 3g); Protein 29g; EXCHANGES: 2 Starch; 2 Vegetable; 1 Medium-Fat Meat; 1½ Fat; CARBOHYDRATE CHOICES: 2½

Expert Tips

■ Use ground turkey instead of ground beef, if you prefer.

■ Start with precooked ground beef, either plain or Italian-seasoned, to trim prep time.

PREP TIME: *15 minutes*

TOTAL TIME: *55 minutes*

MAKES 6 SERVINGS

Pastitsio

MACARONI MIXTURE

- 1 cup uncooked elbow macaroni (3½ ounces)
- 1 egg white
- ¼ cup grated Parmesan cheese
- 2 tablespoons milk

LAMB MIXTURE

- ¾ pound ground lamb
- 1½ cups cubed peeled eggplant
- 1 can (14.5 ounces) Muir Glen® organic diced tomatoes, drained
- 1 medium onion, chopped (½ cup)
- ½ teaspoon salt
- ¼ teaspoon ground cinnamon
- ¼ teaspoon ground nutmeg
- 1 clove garlic, finely chopped

SAUCE

- 1 cup milk
- 1 tablespoon cornstarch
- 2 tablespoons grated Parmesan cheese
- 1 egg, beaten

Heat oven to 350°F. Cook and drain macaroni as directed on package. Stir in remaining macaroni mixture ingredients.

Meanwhile, in 10-inch skillet, cook lamb over medium heat about 10 minutes, stirring occasionally, until no longer pink; drain. Stir in remaining lamb mixture ingredients.

In 1-quart saucepan, cook 1 cup milk and the cornstarch over medium heat, stirring constantly, until mixture thickens and boils. Stir in remaining sauce ingredients.

In ungreased 1½-quart casserole, place half of macaroni mixture. Top with lamb mixture, remaining macaroni mixture and the sauce.

Bake uncovered about 40 minutes or until set in center.

1 SERVING: Calories 270; Total Fat 12g (Saturated Fat 5g, Trans Fat ½g); Cholesterol 80mg; Sodium 510mg; Total Carbohydrate 23g (Dietary Fiber 2g, Sugars 6g); Protein 17g; EXCHANGES: 1 Starch; ½ Other Carbohydrate; CARBOHYDRATE CHOICES: 1½

Expert Tip

Ground beef can be used instead of the ground lamb.

Cheese- and Vegetable-Stuffed Shells

PREP TIME: *40 minutes*

TOTAL TIME: *1 hour 20 minutes*

MAKES 4 SERVINGS

16 uncooked jumbo pasta shells

1 tablespoon olive or vegetable oil

1 medium onion, chopped (½ cup)

1 small bell pepper (any color), chopped (½ cup)

2 cloves garlic, finely chopped

1 small zucchini, diced (about ¾ cup)

1 can (2¼ ounces) sliced ripe olives, drained

1 jar (14 to 15 ounces) tomato pasta sauce

½ cup ricotta cheese

1 egg

¼ cup grated Parmesan cheese

1 cup shredded Italian cheese blend or mozzarella cheese (4 ounces)

Heat oven to 350°F. Spray 11 × 7-inch (2-quart) glass baking dish with cooking spray. Cook and drain pasta shells as directed on package.

Meanwhile, in 10-inch skillet, heat oil over medium heat until hot. Cook onion, bell pepper and garlic in oil 2 to 3 minutes, stirring occasionally, until crisp-tender.

Add zucchini; cook 4 minutes, stirring occasionally. Stir in olives and ¼ cup of the pasta sauce. Cook, stirring frequently, until hot. Remove from heat.

In medium bowl, mix ricotta cheese, egg, Parmesan cheese and ½ cup of the shredded cheese blend. Stir in zucchini mixture until well mixed.

Fill each cooked pasta shell with about 2 tablespoons zucchini mixture. Place in baking dish. Pour remaining pasta sauce over shells.

Cover with foil; bake 30 minutes. Sprinkle with remaining ½ cup shredded cheese blend. Bake uncovered 5 to 10 minutes longer or until bubbly and cheese is melted.

1 SERVING: Calories 510; Total Fat 22g (Saturated Fat 9g, Trans Fat 0g); Cholesterol 85mg; Sodium 1,160mg; Total Carbohydrate 55g (Dietary Fiber 4g, Sugars 13g); Protein 23g; EXCHANGES: 2 Starch; 1½ Other Carbohydrate; 1 Vegetable; 2 High-Fat Meat; 1 Fat; CARBOHYDRATE CHOICES: 3½

Expert Tip

Ricotta is a white, moist, subtly sweet cheese with a slightly grainy texture. It is a popular ingredient in many Italian dishes.

Primavera Ravioli Bake

PREP TIME: *20 minutes*
TOTAL TIME: *1 hour 25 minutes*

MAKES 6 SERVINGS

1 bag (25 ounces) frozen Italian sausage-filled ravioli

6 cups Green Giant® Select® frozen broccoli florets

½ cup chopped drained roasted red bell peppers (from 7-ounce jar)

1 jar (1 pound) Alfredo pasta sauce

¾ cup milk

½ teaspoon Italian seasoning

1 cup Parmesan croutons, crushed

Heat oven to 350°F. Spray 13 × 9-inch (3-quart) glass baking dish with cooking spray. Spread frozen ravioli in baking dish. Top with remaining ingredients except croutons; mix slightly to coat ravioli.

Cover baking dish with foil. Bake 50 minutes; stir. Sprinkle with croutons. Bake uncovered 10 to 15 minutes longer or until bubbly around edges and thoroughly heated.

1 SERVING: Calories 600; Total Fat 30g (Saturated Fat 17g,Trans Fat 1g); Cholesterol 95mg; Sodium 710mg; Total Carbohydrate 59g (Dietary Fiber 6g, Sugars 9g); Protein 22g; EXCHANGES: 3 Starch; ½ Other Carbohydrate; 1 Vegetable; 1½ High-Fat Meat; 3½ Fat; CARBOHYDRATE CHOICES: 4

Expert Tip

Alfredo sauce in a jar works best for this recipe. Refrigerated Alfredo sauce can separate and curdle during baking.

Sausage Ravioli Casserole

PREP TIME: *10 minutes*

TOTAL TIME: *1 hour*

MAKES 6 SERVINGS

1 bag (25 ounces) frozen Italian-style sausage-filled ravioli, thawed

1 jar (4.5 ounces) Green Giant® sliced mushrooms, drained

1 medium zucchini, cut into 1/2-inch slices (about 1 cup)

1/2 cup pepperoni slices (2 1/2 ounces)

1 jar (26 ounces) roasted tomato and garlic pasta sauce

1 cup shredded Swiss cheese (4 ounces)

1/8 teaspoon Italian seasoning, if desired

Heat oven to 350°F. In large bowl, mix all ingredients except cheese and Italian seasoning. Spoon into ungreased 8-inch square (2-quart) glass baking dish.

Sprinkle with cheese and Italian seasoning.

Bake 40 to 50 minutes or until thoroughly heated and bubbly.

1 SERVING: Calories 500; Total Fat 22g (Saturated Fat 9g, Trans Fat 0g); Cholesterol 170mg; Sodium 1,840mg; Total Carbohydrate 52g (Dietary Fiber 4g, Sugars 13g); Protein 23g; EXCHANGES: 2 Starch; 1 1/2 Other Carbohydrate; 2 1/2 High-Fat Meat; CARBOHYDRATE CHOICES: 3 1/2

Expert Tips

■ This recipe can be made the night before. Just cover and store in the refrigerator until it's time to bake.

■ It's a good idea to thaw the ravioli in the refrigerator overnight.

Cheesy Gnocchi Florentine

PREP TIME: *20 minutes*
TOTAL TIME: *50 minutes*
MAKES 4 SERVINGS

- 1 box (9 ounces) Green Giant® frozen spinach
- 1 tablespoon butter or margarine
- $\frac{1}{4}$ cup chopped onion
- 1 tablespoon Gold Medal® all-purpose flour
- $1\frac{1}{4}$ cups half-and-half or milk
- 1 package (16 ounces) shelf-stable gnocchi
- 1 cup shredded Gruyère cheese (4 ounces)
- $\frac{1}{2}$ cup shredded Muenster cheese (2 ounces)
- $\frac{1}{8}$ teaspoon ground nutmeg
- 1 large plum (Roma) tomato, thinly sliced
- 1 teaspoon olive oil

Heat oven to 350°F. Spray $1\frac{1}{2}$-quart casserole with cooking spray. Cook spinach as directed on package; drain in colander or large strainer. Press to remove excess moisture. Set aside.

Meanwhile, in 2-quart saucepan, melt butter. Add onion; cook 2 to 3 minutes, stirring frequently, until tender. Stir in flour. Gradually stir in half-and-half. Stir in gnocchi; heat to boiling. Remove from heat. Stir in cheeses and nutmeg.

Spoon about 2 cups of the gnocchi mixture into casserole. Top with spinach, then remaining gnocchi mixture. Top with tomato slices; brush with olive oil.

Bake about 30 minutes or until bubbly and browned on top and gnocchi is tender.

1 SERVING: Calories 550; Total Fat 40g (Saturated Fat 21g, Trans Fat 3g); Cholesterol 160mg; Sodium 580mg; Total Carbohydrate 19g (Dietary Fiber 2g, Sugars 6g); Protein 27g; EXCHANGES: 1 Starch; $4\frac{1}{2}$ Fat; CARBOHYDRATE CHOICES: 1

Expert Tips

- Use sturdy paper towels or clean kitchen towels to wring as much moisture out of the spinach as possible.
- Three cups frozen gnocchi from a 16-ounce bag can be substituted for the shelf stable. Follow directions above.
- Swiss cheese can be substituted for the Gruyère cheese.

Pizza-Baked Spaghetti

PREP TIME: *15 minutes*
TOTAL TIME: *50 minutes*
MAKES 10 SERVINGS

12 ounces uncooked spaghetti, broken in half

1 pound bulk Italian pork sausage

2 jars (14 ounces each) pizza sauce

1 package (6 ounces) diced pepperoni

1 cup ricotta cheese

⅓ cup shredded Parmesan cheese

2 eggs, beaten

2 cups shredded mozzarella cheese (8 ounces)

Fresh basil, if desired

Heat oven to 350°F. Spray 13 × 9-inch (3-quart) baking dish with cooking spray. In Dutch oven, cook and drain pasta as directed on package, using minimum cook time. Return spaghetti to Dutch oven.

Meanwhile, in 10-inch skillet, cook sausage over medium heat until no longer pink; drain. In Dutch oven, toss spaghetti, sausage, pizza sauce and pepperoni.

In medium bowl, mix ricotta cheese, Parmesan cheese and eggs.

Spoon half of spaghetti mixture into baking dish. Dollop with ricotta mixture; spread evenly over top. Sprinkle with 1 cup of the mozzarella cheese. Top with remaining spaghetti mixture. Sprinkle with remaining 1 cup mozzarella cheese.

Bake uncovered 30 to 35 minutes or until bubbly. Garnish with basil.

1 SERVING: Calories 538; Total Fat 34g (Saturated Fat 14g, Trans Fat 0g); Cholesterol 125; Sodium 1,758mg; Total Carbohydrate 33g (Dietary Fiber 3g, Sugars 6g); Protein 28g; EXCHANGES: 1½ Starch; 1½ High-Fat Meat; 3 Fat; CARBOHYDRATE CHOICES: 2

Bacon Double Cheeseburger Casserole

PREP TIME: *25 minutes*

TOTAL TIME: *50 minutes*

MAKES 8 SERVINGS

3 cups uncooked elbow macaroni (about 10 ounces)

2 pounds (90%) lean ground beef

1 cup milk

1 teaspoon garlic pepper

2 cans (10¾ ounces each) condensed Cheddar cheese soup

1 package (8 ounces) Cheddar cheese cubes

10 strips cooked bacon, chopped

½ cup Progresso® plain bread crumbs

2 tablespoons butter or margarine, melted

Heat oven to 350°F. Cook and drain macaroni as directed on package.

While macaroni is cooking, cook beef in 4-quart Dutch oven over medium-high heat, stirring occasionally, until brown; drain. Stir in macaroni, milk, garlic pepper, soup, cheese cubes and half of the bacon. Spoon into 3-quart casserole.

Bake uncovered 20 minutes. Mix remaining bacon, the bread crumbs and butter; sprinkle over casserole. Bake uncovered 5 minutes.

1 SERVING: Calories 648; Total Fat 33g (Saturated Fat 19g, Trans Fat 1g); Cholesterol 128mg; Sodium 1,124mg; Total Carbohydrate 51g (Dietary Fiber 2g, Sugars 5g); Protein 42g; EXCHANGES: 2½ Starch; 3 Lean Meat; 1 High-Fat Meat; 3 Fat; CARBOHYDRATE CHOICES: 3½

Expert Tips

- Slightly undercook your pasta before adding it to this—or any—casserole mixture. The bake time will continue the cooking process.
- Precooked ground beef shaves minutes off this recipe. Simply heat, then stir in the remaining ingredients as directed.

Mexican Manicotti

12 uncooked manicotti pasta shells

1 pound lean (at least 80%) ground beef

1 can (6 ounces) Muir Glen® organic tomato paste

1 package (1 ounce) Old El Paso® taco seasoning mix

1½ cups water

1 package (3 ounces) cream cheese, softened

1 egg

1½ cups sour cream (12 ounces)

2½ cups shredded sharp Cheddar cheese (10 ounces)

2 cans (4 ounces each) Old El Paso® whole green chiles, drained, chopped

¼ cup chopped fresh cilantro

Heat oven to 350°F. Spray 13 × 9-inch (3-quart) glass baking dish with cooking spray. Cook and drain pasta as directed on package. Rinse with cold water; drain well.

In 10-inch nonstick skillet, cook beef over medium-high heat 5 to 7 minutes, stirring occasionally, until thoroughly cooked; drain. Stir in tomato paste, taco seasoning mix and water. Cook over medium heat 5 to 10 minutes until hot and bubbly.

In medium bowl, mix cream cheese, egg, sour cream, 1½ cups of the cheese, the chiles and 2 tablespoons of the cilantro. Spoon about 3 tablespoons cheese mixture into each pasta shell. Spoon about 1 cup beef mixture into baking dish; top with filled shells and remaining beef mixture.

Cover; bake 40 to 45 minutes or until hot. Uncover; sprinkle remaining 1 cup cheese over shells. Bake 5 minutes longer or until cheese is melted. Sprinkle with remaining 2 tablespoons cilantro.

1 SERVING: Calories 700; Total Fat 42g (Saturated Fat 23g, Trans Fat 1½g); Cholesterol 175mg; Sodium 1,390mg; Total Carbohydrate 45g (Dietary Fiber 3g, Sugars 8g); Protein 35g; EXCHANGES: 2 Starch; 1 Other Carbohydrate; ½ Vegetable; 1 High-Fat Meat; 3½ Fat; CARBOHYDRATE CHOICES: 3

Pumpkin Pastina

PREP TIME: *10 minutes*

TOTAL TIME: *30 minutes*

MAKES 4 SERVINGS

1 carton (32 ounces) Progresso® chicken broth (4 cups)

2 tablespoons olive oil

1 cup finely chopped onion

1 teaspoon finely chopped fresh thyme

¾ pound uncooked pastina or other small pasta, such as riso

Salt and pepper

1 cup winter squash, roasted, or 1 box (9 ounces) frozen winter squash (pumpkin), thawed

1 cup cubed cooked turkey, plain or smoked (about ¼ pound, if desired)

½ cup freshly grated Parmesan cheese and a small piece for garnishing

Bring the broth to a low simmer in a saucepan.

Heat olive oil in a large sauté pan over medium-high heat until hot. Add the onion and cook until soft but not brown, 2 to 3 minutes. Add the thyme, stir and add 2 cups of the simmering broth. Bring to a boil.

Add the pastina, stir well and reduce the heat to maintain a slow simmer.

Season with salt and pepper. Add simmering broth ½ cup at a time as the previous addition is absorbed, stirring occasionally to prevent the pastina from sticking to the bottom of the pan, until the pasta is al dente, about 15 minutes.

Add the squash and turkey to reheat. Stir well. The consistency should be quite loose, like a thick soup. Add more broth if necessary. Add the ½ cup cheese and let melt for a moment before stirring in. Taste for seasoning. If desired, pour into hollowed-out pumpkin for serving. Garnish with cheese.

1 SERVING: Calories 590; Total Fat 14g (Saturated Fat 4g, Trans Fat 0g); Cholesterol 45mg; Sodium 1,540mg; Total Carbohydrate 83g (Dietary Fiber 6g, Sugars 7g); Protein 32g; EXCHANGES: 4½ Starch; ½ Other Carbohydrate; 1 Vegetable; 2½ Lean Meat; 1 Fat; CARBOHYDRATE CHOICES: 5½

PREP TIME: *25 minutes*

TOTAL TIME: *1 hour 15 minutes*

MAKES 4 SERVINGS

Tuna Tetrazzini

8 ounces uncooked spaghetti, broken into 2-inch pieces

1 can (12 ounces) chunk light tuna in water, drained

¼ cup milk

1 jar (1 pound) Alfredo pasta sauce

1 jar (4.5 ounces) Green Giant® sliced mushrooms, drained

1 cup Green Giant® Valley Fresh Steamers® frozen sweet peas (from 12-ounce bag), thawed

1 jar (2 ounces) diced pimientos, drained

2 tablespoons grated Parmesan cheese

Heat oven to 350°F. Cook and drain spaghetti as directed on package.

Meanwhile, in ungreased 2-quart casserole, stir tuna, milk, Alfredo sauce, mushrooms, peas and pimientos. Gently stir in cooked spaghetti.

Cover and bake 40 minutes. Sprinkle cheese on top. Bake uncovered about 10 minutes longer or until top is bubbly and beginning to brown.

1 SERVING: Calories 520; Total Fat 13g (Saturated Fat 7g, Trans Fat 0g); Cholesterol 60mg; Sodium 940mg; Total Carbohydrate 60g (Dietary Fiber 6g, Sugars 7g); Protein 40g; EXCHANGES: 3 Starch; 1½ Other Carbohydrate; 1 Fat; CARBOHYDRATE CHOICES: 4

Expert Tips

■ This casserole also tastes great with 1½ cups chopped cooked chicken or turkey.

■ Use 1½ cups refrigerated reduced-fat Alfredo sauce to reduce the calories to 500 and the fat to 10 grams per serving.

Red Pepper–Spinach Lasagna

PREP TIME: *30 minutes*
TOTAL TIME: *5 hours 30 minutes*
MAKES 6 SERVINGS

1 jar (26 to 28 ounces) tomato pasta sauce

2 red bell peppers, chopped

1 medium onion, chopped (½ cup)

2 boxes (9 ounces each) Green Giant® frozen chopped spinach, thawed, squeezed to drain

1 can (8 ounces) Muir Glen® organic tomato sauce

9 uncooked lasagna noodles

1 jar (16 ounces) Alfredo pasta sauce

15 slices (1 ounce each) provolone cheese

¼ cup grated Parmesan cheese

Spray 5- to 6-quart slow cooker with cooking spray. Spread ¾ cup of the tomato pasta sauce in bottom of slow cooker.

In large bowl, mix bell peppers, onion and spinach; stir in remaining tomato pasta sauce and the tomato sauce.

Layer 3 lasagna noodles, broken into pieces to fit, over sauce in slow cooker. Top with one-third of the Alfredo sauce (about ½ cup), spreading to cover noodles completely. Top with 5 of the cheese slices, overlapping if necessary. Top with one-third of the vegetable mixture (about 2 cups), spreading evenly.

Repeat layers twice. Sprinkle Parmesan cheese over top.

Cover; cook on Low heat setting 5 to 6 hours.

1 SERVING: Calories 630; Total Fat 37g (Saturated Fat 21g, Trans Fat 1g); Cholesterol 95mg; Sodium 1,460mg; Total Carbohydrate 48g (Dietary Fiber 5g, Sugars 15g); Protein 26g; EXCHANGES: 1½ Starch; 1½ Low-Fat Milk; 2 Vegetable; ½ Lean Meat; 5½ Fat; CARBOHYDRATE CHOICES: 3

Expert Tip

Frozen spinach can be quickly thawed using the microwave. Place frozen blocks of spinach in a 10-inch square microwavable dish. Microwave uncovered on High 3 minutes. Break up blocks; microwave 3 more minutes until completely thawed. Drain well, squeezing out as much liquid as possible.

Artichoke–Spinach Lasagna

PREP TIME: *20 minutes*

TOTAL TIME: *1 hour 30 minutes*

MAKES 8 SERVINGS

1 medium onion, chopped (½ cup)

4 cloves garlic, finely chopped

1 can (14 ounces) vegetable broth

1 tablespoon chopped fresh or 1 teaspoon dried rosemary leaves

1 can (14 ounces) artichoke hearts, drained, coarsely chopped

1 box (9 ounces) Green Giant® frozen chopped spinach, thawed, squeezed to drain

1 jar (15 to 17 ounces) roasted garlic Parmesan or Alfredo pasta sauce

9 uncooked lasagna noodles

3 cups shredded mozzarella cheese (12 ounces)

1 package (4 ounces) crumbled herb-and-garlic feta cheese (1 cup)

Rosemary sprigs, if desired

Lemon wedges, if desired

Heat oven to 350°F. Spray 13 × 9-inch (3-quart) glass baking dish with cooking spray.

Spray 12-inch skillet with cooking spray; heat over medium-high heat. Add onion and garlic; cook about 3 minutes, stirring occasionally, until onion is crisp-tender. Stir in broth and rosemary. Heat to boiling. Stir in artichokes and spinach; reduce heat. Cover; simmer 5 minutes. Stir in pasta sauce.

Spread one-quarter of the artichoke mixture in bottom of baking dish; top with 3 noodles. Sprinkle with ¾ cup of the mozzarella cheese. Repeat layers twice. Spread with remaining artichoke mixture; sprinkle with remaining mozzarella cheese. Sprinkle with feta cheese.

Cover and bake 40 minutes. Uncover and bake about 15 minutes longer or until noodles are tender and lasagna is bubbly. Let stand 10 to 15 minutes before cutting. Garnish with rosemary sprigs and lemon wedges.

1 SERVING: Calories 350; Total Fat 13g (Saturated Fat 8g, Trans Fat 0g); Cholesterol 40mg; Sodium 950mg; Total Carbohydrate 38g (Dietary Fiber 5g, Sugars 9g); Protein 20g; EXCHANGES: 2 Starch; 1 Vegetable; 1 Fat; CARBOHYDRATE CHOICES: 2½

Expert Tips

- Warm focaccia or pita bread and a tossed salad with tomatoes would be nice partners for this lasagna.
- Stir in ½ cup cut-up pitted kalamata, Greek or ripe olives with the pasta sauce.

Roasted Vegetable Lasagna with Goat Cheese

PREP TIME: *25 minutes*

TOTAL TIME: *1 hour 30 minutes*

MAKES 8 SERVINGS

- 3 medium bell peppers, cut into 1-inch pieces
- 3 medium zucchini or summer squash, cut in half lengthwise and then into ½-inch slices
- 1 medium onion, cut into 8 wedges, separated into pieces
- 1 package (8 ounces) sliced mushrooms
- ½ teaspoon salt
- ¼ teaspoon black pepper
- 12 uncooked lasagna noodles
- 1 package (5 to 6 ounces) chèvre (goat) cheese
- 1 container (7 ounces) refrigerated basil pesto
- 2 cups tomato pasta sauce
- 2 cups shredded Italian cheese blend (8 ounces)

Heat oven to 450°F. Spray 15 × 10 × 1-inch pan with cooking spray. In pan, place bell peppers, squash, onion and mushrooms in single layer. Spray vegetables with cooking spray; sprinkle with salt and pepper. Bake uncovered 15 to 20 minutes, turning vegetables once, until crisp-tender.

Meanwhile, spray 13 × 9-inch (3-quart) baking dish with cooking spray. Cook and drain noodles as directed on package using minimum cook time. In medium bowl, crumble chèvre into pesto; stir.

Spread ½ cup of the pasta sauce in baking dish; top with 3 noodles. Layer with half the pesto mixture and 2 cups of the vegetables. Top with 3 more noodles. Top with ¾ cup sauce and 1 cup of the shredded cheese blend. Top with 2 cups vegetables, 3 noodles, remaining half of pesto mixture, 2 cups vegetables, 3 noodles and ¾ cup sauce. Sprinkle remaining 1 cup shredded cheese over top.

Reduce oven temperature to 375°F. Bake uncovered 20 to 30 minutes or until hot. Let stand 10 minutes before cutting.

1 SERVING: Calories 520; Total Fat 26g (Saturated Fat 10g, Trans Fat 0g); Cholesterol 30mg; Sodium 990mg; Total Carbohydrate 47g (Dietary Fiber 5g, Sugars 12g); Protein 22g; EXCHANGES: 1½ Starch; 1 Other Carbohydrate; 2 Vegetable; 2 High-Fat Meat; 2 Fat; CARBOHYDRATE CHOICES: 3

Expert Tips

- Switch out the squash by using another package of mushrooms instead of the zucchini.
- Try a unique flavor of pasta sauce, such as those with wine, capers or olives.

Do-Ahead Ravioli Sausage Lasagna

PREP TIME: *20 minutes*

TOTAL TIME: *9 hours 30 minutes*

MAKES 8 SERVINGS

1¼ pounds bulk Italian pork sausage

1 jar (26 to 28 ounces) tomato pasta sauce (any variety)

1 package (25 to 27½ ounces) frozen cheese-filled ravioli

2½ cups shredded mozzarella cheese (10 ounces)

2 tablespoons grated Parmesan cheese

In 10-inch skillet, cook sausage over medium heat, stirring occasionally, until no longer pink; drain.

In ungreased 13 × 9-inch (3-quart) glass baking dish, spread ½ cup of the pasta sauce. Arrange half of the frozen ravioli in single layer over sauce; evenly pour 1 cup pasta sauce over ravioli. Sprinkle evenly with 1½ cups sausage and 1 cup of the mozzarella cheese. Repeat layers with remaining ravioli, pasta sauce and sausage.

Cover tightly with foil; refrigerate at least 8 hours but no longer than 24 hours.

Heat oven to 350°F. Bake covered 45 minutes. Remove foil; sprinkle with remaining 1½ cups mozzarella and the Parmesan cheese. Bake about 15 minutes longer or until cheese is melted and lasagna is hot in center. Let stand 10 minutes before cutting.

1 SERVING: Calories 500; Total Fat 24g (Saturated Fat 10g, Trans Fat 0g); Cholesterol 60mg; Sodium 1,170mg; Total Carbohydrate 49g (Dietary Fiber 2g, Sugars 11g); Protein 23g; EXCHANGES: 1½ Starch; 1½ Other Carbohydrate; 2½ High-Fat Meat; 1 Fat; CARBOHYDRATE CHOICES: 3

Layered Beef-Noodle Bake

PREP TIME: *25 minutes*

TOTAL TIME: *1 hour*

MAKES 6 SERVINGS

2½ cups uncooked mini lasagna (mafalda) noodles (4 ounces)

1 pound lean (at least 80%) ground beef or lean ground turkey

1 jar (14 or 15 ounces) tomato pasta sauce

1 container (8 ounces) chives-and-onion cream cheese

½ cup reduced-fat sour cream

3 tablespoons milk

1 box (9 ounces) Green Giant® frozen spinach, thawed, squeezed to drain*

¼ cup shredded or grated Parmesan cheese (1 ounce)

Heat oven to 350°F. Spray 12 × 8- or 11 × 7-inch (2-quart) glass baking dish with cooking spray. Cook noodles as directed on package. Drain; rinse with hot water.

Meanwhile, in 10-inch skillet, cook beef over medium-high heat 5 to 7 minutes, stirring occasionally, until thoroughly cooked; drain. Stir in pasta sauce and cooked noodles.

In medium bowl, beat cream cheese, sour cream and milk with spoon until smooth.

Spoon half of the noodle mixture into baking dish. Top evenly with cheese mixture. Spoon spinach evenly over cheese mixture. Top with remaining noodle mixture. Cover with foil.

Bake 35 minutes; uncover and sprinkle with Parmesan cheese. Bake about 5 minutes longer or until hot. Cut into squares.

1 SERVING: Calories 460; Total Fat 26g (Saturated Fat 13g, Trans Fat 1g); Cholesterol 95mg; Sodium 800mg; Total Carbohydrate 32g (Dietary Fiber 3g, Sugars 9g); Protein 24g; EXCHANGES: 1½ Starch; ½ Other Carbohydrate; 2 Fat; CARBOHYDRATE CHOICES: 2

Expert Tips

- *To quickly thaw spinach, cut a small slit in the center of the pouch and microwave on High 2 to 3 minutes or until thawed. Remove spinach from pouch and squeeze dry with paper towels.

- Vegetable cream cheese can be used in place of the chives-and-onion cream cheese.

- Assemble this recipe ahead of time, then cover and refrigerate until ready to bake. The bake time will be longer, so watch closely for doneness.

Family-Favorite Macaroni and Cheese

PREP TIME: *25 minutes*

TOTAL TIME: *50 minutes*

MAKES 6 SERVINGS

2 cups uncooked elbow macaroni (7 ounces)

1/4 cup butter or margarine

1/4 cup Gold Medal® all-purpose flour

1/2 teaspoon salt

1/4 teaspoon pepper

1/4 teaspoon ground mustard

1/4 teaspoon Worcestershire sauce

2 cups milk

2 cups shredded or cubed Cheddar cheese (8 ounces)

Heat oven to 350°F.

Cook macaroni as directed on package.

While macaroni is cooking, melt butter in 3-quart saucepan over low heat. Stir in flour, salt, pepper, mustard and Worcestershire sauce. Cook over medium-low heat, stirring constantly, until mixture is smooth and bubbly; remove from heat. Stir in milk. Heat to boiling, stirring constantly. Boil and stir 1 minute. Stir in cheese. Cook, stirring occasionally, until cheese is melted.

Drain macaroni. Gently stir macaroni into cheese sauce. Pour into ungreased 2-quart casserole. Bake uncovered 20 to 25 minutes or until bubbly.

1 SERVING: Calories 424; Total Fat 23g (Saturated Fat 13g, Trans Fat 0g); Cholesterol 68mg; Sodium 529mg; Total Carbohydrate 38g (Dietary Fiber 1g, Sugars 5g); Protein 17g; EXCHANGES: 2 Starch; 1/2 Milk; 1 1/2 High-Fat Meat; 2 Fat; CARBOHYDRATE CHOICES: 2 1/2

Expert Tips

- Purchase the cheese already shredded in an 8-ounce package.
- While stirring the cooked macaroni into the cheese sauce, try adding sliced ripe or green olives or bite-size pieces of cooked vegetables, hot dogs or cooked sausage.
- Add a 4-ounce can of chopped green chiles, drained, for a perked-up version of mac and cheese.

Layered Mac 'n Cheese with Ground Beef

PREP TIME: *30 minutes*

TOTAL TIME: *1 hour*

MAKES 6 SERVINGS

2 cups uncooked elbow macaroni (8 ounces)

1 pound lean (at least 80%) ground beef

1 teaspoon salt

$\frac{1}{8}$ teaspoon pepper

2 tablespoons butter or margarine

2 tablespoons all-purpose flour

2 cups milk

$\frac{1}{2}$ cup Progresso® chicken broth (from 32-ounce carton)

3 cups shredded Cheddar cheese (12 ounces)

1 cup soft bread crumbs (about 2 slices bread)

Heat oven to 350°F. Spray 2-quart casserole with cooking spray. Cook and drain macaroni as directed on package.

Meanwhile, in 10-inch skillet, cook beef, $\frac{1}{2}$ teaspoon of the salt and the pepper over medium-high heat 5 to 7 minutes, stirring occasionally, until beef is thoroughly cooked; drain if desired.

In 2-quart saucepan, melt butter over medium heat. Stir in flour; cook 1 minute, stirring constantly, until bubbly. Stir in milk; cook 5 to 6 minutes, stirring constantly, until mixture thickens slightly. Stir in broth and remaining $\frac{1}{2}$ teaspoon salt. Remove from heat; stir in cheese. Fold in macaroni.

Spoon one-third of the macaroni mixture (about $1\frac{1}{3}$ cups) into casserole; top with half of the beef (about $1\frac{1}{2}$ cups). Layer with another one-third of the macaroni mixture, remaining beef and remaining macaroni mixture. Top with bread crumbs.

Bake uncovered 25 to 30 minutes or until bread crumbs are golden brown.

1 SERVING: Calories 630; Total Fat 34g (Saturated Fat 19g, Trans Fat $1\frac{1}{2}$g); Cholesterol 125mg; Sodium 1,130mg; Total Carbohydrate 43g (Dietary Fiber 2g, Sugars 6g); Protein 37g; EXCHANGES: $2\frac{1}{2}$ Starch; $\frac{1}{2}$ Other Carbohydrate; 4 High-Fat Meat; CARBOHYDRATE CHOICES: 3

Expert Tips

- Use Swiss cheese and a dash of ground nutmeg in place of the Cheddar cheese to bring a whole new flavor to this dish.
- Penne or rotini pasta can be used in place of the elbow macaroni.

PREP TIME: *15 minutes*
TOTAL TIME: *50 minutes*
MAKES 4 SERVINGS

Baked Macaroni and Cheese

7 ounces uncooked penne pasta (rounded 2 cups)

¼ cup butter or margarine

¼ cup all-purpose flour

½ teaspoon seasoned salt

½ teaspoon ground mustard

¼ teaspoon pepper

¼ teaspoon Worcestershire sauce

2 cups milk

2 cups shredded sharp Cheddar cheese (8 ounces)

Heat oven to 350°F. Cook and drain pasta as directed on package.

While pasta is cooking, in 3-quart saucepan, melt butter over low heat. Stir in flour, seasoned salt, mustard, pepper and Worcestershire sauce. Cook over low heat, stirring constantly, until mixture is smooth and bubbly; remove from heat. Stir in milk. Heat to boiling, stirring constantly. Boil and stir 1 minute; remove from heat. Using wire whisk, stir in cheese until melted.

Gently stir pasta into cheese sauce. Spoon into 4 ungreased 8-ounce ramekins/gratin dishes or 10-ounce custard cups. Place filled cups in shallow baking pan (or cookie sheet with sides).

Bake uncovered 20 to 25 minutes or until bubbly.

1 SERVING: Calories 630; Total Fat 34g (Saturated Fat 21g, Trans Fat 1g); Cholesterol 100mg; Sodium 850mg; Total Carbohydrate 55g (Dietary Fiber 2g, Sugars 8g); Protein 27g; EXCHANGES: 3 Starch, ½ Other Carbohydrate; 2½ High-Fat Meat; 2½ Fat; CARBOHYDRATE CHOICES: 3½

Expert Tips

■ We've taken a comfort food classic and given it two taste twists. For over-the-top ooey-gooey goodness, sink your teeth into Bacon–Pepper Mac and Cheese; for zip and crunch, try the Tex-Mex Macaroni and Cheese. Thinking outside the box never tasted so good.

■ Replace 1 cup of the Cheddar with 3 ounces cream cheese, cubed, and 4 ounces shredded Gruyère cheese. Sprinkle 1 tablespoon shredded Parmesan cheese and ¼ teaspoon chopped Italian parsley over the top of each ramekin.

■ Substitute 8 ounces cubed processed cheese spread with jalapeño peppers for the Cheddar cheese. Stir in ¼ cup salsa and top with ½ cup crushed corn chips.

■ Four (4½-inch) foil pie pans can be substituted for the ramekins, gratin dishes or custard cups.

Bacon–Pepper Mac and Cheese

3 cups uncooked penne pasta (10 ounces)

⅓ cup butter

1 medium red bell pepper, thinly sliced (about 1 cup)

4 medium green onions, sliced (¼ cup)

¼ cup Gold Medal® all-purpose flour

½ teaspoon salt

¼ teaspoon black pepper

1 teaspoon Dijon mustard

2¼ cups milk

10 slices packaged precooked bacon (from 2.1-ounce package), cut into ½-inch pieces

1 cup shredded sharp Cheddar cheese (4 ounces)

4 ounces Muenster cheese, shredded (1 cup)

2 ounces Gruyère cheese, shredded (½ cup)

¼ cup Progresso® Italian style bread crumbs

Heat oven to 350°F. Spray 2-quart casserole with cooking spray. Cook and drain pasta as directed on package.

Meanwhile, in 3-quart saucepan, melt butter over low heat. Reserve 1 tablespoon of the butter in small bowl. Stir bell pepper and onions into butter in saucepan. Increase heat to medium; cook and stir 1 minute. Stir in flour, salt, pepper and mustard. Cook, stirring constantly, until mixture is bubbly.

Increase heat to medium-high. Gradually add milk, stirring constantly, until mixture boils and thickens, about 5 minutes. Gently stir in bacon and pasta.

Remove from heat; stir in cheeses until melted. Pour into casserole. Stir bread crumbs into melted butter in small bowl. Sprinkle over pasta mixture.

Bake uncovered 20 to 25 minutes or until edges are bubbly.

1 SERVING: Calories 1,010, Total Fat 51g (Saturated Fat 29g, Trans Fat 1½g); Cholesterol 145mg; Sodium 1,790mg; Total Carbohydrate 91g (Dietary Fiber 5g, Sugars 10g); Protein 45g; EXCHANGES: 5½ Starch; ½ Other Carbohydrate; 4 High-Fat Meat; 3 Fat; CARBOHYDRATE CHOICES: 6

Expert Tip

You can use elbow macaroni in place of the penne. You can also use Swiss cheese instead of the Gruyère, although Gruyère has a more pronounced nutty flavor than regular Swiss.

Smoky Mac 'n Cheese

- 3 cups uncooked elbow macaroni (12 ounces)
- 1½ cups whipping cream
- 1 teaspoon Dijon mustard
- ½ teaspoon coarse (kosher or sea) salt
- ¼ teaspoon ground red pepper (cayenne)
- 8 ounces smoked Cheddar cheese, shredded (2 cups)
- 2 cans (14.5 ounces each) Muir Glen® organic fire roasted diced tomatoes, well drained
- ¼ cup sliced green onions (4 medium)
- ⅓ cup grated Parmesan cheese
- ⅓ cup Progresso® plain bread crumbs
- 2 teaspoons olive oil

Cook and drain macaroni as directed on box. Return to saucepan; cover to keep warm.

Meanwhile, heat oven to 375°F. Spray 13 × 9-inch (3-quart) glass baking dish with cooking spray. In 2-quart saucepan, heat whipping cream, mustard, salt and red pepper to boiling. Reduce heat; stir in Cheddar cheese with wire whisk until smooth.

Pour sauce over macaroni. Stir in tomatoes and onions. Pour into baking dish. In small bowl, mix Parmesan cheese and bread crumbs. Stir in oil. Sprinkle over top of macaroni mixture.

Bake uncovered 15 to 20 minutes or until edges are bubbly and top is golden brown.

1 SERVING: Calories 500; Total Fat 27g (Saturated Fat 16g, Trans Fat ½g); Cholesterol 85mg; Sodium 770mg; Total Carbohydrate 47g (Dietary Fiber 4g, Sugars 5g); Protein 17g; EXCHANGES: 2½ Starch; ½ Other Carbohydrate; 1 Vegetable; 1 High-Fat Meat; 3½ Fat; CARBOHYDRATE CHOICES: 3

Expert Tip

Be sure to use whipping cream when making the sauce for this decadent mac 'n cheese. Milk or half-and-half are more likely to curdle when combined with acidic ingredients like tomatoes.

Tex–Mex Macaroni and Cheese

3 cups uncooked elbow macaroni (12 ounces)

2 tablespoons butter

2 tablespoons Gold Medal® all-purpose flour

2 cups half-and-half

3 cups shredded sharp Cheddar cheese (12 ounces)

1 teaspoon ground cumin

1/2 teaspoon salt

1/4 teaspoon black pepper

1 jar (12 ounces) roasted red bell peppers, drained, chopped

1 can (4 ounces) Old El Paso® whole green chiles, drained, chopped

1 cup crushed nacho-flavored tortilla chips

Cook and drain macaroni as directed on package.

Meanwhile, in 3-quart saucepan, melt butter over medium heat. Stir in flour with whisk until smooth; cook 1 minute. Add half-and-half, cheese, cumin, salt and pepper; cook and stir until cheese is melted.

Add cooked macaroni, roasted peppers and chiles; toss to combine. Serve in bowls; sprinkle with crushed tortilla chips.

1 SERVING: Calories 700; Total Fat 37g (Saturated Fat 21g, Trans Fat 1g); Cholesterol 100mg; Sodium 1,000mg; Total Carbohydrate 65g (Dietary Fiber 4g, Sugars 6g); Protein 26g; EXCHANGES: 3 Starch; 11/2 Other Carbohydrate; 21/2 High-Fat Meat; 3 Fat; CARBOHYDRATE CHOICES: 4

Expert Tips

- To intensify the Tex-Mex flavor, use shredded Mexican blend cheese instead of Cheddar and add 1/2 to 1 teaspoon red pepper sauce.

- We prefer the consistency of whole green chiles, but you can use a 4.5-ounce can of Old El Paso® chopped green chiles.

Bell Pepper Mac and Cheese with Fondue Cheese Sauce

PREP TIME: *30 minutes*

TOTAL TIME: *1 hour 10 minutes*

MAKES 7 SERVINGS

- 3 medium red, yellow, orange or green bell peppers
- 3 cups uncooked penne pasta (9 ounces)
- 10 ounces Gruyère cheese, shredded (2½ cups)
- 3 tablespoons Gold Medal® all-purpose flour
- 1 cup dry white wine
- ¾ cup whipping cream
- 2 cloves garlic, finely chopped
- ½ teaspoon salt
- ¼ teaspoon ground red pepper (cayenne)
- ⅛ teaspoon ground nutmeg
- 2 tablespoons chopped fresh parsley
- ½ cup Progresso® Italian style bread crumbs
- 2 tablespoons butter or margarine, melted

Set oven control to broil. Broil bell peppers with tops about 5 inches from heat about 20 minutes, turning occasionally, until skins are blistered and evenly browned. Place peppers in plastic bag; close tightly. Let stand 20 minutes. Remove skin, stems, seeds and membranes from peppers. Cut peppers into 1-inch pieces; set aside.

Heat oven to 350°F. Spray 3-quart casserole with cooking spray. Cook and drain pasta as directed on package, using minimum cook time.

Meanwhile, in medium bowl, toss cheese with flour until cheese is coated. In 3-quart nonreactive saucepan, heat wine, whipping cream and garlic to simmering; reduce heat. Gradually stir in cheese, salt, red pepper and nutmeg until cheese is melted. Cook and stir 2 minutes longer.

Stir cooked pasta, roasted peppers and parsley into cheese sauce. Spoon into casserole. In small bowl, mix bread crumbs and butter. Sprinkle over pasta mixture.

Bake uncovered 20 to 30 minutes or until edges are bubbly.

1 SERVING: Calories 490; Total Fat 26g (Saturated Fat 14g, Trans Fat ½g); Cholesterol 80mg; Sodium 450mg; Total Carbohydrate 39g (Dietary Fiber 2g, Sugars 4g); Protein 18g; EXCHANGES: 2½ Starch; ½ Vegetable; 3½ Fat; CARBOHYDRATE CHOICES: 2½

Expert Tips

- For a flavor twist, try half Gruyère and half Emmentaler cheese.
- If you like, stir in a 4-ounce can of sliced mushrooms, drained, with the pasta.

Beer-Cheese Mac and Sausages

- 1 package (7 ounces) uncooked elbow macaroni (2 cups)
- 3 tablespoons butter
- 1/4 cup finely chopped onion
- 3 tablespoons Gold Medal® all-purpose flour
- 2 cups half-and-half
- 1 teaspoon ground mustard
- 1/2 teaspoon red pepper sauce
- 1/4 teaspoon salt
- 1 cup beer or nonalcoholic beer
- 2 cups shredded marble jack cheese (8 ounces)
- 1 package (1 pound) cocktail-size fully cooked smoked sausages
- 2 cups popped microwave popcorn

Heat oven to 350°F. Spray 2½-quart casserole with cooking spray. Cook and drain macaroni as directed on package using minimum cook time. Rinse and return to saucepan.

While macaroni is cooking, in 3-quart saucepan, melt butter over medium heat. Cook and stir onion in butter 2 to 3 minutes or until softened. Stir in flour; cook and stir 1 minute. Gradually stir in half-and-half, mustard, pepper sauce and salt. Heat until thickened and bubbly, stirring constantly, about 5 minutes. Stir in beer.

Remove from heat; let stand 2 to 3 minutes. Stir in cheese until melted. Add sausages to cooked macaroni. Stir in cheese sauce. Spoon macaroni mixture into casserole.

Bake 30 to 40 minutes or until bubbly and top begins to brown. Top with popcorn just before serving.

1 SERVING: Calories 500; Total Fat 34g (Saturated Fat 16g, Trans Fat 1g); Cholesterol 80mg; Sodium 1,130mg; Total Carbohydrate 30g (Dietary Fiber 1g, Sugars 5g); Protein 16g; EXCHANGES: 2 Starch; 1½ High-Fat Meat; 4 Fat; CARBOHYDRATE CHOICES: 2

Expert Tips

- Allow the white sauce to cool a couple of minutes before adding the cheese. This keeps the cheese from separating and becoming grainy.

- Serve this perfect football-game casserole with soft pretzels and fresh veggies, such as carrots, celery, pepper strips and cucumber slices.

- Sprinkle top with 1/4 teaspoon paprika or 1 tablespoon chopped fresh parsley.

Spinach and Bacon Mac 'n Cheese

PREP TIME: *25 minutes*
TOTAL TIME: *25 minutes*

MAKES 6 SERVINGS

- 3 cups uncooked bow-tie (farfalle) pasta (8 ounces)
- 1/2 pound sliced bacon, coarsely chopped
- 2 tablespoons butter
- 1 small clove garlic, finely chopped
- 1/4 cup Gold Medal® all-purpose flour
- 1/4 teaspoon salt
- 1/4 teaspoon pepper
- 2 cups milk
- 2 cups shredded sharp Cheddar cheese (8 ounces)
- 1 bag (6 ounces) fresh baby spinach leaves, coarsely chopped

In 5-quart Dutch oven, cook and drain pasta as directed on package. Return to Dutch oven; cover to keep warm.

Meanwhile, in 10-inch skillet, cook bacon over medium heat 5 to 8 minutes, stirring often, until crisp; remove to paper towels. Reserve 2 tablespoons drippings.

In 3-quart saucepan, heat butter and reserved bacon drippings over medium heat until butter is melted. Add garlic; cook 30 seconds or until fragrant. Stir in flour, salt and pepper with whisk until smooth. Stir in milk; heat to boiling. Stir in cheese until melted and sauce is smooth.

Pour cheese sauce over pasta; stir until coated. Stir in spinach. Reserve 1/4 cup of the bacon; stir remaining bacon into pasta mixture. Divide pasta mixture among 6 serving bowls; garnish with reserved bacon.

1 SERVING: Calories 470; Total Fat 24g (Saturated Fat 13g, Trans Fat 1/2g); Cholesterol 70mg; Sodium 810mg; Total Carbohydrate 42g (Dietary Fiber 2g, Sugars 5g); Protein 23g; EXCHANGES: 2 Starch; 1/2 Other Carbohydrate; 1 Vegetable; 2 High-Fat Meat; 1 1/2 Fat; CARBOHYDRATE CHOICES: 3

Expert Tip

If desired, drain all of the bacon drippings and increase the butter by 2 tablespoons. Or substitute 1/4 cup canola or olive oil for the butter and drippings.

Spaghetti with Zucchini and Beans

6 ounces uncooked spaghetti

3 cups chopped zucchini (2 medium)

1/3 cup water

1 tablespoon tomato paste

1/4 teaspoon kosher (coarse) salt

1/8 teaspoon coarse ground black pepper

1 can (15.5 ounces) great northern beans, drained, rinsed

1 can (14.5 ounces) diced tomatoes with basil, garlic and oregano

1/2 cup crumbled feta cheese (2 ounces)

Cook spaghetti as directed on package, omitting salt and oil; drain.

Meanwhile, spray 12-inch skillet with olive oil cooking spray; heat over medium-high heat. Add zucchini; cook 5 minutes, stirring occasionally, until lightly browned. Stir in water, tomato paste, salt, pepper, beans and tomatoes. Cover; simmer 4 minutes or until thoroughly heated.

On each of 4 plates, place about 2/3 cup spaghetti. Top each with 1 cup zucchini mixture and 2 tablespoons cheese.

1 SERVING: Calories 299; Total Fat 4g (Saturated Fat 2½g, Trans Fat 0g); Cholesterol 13; Sodium 708mg; Total Carbohydrate 51g (Dietary Fiber 7g, Sugars 7g); Protein 14g; EXCHANGES: 2½ Starch; 2 Vegetable; ½ Medium-Fat Meat; ½ Fat; CARBOHYDRATE CHOICES: 3½

Linguine with Roasted Vegetables and Pesto

PREP TIME: *15 minutes*

TOTAL TIME: *45 minutes*

MAKES 6 SERVINGS

1 large or 2 medium onions, cut into wedges and separated

3 medium red, green or yellow bell peppers, cut into 1-inch pieces

1 package (8 ounces) whole mushrooms, cut into fourths

½ teaspoon salt

1 cup cherry tomatoes, cut in half, or cut-up tomatoes

12 ounces uncooked linguine

⅓ cup basil pesto

¼ cup shredded Parmesan cheese (1 ounce)

Heat oven to 425°F. Spray 13 × 9-inch (3-quart) glass baking dish with cooking spray. Arrange onion pieces in baking dish. Bake 10 minutes. Add bell peppers and mushrooms to onions; spray with cooking spray and sprinkle with salt. Bake 15 minutes. Stir in tomatoes. Bake about 5 minutes longer or until vegetables are tender.

Meanwhile, cook and drain linguine as directed on package.

Stir pesto into roasted vegetables. Place linguine on large serving platter. Top with vegetable mixture and cheese.

1 SERVING: Calories 350; Total Fat 10g (Saturated Fat 2½g, Trans Fat 0g); Cholesterol 5mg; Sodium 630mg; Total Carbohydrate 55g (Dietary Fiber 6g, Sugars 6g); Protein 13g; EXCHANGES: 3½ Starch; 1½ Fat; CARBOHYDRATE CHOICES: 3

Expert Tips

- Toss Bibb lettuce and red onion with your favorite dressing for a change-of-pace salad.
- Cut up and refrigerate the veggies. Then you're ready to roast them later in the day.

Spicy Italian Tuna and Noodles

PREP TIME: *25 minutes*
TOTAL TIME: *25 minutes*
MAKES 6 SERVINGS

- 8 ounces uncooked yolk-free extra-wide noodles
- 1 jar (26 ounces) tomato-basil pasta sauce
- 2 cans (6 ounces each) albacore tuna in water, drained, flaked
- ¼ cup sliced ripe olives
- 2 teaspoons salt-free extra-spicy seasoning blend
- ¾ cup shredded Italian cheese blend (3 ounces)
- 2 tablespoons chopped fresh parsley

In 4-quart Dutch oven, cook and drain noodles as directed on package. Stir in pasta sauce. Cook until heated through.

Fold in tuna, olives and seasoning. Cook until heated through. Top each serving with cheese and parsley.

1 SERVING: Calories 380; Total Fat 10g (Saturated Fat 3g, Trans Fat 0g); Cholesterol 55mg; Sodium 990mg; Total Carbohydrate 50g (Dietary Fiber 3g, Sugars 10g); Protein 25g; EXCHANGES: 3 Starch; ½ Other Carbohydrate; 2 Very Lean Meat; 1 Fat; CARBOHYDRATE CHOICES: 3

Expert Tip

You can use any combination of these shredded cheeses instead of the cheese blend in this recipe: Parmesan, mozzarella, Asiago, fontina or Romano.

Quick Chicken Scampi

PREP TIME: *25 minutes*
TOTAL TIME: *25 minutes*
MAKES 4 SERVINGS

8 ounces uncooked linguine

1¼ pounds boneless skinless chicken breasts, cut into bite-size pieces

½ teaspoon salt

¼ teaspoon pepper

2 tablespoons butter

2 medium green onions, chopped (2 tablespoons)

2 cloves garlic, finely chopped

¼ cup finely chopped drained roasted red peppers (from 7-ounce jar)

½ pound fresh thin asparagus spears, trimmed, cut into 2-inch pieces

¾ cup Progresso® chicken broth (from 32-ounce carton)

Grated peel of 1 medium lemon (2 to 3 teaspoons)

Cook linguine as directed on package.

Meanwhile, sprinkle chicken with salt and pepper. In 12-inch non-stick skillet, heat 1 tablespoon of the butter over medium-high heat until melted. Cook chicken in butter 5 to 7 minutes, stirring occasionally.

Add onions, garlic, roasted peppers and asparagus; cook 2 to 3 minutes longer, stirring occasionally, until asparagus is crisp-tender and chicken is no longer pink in center. Stir in broth and remaining 1 tablespoon butter; cook until butter is melted.

Drain linguine. Serve chicken mixture over linguine. Sprinkle lemon peel over each serving.

1 SERVING: Calories 500; Total Fat 12g (Saturated Fat 5g, Trans Fat 0g); Cholesterol 105mg; Sodium 800mg; Total Carbohydrate 54g (Dietary Fiber 4g, Sugars 3g); Protein 43g; EXCHANGES: ½ Starch; ½ Vegetable; 4½ Very Lean Meat; 1½ Fat; CARBOHYDRATE CHOICES: 3½

Expert Tips

- If you're not in the mood for pasta, try serving the chicken mixture over your favorite variety of rice.
- When grating the lemon peel, be careful to avoid the pith—the soft white layer between the peel and flesh of the fruit—as it can be bitter.

Bow-Ties with Chicken and Asparagus

PREP TIME: *25 minutes*
TOTAL TIME: *25 minutes*
MAKES 6 SERVINGS

- 4 cups uncooked bow-tie (farfalle) pasta (8 ounces)
- 1 pound fresh asparagus spears
- 1 tablespoon canola oil
- 1 pound boneless skinless chicken breasts, cut into 1-inch pieces
- 1 package (8 ounces) sliced fresh mushrooms (3 cups)
- 2 cloves garlic, finely chopped
- 1 cup Progresso® reduced-sodium chicken broth (from 32-ounce carton)
- 1 tablespoon cornstarch
- 4 medium green onions, sliced (¼ cup)
- 2 tablespoons chopped fresh basil
- Salt, if desired
- ¼ cup finely shredded Parmesan cheese (1 ounce)

Cook and drain pasta as directed on package, omitting salt.

Meanwhile, break off tough ends of asparagus as far down as stalks snap easily. Wash asparagus; cut into 1-inch pieces.

In 12-inch nonstick skillet, heat oil over medium-high heat. Add chicken; cook 2 minutes, stirring occasionally. Stir in asparagus, mushrooms and garlic. Cook 6 to 8 minutes, stirring occasionally, until chicken is no longer pink in center and vegetables are tender.

In small bowl, gradually stir broth into cornstarch. Stir in onions and basil. Stir cornstarch mixture into chicken mixture. Cook and stir 1 to 2 minutes or until thickened and bubbly. Season with salt. Toss with pasta. Sprinkle with cheese.

1 SERVING: Calories 320; Total Fat 7g (Saturated Fat 2g, Trans Fat 0g); Cholesterol 50mg; Sodium 210mg; Total Carbohydrate 37g (Dietary Fiber 3g, Sugars 2g); Protein 27g; EXCHANGES: 2 Starch; 1 Vegetable; 2½ Very Lean Meat; 1 Fat; CARBOHYDRATE CHOICES: 2½

Expert Tip

This light pasta entrée pairs nicely with a glass of crisp white wine such as Pinot Grigio or Sauvignon Blanc.

Vegetable Skillet Tetrazzini

PREP TIME: *25 minutes*
TOTAL TIME: *30 minutes*
MAKES 4 SERVINGS

8 ounces uncooked spaghetti

1/4 cup butter

1 package (8 ounces) sliced fresh mushrooms (about 3 cups)

2 cups chopped fresh broccoli florets

1 medium red bell pepper, thinly sliced

1 clove garlic, finely chopped

1 tablespoon water

2 tablespoons Gold Medal® all-purpose flour

2 1/2 cups half-and-half

1/2 teaspoon salt

2 tablespoons sherry, if desired

2/3 cup shredded Parmesan cheese

Sliced almonds, if desired

In 5-quart Dutch oven, cook and drain spaghetti as directed on package. Return to Dutch oven; cover to keep warm.

Meanwhile, in 10-inch nonstick skillet, melt 2 tablespoons of the butter over medium heat. Cook mushrooms in butter 4 to 6 minutes, stirring frequently, until light brown. Add broccoli, bell pepper, garlic and water. Cover; cook 3 to 4 minutes, until vegetables are crisp-tender. Remove vegetables from skillet to Dutch oven.

In same skillet, melt remaining 2 tablespoons butter over medium heat. Add flour; cook 2 minutes, stirring to make a smooth paste. Add 1 cup of the half-and-half; stir until smooth. Gradually add remaining 1 1/2 cups half-and-half; heat just to boiling, stirring constantly. Remove from heat; stir in salt and sherry.

Pour sauce over spaghetti and vegetables. Stir in cheese. Cover; let stand 5 minutes.

1 SERVING: Calories 680; Total Fat 36g (Saturated Fat 22g, Trans Fat 1g); Cholesterol 100mg; Sodium 980mg; Total Carbohydrate 66g (Dietary Fiber 5g, Sugars 11g); Protein 24g; EXCHANGES: 2 1/2 Starch; 1 Other Carbohydrate; 2 1/2 Vegetable; 1 1/2 Lean Meat; 6 Fat; CARBOHYDRATE CHOICES: 4 1/2

Expert Tips

■ Toast the sliced almonds for sprinkling on top, if desired. Sprinkle almonds in ungreased heavy skillet. Cook over medium heat 5 to 7 minutes, stirring frequently until nuts begin to brown, then stirring constantly until nuts are light brown.

■ Use a combination of cheeses in this dish, if desired. Blend in 1/2 cup shredded Cheddar, Swiss or your favorite cheese with the 1 cup half-and-half; stir until melted and smooth. Proceed as directed. Reduce Parmesan cheese to 2 tablespoons.

Spicy Chicken and Orzo Skillet

PREP TIME: *45 minutes*
TOTAL TIME: *45 minutes*
MAKES 4 SERVINGS

1 tablespoon olive or vegetable oil

4 boneless skinless chicken breasts, cut into thin bite-size strips

1 clove garlic, finely chopped

1 cup ready-to-eat baby-cut carrots, quartered lengthwise

1 small onion, cut into thin wedges

¾ cup uncooked rosamarina or orzo pasta (5½ ounces)

1 teaspoon ground cumin

½ teaspoon Italian seasoning

½ teaspoon crushed red pepper flakes

½ cup water

1 can (15 ounces) Progresso® chickpeas or garbanzo beans, drained, rinsed

1¾ cups Progresso® chicken broth (from 32-ounce carton)

2 cups fresh spinach, cut into thin strips

In 12-inch skillet, heat oil over medium-high heat until hot. Add chicken and garlic; cook and stir 3 minutes. Add carrots and onion; cover and cook 2 to 3 minutes or until vegetables are crisp-tender, stirring once.

Stir in all remaining ingredients except spinach. Heat to boiling. Reduce heat; cover and simmer 12 to 15 minutes, stirring occasionally, until most of liquid is absorbed and orzo is tender.

Stir in spinach; cover and cook 2 to 3 minutes longer or until spinach is wilted.

1 SERVING: Calories 480; Total Fat 11g (Saturated Fat 2g, Trans Fat 0g); Cholesterol 75mg; Sodium 530mg; Total Carbohydrate 52g (Dietary Fiber 8g, Sugars 3g); Protein 42g; EXCHANGES: 2½ Starch; ½ Other Carbohydrate; 1 Vegetable; 4½ Very Lean Meat; 1½ Fat; CARBOHYDRATE CHOICES: 3½

Asparagus and Turkey Sausage Skillet

PREP TIME: *15 minutes*

TOTAL TIME: *25 minutes*

MAKES 4 SERVINGS

- 1 tablespoon olive or vegetable oil
- 1 package (19.5 ounces) lean Italian turkey sausages, casings removed, cut into 1/2-inch slices
- 1 large onion, coarsely chopped (1 cup)
- 1 cup Progresso® chicken broth (from 32-ounce carton)
- 1 cup water
- 1 cup uncooked orzo or rosamarina pasta (6 ounces)
- 1 pound fresh asparagus spears, trimmed, cut into 1-inch pieces
- 2 tablespoons sliced pimientos (from 4-ounce jar)

In 12-inch nonstick skillet, heat oil over medium-high heat. Add sausage and onion; cook 2 minutes, stirring occasionally.

Stir in broth and water. Heat to boiling. Stir in orzo; boil 2 minutes. Add asparagus and pimientos. Reduce heat to medium. Cover; return to boiling. Cook 8 to 10 minutes or until pasta is tender.

1 SERVING: Calories 470; Total Fat 19g (Saturated Fat 4g, Trans Fat 1/2g); Cholesterol 125mg; Sodium 1,140mg; Total Carbohydrate 34g (Dietary Fiber 3g, Sugars 4g); Protein 40g; EXCHANGES: 2 Starch; 1 1/2 Vegetable; 1 1/2 Very Lean Meat; 2 Lean Meat; 2 1/2 Fat; CARBOHYDRATE CHOICES: 2

Expert Tips

- If not using a nonstick skillet, stir often to keep orzo from sticking to the bottom of the skillet.
- Leftover chicken broth can be put into a resealable freezer bag and frozen for later use.
- Coarsely chop onion in a food processor fitted with a chopping blade.

Lemon–Chicken Rigatoni with Broccoli

PREP TIME: *20 minutes*
TOTAL TIME: *45 minutes*
MAKES 4 SERVINGS

2 tablespoons butter or margarine

2 cloves garlic, finely chopped

2 cups uncooked rigatoni pasta (6 ounces)

2 cups Progresso® chicken broth (from 32-ounce carton)

2 cups Green Giant® Valley Fresh Steamers™ frozen broccoli cuts

2 cups chopped deli rotisserie chicken (from 2- to 2½-pound chicken)

1½ teaspoons grated lemon peel

¼ cup shredded Parmesan cheese (1 ounce)

In 12-inch skillet, melt butter over medium heat. Add garlic; cook about 1 minute, stirring occasionally, until softened.

Stir in uncooked pasta and broth. Heat to boiling, stirring occasionally; reduce heat to medium-low. Cover; simmer 11 minutes. Stir well.

Spread broccoli and chicken over pasta. Cover; cook 12 to 14 minutes longer or until pasta is tender.

Stir in lemon peel. Top with cheese.

1 SERVING: Calories 420; Total Fat 14 (Saturated Fat 6g, Trans Fat 0g); Cholesterol 80mg; Sodium 930mg; Total Carbohydrate 41g (Dietary Fiber 4g, Sugars 2g); Protein 32g; EXCHANGES: 2½ Starch; 1 Vegetable; 3 Lean Meat; 1 Fat; CARBOHYDRATE CHOICES: 3

Expert Tips

■ Replace the Parmesan cheese with crumbled feta for a delicious Greek flavor.

■ Add a fresh note by stirring 2 tablespoons chopped fresh herbs, such as parsley, chives or oregano, into the finished dish.

Skillet Spaghetti Pizza

½ pound lean (at least 80%) ground beef

2 ounces sliced pepperoni, chopped (½ cup)

1 can (19 ounces) Progresso® Vegetable Classics hearty tomato soup

2¼ cups water

8 ounces uncooked spaghetti, broken into thirds (about 2 cups)

1 teaspoon Italian seasoning

½ teaspoon garlic salt

1 cup shredded mozzarella cheese (4 ounces)

1 medium tomato, chopped (¾ cup)

¼ cup sliced ripe olives

In 12-inch skillet, cook beef over medium-high heat 5 to 7 minutes, stirring occasionally, until thoroughly cooked. Add pepperoni; cook and stir 1 minute. Drain.

Stir in soup, water, uncooked spaghetti, Italian seasoning and garlic salt; heat to boiling. Stir; reduce heat to medium-low. Cover; cook about 18 minutes, stirring occasionally, until spaghetti is desired doneness.

Sprinkle with cheese, tomato and olives. Remove from heat. Cover; let stand 3 to 5 minutes or until cheese is melted.

1 SERVING: Calories 570, Total Fat 21g (Saturated Fat 9g, Trans Fat ½g); Cholesterol 65mg; Sodium 1,170mg; Total Carbohydrate 66g (Dietary Fiber 5g, Sugars 7g); Protein 31g; EXCHANGES: 4 Starch; ½ Other Carbohydrate; 1 Fat; CARBOHYDRATE CHOICES: 4½

Expert Tip

Customize it! Use your family's favorites to make your spaghetti pizza a new family favorite.

Speedy Pork Skillet

PREP TIME: *10 minutes*
TOTAL TIME: *20 minutes*
MAKES 4 SERVINGS

1 tablespoon vegetable oil

3/4 pound pork tenderloin, cut into 1/2-inch strips

2 packages (3 ounces each) pork flavor ramen noodle soup mix

1 1/2 cups water

1 tablespoon chopped fresh parsley or 2 teaspoons parsley flakes

1 tablespoon soy sauce

1 cup broccoli florets

1 medium red bell pepper, cut into 3/4-inch pieces

4 medium green onions, cut into 1-inch pieces

Heat oil in 12-inch skillet over medium-high heat. Add pork; stir-fry about 5 minutes or until pork is slightly pink.

Gently break apart blocks of noodles. Stir noodles, contents of seasoning packets and remaining ingredients into pork.

Heat to boiling. Boil 3 to 4 minutes, stirring occasionally, until noodles are completely softened.

1 SERVING: Calories 338; Total Fat 13g (Saturated Fat 5g, Trans Fat 0g); Cholesterol 55mg; Sodium 1,147mg; Total Carbohydrate 31g (Dietary Fiber 3g, Sugars 2g); Protein 23g; EXCHANGES: 2 Starch; 1 Vegetable; 2 Lean Meat; 1 1/2 Fat; CARBOHYDRATE CHOICES: 2

Expert Tips

- For a change of taste, use boneless skinless chicken breast halves, cut into strips, instead of the pork and use chicken flavor ramen noodles.
- Freeze pork for about 1 1/2 hours before slicing. Pork is easier to cut when partially frozen.

Sweet-and-Sour Noodles 'n Pork

PREP TIME: *30 minutes*

TOTAL TIME: *30 minutes*

MAKES 4 SERVINGS

1 tablespoon vegetable oil

1 pound boneless pork loin chops, cut into thin strips

$\frac{1}{2}$ teaspoon garlic-pepper blend

$1\frac{3}{4}$ cups Progresso® chicken broth (from 32-ounce carton)

$\frac{1}{2}$ cup sweet-and-sour sauce

2 tablespoons chili sauce

$1\frac{1}{2}$ cups uncooked medium egg noodles (3 ounces)

1 package (8 ounces) fresh sugar snap pea pods

1 small red bell pepper, cut into thin strips

$\frac{1}{4}$ cup cashew pieces

In 12-inch nonstick skillet, heat oil over medium-high heat. Add pork to skillet; sprinkle with garlic-pepper blend. Cook 3 to 5 minutes, stirring frequently, until brown.

Stir in broth, sweet-and-sour sauce and chili sauce. Heat to boiling. Stir in noodles. Cover and cook over medium heat 5 minutes.

Stir in pea pods and bell pepper. Cover and cook 5 to 8 minutes, stirring occasionally, until vegetables and noodles are tender. Sprinkle with cashews.

1 SERVING: Calories 410; Total Fat 18g (Saturated Fat 4½g, Trans Fat 0g); Cholesterol 90mg; Sodium 700mg; Total Carbohydrate 32g (Dietary Fiber 4g, Sugars 11g); Protein 33g; EXCHANGES: 1 Starch; 1 Other Carbohydrate; 1 Vegetable; 4 Lean Meat; 1 Fat; CARBOHYDRATE CHOICES: 2

Expert Tips

▪ Pork tenderloin can be substituted for the pork chops.

▪ Pop some frozen egg rolls into the oven to serve with this easy dish.

Spicy Sausage Lasagna Skillet

1 pound bulk spicy pork sausage

2½ cups hot water

½ cup milk

1 box Hamburger Helper® lasagna

1 cup Green Giant® Valley Fresh Steamers® frozen cut green beans

1 cup shredded pepper Jack or mozzarella cheese (4 ounces)

In 10-inch skillet, cook sausage over medium-high heat 5 to 7 minutes, stirring frequently, until no longer pink; drain. Stir in hot water, milk and sauce mix and uncooked pasta (from Hamburger Helper box). Heat to boiling, stirring occasionally.

Reduce heat; cover and simmer 8 minutes. Stir in frozen green beans. Cover; simmer 6 to 8 minutes longer, stirring occasionally, until beans are tender.

Uncover; sprinkle with cheese. Let stand 1 to 2 minutes or until cheese is melted.

1 SERVING: Calories 290; Total Fat 15g (Saturated Fat 6g, Trans Fat 0g); Cholesterol 40mg; Sodium 1,100mg; Total Carbohydrate 25g (Dietary Fiber 0g, Sugars 5g); Protein 15g; EXCHANGES: 1½ Starch; 1½ Fat; CARBOHYDRATE CHOICES: 1½

Chili Macaroni Skillet

PREP TIME: *30 minutes*

TOTAL TIME: *30 minutes*

MAKES 5 SERVINGS

1 pound bulk pork sausage

1 box Hamburger Helper® chili macaroni

3½ cups hot water

2 teaspoons chili powder

1 can (15 ounces) pinto or Progresso® dark red kidney beans, drained, rinsed

1 can (14.5 ounces) diced tomatoes, undrained

1 can (11 ounces) Green Giant® SteamCrisp® Mexicorn® whole kernel corn with red and green peppers, drained

Shredded Cheddar cheese, if desired

Additional chili powder, if desired

In 12-inch skillet, cook sausage over medium-high heat, stirring occasionally, until no longer pink; drain.

Stir in uncooked pasta and sauce mix (from Hamburger Helper box) and remaining ingredients except cheese and additional chili powder. Heat to boiling, stirring frequently.

Reduce heat, cover and simmer about 10 minutes, stirring occasionally, until pasta is tender. Remove from heat. Spoon into individual serving bowls; sprinkle with cheese and additional chili powder.

1 SERVING: Calories 533; Total Fat 25g (Saturated Fat 8g, Trans Fat 0g); Cholesterol 65mg; Sodium 1,799mg; Total Carbohydrate 52g (Dietary Fiber 5g, Sugars 9g); Protein 23g; EXCHANGES: 3 Starch; 2 High-Fat Meat; 2 Fat; CARBOHYDRATE CHOICES: 3½

Expert Tips

■ Make this tame dish wild by using 1 pound of hot or spicy pork sausage and substituting ¼ cup cayenne pepper sauce (hot sauce) for the chili powder. Your taste buds will definitely be tickled!

■ You'll want to use a 12-inch skillet for this recipe because of the amount of ingredients. If you don't have a skillet that large, use a 4- or 5-quart Dutch oven.

■ One cup of Green Giant® Valley Fresh Steamers™ Niblets® frozen corn can be substituted for the canned corn.

Southwestern Corn Skillet

PREP TIME: *25 minutes*

TOTAL TIME: *25 minutes*

MAKES 6 SERVINGS

8 ounces uncooked rotini pasta (2²⁄₃ cups)

1 pound lean (at least 80%) ground beef

½ cup chopped onion (1 medium)

1 jar (26 ounces) chunky tomato pasta sauce

1 can (11 ounces) Green Giant® SteamCrisp® Southwestern style corn, undrained

½ teaspoon salt

1 cup shredded Cheddar cheese (4 ounces)

4 medium green onions, sliced (¼ cup), if desired

Cook and drain pasta as directed on package. Meanwhile, in 12-inch nonstick skillet, cook beef and onion over medium heat 8 to 10 minutes, stirring occasionally, until beef is thoroughly cooked; drain.

Stir in pasta sauce, corn, salt and cooked pasta. Cook until hot. Sprinkle with cheese; let stand 2 to 3 minutes or until melted. Sprinkle with green onions.

1 SERVING: Calories 560; Total Fat 20g (Saturated Fat 8g, Trans Fat ½g); Cholesterol 65mg; Sodium 1,100mg; Total Carbohydrate 66g (Dietary Fiber 5g, Sugars 15g); Protein 27g; EXCHANGES: 3 Starch; 1 Other Carbohydrate; CARBOHYDRATE CHOICES: 4½

Ground Beef and Mushroom Carbonara

PREP TIME: *30 minutes*
TOTAL TIME: *30 minutes*
MAKES 6 SERVINGS

12 ounces uncooked spaghetti

4 slices bacon

½ pound lean (at least 80%) ground beef

1 package (8 ounces) sliced fresh mushrooms (3 cups)

1 small onion, chopped (¼ cup)

4 cloves garlic, finely chopped

½ teaspoon salt

¼ teaspoon pepper

1 cup whipping cream

3 pasteurized eggs, beaten

1 cup grated Parmesan cheese

2 tablespoons chopped fresh parsley

In 4-quart Dutch oven, cook and drain spaghetti as directed on package. Rinse spaghetti and return to Dutch oven; cover to keep warm.

Meanwhile, in 10-inch skillet, cook bacon over medium-high heat 8 to 9 minutes, turning occasionally, until crisp. Remove bacon from skillet, leaving drippings in skillet. Drain bacon on paper towel. Crumble bacon.

In same skillet, cook beef, mushrooms, onion, garlic, salt and pepper over medium-high heat 5 to 7 minutes, stirring frequently, until beef is thoroughly cooked; drain.

Pour whipping cream over cooked spaghetti in Dutch oven. Cook over medium-high heat 1 to 2 minutes, stirring constantly, until hot.

Add beef mixture, bacon and eggs to spaghetti mixture. Reduce heat to medium. Cook 2 to 3 minutes, tossing mixture constantly, until spaghetti is well coated. Stir in cheese. Garnish with parsley.

1 SERVING: Calories 610, Total Fat 30g (Saturated Fat 15g, Trans Fat 1g); Cholesterol 195mg; Sodium 920mg; Total Carbohydrate 55g (Dietary Fiber 3g, Sugars 4g); Protein 30g; EXCHANGES: 3 Starch; ½ Other Carbohydrate; 2½ Fat; CARBOHYDRATE CHOICES: 3½

Expert Tips

■ If you're not a fan of mushrooms, simply leave them out.

■ Using pasteurized eggs, which have been heat-treated, eliminates the risk of salmonella that can be contracted from raw eggs. Pasteurized eggs can be found in the dairy case at large supermarkets.

Green Bean and Beef Pasta Supper

PREP TIME: *15 minutes*

TOTAL TIME: *30 minutes*

MAKES 5 SERVINGS

1 pound lean (at least 80%) ground beef

2 cups hot water

1 cup milk

1 box Hamburger Helper® beef pasta

1 tablespoon dried minced onion

1½ cups Green Giant® frozen cut green beans

1 can (4.5 ounces) Green Giant® sliced mushrooms, drained

In 10-inch skillet, cook beef over medium-high heat 5 to 7 minutes, stirring frequently, until thoroughly cooked; drain.

Stir in hot water, milk, sauce mix and uncooked pasta (from Hamburger Helper box), onion, frozen green beans and mushrooms. Heat to boiling, stirring occasionally.

Reduce heat, cover and simmer 10 minutes, stirring occasionally. Remove from heat; uncover and let stand 5 minutes (sauce will thicken as it stands). Stir before serving.

1 SERVING: Calories 300; Total Fat 12g (Saturated Fat 4½g, Trans Fat ½g); Cholesterol 60mg; Sodium 870mg; Total Carbohydrate 28g (Dietary Fiber 2g, Sugars 5g); Protein 21g; EXCHANGES: 1½ Starch; 1 Vegetable; CARBOHYDRATE CHOICES: 2

Expert Tip

Any style of green beans can be used in this recipe.

Slow Cooker Beef Stroganoff Stew

PREP TIME: *20 minutes*
TOTAL TIME: *5 hours 50 minutes*
MAKES 5 SERVINGS

1 medium onion, chopped (½ cup)

1 clove garlic, finely chopped

1 pound boneless beef tip steak, cut into ½-inch pieces

2 cans (18 ounces each) Progresso® Vegetable Classics creamy mushroom soup

½ cup water

2½ cups uncooked wide egg noodles (4 ounces)

1 cup sour cream

2 tablespoons chopped fresh parsley, if desired

In 3½- to 4-quart slow cooker, layer onion, garlic and beef. Pour soup and water over beef.

Cover; cook on Low heat setting 5 to 7 hours.

Stir noodles into mixture. Increase heat setting to High. Cover; cook 20 to 30 minutes or until noodles are tender. Stir in sour cream. Garnish individual servings with parsley.

1 SERVING: Calories 430; Total Fat 25g (Saturated Fat 12g, Trans Fat 0g); Cholesterol 125mg; Sodium 880mg; Total Carbohydrate 29g (Dietary Fiber 1g, Sugars 6g); Protein 24g; EXCHANGES: 2 Starch; 2½ Lean Meat; 3 Fat; CARBOHYDRATE CHOICES: 2

Expert Tip

To save precious minutes in the morning, use minced garlic in a jar. You could also cut up the beef the night before and refrigerate.

Slow Cooker Mediterranean Minestrone Casserole

PREP TIME: *20 minutes*

TOTAL TIME: *8 hours 40 minutes*

MAKES 5 SERVINGS

3 medium carrots, sliced (1½ cups)

1 medium onion, chopped (½ cup)

1 cup water

2 teaspoons sugar

1 teaspoon Italian seasoning

½ teaspoon salt

¼ teaspoon pepper

1 can (28 ounces) diced tomatoes, undrained

1 can (15 ounces) Progresso® garbanzo beans, rinsed and drained

1 can (6 ounces) Italian-style tomato paste

2 cloves garlic, finely chopped

1½ cups Green Giant® Valley Fresh Steamers® frozen cut green beans (from 12 ounces bag), thawed

1 cup uncooked elbow macaroni (3½ ounces)

½ cup shredded Parmesan cheese (2 ounces)

Mix all ingredients except green beans, macaroni and cheese in 3- to 4-quart slow cooker.

Cover and cook on Low heat setting 6 to 8 hours.

Stir in green beans and macaroni. Increase heat setting to High. Cover and cook about 20 minutes or until beans and macaroni are tender. Sprinkle with cheese.

1 SERVING: Calories 282; Total Fat 6g (Saturated Fat 2g, Trans Fat 0g); Cholesterol 18mg; Sodium 1,149mg; Total Carbohydrate 48g (Dietary Fiber 7g, Sugars 16g); Protein 19g; EXCHANGES: 1½ Starch; 4 Vegetable; ½ Lean Meat; ½ Fat; CARBOHYDRATE CHOICES: 4½

Expert Tips

■ If you prefer, substitute a can of kidney or great northern beans for the garbanzo beans. If you have cooked beans on hand already, use 1¾ cups instead of the can of beans.

■ Looking to get a healthy dose of vegetables? This vegetarian main dish has carrots, onions, tomatoes and green beans, in addition to fiber-rich garbanzos.

■ Adding sugar, even a small amount, can balance the acid level of the tomatoes and round out the flavor.

Grandma's Slow Cooker Chicken Noodle Soup

PREP TIME: *20 minutes*

TOTAL TIME: *7 hours
20 minutes*

MAKES 4 SERVINGS

¾ pound boneless skinless chicken thighs, cut into 1-inch pieces

2 medium stalks celery, sliced (1 cup)

1 large carrot, chopped (¾ cup)

1 medium onion, chopped (½ cup)

1 can (14.5 ounces) diced tomatoes, undrained

1¾ cups Progresso® chicken broth (from 32-ounce carton)

1 teaspoon dried thyme

2 cups Green Giant® frozen sweet peas, thawed

1 cup frozen home-style egg noodles (from 12-ounce bag)

Spray 10-inch skillet with cooking spray; heat over medium heat. Cook chicken in skillet about 5 minutes, stirring frequently, until brown.

In 3½- to 4-quart slow cooker, mix chicken and remaining ingredients except peas and noodles.

Cover; cook on Low heat setting 6 hours 30 minutes to 7 hours.

Stir in peas and noodles. Increase heat setting to High. Cover; cook about 30 minutes or until noodles are tender.

1 SERVING: Calories 330; Total Fat 9g (Saturated Fat 2½g, Trans Fat 0g); Cholesterol 90mg; Sodium 730mg; Total Carbohydrate 35g (Dietary Fiber 5g, Sugars 9g); Protein 27g; EXCHANGES: 1½ Starch; ½ Other Carbohydrate; 1 Vegetable; 3 Lean Meat; CARBOHYDRATE CHOICES: 2

Expert Tip

If you have a food processor, chop the fresh vegetables quickly by cutting them into chunks and then pulsing in the food processor. Process each vegetable separately because they don't all require the same processing time.

Italian Sausage and Pepper Stew

PREP TIME: *25 minutes*

TOTAL TIME: *25 minutes*

MAKES 4 SERVINGS

1 package (19.5 ounces) Italian turkey sausage (sweet or hot), casings removed, links cut into 2-inch pieces

1 large red bell pepper, cut into bite-size strips

1 large yellow bell pepper, cut into bite-size strips

1 can (14.5 ounces) diced tomatoes, undrained

1 teaspoon dried basil, crushed

8 ounces uncooked penne rigate pasta (2½ cups)

Grated Parmesan cheese, if desired

In 6-quart Dutch oven, cook and stir sausage and bell peppers over medium-high heat about 8 minutes or until sausage is no longer pink; drain.

Reduce heat to medium-low. Stir in tomatoes and basil; cover and simmer 10 minutes.

Meanwhile, cook and drain pasta as directed on package. Serve sausage and peppers over cooked pasta. Top with cheese.

1 SERVING: Calories 550; Total Fat 16g (Saturated Fat 3½g, Trans Fat ½g); Cholesterol 125mg; Sodium 1,070mg; Total Carbohydrate 58g (Dietary Fiber 5g, Sugars 7g); Protein 43g; EXCHANGES: 3½ Starch; 1 Vegetable; 4½ Lean Meat; CARBOHYDRATE CHOICES: 4

Expert Tips

■ Cook the pasta while the stew is simmering; everything will be done at the same time.

■ Italian turkey sausage has less fat than most other Italian sausage, making it easy to use in a stew.

Garden Patch Minestrone

PREP TIME: *30 minutes*

TOTAL TIME: *30 minutes*

MAKES 7 SERVINGS

2 tablespoons extra-virgin olive oil

2 medium carrots, sliced (1 cup)

2 medium stalks celery, sliced (1 cup)

1 small onion, chopped (⅓ cup)

2 cloves garlic, finely chopped

1 medium zucchini or yellow summer squash, cut in half lengthwise, then cut crosswise into ¼-inch pieces

¼ cup chopped fresh basil

1 box Hamburger Helper® beef pasta

1 can (15 ounces) Progresso® cannellini or dark red kidney beans, drained, rinsed

1 can (14.5 ounces) diced tomatoes with basil, garlic and oregano, undrained

5 cups hot water

In 5-quart Dutch oven or stockpot, heat oil over medium heat. Add carrots, celery, onion and garlic; cook about 5 minutes, stirring frequently, until vegetables are almost tender.

Stir in zucchini, basil, uncooked pasta and sauce mix (from Hamburger Helper box), beans, tomatoes and hot water. Heat to boiling. Reduce heat; cover and simmer about 10 minutes or until pasta and vegetables are tender.

1 SERVING: Calories 220; Total Fat 4½g (Saturated Fat ½g, Trans Fat 0g); Cholesterol 0mg; Sodium 790mg; Total Carbohydrate 36g (Dietary Fiber 6g, Sugars 5g); Protein 8g; EXCHANGES: 2 Starch; 1 Vegetable; ½ Fat; CARBOHYDRATE CHOICES: 2½

Chicken Pasta Soup

PREP TIME: *40 minutes*
TOTAL TIME: *40 minutes*
MAKES 6 SERVINGS

2 teaspoons butter or margarine

3 boneless skinless chicken breasts, cut into thin strips

1 package (8 ounces) sliced fresh mushrooms (3 cups)

3 cans (14 ounces each) fat-free chicken broth with 33% less sodium

1½ cups uncooked medium pasta shells (4 ounces)

1 cup sliced yellow summer squash or zucchini

½ cup chopped red bell pepper

1 teaspoon Italian seasoning

In 4-quart nonstick saucepan or Dutch oven, heat butter over medium heat until hot. Cook chicken and mushrooms in butter, stirring occasionally, until chicken is no longer pink. Stir in remaining ingredients. Heat to boiling.

Reduce heat to low; simmer 10 to 13 minutes or until pasta is tender. Serve immediately.

1 SERVING: Calories 190; Total Fat 4g (Saturated Fat 1½g, Trans Fat 0g); Cholesterol 40mg; Sodium 500 mg; Total Carbohydrate 19g (Dietary Fiber 1g, Sugars 1g); Protein 20g; EXCHANGES: 1 Starch; 1 Vegetable; 2 Very Lean Meat; ½ Fat; CARBOHYDRATE CHOICES: 1

Expert Tips

- Rotisserie chicken can be used in place of the raw chicken. It's not necessary to cook the chicken with the mushrooms; instead chop and add with the rest of the ingredients.
- Look in the freezer case for Pillsbury® Oven Baked frozen crusty French dinner rolls. Bake them while the soup is cooking for an accompaniment to this soup.

Sides

Tossed Smoked Gouda Spinach Salad

PREP TIME: *10 minutes*

TOTAL TIME: *10 minutes*

MAKES 8 SERVINGS

3 bags (6 ounces each) washed fresh baby spinach leaves

1 pound sliced Canadian bacon, cut into quarters

1 pound smoked Gouda cheese, cubed

4 medium peaches or nectarines, sliced

1 cup honey Dijon dressing

In large bowl, toss spinach, bacon, cheese and peaches.

Drizzle with dressing; toss.

1 SERVING: Calories 467; Total Fat 32g (Saturated Fat 15g, Trans Fat 0g); Cholesterol 79mg; Sodium 1,980mg; Total Carbohydrate 18g (Dietary Fiber 4g, Sugars 8g); Protein 28g; EXCHANGES: 1 Vegetable; ½ Fruit; 2 Lean Meat; 2½ Fat; CARBOHYDRATE CHOICES: 1

Expert Tips

▥ If you're taking this salad to a picnic or potluck, toss everything except the dressing in a large portable container. Once you arrive, drizzle with dressing, then cover and gently shake or spin to "toss."

▥ Canadian bacon is great for summer salads because it is lower in fat and has terrific flavor. You can also substitute sliced fully cooked ham.

Apple, Blue Cheese and Walnut Salad

PREP TIME: *25 minutes*
TOTAL TIME: *25 minutes*
MAKES 10 SERVINGS

DRESSING

- ½ cup vegetable oil
- 6 tablespoons sugar
- 2 tablespoons white wine vinegar
- 1 tablespoon finely chopped red onion
- ½ teaspoon salt
- ½ teaspoon ground mustard
- ¼ to ½ teaspoon celery seed

SALAD

- 1 large bunch romaine lettuce, torn into bite-size pieces (about 10 cups)
- 1 bag (6 ounces) fresh baby spinach leaves
- 1 cup crumbled blue or Gorgonzola cheese (4 ounces)
- 1 cup walnut halves, toasted
- 2 red apples, cut into bite-size pieces

In medium bowl, mix all dressing ingredients with wire whisk until sugar is dissolved (dressing will be thick). Set aside.

In very large bowl, mix salad ingredients. Pour dressing over salad; toss to coat. Serve immediately.

1 SERVING: Calories 274; Total Fat 22g (Saturated Fat 5g, Trans Fat 0g); Cholesterol 10; Sodium 336mg; Total Carbohydrate 18g (Dietary Fiber 3g, Sugars 12g); Protein 6g; EXCHANGES: ½ Fruit; ½ Vegetable; ½ Other Carbohydrate; ½ High-Fat Meat; 3½ Fat; CARBOHYDRATE CHOICES: 1

Expert Tip

Apples that have a bit of tartness are perfect in this salad because the dressing is sweet.

Mixed Green Salad with Dijon Vinaigrette

PREP TIME: *20 minutes*

TOTAL TIME: *20 minutes*

MAKES 6 SERVINGS

VINAIGRETTE

1 tablespoon Dijon mustard

1 tablespoon red wine vinegar

1/2 teaspoon sugar

3 tablespoons olive oil

Dash salt and pepper

SALAD

1 bag (5 ounces) spring lettuce mix

1 cup grape tomatoes, each cut in half lengthwise

1 cup sliced (1/8 inch) seeded peeled cucumber

1 cup sliced (1/8 inch) halved red onion

In small bowl, mix mustard, vinegar and sugar with wire whisk. Gradually add oil, beating constantly until well blended. Season to taste with salt and pepper.

In large salad bowl, place salad ingredients. Pour vinaigrette over salad; toss gently to mix.

1 SERVING: Calories 90; Total Fat 7g (Saturated Fat 1g, Trans Fat 0g); Cholesterol 0mg; Sodium 95mg; Total Carbohydrate 5g (Dietary Fiber 1g, Sugars 2g); Protein 1g; EXCHANGES: 1 Vegetable; 1½ Fat; CARBOHYDRATE CHOICES: ½

Expert Tip

To remove the seeds from the cucumber, cut it in half lengthwise. With the tip of a spoon, scrape out the seeds.

Mandarin Salad

PREP TIME: *20 minutes*

TOTAL TIME: *20 minutes*

MAKES 6 SERVINGS

SUGARED ALMONDS

¼ cup sliced almonds

4 teaspoons sugar

SWEET-SOUR DRESSING

¼ cup vegetable oil

2 tablespoons sugar

2 tablespoons white or cider vinegar

1 tablespoon chopped fresh parsley

½ teaspoon salt

Dash pepper

Dash red pepper sauce

SALAD

½ small head lettuce, torn into bite-size pieces (3 cups)

½ bunch romaine lettuce, torn into bite-size pieces (3 cups)

2 medium stalks celery, chopped (1 cup)

2 medium green onions, thinly sliced (2 tablespoons)

1 can (11 ounces) mandarin orange segments, drained

In 1-quart saucepan, cook almonds and 4 teaspoons sugar over low heat about 10 minutes, stirring constantly, until sugar is melted and almonds are coated. Cool and break apart.

In tightly covered container, shake all dressing ingredients. Refrigerate until serving time.

In large bowl, toss salad ingredients, dressing and almonds. Serve immediately.

1 SERVING: Calories 170; Total Fat 12g (Saturated Fat 1½g, Trans Fat 0g); Cholesterol 0mg; Sodium 220mg; Total Carbohydrate 15g (Dietary Fiber 2g, Sugars 12g); Protein 2g; EXCHANGES: ½ Fruit; 2 Vegetable; 2 Fat; CARBOHYDRATE CHOICES: 1

Expert Tips

▧ Six cups of any combination of salad greens can be used instead of the head lettuce and romaine.

▧ Be sure to tear the greens by hand instead of chopping with a knife. A chemical reaction between the greens and the metal knife will cause the edges of the greens to brown.

▧ For Crunchy Chicken Mandarin Salad, make salad as directed. Divide among 6 individual serving plates. Top each serving with a grilled boneless skinless chicken breast, sliced (warm or cold). Sprinkle each salad with 2 tablespoons wide or regular chow mein noodles.

Fennel & Three Bean Salad

SALAD

- ⅓ pound green beans
- 1 can (15 ounces) Progresso® cannellini (white kidney) beans, drained, rinsed
- 1 can (15 ounces) Progresso® dark red kidney beans, drained, rinsed
- ½ medium sweet onion, very thinly sliced (½ cup)
- 1 medium bulb fennel, very thinly sliced (1 cup)

DRESSING

- ¼ cup olive oil
- 2 tablespoons red wine vinegar
- 2 tablespoons Dijon mustard
- 1 tablespoon finely chopped fresh basil
- 1 clove garlic, finely chopped
- ¼ teaspoon pepper
- ⅛ teaspoon salt

Remove ends of green beans. Place steamer basket in ½ inch water in 2-quart saucepan or skillet (water should not touch bottom of basket). Place green beans in steamer basket. Cover tightly and heat to boiling; reduce heat. Steam 10 to 12 minutes or until crisp-tender.

In large bowl, stir together green beans and remaining salad ingredients; set aside.

In small jar with tight-fitting lid, shake all dressing ingredients. Pour dressing over salad ingredients; toss gently. Refrigerate 1 hour to blend flavors. Serve at room temperature and refrigerate any leftovers.

1 SERVING: Calories 120; Total Fat 5g (Saturated Fat ½g, Trans Fat 0g); Cholesterol 0mg; Sodium 90mg; Total Carbohydrate 14g (Dietary Fiber 4g, Sugars 1g); Protein 5g; EXCHANGES: 1 Starch; 1 Fat; CARBOHYDRATE CHOICES: 1

Dilled Potato–Bean Salad

PREP TIME: *20 minutes*

TOTAL TIME: *35 minutes*

MAKES 14 SERVINGS

- 2 pounds small red potatoes, cut into ½-inch slices
- ⅔ cup olive or vegetable oil
- ⅓ cup white wine vinegar
- 1 teaspoon salt
- ½ teaspoon pepper
- ½ cup chopped celery
- ¼ cup chopped fresh dill weed
- 2 medium green onions, sliced (2 tablespoons)
- 1 can (15 ounces) Progresso® dark red kidney beans, drained, rinsed
- 4 hard-cooked eggs, halved lengthwise, sliced

In 3-quart saucepan, place potatoes and 4 cups water. Heat to boiling over medium-high heat; reduce heat. Simmer uncovered 8 to 10 minutes or until potatoes are tender; drain.

Meanwhile, in small bowl, beat oil, vinegar, salt and pepper with whisk until blended.

In large bowl, place potatoes, celery, dill, onions, beans and 3 of the eggs. Pour dressing over salad; stir gently to coat. Garnish with remaining egg. Let stand 5 minutes. Serve warm.

1 SERVING: Calories 210; Total Fat 12g (Saturated Fat 2g, Trans Fat 0g); Cholesterol 60mg; Sodium 200mg; Total Carbohydrate 18g (Dietary Fiber 3g, Sugars 1g); Protein 5g; EXCHANGES: 1 Starch; ½ Vegetable; 2½ Fat; CARBOHYDRATE CHOICES: 1

Quinoa and Corn Salad

PREP TIME: *35 minutes*

TOTAL TIME: *35 minutes*

MAKES 12 SERVINGS

SALAD

- ½ cup uncooked quinoa
- 1 cup water
- ¾ cup Green Giant® Valley Fresh Steamers™ Niblets® frozen corn (from 12-ounce bag)
- 1 cucumber, peeled, if desired
- 2 stalks celery, sliced (¾ cup)
- ½ medium red bell pepper, chopped
- ½ cup thinly sliced red onion

DRESSING

- 2 tablespoons white wine vinegar
- 2 tablespoons fresh lime juice
- 1 clove garlic, finely chopped
- 1 teaspoon ground cumin
- ¼ teaspoon salt
- ¼ teaspoon pepper
- ¼ cup olive oil
- 2 tablespoons finely chopped fresh cilantro

Rinse quinoa in cold water; drain in fine-mesh strainer. In 1-quart saucepan, heat quinoa and 1 cup water to boiling. Reduce heat. Cover; simmer 15 to 20 minutes or until water is absorbed and quinoa is tender. Cool slightly. Meanwhile, cook corn as directed on package; cool.

Cut cucumber in half lengthwise; remove seeds and cut into 1½ × ¼-inch strips.

In large salad bowl, stir cucumber, celery, bell pepper, onion, cooked quinoa and corn.

In small bowl, beat vinegar, lime juice, garlic, cumin, salt and pepper with whisk until blended. Beat in oil. Pour dressing over quinoa mixture; toss to coat. Sprinkle with cilantro.

1 SERVING: Calories 80; Total Fat 5g (Saturated Fat ½g, Trans Fat 0g); Cholesterol 0mg; Sodium 55mg; Total Carbohydrate 8g (Dietary Fiber 1g, Sugars 1g); Protein 1g; EXCHANGES: ½ Starch; 1 Fat; CARBOHYDRATE CHOICES: ½

Expert Tips

- When fresh corn is in season, grill or roast it instead of using frozen corn, for an added boost of flavor.
- A lime will yield the maximum amount of juice if allowed to come to room temperature first. Roll the lime firmly on the counter, then cut in half and juice. Typically a lime will yield about 1 to 2 tablespoons of juice. For this recipe, choose a large lime so it will yield the amount of juice needed.
- Quinoa is a very old grain, first used by the Incas. It is popular today because it is a good source of protein.

Quinoa and Vegetable Salad

PREP TIME: *20 minutes*

TOTAL TIME: *1 hour 10 minutes*

MAKES 6 SERVINGS

1 cup uncooked quinoa

2 tablespoons fresh lemon juice

2 tablespoons olive oil

2 tablespoons chopped fresh basil

1 can (15 ounces) gluten-free garbanzo beans, drained, rinsed

1 can (15.25 ounces) gluten-free whole kernel sweet corn, drained

1 can (14.5 ounces) gluten-free diced tomatoes, drained

1 cup chopped red bell pepper

1/3 cup quartered pitted kalamata olives

1/2 cup crumbled gluten-free feta cheese

Basil for garnish

Rinse quinoa under cold water 1 minute; drain. Cook quinoa as directed on package; drain. Cool completely, about 30 minutes.

Meanwhile, in small nonmetal bowl, place lemon juice, oil and basil; mix well. Set aside for dressing.

In large bowl, gently toss cooked quinoa, beans, corn, tomatoes, bell pepper and olives. Pour dressing over quinoa mixture; toss gently to coat. Serve immediately or refrigerate 1 to 2 hours before serving.

Just before serving, sprinkle with cheese. Garnish with basil if desired.

1 SERVING: Calories 350; Total Fat 12g (Saturated Fat 3g, Trans Fat 0g); Cholesterol 10mg; Sodium 580mg; Total Carbohydrate 49g (Dietary Fiber 7g, Sugars 7g); Protein 12g; EXCHANGES: 3 Starch; 1 Vegetable; 2 Fat; CARBOHYDRATE CHOICES: 3

Expert Tips

- Quinoa is a tiny, pearl-shaped, ivory-colored grain that expands to four times its size when cooked. It's rich in nutrients, and unlike other grains, it's a complete protein.

- Always read labels to make sure each recipe ingredient is gluten free. Products and ingredient sources can change.

Green Beans with Feta

PREP TIME: *15 minutes*

TOTAL TIME: *15 minutes*

MAKES 8 SERVINGS

- 1 pound fresh green beans, trimmed
- 2 tablespoons vegetable or olive oil
- 1 tablespoon tarragon vinegar
- 2 tablespoons chopped red onion
- ½ teaspoon salt
- ¼ teaspoon pepper
- 1 clove garlic, finely chopped
- ½ cup crumbled feta cheese (2 ounces)

In 6-quart saucepan, heat 1 inch water and beans to boiling; reduce heat. Simmer uncovered 8 to 10 minutes or until crisp-tender; drain.

In large bowl, place beans. Add remaining ingredients except feta cheese; toss to coat.

Top with feta cheese; serve warm.

1 SERVING: Calories 80; Total Fat 5g (Saturated Fat 2g, Trans Fat 0g); Cholesterol 10mg; Sodium 260mg; Total Carbohydrate 5g (Dietary Fiber 2g, Sugars 2g); Protein 2g; EXCHANGES: 1 Vegetable; 1 Fat; CARBOHYDRATE CHOICES: ½

Peas with Mushrooms and Thyme

PREP TIME: *10 minutes*

TOTAL TIME: *10 minutes*

MAKES 6 SERVINGS

- 1 tablespoon olive or vegetable oil
- 1 medium onion, diced (½ cup)
- 1 cup sliced fresh mushrooms
- 1 bag (16 ounces) Cascadian Farm® frozen organic garden peas
- ¼ teaspoon coarse salt (kosher or sea salt)
- ⅛ teaspoon white pepper
- 1 teaspoon chopped fresh or ¼ teaspoon dried thyme

In 10-inch skillet, heat oil over medium heat. Cook onion and mushrooms in oil 3 minutes, stirring occasionally. Stir in peas. Cook 3 to 5 minutes, stirring occasionally, until tender.

Sprinkle with salt, pepper and thyme. Serve immediately.

1 SERVING: Calories 80; Total Fat 2½g (Saturated Fat 0g, Trans Fat 0g); Cholesterol 0mg; Sodium 150mg; Total Carbohydrate 11g (Dietary Fiber 3g, Sugars 4g); Protein 4g; EXCHANGES: ½ Other Carbohydrate; 1 Vegetable; ½ Fat; CARBOHYDRATE CHOICES: 1

Expert Tip

Purchase presliced mushrooms in the produce section of your supermarket.

Garlic Baby Broccoli

4 bunches baby broccoli, trimmed, tough ends removed (2 pounds)

3 tablespoons extra-virgin olive oil

6 cloves garlic, sliced

¼ cup Progresso® unsalted chicken broth (from 32-ounce carton)

Salt and pepper

In 4-quart saucepan, heat 1 inch water to boiling. Add broccoli; cook over high heat 3 to 4 minutes or just until stalks are crisp-tender. Drain; set aside.

In 12-inch skillet, heat oil over medium-high heat. Add garlic to oil; cook 1 to 2 minutes, stirring occasionally, until light golden brown. Add cooked broccoli and broth; simmer over high heat about 2 minutes or until broth is almost completely reduced. Season with salt and pepper to taste.

1 SERVING: Calories 100; Total Fat 7g (Saturated Fat 1g, Trans Fat 0g); Cholesterol 0mg; Sodium 35mg; Total Carbohydrate 7g (Dietary Fiber 2g, Sugars 2g); Protein 3g; EXCHANGES: 1½ Vegetable; 1½ Fat; CARBOHYDRATE CHOICES: ½

Asparagus with Maple–Mustard Sauce

PREP TIME: *10 minutes*

TOTAL TIME: *10 minutes*

MAKES 8 SERVINGS

2 pounds asparagus

2 tablespoons real maple syrup or maple-flavored syrup

2 tablespoons Dijon mustard

2 tablespoons olive or vegetable oil

Snap off tough ends of asparagus spears. In 12-inch skillet or 4-quart Dutch oven, heat 1 inch water to boiling. Add asparagus. Heat to boiling; reduce heat to medium. Cover and cook 4 to 5 minutes or until asparagus is crisp-tender; drain.

In small bowl, mix maple syrup, mustard and oil. Drizzle over asparagus.

1 SERVING: Calories 70; Total Fat 4g (Saturated Fat ½g, Trans Fat 0g); Cholesterol 0mg; Sodium 95mg; Total Carbohydrate 6g (Dietary Fiber 0g, Sugars 4g); Protein 2g; EXCHANGES: ½ Vegetable; 1 Fat; CARBOHYDRATE CHOICES: ½

Expert Tip

Honey can be used instead of the maple syrup.

Roma Tomatoes with Asparagus and Hollandaise

PREP TIME: *25 minutes*

TOTAL TIME: *30 minutes*

MAKES 12 SERVINGS

6 medium plum (Roma) tomatoes (2½ to 3 inches long)

36 thin asparagus spears (¼ inch diameter)

1 cup milk

1 package (0.9 ounce) hollandaise sauce mix

¼ cup butter or margarine

½ cup shredded Parmesan cheese (2 ounces)

Cut tomatoes in half lengthwise. Seed tomatoes, using teaspoon; remove flesh, leaving ¼-inch-thick shell. Cut thin slice from rounded side of tomato halves, if necessary, so they'll rest level in pan. Drain tomatoes, hollow sides down, on paper towels.

Break off tough ends of asparagus. From tip end, cut off top 3 inches of each spear (reserve remaining portions of spear for another use). In 1-quart saucepan, heat 1 inch water to boiling. Add asparagus tips. Heat to boiling and boil 2 minutes; drain and set aside.

In same 1-quart saucepan, beat milk and sauce mix with wire whisk until smooth.

Add butter. Heat to boiling over medium heat, stirring constantly. Reduce heat to low. Cook 1 minute, stirring constantly, until thickened and smooth.

Set oven control to broil. In 13 × 9-inch pan, place tomato halves hollow side up. In each tomato half, arrange 3 asparagus pieces lengthwise with tips extended over stem end of tomato. Spoon 1 tablespoon sauce over top, allowing some sauce to fill tomato hollow. Sprinkle with cheese.

Broil with tops 4 to 6 inches from heat 2 to 4 minutes or until tomatoes are hot and cheese just begins to brown. If desired, heat remaining sauce until hot; serve with tomatoes.

1 SERVING: Calories 90; Total Fat 6g (Saturated Fat 3g, Trans Fat 0g); Cholesterol 15mg; Sodium 170mg; Total Carbohydrate 5g (Dietary Fiber 0g, Sugars 3g); Protein 4g; EXCHANGES: ½ Vegetable; 1 Fat; CARBOHYDRATE CHOICES: ½

Expert Tip

Isn't it great to find recipes like this? They look fabulous, like you've spent the whole day making them, but they're super easy to make! Serve with roasted beef tenderloin or grilled steak or chicken.

Maple-Glazed Carrots with Pecans

PREP TIME: *10 minutes*
TOTAL TIME: *10 minutes*
MAKES 12 SERVINGS

¼ cup chicken broth

¼ teaspoon salt

2 pounds ready-to-eat baby-cut carrots

¼ cup real maple or maple-flavored syrup

2 tablespoons butter or margarine

¼ cup coarsely chopped pecans

In 12-inch skillet, heat broth and salt to boiling over high heat. Add carrots; reduce heat to medium. Cover; cook 10 to 12 minutes or just until crisp-tender. Drain if necessary.

Add syrup and butter to carrots in saucepan. Cook over medium-high heat 3 to 4 minutes, stirring frequently, until carrots are glazed. Sprinkle with pecans.

1 SERVING: Calories 90; Total Fat 4g (Saturated Fat 1½g, Trans Fat 0g); Cholesterol 5mg; Sodium 135mg; Total Carbohydrate 12g (Dietary Fiber 2g, Sugars 8g); Protein 1g; EXCHANGES: ½ Other Carbohydrate; 1 Vegetable; 1 Fat; CARBOHYDRATE CHOICES: 1

Expert Tips

▪ Substitute purchased sugar-glazed almonds for the pecans.

▪ Real maple syrup is more expensive because it takes 20 gallons of maple sap to make one gallon of syrup! Less costly maple-flavored syrup is a blend of less-expensive syrup and pure maple syrup or flavoring.

Acorn Squash with Dates

PREP TIME: *5 minutes*

TOTAL TIME: *25 minutes*

MAKES 4 SERVINGS

1 acorn squash (1½ to 2 pounds)

2 tablespoons chopped dates or raisins

1 tablespoon packed brown sugar

1½ teaspoons no-trans-fat vegetable oil spread

Pierce squash with knife in several places to allow steam to escape. Place on microwavable paper towel in microwave oven. Microwave uncovered on High about 5 minutes or until squash feels warm to the touch. Cut in half; remove seeds.

In shallow microwavable dish, place squash halves, cut sides down. Cover with microwavable plastic wrap, folding back one edge or corner ¼ inch to vent steam. Microwave on High 5 to 8 minutes, rotating dish every 2 minutes, until tender. Let stand 5 minutes.

In small bowl, mix remaining ingredients. Turn squash cut sides up. Spoon date mixture into centers of squash. Microwave uncovered on High about 1 minute or until sugar is melted. Cut each squash half into 2 serving pieces.

1 SERVING: Calories 45; Total Fat 1½ g (Saturated Fat 0g, Trans Fat 0g); Cholesterol 0mg; Sodium 20mg; Total Carbohydrate 7g (Dietary Fiber 0g, Sugars 7g); Protein 0g; EXCHANGES: 1 Vegetable; CARBOHYDRATE CHOICES: ½

Expert Tips

- You can find a variety of no-trans-fat vegetable oil spreads located in the refrigerated dairy section by the butter.
- Try this with dried cranberries or cherries instead of dates.

Rutabaga Smash with Bacon

2 rutabagas (about 1 pound), peeled, cut into 1-inch cubes

4 large carrots (about ¾ pound), cut into 1-inch cubes

1 teaspoon salt

½ cup butter

1 large sweet onion, thinly sliced, slices cut in half

¼ cup whipping cream

½ teaspoon freshly ground pepper

5 slices thick-sliced bacon, crisply cooked, crumbled (⅓ cup)

Fresh rosemary sprig, if desired

In 3-quart Dutch oven, place rutabagas, carrots and enough water to cover; add ½ teaspoon of the salt. Heat to boiling; reduce heat to low. Cover; simmer 30 to 35 minutes or until tender. Drain.

Meanwhile, in 12-inch nonstick skillet, melt ¼ cup of the butter over medium heat. Cook onion in butter 25 minutes, stirring occasionally, until very tender.

In large bowl, mash rutabagas and carrots until almost no lumps remain. Add onion, whipping cream, pepper, remaining ¼ cup butter and remaining ½ teaspoon salt; stir until well blended. Sprinkle with bacon. Garnish with rosemary.

1 SERVING: Calories 284; Total Fat 25g (Saturated Fat 13g, Trans Fat ½g); Cholesterol 57mg; Sodium 611mg; Total Carbohydrate 12g (Dietary Fiber 3g, Sugars 4g); Protein 4g; EXCHANGES: 2 Vegetable; ½ High-Fat Meat; 4½ Fat CARBOHYDRATE CHOICES: 1

Expert Tip

Rutabagas are easy to peel with a vegetable peeler, or gently scrape them with a knife.

Make–Ahead Sour Cream 'n Chive Mashed Potatoes

PREP TIME: *40 minutes*

TOTAL TIME: *9 hours 30 minutes*

MAKES 16 SERVINGS

3 pounds small red potatoes

1 container (8 ounces) chive-and-onion cream cheese spread

1 container (12 ounces) chive-and-onion sour cream

1½ teaspoons salt

¼ teaspoon pepper

3 tablespoons butter or margarine, melted

½ cup French-fried onions (from 2.8-ounce can)

Spray 13 × 9-inch pan with cooking spray; set aside. In 4-quart Dutch oven, place potatoes; add enough water just to cover potatoes. Cover and heat to boiling; reduce heat. Simmer covered 20 to 25 minutes or until potatoes are tender; drain.

Shake potatoes in Dutch oven over low heat to dry.

Mash potatoes until no lumps remain. Add cream cheese, sour cream, salt and pepper; mix until well blended. Spoon into pan. Cover tightly with foil and refrigerate at least 8 hours but no longer than 24 hours (or bake immediately if desired).

Heat oven to 350°F. Drizzle butter over potatoes. Cover and bake 30 minutes.

Sprinkle onions over potatoes. Bake uncovered 15 to 20 minutes longer or until potatoes are hot.

1 SERVING: Calories 170; Total Fat 11g (Saturated Fat 6g, Trans Fat ½g); Cholesterol 25mg; Sodium 500mg; Total Carbohydrate 17g (Dietary Fiber 2g, Sugars 2g); Protein 3g; EXCHANGES: 1 Starch; 2 Fat; CARBOHYDRATE CHOICES: 1

Expert Tips

■ Eight cups of unseasoned cooked Betty Crocker Potato Buds® mashed potatoes or refrigerated mashed potatoes can be substituted for the fresh potatoes.

■ Stiff mashed potatoes will be better than soft and creamy mashed potatoes.

Roasted Beets and Oranges with Herb Butter

PREP TIME: *50 minutes*

TOTAL TIME: *1 hour 45 minutes*

MAKES 4 SERVINGS

4 medium beets (about 1 pound), peeled, cut into 1-inch pieces

1 small orange, halved, thinly sliced

2 tablespoons olive oil

$\frac{1}{4}$ teaspoon salt

$\frac{1}{4}$ teaspoon freshly ground pepper

3 tablespoons butter

1 tablespoon chopped fresh Italian (flat-leaf) parsley

1 tablespoon chopped fresh rosemary leaves

2 tablespoons orange juice

Heat oven to 400°F. Cut 18 × 12-inch sheet of heavy-duty foil; spray foil with cooking spray. In large bowl, toss beets, orange slices, oil, salt and pepper.

Spoon mixture in center of foil. Bring up 2 sides of foil over mixture so edges meet. Seal edges, making tight $\frac{1}{2}$-inch fold; fold again, allowing space for heat circulation and expansion. Place packet on cookie sheet.

Roast 45 minutes. Carefully unfold foil with tongs; roast 10 minutes longer or until beets are tender and browned.

In 12-inch skillet, melt butter over medium-high heat. Stir in parsley, rosemary and orange juice with whisk; cook 1 to 2 minutes or until slightly thickened.

Remove beets and oranges from foil and add to skillet; cook and stir until coated with butter mixture.

1 SERVING: Calories 188; Total Fat 16g (Saturated Fat 6$\frac{1}{2}$g, Trans Fat 0g); Cholesterol 23; Sodium 271mg; Total Carbohydrate 12g (Dietary Fiber 3g, Sugars 8g); Protein 2g; EXCHANGES: 1 Starch; 1$\frac{1}{2}$ Vegetable; 3 Fat; CARBOHYDRATE CHOICES: 1

Garden Ratatouille

PREP TIME: *25 minutes*

TOTAL TIME: *25 minutes*

MAKES 8 SERVINGS

3 cups ½-inch cubes eggplant (1 pound)

1 small zucchini, cut into ¼-inch slices (1 cup)

1 small onion, sliced

½ medium green bell pepper, cut into strips

2 cloves garlic, finely chopped

2 tablespoons chopped fresh parsley

1 tablespoon chopped fresh or ½ teaspoon dried basil

2 tablespoons water

½ teaspoon salt

¼ teaspoon black pepper

2 medium very ripe tomatoes, cut into eighths

2 tablespoons olive oil if desired

In 10-inch skillet, cook all ingredients except tomatoes and oil over medium heat about 10 minutes, stirring occasionally, until vegetables are tender; remove from heat.

Stir in tomatoes. For added flavor, drizzle with olive oil, if desired. Cover and let stand 2 to 3 minutes until tomatoes are warm.

1 SERVING: Calories 25; Total Fat 0g (Saturated Fat 0g, Trans Fat 0g); Cholesterol 0mg; Sodium 150mg; Total Carbohydrate 5g (Dietary Fiber 2g, Sugars 2g); Protein 0g; EXCHANGES: 1 Vegetable; CARBOHYDRATE CHOICES: ½

Expert Tip

Never cooked eggplant? It is important to understand its structure. An eggplant is—for lack of a better term—a sponge. Looking closely at a cut piece, you'll see thousands of tiny holes. These holes absorb an amazing amount of oil, causing fried eggplant to become heavy and greasy. To help prevent this, cut the eggplant into pieces and then salt them. The salt draws out any bitter juices and collapses some of the holes. Fry salted eggplant quickly over high heat to seal the outside. Because the eggplant isn't fried in this recipe, there is no need to salt it first.

Fruited Tabbouleh with Walnuts and Feta

PREP TIME: *20 minutes*
TOTAL TIME: *4 hours 20 minutes*
MAKES 10 SERVINGS

1 cup uncooked bulgur

1 cup boiling water

¼ cup orange juice

2 tablespoons olive oil

½ medium unpeeled cucumber, seeded, chopped (about 1 cup)

½ cup chopped red onion

½ cup sweetened dried cranberries

⅓ cup loosely packed fresh flat-leaf (Italian) parsley, chopped

⅓ cup loosely packed fresh mint leaves, chopped

1 tablespoon grated orange peel

½ teaspoon salt

1 orange, peeled, sectioned and chopped

⅓ cup chopped walnuts, toasted

½ cup crumbled feta cheese (2 ounces)

Place bulgur in large heatproof bowl. Pour boiling water over bulgur; stir. Let stand about 1 hour or until water is absorbed.

Stir in orange juice, oil, cucumber, onion, cranberries, parsley, mint, orange peel and salt; toss well. Cover; refrigerate 2 to 3 hours or until well chilled.

Just before serving, stir in chopped orange. Sprinkle with walnuts and cheese.

1 SERVING: Calories 151; Total Fat 7g (Saturated Fat 2g, Trans Fat 0g); Cholesterol 5; Sodium 186mg; Total Carbohydrate 21g (Dietary Fiber 4g, Sugars 7g); Protein 4g; EXCHANGES: 1 Starch; ½ Fruit; ½ Vegetable; 1 Fat; CARBOHYDRATE CHOICES: 1½

Expert Tip

To toast walnuts, spread in ungreased shallow pan. Bake uncovered at 350°F 6 to 10 minutes, stirring occasionally, until golden brown.

Onion and Mushroom Quinoa

PREP TIME: *10 minutes*

TOTAL TIME: *30 minutes*

MAKES 4 SERVINGS

1 teaspoon canola or soybean oil

1 cup uncooked quinoa

1 small onion, cut into fourths and sliced

1 medium carrot, shredded ($^2/_3$ cup)

1 small green bell pepper, chopped ($^1/_2$ cup)

1 cup sliced fresh mushrooms (about $2^1/_2$ ounces)

1 teaspoon chopped fresh or $^1/_4$ teaspoon dried thyme

$^1/_4$ teaspoon salt

1 can (14 ounces) fat-free vegetable broth

Heat oil in 2-quart saucepan over medium heat. Cook quinoa and onion in oil 4 to 5 minutes, stirring occasionally, until light brown.

Stir in remaining ingredients. Heat to boiling; reduce heat to low. Cover and simmer about 15 minutes or until liquid is absorbed. Fluff with fork.

1 SERVING: Calories 200; Total Fat 4g (Saturated Fat 0g, Trans Fat 0g); Cholesterol 0mg; Sodium 600mg; Total Carbohydrate 35g (Dietary Fiber 4g, Sugars 6g); Protein 7g; EXCHANGES: 2 Starch; 1 Vegetable; $^1/_2$ Fat; CARBOHYDRATE CHOICES: 2

Expert Tip

This great side dish contains quinoa (KEEN-wa), which has been hailed as a "supergrain" because it contains more protein than any other grain, plus it cooks in only 20 minutes. Like other whole grains, it's low in fat and provides a rich, balanced source of vital nutrients.

Garden-Style Red Rice

1 can (14.5 ounces) fire-roasted crushed tomatoes, undrained

4 cups chicken broth

1 teaspoon tomato bouillon granules with chicken flavor

2 cloves garlic, finely chopped (about 1 teaspoon)

2 tablespoons vegetable oil

1/2 cup finely chopped onion

2 cups uncooked converted white rice

2 large parsley sprigs

2 whole serrano chiles

1 teaspoon salt

2 2/3 cups Green Giant® frozen mixed vegetables

In blender, place tomatoes, 1 cup of the broth, the bouillon and garlic. Cover; blend on low speed 20 to 30 seconds or until smooth.

In 4-quart Dutch oven, heat oil over medium-high heat. Cook onion in oil until tender, stirring constantly. Stir in rice; cook 1 to 2 minutes, stirring constantly, just until rice begins to turn golden.

Carefully stir in tomato mixture. Cook about 1 minute or until mixture starts to bubble. Stir in remaining 3 cups broth, the parsley sprigs, chiles and salt. Return mixture to boiling.

Cover and cook over low heat 20 minutes, stirring occasionally. Stir in frozen vegetables; cook 8 to 10 minutes, stirring frequently, until vegetables are tender and liquid is absorbed. Remove parsley sprigs.

1 SERVING: Calories 270; Total Fat 4 1/2g (Saturated Fat 1g, Trans Fat 0g); Cholesterol 0mg; Sodium 1,610mg; Total Carbohydrate 49g (Dietary Fiber 3g, Sugars 4g); Protein 8g; EXCHANGES: 2 1/2 Starch; 1 Other Carbohydrate; 1/2 Fat; CARBOHYDRATE CHOICES: 3

Expert Tips

- Look for chopped garlic in jars in the produce department. Follow the directions on the jar for the correct amount to use.
- Serve this flavorful rice in yellow, red or green bell peppers that are cut in half lengthwise and seeded.

Confetti Brown Rice

1½ cups sliced fresh mushrooms (4 ounces)

½ cup chopped carrot

½ cup chopped red bell pepper

½ cup uncooked extra-long-grain brown rice

1 cup water

½ teaspoon salt

¼ teaspoon black pepper

1 cup chopped fresh broccoli

Spray 3- to 4-quart slow cooker with cooking spray. In slow cooker, mix all ingredients except broccoli.

Cover; cook on High heat setting 2 hours 30 minutes to 3 hours 30 minutes.

Stir in broccoli. Cover; cook 15 to 20 minutes longer or until broccoli is crisp-tender.

1 SERVING: Calories 80; Total Fat ½g (Saturated Fat 0g, Trans Fat 0g); Cholesterol 0mg; Sodium 410mg; Total Carbohydrate 15g (Dietary Fiber 3g, Sugars 2g); Protein 2g; EXCHANGES: ½ Starch; 1 Vegetable; CARBOHYDRATE CHOICES: 1

Expert Tips

▪ Substitute orange or yellow bell pepper for the red bell pepper if you have one on hand. All of these colors of bell peppers are sweeter than green bell peppers and can be used interchangeably.

▪ If you like the earthy flavor and meaty texture of baby portobello mushrooms, use them in place of the regular white mushrooms.

PREP TIME: *10 minutes*

TOTAL TIME: *40 minutes*

MAKES 4 SERVINGS

Sweet Potato Risotto

2 tablespoons dry white wine or water

1/3 cup chopped onion

1 clove garlic, finely chopped

1 cup uncooked Arborio or other short-grain rice

1/2 cup mashed cooked sweet potato

3 3/4 cups Progresso® chicken broth (from 32-ounce carton), warmed

2 tablespoons grated Parmesan cheese

1/2 teaspoon chopped fresh rosemary leaves or 1/4 teaspoon dried rosemary

1/8 teaspoon ground nutmeg

Spray 3-quart nonstick saucepan with cooking spray. Heat wine to boiling in saucepan over medium-high heat. Cook onion and garlic in wine 3 to 4 minutes, stirring frequently, until onion is tender. Stir in rice. Cook 1 minute, stirring constantly.

Stir in sweet potato and 1/2 cup of the broth. Cook, stirring constantly, until liquid is completely absorbed. Stir in an additional 1/2 cup broth. Continue cooking about 20 minutes, stirring constantly and adding broth 1/2 cup at a time after previous additions have been absorbed, until rice is creamy and just tender; remove from heat.

Stir in remaining ingredients.

1 SERVING: Calories 260; Total Fat 2g (Saturated Fat 1g, Trans Fat 0g); Cholesterol 7mg; Sodium 953mg; Total Carbohydrate 53g (Dietary Fiber 2g, Sugars 4g); Protein 10g; EXCHANGES: 3 Starch; 1/2 Fat; CARBOHYDRATE CHOICES: 3 1/2

Asparagus Risotto

PREP TIME: *45 minutes*

TOTAL TIME: *45 minutes*

MAKES 5 SERVINGS

- 3 cups Progresso® reduced-sodium chicken broth (from 32-ounce carton) or vegetable broth
- 3 cups water
- 1 tablespoon butter or margarine
- 1 medium onion, chopped (½ cup)
- ¼ cup shredded carrot
- 2 cloves garlic, finely chopped
- ¼ cup dry white wine, Progresso® reduced-sodium chicken broth or vegetable broth
- 1 package (12 ounces) uncooked Arborio or other short-grain rice
- ¼ teaspoon coarse salt (kosher or sea salt)
- 1 box (9 ounces) Cascadian Farm® frozen organic asparagus cuts, thawed
- 2 tablespoons pine nuts, toasted
- ½ cup shredded fresh Parmesan cheese (2 ounces)

In 3- to 4-quart saucepan, heat broth and water to boiling. Reduce heat; simmer while preparing risotto.

Meanwhile, in 10-inch skillet, melt butter over medium heat. Add onion, carrot and garlic; cook 2 to 3 minutes, stirring occasionally, until onion and carrot are tender. Stir in wine; cook 1 minute or until wine boils. Stir in rice, salt and 1 cup simmering liquid. Cook until liquid is absorbed into rice, stirring frequently.

Continue to add liquid, 1 cup at a time, cooking until liquid is absorbed and stirring frequently.

When 4 cups liquid have been absorbed, stir in asparagus. Test rice for doneness, and continue adding ½ cup liquid at a time until rice is tender but still firm and creamy (process takes 15 to 20 minutes).

Remove skillet from heat. Stir in pine nuts and cheese. Serve immediately.

1 SERVING: Calories 350; Total Fat 8g (Saturated Fat 3½g, Trans Fat 0g); Cholesterol 15mg; Sodium 780mg; Total Carbohydrate 58g (Dietary Fiber 1g, Sugars 2g); Protein 13g; EXCHANGES: 3 Starch; ½ Other Carbohydrate; 1 Vegetable; 1½ Fat; CARBOHYDRATE CHOICES: 4

Expert Tip

Take your time with risotto—the secret to the creamy texture is a combination of slowly adding the liquid and constantly stirring.

Baked Vegetable Risotto

- 2 tablespoons extra-virgin olive oil
- 2 tablespoons finely chopped onion
- 2 cloves garlic, finely chopped
- 1 package (8 ounces) crimini mushrooms, quartered
- 2 teaspoons chopped fresh rosemary
- 1 cup uncooked Arborio rice
- 1 can (14 ounces) chicken or vegetable broth
- 1/2 cup white wine or water
- 1 1/2 cups Green Giant® frozen cut green beans, thawed and drained
- 1/2 cup roasted red bell peppers (from a jar), cut into strips
- 1 cup grated Parmesan cheese

Heat oven to 400°F. Spray 2 1/2-quart casserole with cooking spray. In 12-inch nonstick skillet, heat olive oil over medium heat. Add onion, garlic, mushrooms and rosemary. Cook 3 to 5 minutes over medium heat, stirring frequently, until mushrooms start to soften.

Add rice. Cook 2 minutes, stirring constantly. Add broth and wine; heat to boiling. Remove from heat; pour into casserole.

Cover casserole. Bake 15 minutes. Stir in green beans, roasted peppers and 1/2 cup of the cheese. Cover; bake 10 to 15 minutes longer or until liquid is absorbed and rice is tender. Stir in remaining 1/2 cup cheese.

1 SERVING: Calories 410; Total Fat 15g (Saturated Fat 6g, Trans Fat 0g); Cholesterol 20mg; Sodium 880mg; Total Carbohydrate 48g (Dietary Fiber 2g, Sugars 4g); Protein 18g; EXCHANGES: 3 Starch; 1 Vegetable; 1 High-Fat Meat; 1 Fat; CARBOHYDRATE CHOICES: 3

Expert Tips

- If your family prefers, you could add a cup of chopped cooked ham or chicken to this meatless dish. Add it when you add the rice to the skillet.
- Crimini mushrooms add a meaty flavor to a meatless main dish. Quartered button mushrooms can be substituted if you prefer.

Cheesy Broccoli–Rice Bake

1 cup uncooked regular long-grain white rice

2 cups water

1 tablespoon butter or margarine

1 large onion, chopped (1 cup)

1 loaf (16 ounces) prepared cheese product, cut into cubes

1 can ($10\frac{3}{4}$ ounces) condensed cream of mushroom soup

$\frac{2}{3}$ cup milk

$\frac{1}{4}$ teaspoon pepper, if desired

2 cups fresh broccoli florets, cut into $\frac{1}{2}$-inch pieces

1 cup fine soft bread crumbs (about $1\frac{1}{2}$ slices bread)

1 tablespoon butter or margarine, melted

Heat oven to 350°F. Spray 13 × 9-inch (3-quart) glass baking dish with cooking spray. Cook rice in water as directed on package.

Meanwhile, in 10-inch skillet, melt 1 tablespoon butter over medium-high heat. Add onion; cook, stirring occasionally, until crisp-tender. Reduce heat to medium. Stir in cheese, soup, milk and pepper. Cook, stirring frequently, until cheese is melted.

Stir in broccoli and rice. Spoon into baking dish. In small bowl, mix bread crumbs and 1 tablespoon melted butter; sprinkle over rice mixture.

Bake uncovered 30 to 35 minutes or until light brown on top and bubbly around edges.

1 SERVING: Calories 410; Total Fat 22g (Saturated Fat 12g, Trans Fat 1g); Cholesterol 65mg; Sodium 1,510mg; Total Carbohydrate 38g (Dietary Fiber 2g, Sugars 9g); Protein 15g; EXCHANGES: 2 Starch; $\frac{1}{2}$ Other Carbohydrate; $1\frac{1}{2}$ High-Fat Meat; $1\frac{1}{2}$ Fat; CARBOHYDRATE CHOICES: $2\frac{1}{2}$

Expert Tips

■ Try this super recipe as a side dish with your favorite vegetarian burgers.

■ Lighter Cheesy Broccoli-Rice Bake: For 9 grams of fat and 275 calories per serving, omit 1 tablespoon butter for cooking onion; instead spray skillet with cooking spray. Use reduced-fat prepared cheese product loaf, condensed 98% fat-free cream of mushroom soup and fat-free (skim) milk.

Slow Cooker Four-Can Baked Beans

PREP TIME: *5 minutes*
TOTAL TIME: *1 hour 5 minutes*
MAKES 12 SERVINGS

1 can (16 ounces) baked beans, undrained

1 can (15 ounces) spicy chili beans, undrained

1 can (15 ounces) Progresso® black beans, drained, rinsed

1 can (10 ounces) diced tomatoes with green chiles, undrained

Heat oven to 350°F. Spray 2-quart casserole with cooking spray. In large bowl, mix all ingredients. Pour into casserole.

Bake 1 hour or until thoroughly heated and flavors are blended.

1 SERVING: Calories 110; Total Fat ½g (Saturated Fat 0g, Trans Fat 0g); Cholesterol 0mg; Sodium 490mg; Total Carbohydrate 23g (Dietary Fiber 6g, Sugars 5g); Protein 7g; EXCHANGES: 1½ Starch; CARBOHYDRATE CHOICES: 1

Expert Tip

Assemble these baked beans in a 3½- to 4-quart slow cooker. Cook them on the Low heat setting until they are thoroughly heated, about 4 hours.

Slow Cooker Chive-and-Onion Creamed Corn

PREP TIME: *20 minutes*

TOTAL TIME: *3 hours*

MAKES 8 SERVINGS

4 slices bacon

4½ cups Green Giant® Niblets® frozen whole kernel corn (from two 1-pound bags), thawed

½ medium red bell pepper, chopped (½ cup)

½ cup milk

¼ cup butter or margarine, melted

1 teaspoon sugar

½ teaspoon salt

⅛ teaspoon black pepper

1 container (8 ounces) reduced-fat chive-and-onion cream cheese

In 12-inch nonstick skillet, cook bacon over medium-high heat, turning occasionally, until crisp. Drain on paper towels. Crumble bacon.

Spray 3- to 4-quart slow cooker with cooking spray. In cooker, mix corn, bell pepper, milk, butter, sugar, salt, pepper and half of the bacon. Refrigerate remaining bacon.

Cover; cook on High heat setting 2 hours to 2 hours 30 minutes.

Stir in cream cheese. Cook on High heat setting 10 minutes longer. Stir well; sprinkle with remaining bacon. Corn can be kept warm on Low heat setting up to 1 hour.

1 SERVING: Calories 220; Total Fat 12g (Saturated Fat 7g, Trans Fat 0g); Cholesterol 35mg; Sodium 460mg; Total Carbohydrate 21g (Dietary Fiber 2g, Sugars 6g); Protein 6g; EXCHANGES: 1½ Starch; 2 Fat; CARBOHYDRATE CHOICES: 1½

Expert Tips

■ Sprinkle with chopped fresh chives for an added burst of color.

■ Company coming? Serve this with baked ham.

Slow Cooker New Potatoes and Spring Vegetables

PREP TIME: *12 minutes*

TOTAL TIME: *6 hours 40 minutes*

MAKES 18 SERVINGS

2 pounds small new potatoes

2 cups baby-cut carrots, cut lengthwise in half

1 large sweet onion (such as Bermuda, Maui, Spanish or Walla Walla), cut in half and thinly sliced

1 teaspoon salt

1 pound asparagus spears, cut into 2-inch pieces

¼ cup olive or vegetable oil

6 tablespoons chopped fresh dill weed

1 to 2 teaspoons grated lemon peel

2 tablespoons Dijon mustard

1 teaspoon salt

Cut large potatoes in half as needed to make similar-size pieces. Place carrots in 5- to 6-quart slow cooker. Top with onion and potatoes; sprinkle with 1 teaspoon salt.

Cover and cook on Low heat setting 5 to 6 hours.

Add asparagus to cooker. Increase heat setting to High. Cover and cook 15 to 20 minutes or until asparagus is crisp-tender.

Mix oil, dill weed, lemon peel, mustard and 1 teaspoon salt in small bowl. Pour over vegetables in cooker; stir to coat. Vegetables will hold on Low heat setting up to 2 hours; stir occasionally.

1 SERVING: Calories 80; Total Fat 3½g (Saturated Fat 0g, Trans Fat 0g); Cholesterol 0mg; Sodium 310mg; Total Carbohydrate 12g (Dietary Fiber 2g, Sugars 2g); Protein 2g; EXCHANGES: ½ Starch; 1 Vegetable; ½ Fat; CARBOHYDRATE CHOICES: 1

Expert Tips

▪ This delicately herbed vegetable dish complements the stronger flavors and textures of dishes including a garlic-spiked turkey breast or London broil beef brisket.

▪ Spoon these spring vegetables on a platter or into a serving bowl, then tuck sprigs of fresh dill weed around the edges.

Okra, Corn and Tomatoes

PREP TIME: *25 minutes*
TOTAL TIME: *25 minutes*
MAKES 8 SERVINGS

4 slices bacon

1 cup coarsely chopped onion (1 large)

2 cups diced tomatoes (from 28-ounce can), undrained

2 cans (15.25 ounces each) Green Giant® whole kernel corn, drained

2½ cups frozen cut okra (from 1-pound bag)

1 teaspoon seasoned salt

¼ teaspoon garlic powder

½ teaspoon hot pepper sauce

In 12-inch skillet, cook bacon over low heat 8 to 10 minutes, turning occasionally, until crisp. Drain on paper towels. Crumble bacon; set aside. Reserve 1 tablespoon bacon drippings in skillet.

Cook onion in bacon drippings over medium heat 2 to 3 minutes, stirring occasionally, until tender. Stir in remaining ingredients except bacon. Heat to boiling. Reduce heat to low; cover and simmer 6 to 8 minutes, stirring occasionally, until okra is tender. Sprinkle with bacon.

1 SERVING: Calories 170; Total Fat 4½g (Saturated Fat 1½g, Trans Fat 0g); Cholesterol 5mg; Sodium 550mg; Total Carbohydrate 26g (Dietary Fiber 4g, Sugars 7g); Protein 6g; EXCHANGES: 1 Starch; ½ Other Carbohydrate; 1 Vegetable; ½ Fat; CARBOHYDRATE CHOICES: 2

Expert Tip

Slash a little fat by trying turkey bacon. It has the same smoky flavor as pork bacon but much less fat. One slice of regular bacon weighs in at about 6 grams of fat per slice versus turkey bacon at roughly ½ gram of fat per slice.

PREP TIME: *20 minutes*

TOTAL TIME: *1 hour 5 minutes*

MAKES 8 SERVINGS

Baked Autumn Vegetables

- 1 small butternut squash (about 1½ pounds)
- 2 medium unpeeled Yukon gold or red potatoes
- 1 medium red onion
- 1 large dark-orange sweet potato or yam (about ½ pound)
- 1 clove garlic or ⅛ teaspoon garlic powder
- 1 pound ready-to-eat baby-cut carrots
- 2 tablespoons olive or vegetable oil
- 1 tablespoon chopped fresh or 1 teaspoon dried sage
- 1 tablespoon chopped fresh or 1 teaspoon crushed dried rosemary
- ½ teaspoon salt

Wash squash. Using chef's knife, carefully cut off bottom and stem ends of squash. Cut narrow part (neck) from rounded bottom part of squash; cut rounded bottom in half. Using spoon, scoop out seeds and fibers from bottom halves and discard. Using sharp vegetable peeler, remove peel from neck and 2 bottom halves. Cut squash into 1-inch pieces.

Scrub potatoes thoroughly with vegetable brush and water to remove any dirt, but do not peel. Cut each potato into eighths. Peel onion; cut into 16 wedges and separate pieces. Peel sweet potato and cut into 1-inch pieces. Peel and finely chop garlic.

Heat oven to 425°F. Spray 15 × 10 × 1-inch pan with cooking spray. Place squash, potatoes, onion, sweet potato and carrots in pan. Pour oil over vegetables. Sprinkle with garlic, sage, rosemary and salt. Stir to coat vegetables.

Roast uncovered 35 to 45 minutes, stirring occasionally, until vegetables are crisp-tender when pierced with fork.

1 SERVING: Calories 150; Total Fat 3½g (Saturated Fat ½g, Trans Fat 0g); Cholesterol 0mg; Sodium 200mg; Total Carbohydrate 26g (Dietary Fiber 4g, Sugars 8g); Protein 3g; EXCHANGES: 1 Starch; ½ Other Carbohydrate; ½ Fat; CARBOHYDRATE CHOICES: 2

Expert Tips

▪ Omit the olive oil and instead spray the pan and vegetables with olive oil–flavored cooking spray to reduce the calories to 90 and the fat to 0 gram per serving.

▪ Butternut squash resembles the shape of a lightbulb or pear— it's wider at one end. It usually weighs between 2 and 3 pounds and has a golden yellow to caramel-colored shell. You can also use about 1½ pounds of other winter squash, such as Hubbard or buttercup.

▪ Sweet potatoes with darker-colored skins are generally more moist and flavorful than the lighter ones.

Baked Butternut Squash with Apples

PREP TIME: *20 minutes*

TOTAL TIME: *1 hour*

MAKES 12 SERVINGS

2 tablespoons butter or margarine

½ teaspoon ground cinnamon

¼ teaspoon ground nutmeg

1½ pounds butternut squash, peeled, seeded and cut into ½-inch cubes (about 5 cups)

2 to 3 large Granny Smith apples, cored, cut into ½-inch cubes (4 cups)

¼ cup real maple or maple-flavored syrup

1 tablespoon balsamic vinegar

¼ cup chopped pecans, toasted*

Heat oven to 375°F. Place butter in 13 × 9-inch (3-quart) glass baking dish; heat in oven 5 to 7 minutes or until melted.

Stir cinnamon and nutmeg into melted butter. Add squash; toss to coat. Cover with foil; bake 20 minutes. Meanwhile, in large bowl, mix apples, syrup and vinegar.

Pour apple mixture over squash. Cover; bake 10 minutes. Stir; bake 5 to 10 minutes longer or until squash is tender. Stir before serving and sprinkle with pecans.

1 SERVING: Calories 100; Total Fat 3½g (Saturated Fat 1½g, Trans Fat 0g); Cholesterol 5mg; Sodium 15mg; Total Carbohydrate 17g (Dietary Fiber 1g, Sugars 11g); Protein 1g; EXCHANGES: ½ Starch; ½ Other Carbohydrate; ½ Fat; CARBOHYDRATE CHOICES: 1

Expert Tips

■ *To toast pecans, sprinkle in ungreased heavy skillet. Cook over medium heat 5 to 7 minutes, stirring frequently until pecans begin to brown, then stirring constantly until light brown.

■ When selecting butternut squash, look for those that have hard, tough rinds and are heavy for their size.

■ Peeling the squash will be easier if you first microwave it on High for 3 minutes.

■ Substitute apple pie spice for the cinnamon and nutmeg.

Balsamic–Glazed Root Vegetables

- 1 pound parsnips, peeled, cut into 2-inch pieces (3 cups)
- 1 pound carrots, cut into 2-inch pieces (3 cups)
- ½ large red onion, thinly sliced, slices cut in half (2 cups)
- 3 tablespoons olive oil
- ½ teaspoon salt
- ¼ teaspoon freshly ground pepper
- ⅔ cup balsamic vinegar
- 3 tablespoons honey
- 1 teaspoon Dijon mustard

Heat oven to 425°F. In large bowl, toss parsnips, carrots, onion, oil, salt and pepper. Arrange vegetables in single layer in ungreased 17 × 12-inch half-sheet pan.

Bake uncovered 35 to 40 minutes, stirring once, until tender and lightly browned.

In 1-quart saucepan, heat vinegar, honey and mustard to boiling; cook 6 to 8 minutes, stirring occasionally, until glaze is reduced to ⅓ cup. Remove from heat; drizzle glaze over vegetables.

1 SERVING: Calories 193; Total Fat 7g (Saturated Fat 1g, Trans Fat 0g); Cholesterol 0mg; Sodium 279mg; Total Carbohydrate 31g (Dietary Fiber 5g, Sugars 19g); Protein 2g; EXCHANGES: ½ Other Carbohydrate; 3 Vegetable; 1 Fat; CARBOHYDRATE CHOICES: 2½

Expert Tip

Cut thicker pieces of carrots and parsnips in half lengthwise to ensure all vegetables are about the same size for even cooking.

Mixed Vegetable Bake

1 pound medium red potatoes (about 4), cut into ¼-inch slices

1 large onion, cut in half and into ¼-inch slices

2 medium carrots, peeled, cut into ¼-inch slices

¼ cup extra-virgin olive oil

2 teaspoons finely chopped garlic

1 teaspoon dried thyme

1 teaspoon dried tarragon

½ teaspoon salt

½ teaspoon black pepper

1 medium red bell pepper, cut into ¼-inch slices

1 medium zucchini, cut into ¼-inch slices

Heat oven to 400°F. Spray bottom of 13 × 9-inch (3-quart) baking dish with cooking spray.

Place potatoes, onion and carrots in baking dish. Toss with half each of the oil, garlic, thyme, tarragon, salt and pepper. Bake 10 minutes.

Meanwhile, in medium bowl, toss bell pepper and zucchini with remaining oil and seasonings. Stir into mixture in baking dish. Bake 30 to 35 minutes longer or until vegetables are tender, stirring halfway through bake time.

1 SERVING: Calories 180; Total Fat 9g (Saturated Fat 1½g, Trans Fat 0g); Cholesterol 0mg; Sodium 220mg; Total Carbohydrate 21g (Dietary Fiber 4g, Sugars 4g); Protein 2g; EXCHANGES: 1 Starch; 1 Vegetable; 1½ Fat; CARBOHYDRATE CHOICES: 1½

Summer Squash au Gratin

2 medium (about 6 inches long each) zucchini squash

1 medium (about 8 inches long) yellow summer squash

4 green onions, chopped (¼ cup)

½ red bell pepper, chopped (½ cup)

1 packet (1.25 to 1.8 ounces) white sauce mix

1½ cups milk

1 cup shredded sharp Cheddar cheese (4 ounces)

1 tablespoon butter or margarine, melted

¼ cup Progresso® plain bread crumbs

Heat oven to 350°F. Cut each squash in half lengthwise; cut into ½-inch-thick slices. Place squash slices, onions and bell pepper in 11 × 7-inch glass baking dish or 2-quart casserole. Add 1 tablespoon water. Cover with microwavable plastic wrap, venting one corner. Microwave on High 5 to 7 minutes or until crisp-tender; drain well.

Meanwhile, in 2-quart saucepan, cook white sauce mix and 1½ cups milk as directed on package. Remove from heat. Stir in cheese. Pour over zucchini mixture in baking dish; stir gently to coat. In small bowl, mix melted butter and bread crumbs. Sprinkle over zucchini mixture.

Bake 30 to 35 minutes or until bubbly and golden brown.

1 SERVING: Calories 130; Total Fat 8g (Saturated Fat 4½g, Trans Fat 0g); Cholesterol 20mg; Sodium 300mg; Total Carbohydrate 10g (Dietary Fiber 1g, Sugars 4g); Protein 7g; EXCHANGES: ½ Other Carbohydrate; 1 Vegetable; ½ High-Fat Meat; ½ Fat; CARBOHYDRATE CHOICES: ½

Expert Tips

▧ This is a great recipe to use when you have lots of summer squash in the garden. Pick them when they are small to medium size for the best texture.

▧ Different brands of white sauce mixes will provide slightly different degrees of thickness, but all will work fine in this recipe.

Cheese Straw– Spinach Casserole

PREP TIME: *25 minutes*
TOTAL TIME: *1 hour*
MAKES 12 SERVINGS

- 3 tablespoons butter or margarine
- 1 large onion, finely chopped (1½ cups)
- 2 cloves garlic, finely chopped
- 2 packages (8 ounces each) cream cheese, softened
- 2 tablespoons Gold Medal® all-purpose flour
- 2 eggs
- ½ teaspoon salt
- ¼ teaspoon pepper
- 1½ cups half-and-half or milk
- 5 boxes (9 ounces each) Green Giant® frozen chopped spinach, thawed, squeezed to drain
- 2 cups shredded Cheddar cheese (8 ounces)
- 2 cups cheese straws, coarsely crushed

Heat oven to 350°F. Spray 13 × 9-inch (3-quart) baking dish with cooking spray. In 10-inch skillet, melt butter over medium-high heat. Cook onion and garlic in butter, stirring frequently, until golden.

In large bowl, mix cream cheese and flour until smooth. Add eggs, one at a time. Stir in salt and pepper. Beat in half-and-half with wire whisk until blended. Add spinach, Cheddar cheese and onion mixture. Spoon mixture into baking dish. Sprinkle with cheese straws.

Bake uncovered 30 to 35 minutes or until hot and bubbly.

1 SERVING: Calories 312; Total Fat 21g (Saturated Fat 13g, Trans Fat 0g); Cholesterol 106mg; Sodium 728mg; Total Carbohydrate 10g (Dietary Fiber 2g, Sugars 4g); Protein 15g; EXCHANGES: ½ Starch; 1 Vegetable; 1 Lean Meat; 3½ Fat; CARBOHYDRATE CHOICES: 1

Expert Tip

Use your favorite brand of cheese straws for this casserole. For a kid-friendly version, use cheese-flavored tiny fish-shaped crackers.

Crunchy-Topped Broccoli Casserole

- 1 bag (24 ounces) Green Giant® frozen broccoli & three cheese sauce
- ¼ cup coarsely chopped drained roasted red bell peppers (from 7-ounce jar)
- ¾ cup Fiber One® original bran cereal
- 2 tablespoons grated Parmesan cheese
- ½ teaspoon Italian seasoning
- 1 tablespoon olive or vegetable oil

Heat oven to 350°F. In ungreased 8-inch square microwavable dish or 2-quart microwavable casserole, place broccoli and cheese sauce. Microwave on High 7 to 8 minutes or until cheese is melted and mixture is very hot; stir well. Stir in roasted peppers.

Place cereal in resealable food-storage plastic bag. Seal bag and slightly crush with rolling pin or meat mallet (or slightly crush in food processor). In small bowl, mix crushed cereal and remaining ingredients until blended. Sprinkle over broccoli mixture in casserole.

Bake 20 to 25 minutes or until broccoli is crisp-tender and topping is crisp.

1 SERVING: Calories 120; Total Fat 4½g (Saturated Fat 1g, Trans Fat 0g); Cholesterol 0mg; Sodium 480mg; Total Carbohydrate 14g (Dietary Fiber 5g, Sugars 4g); Protein 4g; EXCHANGES: 1 Starch; ½ Vegetable; ½ Fat; CARBOHYDRATE CHOICES: 1

Expert Tips

- Experiment with other seasonings. Instead of Italian, try herbes de Provence or dried basil or sage leaves.
- Serving a crowd? Double the recipe, and bake it in a 13 x 9-inch baking dish.

Swiss Vegetable Casserole

2 tablespoons butter or margarine

6 green onions, cut into ½-inch pieces (½ cup)

2 tablespoons all-purpose flour

¼ teaspoon salt

⅛ teaspoon pepper

1½ cups milk

1 cup shredded Swiss cheese (4 ounces)

1 bag (1 pound) frozen broccoli, carrots and cauliflower, cooked, drained

¼ cup crushed round buttery crackers

Heat oven to 350°F. Spray 1- to 1½-quart casserole with cooking spray. In 2-quart saucepan, melt butter over medium heat. Add onions; cook and stir 2 to 3 minutes or until tender.

Stir in flour, salt and pepper. Gradually add milk, stirring constantly. Cook and stir until mixture is bubbly and thickened. Remove from heat.

Add ¾ cup of the cheese; stir until melted. Stir in cooked vegetables. Spoon mixture into casserole. Sprinkle with crushed crackers and remaining ¼ cup cheese.

Bake 25 to 30 minutes or until topping is golden brown and casserole is bubbly.

1 SERVING: Calories 140; Total Fat 9g (Saturated Fat 5g, Trans Fat 0g); Cholesterol 25mg; Sodium 170mg; Total Carbohydrate 9g (Dietary Fiber 2g, Sugars 4g); Protein 7g; EXCHANGES: ½ Other Carbohydrate; 1 Vegetable; ½ High-Fat Meat; 1 Fat; CARBOHYDRATE CHOICES: ½

Expert Tips

- To lower the fat in this casserole by about 2 grams per serving, use skim milk and reduced-fat Swiss cheese.
- To make ahead, prepare this casserole as directed, reserving the crushed crackers. Cover and refrigerate up to one day. Then, sprinkle the casserole with the cheese and crackers, and bake it for 30 to 40 minutes.

Scalloped Potatoes Supreme

1 box (4.7 ounces) Betty Crocker® scalloped potatoes

1²⁄₃ cups boiling water

1 cup half-and-half

1 tablespoon margarine or butter

¹⁄₈ teaspoon ground red pepper (cayenne)

2 cups Green Giant® Valley Fresh Steamers™ frozen cut green beans

¹⁄₄ teaspoon paprika

Heat oven to 400°F.

Stir sauce mix (from scalloped potatoes box), boiling water, half-and-half, margarine and red pepper with whisk in 2-quart casserole. Stir in potatoes (from box) and green beans.

Bake uncovered about 30 minutes or until potatoes are tender. Sprinkle with paprika.

1 SERVING: Calories 120; Total Fat 5g (Saturated Fat 2¹⁄₂g, Trans Fat 0g); Cholesterol 10mg; Sodium 400mg; Total Carbohydrate 16g (Dietary Fiber 1g, Sugars 2g); Protein 2g; EXCHANGES: 1 Starch; ¹⁄₂ Vegetable; 1 Fat; CARBOHYDRATE CHOICES: 1

Desserts

Berry–Peach Cobbler

BISCUITS

1¼ cups all-purpose flour

⅓ cup sugar

1½ teaspoons baking powder

½ teaspoon salt

¼ teaspoon ground nutmeg

¼ cup cold butter or margarine, cut into pieces

½ cup milk

1 teaspoon decorator sugar crystals, if desired

FRUIT MIXTURE

¾ cup sugar

2 tablespoons all-purpose flour

1 cup fresh blueberries

1 cup fresh raspberries

3 medium peaches, peeled, sliced (about 3 cups)

2 teaspoons grated lemon peel

1 tablespoon lemon juice

Heat oven to 400°F. Grease 2-quart glass casserole with butter or cooking spray.

In medium bowl, stir together 1¼ cups flour, ⅓ cup sugar, the baking powder, salt and nutmeg. Cut in butter, using pastry blender or fork, until mixture looks like coarse crumbs. Stir in milk just until combined; set aside.

In 2½-quart saucepan, stir together ¾ cup sugar and 2 table-spoons flour. Stir in blueberries, raspberries, peaches, lemon peel and lemon juice. Heat to boiling over medium-high heat, stirring constantly. Spoon fruit mixture into baking dish.

Immediately drop biscuit dough by 8 spoonfuls onto hot mixture. Sprinkle sugar crystals over dough.

Bake 25 to 35 minutes or until biscuits are golden brown. Cool at least 15 minutes before serving.

1 SERVING: Calories 290; Total Fat 7g (Saturated Fat 4g, Trans Fat 0g); Cholesterol 15mg; Sodium 290mg; Total Carbohydrate 55g (Dietary Fiber 3g, Sugars 35g); Protein 3g; EXCHANGES: 1 Starch; ½ Fruit; 2 Other Carbohydrate; 1½ Fat; CARBOHYDRATE CHOICES: 3½

Expert Tips

■ Serve this luscious cobbler with a scoop of vanilla or cinnamon ice cream or a dollop of sweetened whipped cream.

■ Make 8 individual cobblers in 10-inch custard cups. Bake 20 to 25 minutes.

Chocolate Raspberry Cobbler

1 can (21 ounces) raspberry pie filling

1 pouch (1 pound 1.5 ounces) Betty Crocker® double chocolate chunk cookie mix

¾ cup butter or margarine, melted

Heat oven to 350°F. Spray bottom and sides of 11 × 7-inch (2-quart) glass baking dish with cooking spray.

Spread pie filling in bottom of baking dish. Sprinkle cookie mix evenly over pie filling. Pour melted butter evenly over cookie mix. Using small metal spatula, gently spread melted butter over cookie mix just to cover the dry mix.

Bake 28 to 30 minutes or until topping is set. To serve warm, cool 15 minutes or serve at room temperature. Store covered in refrigerator.

1 SERVING: Calories 566; Total Fat 18g (Saturated Fat 11g, Trans Fat ½g); Cholesterol 35mg; Sodium 320mg; Total Carbohydrate 65g (Dietary Fiber 2g, Sugars 44g); Protein 2g; EXCHANGES: 1 Starch; 3½ Other Carbohydrate; 3½ Fat; CARBOHYDRATE CHOICES: 4

Expert Tip

Serve with ice cream or whipped cream.

Cornbread–Apple Cobbler

PREP TIME: *15 minutes*

TOTAL TIME: *40 minutes*

MAKES 6 SERVINGS

FILLING

- 2 tablespoons butter or margarine
- 5 large firm apples, peeled, cored and sliced (Golden Delicious or Gala)
- ¾ cup packed light brown sugar
- ¼ cup dark rum; or 1 tablespoon rum extract plus water to measure ¼ cup
- ½ teaspoon ground cinnamon
- ½ teaspoon ground nutmeg
- ¼ teaspoon ground ginger

CORNBREAD TOPPING

- 1 pouch Betty Crocker® cornbread and muffin mix
- ⅓ cup milk
- 2 tablespoons butter or margarine, melted
- 1 egg

Heat oven to 375°F. Grease 8-inch square or round glass baking dish with shortening or cooking spray. In 12-inch skillet, melt 2 tablespoons butter over medium-high heat. Gently stir in remaining filling ingredients with wooden spoon.

Cook about 5 minutes, stirring occasionally, until apples are tender. Pour into baking dish.

In medium bowl, stir together cornbread topping ingredients. Spread over apples, covering them completely.

Bake 20 to 25 minutes or until topping is golden brown.

1 SERVING: Calories 400; Total Fat 10g (Saturated Fat 5g, Trans Fat 0g); Cholesterol 55mg; Sodium 290mg; Total Carbohydrate 73g (Dietary Fiber 2g, Sugars 50g); Protein 4g; EXCHANGES: 1 Starch; 1 Fruit; 3 Other Carbohydrate; 2 Fat; CARBOHYDRATE CHOICES: 5

Expert Tip

Serve with whipped cream sweetened with brown sugar and a touch of cinnamon.

Cranberry–Apple Cobbler

TOPPING

1 cup Gold Medal® all-purpose flour

¾ cup granulated sugar

¼ cup butter or margarine, softened

1 egg, beaten

FILLING

2 cups packed brown sugar

1 cup chopped pecans, toasted

1 teaspoon ground cinnamon

4 large tart red apples, peeled, cored and sliced

1 bag (12 ounces) fresh cranberries, rinsed

Heat oven to 400°F. Grease 2-quart casserole. In medium bowl, mix flour and granulated sugar. Cut in butter, using fork or pastry blender, until crumbly. Stir in egg until blended.

In casserole, mix all filling ingredients. Crumble topping over fruit mixture.

Bake uncovered 25 to 30 minutes or until topping is golden brown.

1 SERVING: Calories 566, Total Fat 17g (Saturated Fat 5g, Trans Fat 0g); Cholesterol 42mg; Sodium 66mg; Total Carbohydrate 107g (Dietary Fiber 5g, Sugars 86g); Protein 4g; EXCHANGES: 1 Starch; 1 Fruit; 4 Other Carbohydrates; 3 Fat; CARBOHYDRATE CHOICES: 7

Expert Tips

■ Think of cobblers as first cousins to deep-dish pies. The cobbled, or bumpy, topping gives this favorite fruit dessert its name.

■ With fruit desserts such as this one, using the right size of dish is important. The fruit filling bubbles during baking and can spill out if the baking dish is too small. For extra insurance, place a baking sheet under the dish to catch any spills.

PREP TIME: *15 minutes*

TOTAL TIME: *1 hour 25 minutes*

MAKES 12 SERVINGS

Pecan Pie Cobbler

1 box Pillsbury® refrigerated pie crusts, softened as directed on box

2½ cups light corn syrup

2½ cups packed brown sugar

½ cup butter, melted

4½ teaspoons vanilla

6 eggs, slightly beaten

2 cups coarsely chopped pecans

2 cups pecan halves

Vanilla ice cream, if desired

Heat oven to 425°F. Grease 13 × 9-inch (3-quart) glass baking dish with shortening or cooking spray. Remove 1 pie crust from pouch; unroll on work surface. Roll into 13 × 9-inch rectangle; trim sides to fit baking dish. Place crust in dish.

In large bowl, stir corn syrup, brown sugar, butter, vanilla and eggs with wire whisk. Stir in chopped pecans. Spoon half of filling into pastry-lined dish. Remove second pie crust from pouch; unroll on work surface. Roll into 13 × 9-inch rectangle; trim sides to fit baking dish. Place crust over filling. Spray crust with butter-flavor cooking spray.

Bake 14 to 16 minutes or until browned. Reduce oven temperature to 350°F.

Carefully spoon remaining filling over baked pastry; arrange pecan halves on top in decorative fashion. Bake 30 minutes longer or until set. Cool 20 minutes on cooling rack. Serve warm cobbler with vanilla ice cream.

1 SERVING: Calories 877; Total Fat 45g (Saturated Fat 12g, Trans Fat 0g); Cholesterol 130mg; Sodium 335mg; Total Carbohydrate 123g (Dietary Fiber 3g, Sugars 6g); Protein 8g; EXCHANGES: ½ Protein; 1 Starch; 6½ Other Carbohydrate; ½ Medium-Fat Meat; 8 Fat; CARBOHYDRATE CHOICES: 8½

Peach Crisp

1 pouch (1 pound 1.5 ounces) Betty Crocker® oatmeal cookie mix

½ cup cold butter

5 cups frozen sliced peaches, thawed and drained, or 1 can (29 ounces) sliced peaches, drained

Heat oven to 375°F. In large bowl, place cookie mix. Cut in butter, using pastry blender or fork, until mixture looks like coarse crumbs.

In ungreased 8-inch square baking dish or 2-quart round casserole, place peaches. Sprinkle cookie mixture over peaches.

Bake 25 to 30 minutes or until topping is golden brown. Serve warm or cool.

1 SERVING: Calories 650; Total Fat 19g (Saturated Fat 10g, Trans Fat ½g); Cholesterol 40mg; Sodium 440mg; Total Carbohydrate 113g (Dietary Fiber 5g, Sugars 77g); Protein 7g; EXCHANGES: 2 Starch; 1 Fruit; 4½ Other Carbohydrate; 3½ Fat; CARBOHYDRATE CHOICES: 7½

Expert Tip

Why just use peaches? Experiment with other fruits or fruit combos.

Apple–Cranberry Dessert

6 cups sliced peeled apples
(about 6 medium)

⅔ cup sweetened dried
cranberries

1 teaspoon ground cinnamon

2 tablespoons maple-
flavored syrup

1 tablespoon lemon juice

⅔ cup quick-cooking oats

½ cup packed brown sugar

½ cup Original Bisquick® mix

¼ cup chopped walnuts

¼ cup butter or margarine,
softened

Vanilla ice cream, if desired

Heat oven to 375°F. In large bowl, mix apples, cranberries, cinnamon, syrup and lemon juice. Spoon into ungreased 8-inch square baking dish.

In medium bowl, mix remaining ingredients except ice cream with fork until crumbly. Sprinkle over fruit mixture.

Bake 35 to 40 minutes or until apples are tender, juices are bubbly and topping is golden brown. Cool about 30 minutes. Serve warm with ice cream.

1 SERVING: Calories 280; Total Fat 10g (Saturated Fat 3½g, Trans Fat ½g); Cholesterol 15mg; Sodium 150mg; Total Carbohydrate 47g (Dietary Fiber 3g, Sugars 32g); Protein 2g; EXCHANGES: 1 Starch; 1 Fruit; 1 Other Carbohydrate; 2 Fat; CARBOHYDRATE CHOICES: 3

Expert Tips

- Unlike fresh cranberries, dried cranberries are available year-round and can be used like raisins when baking.

- Tart cooking or baking apples work best in this dessert. Choose from these varieties: Braeburn, Cortland, Empire, Granny Smith, Greening, Haralson, Ida Red, Newtown Pippin, Prairie Spy, Rome and York Imperial. Try them all to find your favorites!

Triple-Berry Granola Crisp

PREP TIME: *10 minutes*

TOTAL TIME: *1 hour*

MAKES 9 SERVINGS

1 bag (8 ounces) Cascadian Farm® frozen organic blueberries

1 bag (10 ounces) Cascadian Farm® frozen organic strawberries

1 bag (10 ounces) Cascadian Farm® frozen organic raspberries

1/4 cup sugar

2 tablespoons Gold Medal® all-purpose flour

1 1/2 cups Cascadian Farm® organic oats and honey granola

Ice cream or whipped cream, if desired

Heat oven to 375°F. In ungreased 8-inch square (2-quart) glass baking dish, mix frozen berries, sugar and flour until fruit is coated.

Bake uncovered 20 minutes. Stir fruit mixture. Sprinkle with granola.

Bake 15 to 20 minutes longer or until light golden brown and bubbly. Let stand 5 to 10 minutes before serving. Serve warm with ice cream.

1 SERVING: Calories 130; Total Fat 2g (Saturated Fat 0g, Trans Fat 0g); Cholesterol 0mg; Sodium 30mg; Total Carbohydrate 27g (Dietary Fiber 4g, Sugars 14g); Protein 2g; EXCHANGES: 1 Starch; 1/2 Fruit; 1/2 Fat; CARBOHYDRATE CHOICES: 2

Expert Tip

If you like, use 3 bags (10 ounces each) Cascadian Farm® frozen harvest berries in place of the blueberries, strawberries and raspberries.

Apple and Caramel Bread Pudding

1 cup unsweetened applesauce

1 cup vanilla soymilk

½ cup fat-free egg product

¼ cup packed brown sugar

1 teaspoon ground cinnamon

1 teaspoon vanilla

5 cups 1-inch cubes French bread

3 tablespoons sliced almonds

¼ cup fat-free caramel topping, heated

Heat oven to 350°F. Spray 9-inch quiche dish or pie plate with cooking spray.

In large bowl, mix all ingredients except bread, almonds and caramel topping with wire whisk until smooth. Fold in bread. Pour into quiche dish; sprinkle with almonds.

Bake 30 to 35 minutes or until golden brown and set. Cut into wedges. Drizzle caramel topping over each serving.

1 SERVING: Calories 160; Total Fat 2½g (Saturated Fat 0g, Trans Fat 0g); Cholesterol 0mg; Sodium 220mg; Total Carbohydrate 29g (Dietary Fiber 1g, Sugars 15g); Protein 5g; EXCHANGES: 1 Starch; 1 Other Carbohydrate; ½ Fat; CARBOHYDRATE CHOICES: 2

Expert Tip

Bread pudding made with a bread that's too soft can be almost mushy. Gently squeeze bread loaves to choose the one that has some resistance and doesn't feel like a marshmallow!

Vermont Maple Bread Pudding

PUDDING

- 1 bag (12.4 ounces) Pillsbury® Oven Baked frozen crusty French dinner rolls
- 6 eggs
- ½ cup maple-flavored or real maple syrup
- ¾ cup granulated sugar
- 1½ teaspoons baking powder
- 1 pint (2 cups) half-and-half
- 1 cup milk
- ¼ cup butter or margarine, melted
- ½ cup Rich & Creamy cream cheese ready-to-spread frosting (from 16-ounce container)
- ⅔ cup Yoplait® 99% Fat Free creamy vanilla yogurt (from 2-pound container)

GARNISHES, IF DESIRED

Vanilla ice cream

Fresh mint sprigs

Powdered sugar

Heat oven to 350°F. Spray 13 × 9-inch pan with cooking spray. Let frozen rolls stand at room temperature 10 minutes. Cut each roll into 12 pieces; place in large bowl.

In another large bowl, slightly beat eggs. Reserve 1 tablespoon of the syrup in small microwavable bowl; add remaining syrup to eggs. Stir in sugar, baking powder, half-and-half, milk and melted butter until well blended. Pour mixture over roll pieces in bowl; stir to coat well. Pour mixture into pan, pressing bread into liquid with back of spoon. Let stand 5 minutes; press down bread again.

Bake 45 to 55 minutes or until top is golden brown and knife inserted in center comes out clean. Cool 20 minutes before serving.

To reserved maple syrup, stir in frosting and yogurt. Microwave on High about 20 seconds or until melted. Stir; pour over warm bread pudding and spread to cover. Cut into 12 servings. Serve warm with ice cream; garnish with mint and sprinkle with powdered sugar.

1 SERVING: Calories 350; Total Fat 14g (Saturated Fat 7g, Trans Fat 1g); Cholesterol 120mg; Sodium 340mg; Total Carbohydrate 48g (Dietary Fiber 0g, Sugars 30g); Protein 7g; EXCHANGES: 2 Starch; 1 Other Carbohydrate; 2½ Fat; CARBOHYDRATE CHOICES: 3

Expert Tips

- You can use 1 (6-ounce) container of Yoplait® Original 99% fat free French vanilla yogurt instead of the yogurt in the recipe if you like.
- A kitchen scissors makes cutting the biscuit dough easier.

Rhubarb Oven Pudding

4 teaspoons butter (do not use margarine)

⅓ cup all-purpose flour

½ cup fat-free (skim) milk

1 egg or 2 egg whites

⅛ teaspoon salt

¾ cup frozen cut rhubarb (from 16-ounce bag), thawed, drained and finely chopped

⅓ cup packed brown sugar

¼ teaspoon ground nutmeg

Heat oven to 425°F. In each of 2 (10-ounce) custard cups, place 2 teaspoons butter. Heat in oven until bubbling.

Meanwhile, in small bowl, beat flour, milk, egg and salt with wire whisk just until smooth. Pour mixture into bubbling butter. Sprinkle rhubarb over batter. In small bowl, mix brown sugar and nutmeg; sprinkle over batter and rhubarb. Place cups in 11 × 7-inch glass baking dish.

Bake 20 to 25 minutes or until puffed and golden brown. Serve warm.

1 SERVING: Calories 460; Total Fat 11g (Saturated Fat 6g, Trans Fat 0g); Cholesterol 130mg; Sodium 270mg; Total Carbohydrate 83g (Dietary Fiber 2g, Sugars 65g); Protein 8g; EXCHANGES: 2 Starch; 3½ Other Carbohydrate; 2 Fat; CARBOHYDRATE CHOICES: 5½

Expert Tip

You'll agree with the taste testers in the Betty Crocker Kitchens: This rhubarb pudding is scrumptious! Serve with frozen (thawed) fat-free whipped topping or reduced-fat frozen yogurt.

Individual Black Forest Bread Puddings

PREP TIME: *10 minutes*

TOTAL TIME: *50 minutes*

MAKES 6 SERVINGS

6 slices French bread, cut into small cubes

4 eggs

1 cup fat-free (skim) milk

2 containers (6 ounces each) Yoplait® Light fat free black forest cake yogurt

CHERRY SAUCE

½ cup frozen dark sweet or tart cherries, thawed, cut in half

1 tablespoon cherry-flavored liqueur, if desired

Place 1 slice bread, cubed, in each of six 6-ounce custard cups. In medium bowl, mix eggs, milk and yogurt until well blended. Spoon yogurt mixture over bread; let stand about 30 minutes or until bread absorbs some of the yogurt mixture. Heat oven to 350°F.

Bake 25 to 30 minutes or until knife inserted in center comes out clean. Cool 5 minutes.

Mix sauce ingredients. Serve over warm bread pudding.

1 SERVING: Calories 290; Total Fat 5g (Saturated Fat 1½g, Trans Fat 0g); Cholesterol 125mg; Sodium 420mg; Total Carbohydrate 47g (Dietary Fiber 2g, Sugars 13g); Protein 15g; EXCHANGES: 2 Starch; 1 Other Carbohydrate; 1 Very Lean Meat; ½ Fat; CARBOHYDRATE CHOICES: 3

Lattice Peach-Apple Pie

PASTRY

- 2 cups Gold Medal® all-purpose flour
- 1 teaspoon salt
- ²⁄₃ cup plus 2 tablespoons shortening
- 4 to 6 tablespoons cold water

FILLING

- 1 cup sugar
- ¼ cup Gold Medal® all-purpose flour
- ¼ teaspoon ground cinnamon
- 3 medium fresh peaches, sliced (2 cups)
- 2 medium green cooking apples, peeled and thinly sliced (2 cups)
- ¼ cup sliced almonds
- 1 tablespoon butter or margarine

In medium bowl, mix 2 cups flour and the salt. Cut in shortening, using pastry blender (or pulling 2 table knives through ingredients in opposite directions), until particles are size of small peas. Sprinkle with cold water, 1 tablespoon at a time, tossing with fork until all flour is moistened and pastry almost clears side of bowl (1 to 2 teaspoons more water can be added if necessary).

Gather pastry into a ball. Divide in half. On lightly floured surface, shape each half into flattened round. Wrap in plastic wrap; refrigerate about 45 minutes or until dough is firm and cold, yet pliable. This allows the shortening to become slightly firm, which helps make the baked pastry more flaky. If refrigerated longer, let pastry soften slightly before rolling.

Heat oven to 425°F. With floured rolling pin, roll 1 pastry round into round 2 inches larger than upside-down 9-inch glass pie plate. Fold pastry into fourths; place in pie plate. Unfold and ease into plate, pressing firmly against bottom and side.

In large bowl, mix sugar, ¼ cup flour and the cinnamon. Stir in peaches and apples. Spoon into pastry-lined pie plate. Sprinkle with almonds. Cut butter into small pieces; sprinkle over filling. Trim overhanging edge of pastry 1 inch from rim of plate.

Roll other pastry round into 10-inch round. Cut into ½-inch strips. Place 6 strips across filling. To make lattice top, weave a cross-strip through center by first folding back every other strip going the other way. Continue weaving lattice, folding back alternate strips before adding each cross-strip, until lattice is complete. Trim ends of strips. Fold trimmed edge of bottom crust over ends of strips, building up a high edge; seal and flute. Cover edge of pastry with 2- to 3-inch strip of foil to prevent excessive browning.

Bake 35 to 45 minutes or until crust is brown and filling is bubbly, removing foil for last 15 minutes of baking. Cool on cooling rack. Serve slightly warm.

1 SERVING: Calories 468; Total Fat 24g (Saturated Fat 6g, Trans Fat 7g); Cholesterol 4mg; Sodium 302mg; Total Carbohydrate 61g (Dietary Fiber 2g, Sugars 32g); Protein 5g; EXCHANGES: 2 Starches; ½ Fruit; 1½ Other Carbohydrate; 4½ Fat; CARBOHYDRATE CHOICES: 5

Expert Tip

Peaches out of season? Substitute 2 cups frozen sliced peaches, partially thawed and drained, for the fresh peaches.

Easy-as-Peach-Pie Wedges

1 box Pillsbury® refrigerated pie crusts, softened as directed on box

1 can (21 ounces) peach pie filling with more fruit

1/8 teaspoon ground nutmeg

2 teaspoons sugar

Heat oven to 450°F. Spray large cookie sheet with cooking spray. Remove pie crusts from pouches; unroll crusts onto opposite ends of cookie sheet (edges of crusts may hang over sides of cookie sheet).

Spoon half of pie filling onto one half of each crust to within 1 inch of edge. Sprinkle with nutmeg. Fold other half of each crust over filling; press 1/2-inch edge with fork to seal. Cut several slits in top crust of each. Sprinkle with sugar.

Bake 10 minutes. Cover edges of crusts with strips of foil. Bake 5 to 8 minutes longer or until crusts are golden brown. Cool at least 30 minutes. Cut into wedges to serve.

1 SERVING: Calories 300; Total Fat 12g (Saturated Fat 5g, Trans Fat 0g); Cholesterol 5mg; Sodium 260mg; Total Carbohydrate 45g (Dietary Fiber 0g, Sugars 19g); Protein 1g; EXCHANGES: 1 Starch; 2 Other Carbohydrate; 2 1/2 Fat; CARBOHYDRATE CHOICES: 3

Expert Tip

For a small family, it's easy to prepare half of this recipe for 4 servings. Keep the second pie crust in the refrigerator for another one-crust pie at a later date. Use the other half of the pie filling as a topping for ice cream or cake.

Apple–Blueberry Pie with Strawberry Sauce

PIE

- 5 cups peeled, cored and thinly sliced apples

- 2 cups fresh or frozen (thawed) blueberries

- 1 cup sugar

- 1/2 teaspoon ground cinnamon

- 3 tablespoons quick-cooking tapioca

- 1 box Pillsbury® refrigerated pie crusts, softened as directed on box

- 2 tablespoons butter or margarine

- 1 egg

- 1 teaspoon water

STRAWBERRY SAUCE

- 2 cups fresh strawberries

- 1/2 cup sugar

- 1 tablespoon sweet Marsala wine or water

- 1 tablespoon cornstarch

- 2 tablespoons water

- 1/2 cup whipping cream

Heat oven to 400°F. In large bowl, stir together apples, blueberries, 1 cup sugar, the cinnamon and tapioca; let stand 15 minutes. Make pie crusts as directed on box for Two-Crust Pie, using 9-inch glass pie plate.

Spoon apple mixture into crust-lined pie plate. Dot with butter. Top with second crust; seal edges and flute. Cut slits in several places in top crust. Stir together egg and 1 teaspoon water; brush on top of crust.

Bake 15 minutes. Cover edge of crust with strips of foil; reduce oven temperature to 350°F. Bake 40 to 45 minutes longer or until apples are tender. Cool on cooling rack at least 2 hours.

Meanwhile, in 1-quart saucepan, crush enough strawberries to make 1/3 cup. Stir in 1/2 cup sugar and the wine. Heat to boiling over medium heat. Dissolve cornstarch in 2 tablespoons water; stir into strawberry mixture. Boil and stir 2 minutes. Remove from heat; cool to room temperature. Stir in whipping cream. Slice remaining strawberries; stir into sauce. Refrigerate until serving time. Top individual servings with sauce.

1 SERVING: Calories 530; Total Fat 20g (Saturated Fat 10g, Trans Fat 0g); Cholesterol 55mg; Sodium 290mg; Total Carbohydrate 83g (Dietary Fiber 2g, Sugars 50g); Protein 3g; EXCHANGES: 1½ Starch; 1 Fruit; 3 Other Carbohydrate; 4 Fat; CARBOHYDRATE CHOICES: 5½

Expert Tips

- Adjust the level of sugar according to how sweet your apples are. If using a very sweet variety of apple, decrease the sugar to 3/4 cup.

- Paula M. Reed, from Cantonsville, Maryland, won first place for this recipe at the 2004 Maryland State Fair. She went on to place in the national Pillsbury® Refrigerated Pie Crust Championship.

Wild Berry Pie

- 1 box Pillsbury® refrigerated pie crusts
- 1 tablespoon sour cream
- 1½ quarts wild berries, such as black raspberries, blackberries, black mulberries, blueberries, red huckleberries, black huckleberries, strawberries
- 1 cup sugar
- 6 tablespoons cornstarch
- 1 teaspoon fresh lemon juice

Heat oven to 400°F. Remove pie crusts from box, but leave in pouches. Microwave 20 seconds in pouches to soften. Remove crusts from pouches. Mix sour cream into crust dough using hands. Divide dough in half. On lightly floured surface, roll out thin. Place 1 pie crust into 9-inch pie plate.

To make filling, mix berries, sugar and cornstarch together in large bowl. Add lemon juice. Place in crust-lined pie plate. Add second crust to top of pie and seal; cut slits in pastry. If you like, brush top with cream and sprinkle with sugar. Place pie on middle oven rack; place sheet of foil on rack below pie in case of spillover.

Bake 45 to 55 minutes or until crust is golden brown. Cool at least 3 hours before serving.

1 SERVING: Calories 390; Total Fat 13g (Saturated Fat 5g, Trans Fat 0g); Cholesterol 10mg; Sodium 260mg; Total Carbohydrate 67g (Dietary Fiber 3g, Sugars 33g); Protein 2g; EXCHANGES: 2½ Starch; 2 Other Carbohydrate; 2 Fat; CARBOHYDRATE CHOICES: 4½

Expert Tips

- If you don't have wild berries, you can purchase any combination of fresh berries from your local supermarket.
- If using wild berries such as huckleberries or mulberries, you may want to increase the sugar slightly due to the tartness.

Lemon Meringue Pie

CRUST

1 box Pillsbury® refrigerated pie crusts, softened as directed on box

FILLING

1¼ cups sugar

⅓ cup cornstarch

½ teaspoon salt

1½ cups cold water

3 egg yolks

2 tablespoons butter or margarine

1 tablespoon grated lemon peel

½ cup fresh lemon juice

MERINGUE

3 egg whites

¼ teaspoon cream of tartar

½ teaspoon vanilla

¼ cup sugar

Heat oven to 450°F. Make pie crust as directed on box for One-Crust Baked Shell using 9-inch glass pie pan. Bake 9 to 11 minutes or until light golden brown. Cool completely, about 30 minutes.

Meanwhile, in 2-quart saucepan, mix 1¼ cups sugar, the cornstarch and salt. Gradually stir in cold water until smooth. Cook over medium heat, stirring constantly, until mixture boils. Boil 1 minute, stirring constantly. Remove from heat.

In small bowl, beat egg yolks with fork. Stir about ¼ cup of hot mixture into egg yolks. Gradually stir yolk mixture into hot mixture. Cook over low heat, stirring constantly, until mixture boils. Boil 1 minute, stirring constantly.

Remove from heat. Stir in butter, lemon peel and lemon juice. Cool slightly, about 15 minutes. Pour into cooled baked shell.

Reduce oven temperature to 350°F. In small deep bowl with electric mixer, beat egg whites, cream of tartar and vanilla on medium speed about 1 minute or until soft peaks form. On high speed, gradually beat in sugar 1 tablespoon at a time until stiff glossy peaks form and sugar is dissolved. Spoon meringue onto hot filling; spread to edge of crust to seal well and prevent shrinkage.

Bake 12 to 15 minutes or until meringue is light golden brown. Cool completely, about 1 hour. Refrigerate until filling is set, about 3 hours. Store in refrigerator.

1 SERVING: Calories 330; Total Fat 11g (Saturated Fat 5g, Trans Fat 0g); Cholesterol 90mg; Sodium 320mg; Total Carbohydrate 56g (Dietary Fiber 0g, Sugars 38g); Protein 3g; EXCHANGES: 1 Starch; 2½ Other Carbohydrate; 2 Fat; CARBOHYDRATE CHOICES: 4

Expert Tip

Eggs separate most easily when they are cold, but the whites will whip best at room temperature. To take off the chill, set the bowl of whites into a larger pan filled with warm water.

Key Lime Cheesecake Pie

1 box Pillsbury® refrigerated pie crusts, softened as directed on box

FILLING

1 envelope unflavored gelatin

½ cup fresh lime juice

1 cup sugar

2 eggs, beaten

2 packages (3 ounces each) cream cheese, softened

¼ cup butter or margarine, softened

1 cup whipping cream

1½ teaspoons grated lime peel

½ cup whipping cream, whipped, sweetened

Lime slices

Heat oven to 450°F. Make pie crust as directed on box for One-Crust Baked Shell. Cool completely on cooling rack, about 15 minutes.

In 1-quart saucepan, sprinkle gelatin on lime juice. Let stand 5 minutes to soften. Using wire whisk, beat in sugar and eggs. Heat mixture to boiling over medium heat. Reduce heat; boil gently 3 minutes, stirring constantly.

In medium bowl, beat cream cheese and butter. Pour in hot lime juice mixture; beat until smooth and well blended. Refrigerate about 45 minutes or until cool, stirring occasionally.

In medium bowl, beat 1 cup whipping cream until stiff peaks form. Fold in cooled lime juice mixture and grated lime peel. Spoon into cooled pie shell. Refrigerate until firm, about 2 hours. Garnish with ½ cup whipped cream and lime slices as desired. Cover and refrigerate any remaining pie.

1 SERVING: Calories 500; Total Fat 35g (Saturated Fat 20g, Trans Fat 1g); Cholesterol 145mg; Sodium 250mg; Total Carbohydrate 41g (Dietary Fiber 0g, Sugars 27g); Protein 5g; EXCHANGES: 1½ Starch; 1½ Other Carbohydrate; 6½ Fat; CARBOHYDRATE CHOICES: 3

Expert Tips

- For authenticity, use Key limes for the fresh juice and peel. If needed, Key lime juice is available bottled.
- To soften cream cheese, simply let it come to room temperature.

Peppermint Truffle Pie

1 bag (12 ounces) semisweet chocolate chips

1 cup half-and-half

¼ cup butter, cut into pieces

1½ teaspoons peppermint extract

1 box Pillsbury® refrigerated pie crusts, softened as directed on box

1 cup white chocolate chunks or white vanilla baking chips

1½ cups whipping cream

12 hard peppermint candies, crushed

Heat oven to 450°F. In medium microwavable bowl, place chocolate chips, half-and-half and butter. Microwave on High 2 minutes to 2 minutes 30 seconds or until melted, stirring once or twice. Stir in peppermint extract. Beat with electric mixer or wire whisk until well blended. Refrigerate 45 to 60 minutes or until thickened.

Meanwhile, make pie crust as directed on box for One-Crust Baked Shell using 9-inch glass pie plate. Bake 9 to 11 minutes or until golden brown. Cool completely, about 30 minutes.

In small microwavable bowl, place white chocolate chunks and whipping cream. Microwave on High 1 minute 30 seconds or until smooth, stirring once or twice. Cover and refrigerate 2 hours or until chilled.

Pour semisweet chocolate mixture into cooled baked shell. Reserve 3 peppermint candies. Crush remaining candies and sprinkle over top. Refrigerate 2 hours or until firm.

In medium bowl, beat white chocolate mixture with electric mixer on high speed until light and fluffy. Do not overbeat. Carefully spoon and spread over chocolate. Refrigerate at least 4 hours or until firm. Just before serving, garnish with peppermint candies or fresh mint. Store in refrigerator.

1 SERVING: Calories 530; Total Fat 36g (Saturated Fat 21g, Trans Fat ½g); Cholesterol 55mg; Sodium 140mg; Total Carbohydrate 47g (Dietary Fiber 2g, Sugars 37g); Protein 4g; EXCHANGES: ½ Starch; 2½ Other Carbohydrate; 6½ Fat; CARBOHYDRATE CHOICES: 3

Expert Tip

The pie can be made and stored in the refrigerator up to 24 hours before serving.

PREP TIME: *40 minutes*

TOTAL TIME: *3 hours 45 minutes*

MAKES 8 SERVINGS

Triple-Threat Coconut Cream Pie

1 Pillsbury® refrigerated pie crust, softened as directed on box

1 can (13½ ounces) coconut milk, shaken well

½ cup plus 1 tablespoon sweetened shredded or flaked coconut, toasted

1 cup whole milk

½ vanilla bean, split (or 1 teaspoon vanilla)

⅔ cup sugar

¼ teaspoon salt

5 large egg yolks

¼ cup cornstarch

½ teaspoon coconut extract

2 tablespoons unsalted butter, cut into four pieces

TOPPING

1½ cups heavy whipping cream, well chilled

1½ tablespoons sugar

2 teaspoons dark rum (or 1 teaspoon vanilla)

¼ cup sweetened shredded or flaked coconut, toasted

1 ounce white chocolate, shaved

Heat oven to 450°F. Unroll pie crust onto cooking parchment or waxed paper. Brush small amount of coconut milk onto dough (just enough to moisten it). Sprinkle ½ tablespoon of the toasted coconut evenly on dough, then press it lightly into dough, just enough to make it stick.

Sprinkle ½ tablespoon toasted coconut onto bottom of 9-inch pie plate, then form dough into plate. Prick bottom and side with fork. Bake 10 to 12 minutes or until light brown. Cool.

In 2-quart saucepan, simmer remaining coconut milk and ½ cup toasted coconut, the whole milk, vanilla bean, ⅓ cup of the sugar and the salt over medium heat, stirring occasionally with wooden spoon, about 5 minutes to dissolve sugar.

In separate large bowl, with whisk, beat egg yolks, remaining ⅓ cup sugar and the cornstarch until well combined. Gradually beat simmering liquid into yolk mixture to temper it, then return entire mixture to saucepan, scraping bowl with rubber spatula. Discard vanilla bean.

Simmer mixture over medium heat, beating constantly with whisk, 5 to 6 minutes or until mixture is thickened.

Remove from heat; beat in coconut extract and butter. Pour into cooled crust; press sheet of plastic wrap directly on surface of filling and refrigerate until filling is cold and firm, at least 3 hours or overnight.

Just before serving, beat whipping cream and 1½ tablespoons sugar in chilled bowl using electric mixer at medium speed until soft peaks form. Add rum and continue to beat until slightly stiff peaks are formed. Spread or pipe whipped cream over chilled filling. Sprinkle ¼ cup toasted coconut and shaved chocolate over top. Store in refrigerator.

1 SERVING: Calories 580; Total Fat 41g (Saturated Fat 27g, Trans Fat ½g); Cholesterol 190mg; Sodium 270mg; Total Carbohydrate 47g (Dietary Fiber 1g, Sugars 29g); Protein 5g; EXCHANGES: 1½ Starch; 1½ Other Carbohydrate; 8 Fat; CARBOHYDRATE CHOICES: 3

Expert Tip

After opening, bagged coconut is best stored for only up to 6 months.

Fudgy Dark Chocolate Tart

PREP TIME: *10 minutes*

TOTAL TIME: *1 hour 50 minutes*

MAKES 12 SERVINGS

CRUST

- 1 cup Gold Medal® white whole wheat flour
- 2 tablespoons sugar
- ½ cup butter or margarine, softened

FILLING

- 2 tablespoons butter or margarine
- 1 can (14 ounces) sweetened condensed milk (not evaporated)
- 1 bag (12 ounces) dark, bittersweet or semisweet chocolate chips (2 cups)
- 1 teaspoon vanilla
- ¼ teaspoon salt
- ½ cup chopped walnuts, toasted if desired
- Whipped cream, if desired
- Chocolate curls or grated chocolate, if desired

Heat oven to 400°F. In medium bowl, mix crust ingredients until soft dough forms. Press firmly and evenly against bottom and side of ungreased 9-inch tart pan with removable bottom.

Bake 10 to 13 minutes or until light golden brown; cool on cooling rack. Reduce oven temperature to 350°F.

In 2-quart saucepan, melt 2 tablespoons butter over low heat. Stir in condensed milk and chocolate chips. Cook over low heat, stirring occasionally, until chocolate is melted. Stir in vanilla and salt; stir in walnuts. Spread in baked crust.

Bake about 20 minutes or just until edge is set. Cool in pan on cooling rack, about 1 hour to serve warm, or serve at room temperature. To serve, spoon whipped cream onto center of tart and top with chocolate curls, or top each slice with whipped cream and chocolate curls.

1 SERVING: Calories 367; Total Fat 20g (Saturated Fat 12g, Trans Fat ½g); Cholesterol 37mg; Sodium 166mg; Total Carbohydrate 46g (Dietary Fiber 1g, Sugars 20g); Protein 5g; EXCHANGES: ½ Starch; 1½ Other Carbohydrate; 2½ Fat; CARBOHYDRATE CHOICES: 3

Expert Tips

- To make chocolate curls, let a large bar of chocolate stand in a warm place (80°F to 85°F) until slightly softened. Using vegetable peeler, shave chocolate in long strands along smooth side of chocolate. Transfer curls with toothpick to dessert.
- To make ahead, tightly cover the completely cooled tart and refrigerate up to 3 days or freeze up to 2 months. About 1 hour before serving, uncover frozen tart and let stand at room temperature to thaw.

Mixed-Berry Cream Tart

2 cups sliced fresh
strawberries

½ cup boiling water

1 box (4-serving size) sugar-
free strawberry-flavored
gelatin

3 pouches (1.5 ounces each)
Nature Valley® roasted
almond crunchy granola
bars (from 8.9-ounce box)

1 package (8 ounces) fat-free
cream cheese

¼ cup sugar

¼ teaspoon almond extract

1 cup fresh blueberries

1 cup fresh raspberries

Fat-free whipped topping,
if desired

In small bowl, crush 1 cup of the strawberries with pastry blender or fork. Reserve remaining 1 cup strawberries.

In medium bowl, pour boiling water over gelatin; stir about 2 minutes or until gelatin is completely dissolved. Stir crushed strawberries into gelatin. Refrigerate 20 minutes.

Meanwhile, crush granola bars in their pouches with rolling pin. Sprinkle crushed granola in bottom of 9-inch ungreased glass pie plate, pushing crumbs up side of plate to make crust.

In small bowl, beat cream cheese, sugar and almond extract with electric mixer on medium-high speed until smooth. Drop by spoonfuls over crushed granola; gently spread to cover bottom of crust.

Gently fold blueberries, raspberries and remaining 1 cup strawberries into gelatin mixture. Spoon over cream cheese mixture. Refrigerate about 3 hours or until firm. Serve topped with whipped topping.

1 SERVING: Calories 200; Total Fat 3½g (Saturated Fat ½g, Trans Fat 0g); Cholesterol 0mg; Sodium 270mg; Total Carbohydrate 36g (Dietary Fiber 3g, Sugars 26g); Protein 7g; EXCHANGES: 2 Starch; ½ Fruit; ½ Fat; CARBOHYDRATE CHOICES: 2½

Expert Tips

■ The same pigments that give strawberries and blueberries their intense colors are thought to help prevent disease.

■ The great thing about having fruit in dessert is that it is likely to be eaten!

Rhubarb Upside–Down Desserts

⅓ cup packed brown sugar

2 tablespoons butter or margarine, melted

2 tablespoons dark or light corn syrup

½ teaspoon grated orange peel

1½ cups chopped fresh rhubarb

4 Pillsbury® Grands!® frozen Southern style biscuits (from 25-ounce bag)

½ teaspoon granulated sugar

⅛ teaspoon ground cinnamon

1 cup vanilla ice cream

Heat oven to 375°F. Spray insides of 4 (6-ounce) custard cups with cooking spray. Place custard cups on cookie sheet with sides.

In medium bowl, mix brown sugar, butter, corn syrup, orange peel and rhubarb; divide evenly among custard cups. Top each with 1 biscuit. In small bowl, mix granulated sugar and cinnamon; sprinkle over biscuits.

Bake 25 to 28 minutes or until deep golden brown; cool 1 minute. Turn upside down onto 4 serving plates; remove custard cups. Serve warm with ice cream.

1 SERVING: Calories 420; Total Fat 19g (Saturated Fat 9g, Trans Fat 4½g); Cholesterol 30mg; Sodium 640mg; Total Carbohydrate 57g (Dietary Fiber 0g, Sugars 31g); Protein 6g; EXCHANGES: 2 Starch; 2 Other Carbohydrate; 3 Fat; CARBOHYDRATE CHOICES: 4

Expert Tips

▨ To prepare fresh rhubarb, trim the ends and discard all traces of the leaves (rhubarb leaves are poisonous). Scrub the stalks and cut into pieces about 1 inch in length.

▨ Instead of vanilla ice cream, serve these desserts with cinnamon ice cream.

Double-Chocolate Lava Cake

1 cup Gold Medal® white whole wheat flour

¾ cup granulated sugar

2 tablespoons unsweetened baking cocoa

2 teaspoons baking powder

¼ teaspoon salt

½ cup milk

3 tablespoons butter or margarine, melted

1 teaspoon vanilla

1 cup semisweet, bittersweet or milk chocolate chips (6 ounces)

½ cup packed brown sugar

¼ cup unsweetened baking cocoa

1¾ cups very hot water

Ice cream, if desired

Chopped toasted walnuts or pecans, if desired

Heat oven to 350°F. In ungreased 9-inch square pan, mix flour, granulated sugar, 2 tablespoons cocoa, baking powder and salt. Stir in milk, butter and vanilla with fork until smooth, making sure to incorporate dry ingredients in corners of pan. Stir in chocolate chips.

Spread batter in pan. Sprinkle with brown sugar and ¼ cup cocoa. Pour hot water evenly over batter.

Bake about 40 minutes or until top is dry. Cool 10 minutes. Spoon warm cake into dessert dishes. Spoon sauce from pan onto each serving. Top with ice cream; sprinkle with nuts.

1 SERVING: Calories 300; Total Fat 10g (Saturated Fat 6g, Trans Fat 0g); Cholesterol 12mg; Sodium 214mg; Total Carbohydrate 54g (Dietary Fiber 3g, Sugars 40g); Protein 4g; EXCHANGES: ½ Starch; 2½ Other Carbohydrate; 1½ Fat; CARBOHYDRATE CHOICES: 4

Expert Tip

Gold Medal® white whole wheat flour can be used in any recipe. It's the best of both worlds—100% whole grain but with a lighter taste and color. Start substituting 25 percent or 50 percent of the all-purpose flour with Gold Medal® White whole wheat flour, gradually increasing proportion as desired.

Streusel-Topped Banana-Chocolate Snack Cake

PREP TIME: *15 minutes*

TOTAL TIME: *35 minutes*

MAKES 12 SERVINGS

1½ cups Original Bisquick® mix

½ cup Gold Medal® whole wheat flour

½ cup packed brown sugar

2 ripe medium bananas, mashed (about 1 cup)

½ cup milk

1 teaspoon vanilla

½ cup semisweet chocolate chips

STREUSEL TOPPING

¼ cup packed brown sugar

¼ cup Gold Medal® whole wheat flour

¼ teaspoon ground cinnamon

2 tablespoons cold butter or margarine

Heat oven to 425°F. Grease bottom and sides of 9-inch square pan with shortening or cooking spray.

In large bowl, stir Bisquick mix, ½ cup flour, ½ cup brown sugar, the bananas, milk and vanilla. Gently fold in chocolate chips. Pour into pan.

In medium bowl, mix ¼ cup brown sugar, ¼ cup flour and the cinnamon. Cut in butter, using pastry blender (or pulling 2 table knives through ingredients in opposite directions), until mixture is crumbly. Sprinkle topping evenly over batter in pan.

Bake 17 to 20 minutes or until toothpick inserted in center comes out clean. Cool on cooling rack.

1 SERVING: Calories 110; Total Fat 3g (Saturated Fat 1½g, Trans Fat 0g); Cholesterol 0mg; Sodium 105mg; Total Carbohydrate 19g (Dietary Fiber 1g, Sugars 10g); Protein 1g; EXCHANGES: ½ Starch; 1 Other Carbohydrate; ½ Fat; CARBOHYDRATE CHOICES: 1

Expert Tips

- For a more rustic version, use chocolate chunks or chopped chocolate bars instead of chips.
- Cut into smaller squares for party-size bites.

Brown Sugar–Spice Cake with Caramelized Apples

CAKE

- ½ cup butter or margarine, softened
- ½ cup packed brown sugar
- 2 eggs
- 1¼ cups Gold Medal® all-purpose flour
- 1 teaspoon baking powder
- ½ teaspoon baking soda
- ½ teaspoon ground ginger
- ½ teaspoon ground nutmeg
- ¼ teaspoon ground cloves
- ¼ teaspoon salt
- ½ cup sour cream
- 1 cup finely chopped peeled apple (1 medium)

CARAMELIZED APPLES

- 6 medium apples, peeled, sliced (about 8 cups)
- 1 cup packed brown sugar

WHIPPED CREAM

- 1 cup heavy whipping cream

Heat oven to 350°F. Spray bottom only of 9-inch square pan with baking spray with flour.

In large bowl, beat butter, ½ cup brown sugar and the eggs with electric mixer on low speed until blended; beat on medium speed until well combined. On low speed, beat in flour, baking powder, baking soda, ginger, nutmeg, cloves, salt and sour cream until mixed; beat on medium speed 1 minute. Stir in chopped apple. Spoon batter evenly into pan.

Bake 35 to 40 minutes or until toothpick inserted in center comes out clean and top is golden brown. Cool 10 minutes. Run knife around pan to loosen cake. Remove cake to heatproof serving plate. Cool cake about 30 minutes.

Meanwhile, in 12-inch skillet, cook sliced apples and 1 cup brown sugar over medium-high heat 20 to 25 minutes, stirring occasionally, or until apples are tender and caramelized.

In chilled large deep bowl, beat whipping cream with electric mixer on low speed until cream begins to thicken. Gradually increase speed to high and beat just until soft peaks form. Spoon caramelized apples over cake. Top with dollops of whipped cream.

1 SERVING: Calories 370; Total Fat 18g (Saturated Fat 11g, Trans Fat ½g); Cholesterol 90mg; Sodium 230mg; Total Carbohydrate 49g (Dietary Fiber 1g, Sugars 36g); Protein 3g; EXCHANGES: ½ Starch; ½ Fruit; 2½ Other Carbohydrate; 3½ Fat; CARBOHYDRATE CHOICES: 3

Expert Tips

- Chilling the bowl and beaters before whipping cream will make the cream whip faster. If you use the whisk attachment rather than regular beaters, the cream will thicken and form soft peaks more quickly. Don't overbeat, or the cream will curdle.
- If the brown sugar in your pantry has hardened, you can soften it by placing an apple wedge with the brown sugar in a plastic bag and sealing tightly for 1 to 2 days.

Coconut–Carrot Cake

1 cup flaked coconut

1 box Betty Crocker®
SuperMoist® carrot
cake mix

Water, vegetable oil and
eggs called for on cake
mix box

½ cup Betty Crocker® Rich &
Creamy vanilla frosting

Heat oven to 325°F. Grease and flour 12-cup fluted tube cake pan, or spray with baking spray with flour.

In ungreased shallow pan, spread coconut. Bake uncovered 5 to 7 minutes, stirring occasionally, until golden brown. Reserve 2 tablespoons toasted coconut for garnish.

Make cake batter using water, oil and eggs as directed on box. Fold remaining toasted coconut into batter. Pour into cake pan. Bake as directed on box for fluted tube pan. Cool 15 minutes; remove from pan to cooling rack. Cool completely, about 1 hour.

In small microwavable bowl, microwave frosting uncovered on Medium 15 seconds. Drizzle frosting over top of cake. Sprinkle with reserved toasted coconut. Cut cake with serrated knife. Store loosely covered.

1 SERVING: Calories 260; Total Fat 14g (Saturated Fat 4½g, Trans Fat ½g); Cholesterol 40mg; Sodium 240mg; Total Carbohydrate 30g (Dietary Fiber 0g, Sugars 18g); Protein 2g; EXCHANGES: 1 Starch; 1 Other Carbohydrate; 2½ Fat; CARBOHYDRATE CHOICES: 2

Expert Tips

■ For best results, do not spray fluted tube cake pans with cooking spray. Use shortening and flour or baking spray with flour.

■ For extra coconut flavor, stir ½ teaspoon coconut extract into the frosting.

White Texas Sheet Cake

CAKE

- 3 ounces white chocolate baking bars or squares, chopped
- 2 tablespoons whipping cream
- 1 box Betty Crocker® SuperMoist® white cake mix
- 1 cup sour cream
- ½ cup vegetable oil
- 3 eggs

WHITE CHOCOLATE FROSTING

- 3 ounces white chocolate baking bars or squares, chopped
- 3 tablespoons whipping cream
- ½ cup butter or margarine, softened
- 3 cups powdered sugar

GARNISH

- ½ cup chopped pecans, toasted if desired

Heat oven to 350°F (325°F for dark or nonstick pan). Spray bottom and sides of 15 × 10 × 1-inch pan with baking spray with flour.

In small microwavable bowl, microwave 3 ounces white chocolate and 2 tablespoons cream uncovered on High 1 minute, stirring once midway, until smooth. Stir, then cool 10 to 15 minutes.

In large bowl, beat cake mix, sour cream, oil, eggs and chocolate mixture with electric mixer on low speed 30 seconds, then on medium speed 2 minutes, scraping bowl occasionally. Pour into pan.

Bake 21 to 25 minutes or until toothpick inserted in center comes out clean. Cool completely, about 1 hour.

In small microwavable bowl, microwave 3 ounces white chocolate and 3 tablespoons whipping cream uncovered on High 1 minute, stirring once midway, until smooth. Stir, then cool 10 to 15 minutes.

In medium bowl, beat butter and 2 cups of the powdered sugar with electric mixer on medium speed until blended. Add white chocolate mixture; blend well. Add remaining 1 cup powdered sugar; beat until smooth. Spread frosting over cake; sprinkle with pecans. Store loosely covered.

1 SERVING: Calories 280; Total Fat 15g (Saturated Fat 7g, Trans Fat 0g); Cholesterol 45mg; Sodium 180mg; Total Carbohydrate 35g (Dietary Fiber 0g, Sugars 27g); Protein 2g; EXCHANGES: ½ Starch; 2 Other Carbohydrate; 3 Fat; CARBOHYDRATE CHOICES: 2

Expert Tips

- Toasting pecans or other nuts intensifies their flavor. To toast pecans, heat oven to 350°F. Spread pecans in ungreased shallow pan. Bake uncovered 6 to 10 minutes, stirring occasionally until light brown.

- White chocolate is made from cocoa butter and adds a wonderful rich flavor to this cake. Find white chocolate in the baking section of the grocery store, and use half of the 6-ounce package (3 squares, 1 ounce each) for the cake and the other half for the frosting. Melting the white chocolate in the microwave oven is quick and easy, but if you melt it in a pan on the stove, be sure to use very low heat to avoid scorching it.

PREP TIME: *40 minutes*

TOTAL TIME: *4 hours 40 minutes*

MAKES 12 SERVINGS

Lemon Buttercream Cake with Blueberries

- 2¾ cups Gold Medal® all-purpose flour
- 2½ teaspoons baking powder
- 1 teaspoon salt
- 1½ cups granulated sugar
- ¾ cup butter, softened
- 3 eggs
- 1¼ cups milk
- 1 cup powdered sugar
- ⅓ cup fresh lemon juice
- 1½ cups butter, softened
- 4 cups powdered sugar
- 3 tablespoons milk
- 2 tablespoons fresh lemon juice
- 3 cups fresh blueberries
- 3 teaspoons grated lemon peel

Heat oven to 350°F. Grease and flour 2 (8-inch or 9-inch) round cake pans.

In medium bowl, mix flour, baking powder and salt. In large bowl, beat granulated sugar and ¾ cup butter with electric mixer on medium speed until fluffy. Add eggs, one at a time, beating well. On low speed, alternately beat in flour mixture and 1¼ cups milk until blended. Pour into pans.

Bake 25 to 35 minutes or until toothpick comes out clean. Cool 10 minutes. With fork, poke tops every 1 inch.

Mix 1 cup powdered sugar and ⅓ cup lemon juice until smooth. Spoon over cakes. Let stand 10 minutes. Remove from pans; place top side up on cooling racks. Cool.

In large bowl, beat 1½ cups butter, 4 cups powdered sugar, 3 tablespoons milk and 2 tablespoons lemon juice on low speed until blended. Beat 3 minutes on medium speed until fluffy.

On plate, place 1 cake layer, rounded side up. Spread with ½ cup frosting. Top with 1½ cups of the berries. Spoon ¾ cup frosting over berries; carefully spread to cover. Place remaining layer, top side up, over frosted berries. Frost top and side. Arrange remaining berries on cake. Sprinkle with lemon peel.

Refrigerate 2 hours. Before serving, let cake stand at room temperature 15 minutes. Cover; refrigerate any remaining cake.

1 SERVING: Calories 770; Total Fat 37g (Saturated Fat 23g, Trans Fat 1½g); Cholesterol 145mg; Sodium 570mg; Total Carbohydrate 104g (Dietary Fiber 2g, Sugars 79g); Protein 6g; EXCHANGES: 2 Starch; 5 Other Carbohydrate; 7 Fat; CARBOHYDRATE CHOICES: 7

Expert Tips

- One medium lemon yields about 3 tablespoons juice and 2 to 3 teaspoons grated lemon peel.
- A handheld plane grater makes grating citrus peel easier than ever. This kitchen tool is available in stores that carry specialty kitchen utensils.

Banana Tres Leches Dessert

1 box Betty Crocker® SuperMoist® white cake mix

1¼ cups water

2 tablespoons vegetable oil

3 eggs

1 cup mashed bananas (2 medium)

1 can (14 ounces) sweetened condensed milk (not evaporated)

½ cup (from 14-ounce can) coconut milk (not cream of coconut)

½ cup whipping cream

1 container Betty Crocker® whipped fluffy white frosting

Banana slices and/or toasted coconut, if desired

Heat oven to 350°F (325°F for dark or nonstick pan). Grease bottom only of 13 × 9-inch pan.

In large bowl, beat cake mix, water, oil, eggs and mashed bananas with electric mixer on low speed 30 seconds, then on medium speed 2 minutes, scraping bowl occasionally. Pour into pan.

Bake 33 to 38 minutes or until toothpick inserted in center comes out clean. Cool completely, about 1 hour.

Poke top of cake every ½ inch with long-tined fork, wiping fork occasionally to reduce sticking. In large bowl, stir together condensed milk, coconut milk and whipping cream. Carefully pour evenly over top of cake. Cover; refrigerate at least 2 hours or overnight until mixture is absorbed into cake.

Spread frosting over cake. Garnish each serving with banana slices and/or toasted coconut. Store loosely covered in refrigerator.

1 SERVING: Calories 360; Total Fat 14g (Saturated Fat 7g, Trans Fat 1½g); Cholesterol 50mg; Sodium 280mg; Total Carbohydrate 54g (Dietary Fiber 0g, Sugars 40g); Protein 4g; EXCHANGES: 1 Starch; 2½ Other Carbohydrate; 2½ Fat; CARBOHYDRATE CHOICES: 3½

Expert Tip

Sprinkle your favorite toasted nuts over the top of the cake.

Chocolate Sandwich Cookie Cake

1¼ cups Gold Medal® all-purpose flour

⅔ cup sugar

½ teaspoon baking soda

½ cup butter or margarine, softened

¼ cup water

1 ounce unsweetened baking chocolate, melted, cooled

1 egg

6 creme-filled chocolate sandwich cookies, coarsely broken

1 container (12 ounces) Betty Crocker® whipped fluffy white frosting

¼ cup semisweet chocolate chips

½ teaspoon shortening

Coarsely broken cookies, if desired

Heat oven to 375°F. Grease bottom and side of 8-inch round pan with shortening; lightly flour.

In medium bowl, beat flour, sugar, baking soda, butter, water, chocolate and egg with electric mixer on low speed 30 seconds, scraping bowl constantly. Beat on medium speed 1 minute, scraping bowl occasionally. Stir in 6 broken cookies. Spread in pan.

Bake 25 to 30 minutes or until cake springs back when touched lightly in center. Cool 10 minutes. Remove from pan to cooling rack. Cool completely, about 1 hour.

Cut cake horizontally in half. Place bottom layer on serving plate. Spread with frosting. Top with remaining layer.

In small microwavable bowl, microwave chocolate chips and shortening uncovered on High 10 to 15 seconds or until chocolate can be stirred smooth and is thin enough to drizzle. Drizzle chocolate over top of cake. Sprinkle with coarsely broken cookies.

1 SERVING: Calories 520; Total Fat 26g (Saturated Fat 13g, Trans Fat 3½g); Cholesterol 55mg; Sodium 260mg; Total Carbohydrate 68g (Dietary Fiber 2g, Sugars 45g); Protein 4g; EXCHANGES: 1 Starch; 3½ Other Carbohydrate; 5 Fat; CARBOHYDRATE CHOICES: 4½

Layered Pumpkin Cheesecake

CRUST

- 2 cups gingersnap cookie crumbs (about 32)
- 1/4 cup butter or margarine, melted

CHEESECAKE

- 4 packages (8 ounces each) cream cheese, softened
- 1 1/2 cups sugar
- 4 eggs
- 1 cup canned pumpkin (not pumpkin pie mix)
- 1 1/2 teaspoons ground ginger
- 1 teaspoon ground cinnamon
- 1/4 teaspoon ground nutmeg

Heat oven to 300°F. Grease 9-inch springform pan with shortening or cooking spray. Wrap foil around pan to catch drips. In small bowl, mix cookie crumbs and butter. Press crumb mixture in bottom and 1 inch up side of pan. Bake 8 to 10 minutes or until set. Cool 5 minutes.

In large bowl, beat cream cheese with electric mixer on medium speed just until smooth and creamy; do not overbeat. On low speed, gradually beat in sugar. On low speed, beat in eggs, one at a time, just until blended. Spoon 3 cups of the cream cheese mixture into pan; spread evenly.

Stir pumpkin, ginger, cinnamon and nutmeg into remaining cream cheese mixture; mix with wire whisk until smooth. Spoon over mixture in pan.

Bake 1 hour 25 minutes to 1 hour 30 minutes or until edges are set but center of cheesecake still jiggles slightly when moved.

Turn oven off; open oven door at least 4 inches. Leave cheesecake in oven 30 minutes longer. Remove from oven; place on cooling rack. Without releasing side of pan, run knife around edge of pan to loosen cheesecake. Cool in pan on cooling rack 30 minutes. Cover loosely; refrigerate at least 6 hours but no longer than 24 hours.

Run knife around edge of pan to loosen cheesecake again; carefully remove side of pan. Place cheesecake on serving plate. Store cheesecake covered in refrigerator.

1 SERVING: Calories 390; Total Fat 26g (Saturated Fat 15g, Trans Fat 1g); Cholesterol 125mg; Sodium 290mg; Total Carbohydrate 34g (Dietary Fiber 0g, Sugars 27g); Protein 7g; EXCHANGES: 2 Other Carbohydrate; 4 1/2 Fat; CARBOHYDRATE CHOICES: 2

Expert Tips

- The key to a smooth top on a cheesecake is using the correct oven temperature and bake time, and beating the cream cheese mixture just until smooth.
- Garnish this luscious dessert with whipping cream.

PREP TIME: *20 minutes*

TOTAL TIME: *8 hours
35 minutes*

MAKES 16 SERVINGS

Red Velvet Cheesecake

1 box Betty Crocker® SuperMoist® devil's food cake mix

½ cup butter or margarine, softened

3 packages (8 ounces each) cream cheese, softened

1 cup semisweet chocolate chips (6 ounces), melted, cooled slightly

½ cup sour cream

¾ cup sugar

1 tablespoon red food color

3 eggs

2 cups frozen (thawed) whipped topping

Heat oven to 300°F. Wrap outside bottom and side of 10-inch springform pan with heavy-duty foil. Spray inside of pan with baking spray with flour.

Reserve ¼ cup of the cake mix for filling; set aside. In large bowl, beat remaining cake mix and the butter with electric mixer on low speed. Press in bottom and 1½ inches up side of pan.

In large bowl, beat reserved ¼ cup cake mix, the cream cheese, chocolate, sour cream, sugar and food color with electric mixer on medium speed until smooth. Beat in eggs, one at a time, just until blended. Pour over crust.

Bake 1 hour 5 minutes to 1 hour 15 minutes or until edges of cheesecake are set at least 2 inches from edge of pan but center of cheesecake still jiggles slightly when moved. Turn off oven; open oven door 4 inches. Leave cheesecake in oven 30 minutes. Remove from oven and cool in pan on cooling rack 30 minutes.

Refrigerate 6 hours or overnight. Run small metal spatula around edge of pan; remove side of pan. Pipe whipped topping around outer edge of cheesecake. Store covered in refrigerator.

1 SERVING: Calories 450; Total Fat 29g (Saturated Fat 17g, Trans Fat ½g); Cholesterol 105mg; Sodium 420mg; Total Carbohydrate 42g (Dietary Fiber 1g, Sugars 30g); Protein 6g; EXCHANGES: 2 Starch; 1 Other Carbohydrate; 5½ Fat; CARBOHYDRATE CHOICES: 3

Expert Tip

If you'd prefer, the whipped topping can be spread over the top of the cheesecake.

Pumpkin Chocolate Chip Bread

BREAD

- ½ cup butter, softened
- 1 cup granulated sugar
- 2 eggs
- 1 cup canned pumpkin (not pumpkin pie mix)
- 2 cups Gold Medal® all-purpose flour
- 1 teaspoon baking soda
- 1 teaspoon ground cinnamon
- 1 teaspoon pumpkin pie spice
- ½ cup miniature semisweet chocolate chips
- ¼ cup chopped walnuts

GLAZE

- ½ cup powdered sugar
- 2 to 3 teaspoons milk or whipping cream

Heat oven to 350°F. Grease bottom only of 9 × 5-inch loaf pan with shortening or cooking spray.

In large bowl, mix butter, granulated sugar, eggs and pumpkin with wire whisk. Stir in flour, baking soda, cinnamon and pumpkin pie spice. Stir in chocolate chips and walnuts. Spread in pan.

Bake 55 to 65 minutes or until toothpick inserted in center comes out clean. Cool 10 minutes; remove from pan to cooling rack. Cool completely, about 2 hours.

In small bowl, stir powdered sugar and milk until smooth and thin enough to drizzle. Drizzle over loaf. Let glaze set up before slicing, about 30 minutes.

1 SERVING: Calories 230; Total Fat 9g (Saturated Fat 5g, Trans Fat 0g); Cholesterol 40mg; Sodium 130mg; Total Carbohydrate 33g (Dietary Fiber 1g, Sugars 20g); Protein 3g; EXCHANGES: ½ Starch; 1½ Other Carbohydrate; 2 Fat; CARBOHYDRATE CHOICES: 2

Expert Tips

- For a different flavor, try sweetened dried cranberries instead of chocolate chips.
- Instead of the glaze, sprinkle some brown sugar and additional chopped walnuts on top of the bread before baking.

Easy Apple–Cranberry Dessert Squares

CRUST

2½ cups Original Bisquick® mix

1½ cups quick-cooking oats

1 cup packed brown sugar

1 cup cold butter or margarine

½ cup chopped pecans

FILLING

8 cups thinly sliced peeled apples (about 5 large)

1 bag (6 ounces) sweetened dried cranberries

½ cup granulated sugar

1 tablespoon ground cinnamon

1 container (8 ounces) sour cream

3 eggs

½ gallon vanilla ice cream

Heat oven to 375°F. Spray 15 × 10-inch pan with cooking spray.

In large bowl, mix Bisquick, oats and brown sugar. Cut in butter, using pastry blender (or pulling 2 table knives through ingredients in opposite directions), until mixture is crumbly. Remove 1½ cups crumb mixture to small bowl; stir in pecans. Set aside for topping. Pat remaining crumb mixture into bottom of pan.

In large bowl, toss apples, cranberries, granulated sugar and cinnamon. In small bowl, whisk together sour cream and eggs. Pour over apple mixture; toss to coat. Spoon filling over crust; sprinkle reserved crumb/nut mixture over filling.

Bake 45 to 55 minutes or until topping is golden brown and apples are tender. Cool 30 minutes. Cut into 8 rows by 4 rows. Serve warm with ice cream.

1 SERVING: Calories 280; Total Fat 14g (Saturated Fat 7g, Trans Fat ½g); Cholesterol 55mg; Sodium 210mg; Total Carbohydrate 35g (Dietary Fiber 2g, Sugars 23g); Protein 3g; EXCHANGES: ½ Fruit; 1½ Other Carbohydrate; ½ Low-Fat Milk; 2½ Fat; CARBOHYDRATE CHOICES: 2

Expert Tip

When choosing apples for this recipe, try 4 cups of a tart apple type (such as Granny Smith) and 4 cups of a sweeter apple (such as Gala) for a flavor variation.

Carrot Cake Bars with Cinnamon–Cream Cheese Frosting

PREP TIME: *20 minutes*

TOTAL TIME: *1 hour 4 minutes*

MAKES 48 SERVINGS

BARS

- 1 box Betty Crocker® SuperMoist® carrot cake mix
- 1 cup butter or margarine, softened
- 2 eggs
- 3 tablespoons milk
- 1 teaspoon ground cinnamon
- $\frac{1}{2}$ teaspoon maple flavor

FROSTING

- 1 package (8 ounces) cream cheese, softened
- $\frac{1}{4}$ cup butter or margarine, softened
- 1 teaspoon vanilla
- $\frac{1}{2}$ teaspoon ground cinnamon
- 2 to 3 teaspoons milk
- 4 cups powdered sugar

Heat oven to 350°F (325°F for dark or nonstick pan). Spray 15 × 10 × 1-inch pan with baking spray with flour.

In large bowl, beat bar ingredients with electric mixer on medium speed until well blended. Spread evenly in pan.

Bake 19 to 24 minutes or until top is evenly golden brown and toothpick inserted in center comes out clean. Cool completely, about 1 hour.

In medium bowl, beat cream cheese, $\frac{1}{4}$ cup butter, vanilla, $\frac{1}{2}$ teaspoon cinnamon and 2 teaspoons of the milk, with electric mixer on low speed until smooth, adding more milk if the mixture is too thick. Gradually beat in powdered sugar, 1 cup at a time, until smooth and spreadable. Spread frosting evenly over cooled bars. Store covered in refrigerator.

1 SERVING: Calories 140; Total Fat 7g (Saturated Fat 4g, Trans Fat 0g); Cholesterol 25mg; Sodium 115mg; Total Carbohydrate 18g (Dietary Fiber 0g, Sugars 14g); Protein 1g; EXCHANGES: 1 Other Carbohydrate; 1½ Fat; CARBOHYDRATE CHOICES: 1

Praline Crumb Caramel Cheesecake Bars

PREP TIME: *25 minutes*

TOTAL TIME: *3 hours 35 minutes*

MAKES 36 SERVINGS

COOKIE BASE AND TOPPING

- 1 pouch (1 pound 1.5 ounces) Betty Crocker® sugar cookie mix
- $\frac{1}{2}$ cup cold butter or margarine
- $\frac{1}{2}$ cup chopped pecans
- $\frac{1}{2}$ cup toffee bits

FILLING

- 2 packages (8 ounces each) cream cheese, softened
- $\frac{1}{2}$ cup sugar
- 2 tablespoons Gold Medal® all-purpose flour
- $\frac{1}{2}$ cup caramel topping
- 1 teaspoon vanilla
- 1 egg

Heat oven to 350°F. Spray bottom and sides of 13 × 9-inch pan with cooking spray. Place cookie mix in bowl; cut in butter using pastry blender or fork until mixture is crumbly. Reserve $1\frac{1}{2}$ cups mixture for topping. Press remaining mixture in bottom of pan. Bake 10 minutes.

Meanwhile, in large bowl, beat cream cheese, sugar, flour, $\frac{1}{4}$ cup of the caramel topping, vanilla and egg with electric mixer on medium speed until smooth.

Spread cream cheese mixture evenly over partially baked cookie base. Sprinkle with reserved crumb topping, pecans and toffee bits.

Bake 35 to 40 minutes or until light golden brown. Cool 30 minutes. Refrigerate about 2 hours or until chilled. Drizzle with remaining $\frac{1}{4}$ cup caramel topping. For bars, cut into 9 rows by 4 rows. Store covered in refrigerator.

1 SERVING: Calories 190; Total Fat 11g (Saturated Fat 5g, Trans Fat 1g); Cholesterol 30mg; Sodium 125mg; Total Carbohydrate 21g (Dietary Fiber 0g, Sugars 15g); Protein 1g; EXCHANGES: $\frac{1}{2}$ Starch; 1 Other Carbohydrate; 2 Fat; CARBOHYDRATE CHOICES: $1\frac{1}{2}$

Expert Tip

Cold butter is needed to create a just-right streusel and crust texture.

Blueberry Cheesecake Squares

CHEESECAKE

- 2 cups Wheaties® cereal, crushed

- 1 tablespoon butter or margarine, melted

- 2 packages (8 ounces each) reduced-fat cream cheese (Neufchâtel)

- 1 can (14 ounces) fat-free sweetened condensed milk

- ½ cup fat-free sour cream

- 2 eggs or ½ cup fat-free egg product

- 1 teaspoon vanilla

BLUEBERRY TOPPING

- ¼ cup sugar

- 1½ teaspoons cornstarch

- 2 tablespoons water

- 1 tablespoon lemon juice

- 2 cups fresh or frozen (unsweetened) blueberries

Heat oven to 375°F. In 8- or 9-inch square pan, toss cereal and melted butter until cereal is well coated. Spread evenly in pan. Bake 5 to 11 minutes or until golden brown.

Meanwhile, in large bowl, beat cream cheese and milk with electric mixer on medium speed until smooth. Beat in sour cream, eggs and vanilla until well blended. Pour over crust.

Bake 35 to 40 minutes or until center is jiggly but sides are set. Cool 1 hour at room temperature. Refrigerate about 2 hours or until chilled.

Meanwhile, in 1-quart saucepan, mix sugar and cornstarch. Stir in water and lemon juice until smooth. Add 1 cup of the blueberries. Heat to boiling over medium heat, stirring constantly. Boil about 2 minutes or until thickened; remove from heat. Stir in remaining 1 cup blueberries. Place blueberry topping in small bowl; let stand at room temperature 5 minutes. Cover and refrigerate until chilled.

For squares, cut cheesecake into 4 rows by 4 rows. Serve blueberry topping over cheesecake.

1 SERVING: Calories 200; Total Fat 8g (Saturated Fat 5g, Trans Fat 0g); Cholesterol 50mg; Sodium 190mg; Total Carbohydrate 26g (Dietary Fiber 0g, Sugars 21g); Protein 6g; EXCHANGES: ½ Starch; 1½ Other Carbohydrate; ½ Very Lean Meat; 1½ Fat; CARBOHYDRATE CHOICES: 2

Crème Brulee Cheesecake Bars

PREP TIME: *15 minutes*

TOTAL TIME: *3 hours 25 minutes*

MAKES 36 SERVINGS

1 pouch (1 pound 1.5 ounces) Betty Crocker® sugar cookie mix

1 box (4-serving size) French vanilla instant pudding and pie filling mix

2 tablespoons packed brown sugar

$\frac{1}{2}$ cup butter or margarine, melted

$2\frac{1}{2}$ teaspoons vanilla

2 eggs plus 3 egg yolks

2 packages (8 ounces each) cream cheese, softened

$\frac{1}{2}$ cup sour cream

$\frac{1}{2}$ cup sugar

$\frac{2}{3}$ cup toffee bits, finely crushed

Heat oven to 350°F. Lightly spray bottom and sides of 13 × 9-inch pan with cooking spray. In large bowl, stir cookie mix, pudding mix, brown sugar, melted butter, 1 teaspoon of the vanilla and 1 whole egg until soft dough forms. Press dough in bottom and $\frac{1}{2}$ inch up sides of pan.

In small bowl, beat cream cheese, sour cream and sugar with electric mixer on medium speed until smooth. Add remaining whole egg, 3 egg yolks and remaining $1\frac{1}{2}$ teaspoons vanilla; beat until smooth. Spread over crust in pan.

Bake 30 to 35 minutes or until set in center. Immediately sprinkle top with crushed toffee bits. Cool 30 minutes. Refrigerate about 3 hours or until chilled. For bars, cut into 9 rows by 4 rows. Store covered in refrigerator.

1 SERVING: Calories 200; Total Fat 11g (Saturated Fat 6g, Trans Fat 1g); Cholesterol 55mg; Sodium 150mg; Total Carbohydrate 22g (Dietary Fiber 0g, Sugars 16g); Protein 2g; EXCHANGES: $\frac{1}{2}$ Starch; 1 Other Carbohydrate; 2 Fat; CARBOHYDRATE CHOICES: $1\frac{1}{2}$

Expert Tip

To easily crush the toffee bits, put them in a food-safe plastic bag. Seal the bag and finely crush with a rolling pin or meat mallet.

Ultimate Turtle Cookie Bars

1 pouch (1 pound 1.5 ounces) Betty Crocker® chocolate chip cookie mix

½ cup butter or margarine, softened

1 egg

½ cup coarsely chopped pecans

24 caramels, unwrapped

1 tablespoon milk

¾ cup pecan halves

3 tablespoons semisweet chocolate chips

1 teaspoon shortening

Heat oven to 350°F. In medium bowl, stir together cookie mix, butter, egg and ½ cup chopped pecans until soft dough forms. Press evenly in ungreased 8-inch square pan. Bake 28 to 33 minutes or until golden brown.

Meanwhile, in 1-quart saucepan, heat caramels and milk over low heat, stirring frequently, until melted and smooth. Remove from heat.

Carefully spread melted caramels evenly over warm bars; sprinkle with pecan halves. Cool completely on cooling rack, about 1 hour.

In small microwavable bowl, microwave chocolate chips and shortening uncovered on High 30 to 60 seconds, stirring every 15 seconds, until melted and smooth. Drizzle over bars. Let stand about 30 minutes or until chocolate is set. For bars, cut into 4 rows by 4 rows.

1 SERVING: Calories 320; Total Fat 17g (Saturated Fat 7g, Trans Fat 0g); Cholesterol 30mg; Sodium 170mg; Total Carbohydrate 38g (Dietary Fiber 1g, Sugars 24g); Protein 3g; EXCHANGES: ½ Starch; 2 Other Carbohydrate; 3½ Fat; CARBOHYDRATE CHOICES: 2½

Expert Tips

▪ To microwave caramels (for step 2), place caramels and milk in 2-cup microwavable measuring cup and microwave uncovered on Medium-High 2 minutes; stir. Microwave 30 to 60 seconds longer, stirring every 15 seconds, until melted and smooth.

▪ Use a wet, sharp knife to cut bars easily.

▪ Use your favorite nut in place of the pecans.

Cranberry–Apple Butter Bars

FILLING

- 1 bag (12 ounces) fresh or frozen cranberries
- 1 cup granulated sugar
- 1 teaspoon grated orange peel
- 1/4 cup orange juice
- 1/2 cup apple butter
- 2 tablespoons butter or margarine

BASE AND TOPPING

- 3/4 cup butter or margarine, softened
- 1 cup packed brown sugar
- 1 1/2 cups Gold Medal® all-purpose flour
- 1 teaspoon salt
- 1/2 teaspoon baking soda
- 1 1/4 cups quick-cooking oats

Heat oven to 400°F. Spray 13 × 9-inch pan with cooking spray.

In 4-quart saucepan, mix cranberries, granulated sugar, orange peel and orange juice. Heat to boiling over high heat, stirring constantly. Cook over high heat 6 to 8 minutes, stirring frequently, until cranberries pop and lose their round shape and mixture thickens. Stir in apple butter and 2 tablespoons butter; remove from heat.

In large bowl, beat 3/4 cup butter and the brown sugar with electric mixer on medium speed, scraping bowl occasionally, until fluffy. Stir in flour, salt, baking soda and oats. Press 3 cups of the oat mixture in pan.

Spread cranberry filling over base. Crumble remaining 2 cups oat mixture over filling; press lightly.

Bake 25 to 30 minutes or until golden brown. Cool completely, about 1 hour 30 minutes. For bars, cut into 8 rows by 4 rows.

1 SERVING: Calories 150; Total Fat 5g (Saturated Fat 3g, Trans Fat 0g); Cholesterol 15mg; Sodium 130mg; Total Carbohydrate 23g (Dietary Fiber 1g, Sugars 16g); Protein 1g; EXCHANGES: 1/2 Starch; 1 Other Carbohydrate; 1 Fat; CARBOHYDRATE CHOICES: 1 1/2

Expert Tips

- One medium orange will provide enough grated peel and the 1/4 cup of juice.
- Homemade or purchased apple butter will work in this recipe.

Pumpkin-Ginger Bars

BARS

1½ cups packed brown sugar

1 cup Gold Medal® all-purpose flour

1 cup Gold Medal® whole wheat flour

¼ cup finely chopped crystallized ginger

2 teaspoons baking powder

1½ teaspoons ground cinnamon

1 teaspoon baking soda

¼ teaspoon salt

½ cup vegetable oil

½ cup milk

1 teaspoon vanilla

1 can (15 ounces) pumpkin (not pumpkin pie mix)

2 eggs

FROSTING

1 package (3 ounces) cream cheese, softened

2 tablespoons butter or margarine, softened

½ teaspoon vanilla

3 cups powdered sugar

1 to 2 tablespoons milk

Ground nutmeg, if desired

Heat oven to 350°F. Grease 15 × 10 × 1-inch pan with shortening or cooking spray; lightly flour. In large bowl, beat bar ingredients with electric mixer on low speed until moistened. Beat on medium speed 2 minutes. Spread in pan.

Bake 20 to 30 minutes or until toothpick inserted in center comes out clean. Cool completely, about 1 hour.

In small bowl, beat cream cheese and butter on low speed until blended. Beat in ½ teaspoon vanilla. Gradually beat in powdered sugar, 1 cup at a time, and 1 to 2 tablespoons milk until frosting is smooth and spreadable. Frost cooled bars. Sprinkle with nutmeg. Refrigerate about 30 minutes or until set. For bars, cut into 8 rows by 6 rows. Store in refrigerator.

1 SERVING: Calories 120; Total Fat 4g (Saturated Fat 1g, Trans Fat 0g); Cholesterol 10mg; Sodium 75mg; Total Carbohydrate 19g (Dietary Fiber 0g, Sugars 14g); Protein 1g; EXCHANGES: 1 Starch; 1 Fat; CARBOHYDRATE CHOICES: 1

Expert Tip

One-half teaspoon ground ginger can be used in place of the crystallized ginger, but expect a different texture and flavor.

Cherry-Chocolate Ice Cream Pie

15 creme-filled chocolate sandwich cookies, crumbled

¼ cup butter or margarine, melted

¾ cup hot fudge topping (room temperature)

1 quart (4 cups) vanilla ice cream, softened

¼ cup sugar

1 tablespoon cornstarch

½ cup water

2 tablespoons frozen cranberry juice cocktail concentrate

2 cups fresh or frozen dark sweet cherries, halved, pitted

1 tablespoon cherry-flavored liqueur, if desired

Heat oven to 375°F. In food processor, place crumbled cookies. Cover; process 10 to 15 seconds or until finely crushed. Add melted butter. Cover; process 5 to 10 seconds or until mixed. Press in bottom and up side of ungreased 9-inch pie plate. Bake 8 to 10 minutes or until set. Cool completely, about 30 minutes.

Stir hot fudge topping until smooth. Carefully spread over bottom of crust. Freeze 30 minutes. Spread ice cream over hot fudge topping. Cover; freeze at least 1 hour until firm.

Meanwhile, in 2-quart saucepan, mix sugar, cornstarch, water and frozen juice concentrate. Heat to boiling over medium heat, stirring occasionally. Stir in cherries; reduce heat. Simmer 5 minutes. Stir in liqueur. Cool completely, about 30 minutes. Let pie stand 10 minutes before cutting. Serve sauce over slices of frozen pie.

1 SERVING: Calories 460; Total Fat 20g (Saturated Fat 11g, Trans Fat 1½g); Cholesterol 50mg; Sodium 320mg; Total Carbohydrate 63g (Dietary Fiber 3g, Sugars 46g); Protein 5g; EXCHANGES: 1 Starch; 3 Other Carbohydrate; 4 Fat; CARBOHYDRATE CHOICES: 4

Expert Tip

Experiment with different variations of chocolate, vanilla or cherry ice creams in this pie.

Peanutty Ice Cream Cookie Cake

1 pouch (1 pound 1.5 ounces) Betty Crocker® double chocolate chunk cookie mix

⅓ cup hot fudge topping

¼ cup vegetable oil

1 egg

4 cups vanilla ice cream or frozen yogurt

¼ cup caramel topping

1 cup peanuts

Heat oven to 350°F. Lightly spray 10-inch springform pan with cooking spray. Or line 9-inch square baking pan with foil, leaving about 2 inches of the foil overhanging sides of pan; lightly spray with cooking spray.

In large bowl, stir cookie mix, 2 tablespoons of the hot fudge topping, the oil and egg until soft dough forms. Press dough in bottom and 1 inch up sides of pan. Bake 13 to 15 minutes or until top of crust is no longer shiny. Cool completely, about 1 hour.

Remove ice cream from freezer to soften. Spread softened ice cream over cookie crust. Freeze 2 hours. Remove from freezer. Drizzle with caramel topping and remaining hot fudge topping; sprinkle with peanuts. Freeze at least 2 hours or until firm.

To serve, remove sides of springform pan or lift dessert using foil out of 9-inch pan. Let stand 10 minutes. Use hot wet knife to cut into wedges or squares. Store covered in freezer.

1 SERVING: Calories 330; Total Fat 15g (Saturated Fat 5g, Trans Fat 0g); Cholesterol 30mg; Sodium 280mg; Total Carbohydrate 42g (Dietary Fiber 1g, Sugars 26g); Protein 5g; EXCHANGES: 1 Starch; 2 Other Carbohydrate; 3 Fat; CARBOHYDRATE CHOICES: 3

Expert Tip

If caramel and hot fudge toppings are too thick to drizzle, place in separate small microwavable bowls. Microwave each on High for 20 to 30 seconds until of drizzling consistency.

PREP TIME: *40 minutes*

TOTAL TIME: *3 hours 25 minutes*

MAKES 15 SERVINGS

Chocolate Chip Ice Cream Dessert

1 pouch (1 pound 1.5 ounces) Betty Crocker® chocolate chip cookie mix

½ cup butter or margarine, softened

1 egg

1 bottle (7.25 ounces) chocolate topping that forms hard shell

1 container (1.5 quarts) chocolate chip-cookie dough ice cream (6 cups)

Heat oven to 375°F. Spray bottom and sides of 13 × 9-inch pan with cooking spray. In large bowl, stir cookie mix, butter and egg until soft dough forms.

On ungreased cookie sheet, make 5 cookies by dropping dough by tablespoonfuls. Bake 9 to 11 minutes or until edges are golden brown. Cool 2 minutes; remove from cookie sheet to cooling rack.

Meanwhile, press remaining dough in pan, using moistened fingers (dough will be sticky). Bake 8 to 10 minutes or until set. Cool completely, about 30 minutes.

Spread ⅓ cup chocolate topping over baked crust. Freeze 10 to 15 minutes or until chocolate is set.

Meanwhile, remove ice cream from freezer to soften. Spread softened ice cream evenly over chocolate-topped crust.

Crumble 5 baked cookies; sprinkle over ice cream layer. Drizzle remaining chocolate topping over cookie crumbs. Cover; freeze 2 hours. To serve, let stand at room temperature 5 minutes before cutting. For serving pieces, cut into 5 rows by 3 rows. Store covered in freezer.

1 SERVING: Calories 410; Total Fat 23g (Saturated Fat 12g, Trans Fat 0g); Cholesterol 55mg; Sodium 220mg; Total Carbohydrate 46g (Dietary Fiber 2g, Sugars 32g); Protein 4g; EXCHANGES: 1 Starch; 2 Other Carbohydrate; 4½ Fat; CARBOHYDRATE CHOICES: 3

Expert Tip

To cut the cake easily, line the bottom and sides of the pan with foil, leaving foil overhanging at the opposite sides of the pan. Spray the bottom only of the foil-lined pan with cooking spray. Use the foil to lift the cake out of the pan. Pull the foil from the sides of the cake before cutting into serving pieces.

Index

Boldfaced page references indicate photographs.

Conversion Chart

These equivalents have been slightly rounded to make measuring easier.

VOLUME MEASUREMENTS

U.S.Imperial	Metric	U.S.	Metric
¼ tsp	—		1 ml
½ tsp	—		2 ml
1 tsp	—		5 ml
1 Tbsp	—		15 ml
2 Tbsp (1 oz)	1 fl oz		30 ml
¼ cup (2 oz)	2 fl oz		60 ml
⅓ cup (3 oz)	3 fl oz		80 ml
½ cup (4 oz)	4 fl oz		120 ml
⅔ cup (5 oz)	5 fl oz		160 ml
¾ cup (6 oz)	6 fl oz		180 ml
1 cup (8 oz)	8 fl oz		240 ml

WEIGHT MEASUREMENTS

U.S.	Metric
1 oz	30 g
2 oz	60 g
4 oz (¼ lb)	115 g
5 oz (⅓ lb)	145 g
6 oz	170 g
7 oz	200 g
8 oz (½ lb)	230 g
10 oz	285 g
12 oz (¾ lb)	340 g
14 oz	400 g
16 oz (1 lb)	455 g
2.2 lb	1 kg

LENGTH MEASUREMENTS

¼"	0.6 cm
½"	1.25 cm
1"	2.5 cm
2"	5 cm
4"	11 cm
6"	15 cm
8"	20 cm
10"	25 cm
12" (1')	30 cm

PAN SIZES

U.S.	Metric
8" cake pan	20 × 4 cm sandwich or cake tin
9" cake pan	23 × 3.5 cm sandwich or cake tin
11" × 7" baking pan	28 × 18 cm baking tin
13" × 9" baking pan	32.5 × 23 cm baking tin
15" × 10" baking pan	38 × 25.5 cm baking tin (Swiss roll tin)
1½ qt baking dish	1.5 liter baking dish
2 qt baking dish	2 liter baking dish
2 qt rectangular baking dish	30 × 19 cm baking dish
9" pie plate	22 × 4 or 23 × 4 cm pie plate
7" or 8" springform pan	18 or 20 cm springform or loose-bottom cake tin
9" × 5" loaf pan	23 × 13 cm or 2 lb narrow loaf tin or pâté tin

TEMPERATURES

Fahrenheit	Centigrade	Gas
140°	60°	—
160°	70°	—
180°	80°	—
225°	105°	¼
250°	120°	½
275°	135°	1
300°	150°	2
325°	160°	3
350°	180°	4
375°	190°	5
400°	200°	6
425°	220°	7
450°	230°	8
475°	245°	9
500°	260°	—